First World War
and Army of Occupation

War Diary
France, Belgium and Germany

1 DIVISION
2 Infantry Brigade
King's Royal Rifle Corps 2nd Battalion,
Welsh Regiment 51st Battalion,
Welsh Regiment 52nd Battalion,
Welsh Regiment 53rd Battalion,
Trench Mortar Battery and Machine Gun Company
26 January 1916 - 28 February 1918

WO95/1273

The Naval & Military Press Ltd
www.nmarchive.com
Published in association with The National Archives

Published by

The Naval & Military Press Ltd

Unit 10 Ridgewood Industrial Park,
Uckfield, East Sussex,
TN22 5QE England
Tel: +44 (0) 1825 749494

www.naval-military-press.com
www.nmarchive.com

This diary has been reprinted in facsimile from the original. Any imperfections are inevitably reproduced and the quality may fall short of modern type and cartographic standards.

© Crown Copyright
Images reproduced by permission of The National Archives, London, England, 2015.

Contents

Document type	Place/Title	Date From	Date To
Heading	2nd Battalion King's Royal Rifle Corps Jan-Dec 1917		
Heading	2nd. King's Royal Rifle Corps. 2nd. Infantry Brigade. 1st Division. January 1917		
War Diary		01/01/1917	31/01/1917
Heading	2nd. Bn. The King's Rifle Corps. 2nd Infantry Brigade. 1st Division February 1917		
War Diary		01/02/1917	28/02/1917
Miscellaneous	Instructions Regarding The Relief of the 24th French Division.	30/01/1917	30/01/1917
Operation(al) Order(s)	Battalion Order No. 6. by Lieutenant-Colonel R.N. Abadie, D.S.O. Commanding, in the Field. App. I	02/02/1917	02/02/1917
Operation(al) Order(s)	Battalion Order No. 7. by Lieutenant-Colonel R. N. Abadie, D.S.O. Commanding, in the Field. App II	04/02/1917	04/02/1917
Operation(al) Order(s)	Battalion Order No. 8. App III	06/02/1917	06/02/1917
Miscellaneous	Copy of letter from General Hirschauer, K.C.B. to H.Q. III Corps. App IV		
Miscellaneous	1st Div. No. G. 247/16. 2nd Bde. No. G. 38/19. App IV	08/02/1917	08/02/1917
Operation(al) Order(s)	2nd Infantry Brigade Order No. 121. App IV (A)	02/02/1917	02/02/1917
Miscellaneous	March Table To Accompany 2nd Infantry Brigade Order No. 121.	02/02/1917	02/02/1917
Operation(al) Order(s)	Battalion Orders No. 8. App V	06/02/1917	06/02/1917
Miscellaneous			
Miscellaneous	Proposals for the relieve of the 7th February.		
Operation(al) Order(s)	2nd Infantry Brigade Order No. 123.	05/02/1917	05/02/1917
Operation(al) Order(s)	Move Table to Accompany 2nd Infantry Brigade Order No. 123.	05/02/1917	05/02/1917
Operation(al) Order(s)	2nd Infantry Brigade Order No. 124. App V A	10/02/1917	10/02/1917
Operation(al) Order(s)	Battalion Order No. 4. Reference trench map & 1/20,000 62c. S.W. App VI	09/02/1917	09/02/1917
Operation(al) Order(s)	2nd Infantry Brigade Order No. 125. App VI A	11/02/1917	11/02/1917
Operation(al) Order(s)	2nd Infantry Brigade Order No. 126. App VI A	13/02/1917	13/02/1917
Miscellaneous	Table To Accompany 2nd Infantry Brigade Order No. 126. dated 13th February, 1917	13/02/1917	13/02/1917
Operation(al) Order(s)	2nd Infantry Brigade Order No. 127. App VII A	21/02/1917	21/02/1917
Miscellaneous	Table To Accompany 2nd Infantry Brigade Order No. 127.	21/02/1917	21/02/1917
Operation(al) Order(s)	Battalion Order No. 9. App VII	22/02/1917	22/02/1917
Operation(al) Order(s)	Battalion Order No. 9.	25/02/1917	25/02/1917
Miscellaneous	O.C. Royal Sussex. O.C. Loyal N. Lancs. O.C. Northamptons. O.C. K.R.R.C. O.C. No.2 M.G. Coy. O.C. 2nd T.M. Battery. H.Q. 1st Division. 1st Brigade. 145th Brigade. 2nd Bde. No. G. 38/29.	27/02/1917	27/02/1917
Miscellaneous	All Corps	27/02/1917	27/02/1917
Miscellaneous	Reference this office No. G.38/29 and B.M. 279 of Today's date. 2nd Bde. No. G. 38/29.	27/02/1917	27/02/1917
Operation(al) Order(s)	Battalion Order No. 10	27/02/1917	27/02/1917
Heading	2nd Bn. The King's Royal Rifle Corps. 2nd Infantry Brigade. 1st Division March. 1917		
War Diary		01/03/1917	31/03/1917
Operation(al) Order(s)	Battn Order No. 11 App I	01/03/1917	01/03/1917

Operation(al) Order(s)	Battn Order No. 13 App II	07/03/1917	07/03/1917
Operation(al) Order(s)	Battn Order No. 14 App III	08/03/1917	08/03/1917
Operation(al) Order(s)	2nd Bn. K.R.R.C. Order No. 15 App IV	18/03/1917	18/03/1917
Heading	2nd Bn. The King's Royal Rifle Corps. 2nd Infantry Brigade. 1st Division. April 1917		
War Diary		01/04/1917	30/04/1917
Heading	2nd. Bn. The King's Royal Rifle Corps. 2nd Infantry Brigade. 1st Division. May. 1917		
War Diary	Roisel	01/05/1917	31/05/1917
Miscellaneous	Fourth Army No. G.S. 697 A.P. I	20/05/1917	20/05/1917
Miscellaneous	T.O.		
Heading	2nd. Bn. The King's Royal Rifle Corps. 2nd Infantry Brigade. 1st Division June. 1917		
War Diary	Meteren	01/06/1917	30/06/1917
Operation(al) Order(s)	Battalion Order No. 108 App I	19/06/1917	19/06/1917
Heading	2nd. Bn. The King's Royal Rifle Corps. 2nd Infantry Brigade. 1st Division. July 1917		
War Diary	In The Field	01/07/1917	31/07/1917
Miscellaneous	Report on The Operations of July, 10th, 1917	14/07/1917	14/07/1917
Miscellaneous	Officer Commanding:- 1st South Wales Borderers, 2nd Welsh Regt. 1st Northants Regt. 2nd K.R.R. Corps, 2nd Machine Gun Coy, 3rd Machine Gun Coy. 3rd Brigade No. B.M. 522	18/07/1917	18/07/1917
Operation(al) Order(s)	Addendum and Corrigendum to March Table issued with 3rd Infantry Brigade Order No 118	17/07/1917	17/07/1917
Operation(al) Order(s)	3rd Infantry Brigade Order No 117	16/07/1917	16/07/1917
Operation(al) Order(s)	3rd Infantry Brigade Administrative Orders No 14	16/07/1917	16/07/1917
Miscellaneous	1st Division Administrative Instructions No. 10. Move of 1st Division to Le Clipon Camp.	15/07/1917	15/07/1917
Miscellaneous	Supply Arrangements.		
Operation(al) Order(s)	Reference 3rd Brigade Order No. 116	15/07/1917	15/07/1917
Operation(al) Order(s)	Corrigendum to 1st Division R.A.M.C. Order No 107.	15/07/1917	15/07/1917
Operation(al) Order(s)	Addenda and Corrigenda No. 2 to 2nd Infantry Brigade Order No. 148.	15/07/1917	15/07/1917
Operation(al) Order(s)	3rd Infantry Brigade Administrative Orders No 13	14/07/1917	14/07/1917
Operation(al) Order(s)	3rd Infantry Brigade Order No 115	14/07/1917	14/07/1917
Miscellaneous	March Table To Accompany 3rd Brigade Order No. 118		
Operation(al) Order(s)	Addenda and Corrigenda No. 1 to 2nd Infantry Brigade Order No. 148.	14/07/1917	14/07/1917
Operation(al) Order(s)	3rd Infantry Brigade Order No 115	14/07/1917	14/07/1917
Miscellaneous	March Table To Accompany 3rd Brigade Order No. 115		
Miscellaneous	Routes		
Operation(al) Order(s)	1st Division R.A.M.C. Order No. 107.	14/07/1917	14/07/1917
Miscellaneous	A Form. Messages And Signals.		
Miscellaneous			
Miscellaneous	2nd Battalion King's Royal Rifle Corps.	07/07/1917	07/07/1917
Map	Squares M		
Diagram etc	2nd Royal Sussex		
Heading	2nd Bn The King's Royal Rifle Corps. 2nd Infantry Brigade. 1st Division. August 1917		
War Diary	In The Field	01/08/1917	31/08/1917
Heading	2nd. Bn. The King's Royal Rifle Corps. 2nd Infantry Brigade 1st Division September 1917		
War Diary	In The Field	01/09/1917	30/09/1917

Heading	2nd. Bn. The King's Royal Rifle Corps. 2nd Infantry Brigade. 1st Division. October 1917		
War Diary		01/10/1917	31/10/1917
Heading	2nd. Bn. The King's Royal Rifle Corps. 2nd Infantry Brigade. 1st Division November. 1917		
War Diary		01/11/1917	16/11/1917
War Diary	In The Field	17/11/1917	30/11/1917
Heading	2nd. Bn. The King's Royal Rifle Corps. 2nd Infantry Brigade. 1st Division December 1917		
War Diary	France Herzeele	01/12/1917	05/12/1917
War Diary	Belgium Crombene	06/12/1917	11/12/1917
War Diary	Woesten	12/12/1917	18/12/1917
War Diary	In The Line	19/12/1917	26/12/1917
War Diary	Woesten Crombeke	27/12/1917	31/12/1917
Heading	1st Division 2nd Brigade 2nd Btn. Kings Royal Rifle Corps from 1st January 1918 to 1919 June		
War Diary	Combeke	01/01/1918	04/01/1918
War Diary	Woesten	05/01/1918	11/01/1918
War Diary	In The Line	12/01/1918	20/01/1918
War Diary	Crombeke	21/01/1918	26/01/1918
War Diary	Woesten	27/01/1918	07/02/1918
War Diary	In The Line	08/02/1918	28/02/1918
War Diary	Caribou Camp	01/03/1918	02/03/1918
War Diary	Kempton Park.	03/03/1918	15/03/1918
War Diary	Front Line	16/03/1918	27/03/1918
War Diary	California Dugouts	28/03/1918	30/03/1918
War Diary	Canal Bank & Battle Zone	31/03/1918	31/03/1918
Heading	2nd Battalion King's Royal Rifle Corps April 1918		
War Diary	Canal Bank	01/04/1918	05/04/1918
War Diary	Lapugnoy	06/04/1918	07/04/1918
War Diary	In The Line	07/04/1918	30/04/1918
War Diary	Cambrin	01/05/1918	08/05/1918
War Diary	Noeux-Les Mines	08/05/1918	11/05/1918
War Diary	Hohenzollern Sector	12/05/1918	15/05/1918
War Diary	Annequin	16/05/1918	19/05/1918
War Diary	Hohenzollern Sector	20/05/1918	27/05/1918
War Diary	Noeux-Les-Mines	28/05/1918	31/05/1918
Operation(al) Order(s)	2nd Battn. King's Royal Rifle Corps. Order No. 33.C.	23/05/1918	23/05/1918
Miscellaneous	Formations.		
Map	A28c-Scale-D-2.500		
Operation(al) Order(s)	2nd d K.R.R.C. Order No. 33	20/05/1918	20/05/1918
Heading	War Diary		
Operation(al) Order(s)	2nd Bn. K.R.R.C. Order No. 33A.	21/05/1918	21/05/1918
Diagram etc	Diagram of Barrage (not to scale)		
Operation(al) Order(s)	2nd Bn. King's Royal Rifle Corps. Order No. 33. B.	22/05/1918	22/05/1918
War Diary	Noeux Les Mines	01/06/1918	04/06/1918
War Diary	Cambrin	05/06/1918	12/06/1918
War Diary	Cuinchy	13/06/1918	20/06/1918
War Diary	Noeux Les Mines	21/06/1918	01/07/1918
War Diary	Hohenzollern Sector	02/07/1918	06/07/1918
War Diary	Annequin	07/07/1918	11/07/1918
War Diary	Cambrin Sector	12/07/1918	21/07/1918
War Diary	Noeux Les Mines	22/07/1918	31/07/1918
War Diary	Cambrin	01/08/1918	03/08/1918
War Diary	Left Subsector	04/08/1918	07/08/1918
War Diary	Cambrin	08/08/1918	11/08/1918

War Diary	Right Subsector	12/08/1918	14/08/1918
War Diary	Cambrin	15/08/1918	15/08/1918
War Diary	Right Subsector	16/08/1918	22/08/1918
War Diary	Beugin	22/08/1918	31/08/1918
War Diary	Arras	01/09/1918	31/10/1918
War Diary	Vaux-Andigny	01/11/1918	06/11/1918
War Diary	Fresnoy Le Grand	07/11/1918	13/11/1918
War Diary	Favril	14/11/1918	14/11/1918
War Diary	Dompierre	15/11/1918	15/11/1918
War Diary	Sars-Poteries	16/11/1918	17/11/1918
War Diary	Thirimont	18/11/1918	18/11/1918
War Diary	Walcourt	19/11/1918	22/11/1918
War Diary	Morialme	23/11/1918	23/11/1918
War Diary	Falaen	24/11/1918	30/11/1918
War Diary	Chestruvin	01/12/1918	01/12/1918
War Diary	Foy Nr Dame	02/12/1918	02/12/1918
War Diary	Ciergnon	03/12/1918	08/12/1918
War Diary	Haversin	09/12/1918	09/12/1918
War Diary	Melreux	10/12/1918	10/12/1918
War Diary	Erezee	11/12/1918	13/12/1918
War Diary	Odeigne	14/12/1918	14/12/1918
War Diary	Ottre	15/12/1918	15/12/1918
War Diary	Courtil	16/12/1918	16/12/1918
War Diary	Krombach	17/12/1918	17/12/1918
War Diary	Manderfeld	18/12/1918	18/12/1918
War Diary	Dahlem	19/12/1918	20/12/1918
War Diary	Blankenheim	21/12/1918	21/12/1918
War Diary	Munstereifel	22/12/1918	22/12/1918
War Diary	Palmersheim	23/12/1918	23/12/1918
War Diary	Lengsdorf	24/12/1918	29/12/1918
War Diary	Alfter	30/12/1918	25/03/1919
War Diary	Dransdorf	26/03/1918	31/03/1918
War Diary	Witterschlick	02/04/1919	10/04/1919
War Diary	Jolimetz	11/04/1919	21/04/1919
Miscellaneous	The Deputy Adjutant General. British Troops in France & Flanders.	23/07/1919	23/07/1919
War Diary			
Heading	BEF 1 Division 2 Brigade 51 Welsh R. 1919 Mar to 1919 July		
War Diary	Munstereifel	17/03/1919	25/03/1919
War Diary	Flamersheim	25/03/1919	31/03/1919
War Diary	Meckenheim	31/03/1919	30/04/1919
Heading	War Diary of the 51st Battalion, the Welsh Regiment, from 1st May 1919 to 31st May 1919		
War Diary	Meckenheim	01/05/1919	31/05/1919
Heading	War Diary of 51st Battalion The Welsh Regiment. from 1st June 1919 to 30th June 1919		
War Diary	Meckenheim	01/06/1919	17/06/1919
War Diary	Bonn	18/06/1919	18/06/1919
War Diary	Troisdorf	19/06/1919	30/06/1919
Heading	War Diary of 51st Battn. The Welsh Regt. from 1st July 1919 to 31st July 1919		
War Diary	Meckenheim	01/07/1919	31/07/1919
Heading	BEF 1 Division 2 Brigade 52 Welsh R. 1919 Mar to 1919 July		

Heading	War Diary of the 52nd Battalion, The Welsh Regiment. from March 1919 to 31st May, 1919		
War Diary	Lowestoft	01/03/1919	02/03/1919
War Diary	Dover	03/03/1919	03/03/1919
War Diary	Dunkirk	03/03/1919	04/03/1919
War Diary	Cologne	05/03/1919	05/03/1919
War Diary	Duisdorf	06/03/1919	31/03/1919
Miscellaneous	Defence of Bonn 52nd Battalion Welsh Regiment.	16/03/1919	16/03/1919
War Diary	Duisdorf	01/04/1919	31/05/1919
Miscellaneous	Orderly Room 52nd Batt Welsh Regt	02/06/1919	02/06/1919
Heading	War Diary of 52nd Batt. Welsh Regiment from 1st June 1919 to 30th June 1919 (Volume IV)		
War Diary	Duisdorf	01/06/1919	19/06/1919
War Diary	Bonn	19/06/1919	30/06/1919
Heading	War Diary of 52nd Battalion The Welsh Regiment from 1-7-1919 to 31-7-1919 Volume V		
War Diary	Duisdorf	01/07/1919	31/07/1919
Heading	BEF 1 Division 2 Brigade 53 Welsh R. 1919 Mar to 1919 July		
Heading	War Diary of the 53rd Batt The Welsh Regt from 23rd March 1919 to 31st March 1919		
War Diary	Shoreham By Sea	22/03/1919	22/03/1919
War Diary	Dover	22/03/1919	23/03/1919
War Diary	Dunkerque	23/03/1919	25/03/1919
War Diary	Duisdorf	26/03/1919	26/03/1919
War Diary	Alfter	27/03/1919	31/03/1919
War Diary	Shoreham By Sea	22/03/1919	22/03/1919
War Diary	Dover	22/03/1919	23/03/1919
War Diary	Dunkerque	23/03/1919	25/03/1919
War Diary	Duisdorf	26/03/1919	26/03/1919
War Diary	Alfter	27/03/1919	31/03/1919
Heading	War Diary of 53rd Batt Welsh Regiment 1st-30th April 1919		
War Diary	Alfter	01/04/1919	29/04/1919
Miscellaneous	Reference Provisional Scheme For Defence of Bonn		
Miscellaneous	Provisional Scheme for Defence of Bonn		
Heading	War Diary of 53rd Batt. The Welsh Regiment from 1st May 1919 to 31st May 1919 Vol I		
War Diary	Alfter	01/05/1919	01/05/1919
War Diary	Germany	01/05/1919	31/05/1919
Heading	War Diary of 53rd Batt The Welsh Regt from 1st June 1919 to 30th June 1919		
War Diary	Alfter	01/06/1919	30/06/1919
Operation(al) Order(s)	Operation Order No. 1. 53rd Batt. The Welsh Regiment. Appendix I		
Miscellaneous	53rd Batt The Welsh Regiment Appendix 1.		
Heading	War Diary of 53rd Batt The Welsh Regt from 1st July 1919 to 31st July 1919		
War Diary	Alfter	01/07/1919	30/07/1919
Heading	2nd Trench Mortar Battery 1917 Jul-1918 Dec		
Heading	2nd T.M. Battery. 2nd Infantry Brigade. 1st Division. July 1917		
Miscellaneous	2nd Brigade No. G. 20/6.	10/08/1917	10/08/1917
War Diary	Bador Camps	01/07/1917	01/07/1917
War Diary	Coxyde Bains Area	02/07/1917	02/07/1917
War Diary	Nieuport Bains Area	03/07/1917	10/07/1917

War Diary	Coxyde Bains Area	14/07/1917	16/07/1917
War Diary	Leffrinckhoucke Area	17/07/1917	17/07/1917
War Diary	St. Pol. Sur Mer Area	18/07/1917	30/07/1917
War Diary	Le Clipon Camp Area	30/07/1917	30/07/1917
Heading	2nd T.M. Battery. 2nd Infantry Brigade. 1st Division. September 1917		
War Diary	Le Clipon Camp	01/09/1917	30/09/1917
Heading	2nd T. M. Battery. 2nd Infantry Brigade. 1st Division. October 1917		
War Diary	Le Clipon Camp	01/10/1917	22/10/1917
War Diary	Beggars Cappel	23/10/1917	24/10/1917
War Diary	Herzelle	25/10/1917	25/10/1917
War Diary	School Camp	26/10/1917	31/10/1917
Heading	2nd T. M. Battery. 2nd Infantry Brigade. 1st Division. November 1917		
War Diary	School Camp	01/11/1917	06/11/1917
War Diary	Poperinghe	07/11/1917	07/11/1917
War Diary	Reigersberg	09/11/1917	25/11/1917
War Diary	Tunnelling Camp	26/11/1917	28/11/1917
War Diary	Herzule	30/11/1917	30/11/1917
Heading	2nd T. M. Battery 2nd. Infantry Brigade. 1st Division. December 1917		
War Diary	Herzeele	01/12/1917	06/12/1917
War Diary	Crombeke	07/12/1917	07/12/1917
War Diary	Woesten	08/12/1917	10/12/1917
War Diary	Canal Bank	12/12/1917	14/12/1917
War Diary	Charpentier Cross Roads	14/12/1917	31/12/1917
Heading	1st Division War Diaries 2nd French Mortar Battery from 1st January to 31st December 1918		
War Diary	Charpentier Cross Roads	01/01/1918	31/03/1918
War Diary	Canal Bank Ypres	01/04/1918	04/04/1918
War Diary	Marles Les Mines	05/04/1918	06/04/1918
War Diary	Line and Annequin	07/04/1918	07/04/1918
War Diary	Line	08/04/1918	30/04/1918
War Diary	In The Line Cambrin Sector	01/05/1918	01/05/1918
War Diary	Noeux Les Mines	02/05/1918	11/05/1918
War Diary	In The Line Hohenzollern	12/05/1918	27/05/1918
War Diary	Noeux Les Mines	28/05/1918	04/06/1918
War Diary	Cambrin Sector	05/06/1918	20/06/1918
War Diary	Noeux Les Mines	21/06/1918	01/07/1918
War Diary	Hohenzollern Sector	02/07/1918	21/07/1918
War Diary	Noeux Les Mines	22/07/1918	29/07/1918
War Diary	Cambrin Sector	31/07/1918	22/08/1918
War Diary	Dieval	22/08/1918	31/08/1918
War Diary	Arras	01/09/1918	03/09/1918
War Diary	Enterpigng	04/09/1918	08/09/1918
War Diary	Harbucq	09/09/1918	11/09/1918
War Diary	Athies	13/09/1918	13/09/1918
War Diary	Tertery	15/09/1918	16/09/1918
War Diary	Gricourt Sector	18/09/1918	19/09/1918
War Diary	Vermand	20/09/1918	20/09/1918
War Diary	Gricourt Sector	23/09/1918	28/09/1918
War Diary	Vermand	28/09/1918	30/09/1918
War Diary	Marteville	01/10/1918	03/10/1918
War Diary	Caullincourt	04/10/1918	08/10/1918
War Diary	Bellinglase	09/10/1918	15/10/1918

War Diary	Bohain	16/10/1918	16/10/1918
War Diary	Vaux Andigny	17/10/1918	19/10/1918
War Diary	Arbre Deguise	20/10/1918	24/10/1918
War Diary	Lavalee Mulatre	24/10/1918	27/10/1918
War Diary	Mazinghen	28/10/1918	29/10/1918
War Diary	Vaux Audigny	30/10/1918	02/11/1918
War Diary	Mazinghen	03/11/1918	04/11/1918
War Diary	Fermy	04/11/1918	04/11/1918
War Diary	Layalee Mulatre	05/11/1918	05/11/1918
War Diary	Fernoy Le Grand	06/11/1918	11/11/1918
War Diary	Favril	13/11/1918	13/11/1918
War Diary	Dompierre	15/11/1918	15/11/1918
War Diary	Sars Pottlers	16/11/1918	16/11/1918
War Diary	Marzelle	18/11/1918	18/11/1918
War Diary	Walcourt	19/11/1918	22/11/1918
War Diary	Moraline	23/11/1918	23/11/1918
War Diary	Anthee	24/11/1918	30/11/1918
War Diary	Whiellen	01/12/1918	01/12/1918
War Diary	Soinne	02/12/1918	02/12/1918
War Diary	Jamblinne	03/12/1918	08/12/1918
War Diary	Sin Sin	09/12/1918	09/12/1918
War Diary	Hutton	10/12/1918	10/12/1918
War Diary	Erqzec	11/12/1918	13/12/1918
War Diary	Grandmil	14/12/1918	14/12/1918
War Diary	Hubronvale	15/12/1918	15/12/1918
War Diary	Beho	16/12/1918	16/12/1918
War Diary	Gruffling	17/12/1918	17/12/1918
War Diary	Losheim	18/12/1918	18/12/1918
War Diary	Hammerhutte	19/12/1918	20/12/1918
War Diary	Schmidtheim	21/12/1918	21/12/1918
War Diary	Munsterfel	22/12/1918	22/12/1918
War Diary	Essig	23/12/1918	23/12/1918
War Diary	Duisdorf	24/12/1918	31/12/1918
Heading	2nd Machine Gun Company Jan-Dec 1916		
Heading	2nd Brigade 1st Division Formed in France 26.1.16. 2nd Machine Gun Company 26th January to 30th April 1916		
War Diary	Lillers Pas-De-Calais France	26/01/1916	26/01/1916
War Diary	Ecquedecques	27/01/1916	13/02/1916
War Diary	Burbure	14/02/1916	15/02/1916
War Diary	Les Brebis	15/02/1916	15/03/1916
War Diary	Grenay	15/03/1916	16/03/1916
War Diary	Les Brebis	16/03/1916	28/03/1916
War Diary	Grenay	28/03/1916	03/04/1916
War Diary	Les Brebis	04/04/1916	15/04/1916
War Diary	Grenay	15/04/1916	21/04/1916
War Diary	Les Brebis	22/04/1916	03/05/1916
War Diary	Grenay	03/05/1916	09/05/1916
War Diary	Les Brebis	10/05/1916	18/05/1916
War Diary	Grenay	19/05/1916	26/05/1916
War Diary		10/04/1916	18/04/1916
War Diary	Erquinhem	19/04/1916	28/04/1916
War Diary	Fleurbaix	29/04/1916	30/04/1916
Heading	2nd Machine Gun Company May 1916		
War Diary	Fleurbaix	01/05/1916	31/05/1916

Heading	War Diary 2nd Machine Gun Company June & July 1916		
Heading	2nd Infantry Brigade attached I beg to hand for A F 2118-War Diary-in duplicate from 26/5/16 to 30/7/16		
War Diary	Grenay	26/05/1916	26/05/1916
War Diary	Les Brebis	27/05/1916	11/06/1916
War Diary	Bully-Grenay	11/06/1916	18/06/1916
War Diary	Les Brebis	19/06/1916	03/07/1916
War Diary	Grenay	26/05/1916	26/05/1916
War Diary	Les Brebis	27/05/1916	11/06/1916
War Diary	Bully-Grenay	11/06/1916	19/06/1916
War Diary	Les Brebis	19/06/1916	03/07/1916
War Diary	Haillicourt	04/07/1916	04/07/1916
War Diary	Bruay	06/07/1916	06/07/1916
War Diary	Flesselles	08/07/1916	08/07/1916
War Diary	Frechencourt (Ref 1/100,000 Amiens 17.)	09/07/1916	09/07/1916
War Diary	Bresle (Ref 1/100,000 Amiens 17.)	10/07/1916	10/07/1916
War Diary	Maxse Redoubt	11/07/1916	17/07/1916
War Diary	Les Brebis	03/07/1916	03/07/1916
War Diary	Haillicourt	04/07/1916	04/07/1916
War Diary	Bruay	06/07/1916	06/07/1916
War Diary	Flesselles	08/07/1916	08/07/1916
War Diary	Frechencourt (Ref 1/100,000 Amiens 17.)	09/07/1916	09/07/1916
War Diary	Bresle (Ref 1/100,000 Amiens 17.)	10/07/1916	10/07/1916
War Diary	Maxse Redoubt	11/07/1916	23/07/1916
War Diary	Albert	23/07/1916	26/07/1916
War Diary	Franvillers	26/07/1916	30/07/1916
War Diary		18/07/1916	23/07/1916
War Diary	Albert	23/07/1916	26/07/1916
War Diary	Franvillers	26/07/1916	30/07/1916
Heading	2nd Brigade Machine Gun Company August 1916		
War Diary	Henencourt Wood	30/07/1916	13/08/1916
War Diary	Maxse Redoubt	14/08/1916	14/08/1916
War Diary	Mametz Wood.	14/08/1916	28/08/1916
War Diary		18/08/1916	19/08/1916
War Diary	Henencourt Wood	30/07/1916	13/08/1916
War Diary	Maxse Redoubt	14/08/1916	14/08/1916
War Diary	Mametz Wood.	14/08/1916	28/08/1916
War Diary		18/08/1916	20/08/1916
War Diary	Maxse Redoubt	20/08/1916	27/08/1916
War Diary	Mametz Wood.	27/08/1916	31/08/1916
War Diary	Bazentin Le Grand	31/08/1916	02/09/1916
War Diary	Maxse Redoubt	20/08/1916	20/08/1916
War Diary	Mametz Wood	27/08/1916	31/08/1916
War Diary	Bazentin Le Grand	31/08/1916	02/09/1916
Heading	2nd Machine Gun Company September 1916		
War Diary	Maxse Redoubt	02/09/1916	08/09/1916
War Diary	Bazentin Le Grand	08/09/1916	12/09/1916
War Diary	Baizieux	12/09/1916	19/09/1916
War Diary	Maxse Redoubt	02/09/1916	08/09/1916
War Diary	Bazentin Le Grand	08/09/1916	12/09/1916
War Diary	Baizieux	12/09/1916	19/09/1916
War Diary	Mametz Wood	19/09/1916	26/09/1916
War Diary	Bazentin Le Grand	26/09/1916	29/09/1916
War Diary	Millencourt	29/09/1916	02/10/1916
War Diary	Baizieux	19/09/1916	19/09/1916

War Diary	Mametz Wood	19/09/1916	26/09/1916
War Diary	Bazentin Le Grand	26/09/1916	29/09/1916
War Diary	Millencourt	29/09/1916	02/10/1916
Heading	2nd Machine Gun Company : : : October 1916		
War Diary	Millencourt	03/10/1916	03/10/1916
War Diary	Tours	03/10/1916	31/10/1916
War Diary	Bresle	01/11/1916	02/11/1916
Heading	2nd Machine Gun Company : : November 1916		
War Diary	Bresle	05/11/1916	05/11/1916
War Diary	Albert	05/11/1916	18/11/1916
War Diary	Bazentin Le Grand	22/11/1916	01/12/1916
War Diary	Mametz Wood	03/12/1916	03/12/1916
Heading	2nd Machine Gun Company : : : December 1916		
War Diary	Mametz Wood	05/12/1916	05/12/1916
War Diary	High Wood	05/12/1916	01/01/1917
Heading	2nd Machine Gun Company. 1917 Jan-1918 Feb		
Heading	2nd M.G. Company. 2nd Infantry Brigade. 1st Division. January 1917		
War Diary	Millencourt	02/01/1917	23/01/1917
War Diary	Bresle	24/01/1917	31/01/1917
Heading	No. 2. M.G. Company. 2nd. Infantry Brigade. 1st. Division. February 1917		
War Diary	Mericourt	03/02/1917	03/02/1917
War Diary	Chignolles	04/02/1917	26/02/1917
Heading	No. 2. M.G. Company. 2nd. Infantry Brigade. 1st. Division. March 1917		
War Diary	Chuignes	03/03/1917	02/04/1917
Heading	No.2. M.G. Company. 2nd Infantry Brigade. 1st Division April 1917		
War Diary	Grand Bois Nr Assevillers	03/04/1917	06/04/1917
War Diary	Chuignes	07/04/1917	14/04/1917
War Diary	Morcourt	15/04/1917	30/04/1917
Heading	No.2. M.G. Company.2nd Infantry Brigade. 1st Division May 1917		
War Diary	Morcourt	01/05/1917	20/05/1917
War Diary	Villers-Bretonneux	21/05/1917	28/05/1917
War Diary	Meteren	28/05/1917	31/05/1917
Heading	No.2. M.G. Company.2nd Infantry Brigade. 1st Division. June 1917.		
War Diary	Fontaine Houck	01/06/1917	11/06/1917
War Diary	Saint Marie Capelle	12/06/1917	15/06/1917
War Diary	Wormhoudt	16/06/1917	16/06/1917
War Diary	Mald	17/06/1917	17/06/1917
War Diary	Camp Zeepanne	18/06/1917	24/06/1917
War Diary	La Fevre Camp	25/06/1917	30/06/1917
Heading	War Diary No.2. M.G. Company.2nd Infantry Brigade. 1st Division. July 1917		
War Diary	La Levre Camp	01/07/1917	03/07/1917
War Diary	Nieuport Bains	07/07/1917	10/07/1917
War Diary	Rinckcamp	11/07/1917	15/07/1917
War Diary	Ghyvelde	16/07/1917	16/07/1917
War Diary	Pont De Pte Synthe	19/07/1917	30/07/1917
War Diary	St. Pol Sur Mer	30/07/1917	31/07/1917
War Diary	Le Clipon	31/07/1917	31/07/1917
Heading	War Diary. No.2. M.G. Company. 2nd Infantry Brigade. 1st Division. August 1917		

Miscellaneous	2nd Infantry Bde. 1917	01/09/1917	01/09/1917
War Diary	Le Clipon Camp	01/05/1917	31/05/1917
Heading	War Diary. No.2. M.G. Company. 2nd Infantry Brigade. 1st Division. September 1917		
War Diary	Le Clipon Camp	01/09/1917	30/09/1917
Heading	War Diary. No.2. M.G. Company. 2nd Infantry Brigade. 1st Division. October 1917.		
War Diary	Le Clipon Camp	01/10/1917	22/10/1917
War Diary	Eringham	24/10/1917	24/10/1917
War Diary	Herzeele	25/10/1917	25/10/1917
War Diary	St. Jan	26/10/1917	31/10/1917
Heading	War Diary. No. 2. M.G. Company. 2nd Infantry Brigade. 1st Division. November 1917		
War Diary		01/11/1917	30/11/1917
Heading	War Diary. No. 2. M.G. Company. 2nd Infantry Brigade. 1st Division. December 1917		
War Diary		01/12/1917	31/12/1917
Heading	1st Division War Diaries No. 2 Machine Gun Company Jan 1918		
War Diary		01/01/1918	28/02/1918

1ST DIVISION
2ND INFY BDE

2ND BATTALION

KING'S ROYAL RIFLE CORPS

JAN - DEC 1917

WAR DIARY.

2nd. KING'S ROYAL RIFLE CORPS.

2nd. INFANTRY BRIGADE.

1st. DIVISION.

JANUARY. 1917.

Army Form C. 2118.

Instructions regarding War Diaries and Intelligence Summaries are contained in F. S. Regs., Part II. and the Staff Manual respectively. Title Pages will be prepared in manuscript.

WAR DIARY
or
INTELLIGENCE SUMMARY
(Erase heading not required.)

1/2 2nd. King's Royal Rifle Corps.

Vol 28

Place	Date	Hour	Summary of Events and Information	Remarks and references to Appendices
	Jan 1 1917		At 1.15 pm the Battalion marched from BAZENTIN to billets in ALBERT. Going to the same that we occupied 6 weeks ago in the RUE de BOULANS	
	2		Engaged in cleaning up & training – also finding working parties of 1 officer & 105 O.R.	
	3.		ditto but had to find 155 OR.	
	4		Working parties as on 2nd – Lt W.C. Smith & 20 OR joined the Bn.	
	5		ditto. 5 NCOs & men were wounded while taking detonators out of Mills Bombs.	
	6		Working parties as on 3rd – Sgt Kelly who was wounded yesterday died of wounds.	
	7		Church parade. Working parties as on 2nd. CAPT. T.R.F. FORREST returned from leave & went to 4th Army School. FLEXICOURT.	
	8.		Working parties as on 2nd.	
	9.		Working parties as on 2nd Major J. Wormald MC left for England 2nd Lt. T.P. McDowell arrived.	
	10.		Battalion relieved 10th Gloucesters at FRICOURT FARM. 2nd Lt G.E. McCabe and 169 O.R.s left for Musketry Course at PONT REMY.	

2449 Wt. W14957/M90 750,000 1/16 J.B.C. & A. Forms/C.2118/12.

Army Form C. 2118.

WAR DIARY
or
INTELLIGENCE SUMMARY
(Erase heading not required.)

Instructions regarding War Diaries and Intelligence Summaries are contained in F. S. Regs., Part II. and the Staff Manual respectively. Title Pages will be prepared in manuscript.

Place	Date	Hour	Summary of Events and Information	Remarks and references to Appendices
	11.		2nd Lt E. A. Warner rejoined Battalion. Lt. Hon L. St. Aubyn joined Battalion. All available men on fatigue; clearing mud &c. Draft of 13 ORs arrived	
	12.		Battalion moved into C camp across the road. Larger camp & more concentrated. Working parties as on 11th. Rain in afternoon. H.Q. coy improved camp drains &c	
	13		Working parties as on 12th. Cold with sleet in the evening.	
	14		Working parties as on 13th.	
	15		Working parties as on 14th. Slight shelling at night. One latrine demolished	
	16		Working Parties as for 15th. Shelled at night. 8 inch(?) crater 6 yds from Sgts Mess. Heavy fall of snow during the night	
	17		Working parties as usual. Lt. J. L. Muscat arrived to join the Battn. More snow and shelling at night. Very cold.	
	18		2nd Lt Warner & 2nd Lt Sheepshanks and 200 ORs left for musketry course at Pont Remy. 2nd Lt McCabe's party returned.	
	19		Working parties as on 17th. Very cold.	
	20		Working parties as usual. Still very cold	
	21		Capt H. K. Ward (R.A.M.C.) rejoined the Battn. Capt. Collier (RAMC) left. 2nd Lt. A L Gracie joined the Battn. Draft of 15 ORs arrived. Working parties as usual	767c

2449 Wt. W14957/M90 750,000 1/16 J.B.C. & A. Forms/C.2118/12.

Instructions regarding War Diaries and Intelligence Summaries are contained in F. S. Regs., Part II. and the Staff Manual respectively. Title Pages will be prepared in manuscript.

WAR DIARY
or
INTELLIGENCE SUMMARY
(Erase heading not required.)

Army Form C. 2118

Place	Date	Hour	Summary of Events and Information	Remarks and references to Appendices
	22		Working parties as usual. Very cold.	
	23		Clear fine day but extremely cold. ~~Working parties as usual~~	
	24		Relieved by 11th Australian Regt. Batt. marched to billets in BRESLE. A bomb nearly caught A & D coys while marching through ALBERT. Left FRICOURT at 10 am arrived BRESLE about 1.45 pm. Weather getting colder than ever. 2nd Lt E.R. Vincers joined the Batt. 2nd Lt. Warne's & Sheepshanks' musketry party rejoined the Batt.	
	25		Coy. training. Very severe frost. Capt. A.C. Oppenheim appointed Tmpy. Major from 11th Jan.	
	26.		Ditto – Ditto. Lecture by G.O.C. to all officers of brigade on discipline	ACO Maj
	27.		Brigade route march. Ditto. 2nd Lt. A.L. KELLY joined	
	28		Very severe frost. 2/Lt AMBLER and LINDSAY rejoined Battn from Div. school	
	29.		Attack scheme with L.N. LANCS. BDE Boxing tournament in Battn dig 3.PM. Very severe frost	
	30		Coy. training – Ditto – 2/Lt AMBLER started being trained as a/Adj.	[illegible]
	31		Bde. route march. Very severe frost and a little snow.	

1875 Wt. W593/826 1,000,000 4/15 J.B.C. & A. A.D.S.S./Forms/C. 2118.

768c

W A R D I A R Y.

(WITH APPENDICES).

2nd. Bn. THE KING'S RIFLE CORPS.

2nd. INFANTRY BRIGADE.

1st. DIVISION.

FEBRUARY. 1917.

Instructions regarding War Diaries and Intelligence Summaries are contained in F. S. Regs., Part II. and the Staff Manual respectively. Title Pages will be prepared in manuscript.

WAR DIARY or INTELLIGENCE SUMMARY

(Erase heading not required.)

Army Form C. 2118

2nd Bn K.R.R.C.

1/2

Vol 29

Place	Date	Hour	Summary of Events and Information	Remarks and references to Appendices
	1 Feb		Training 2/Lt. FARNAN to Div. training school 2/Lt Sheepshanks – – – 2/Lt RAVENSCROFT to Brigade for instruction in Q Duties Very severe cold	APP A.
	2		Training. V. cold	
	3		Bn marched to MERICOURT-SUR-SOMME and went into huts. Very cold	APP. I
	4		The C.O. and 2nd in c. and went up to French support Bn to arrange about the relief. The French regiment is the 108th Reg. and the Battn. to relieve is 2nd BATAILLON of 9th Corps. Cold intense. Battn. washed feet for the first time according to the French method which has given such wonderful results in preventing trench foot.	
	5.		Marched to CHUIGNES. French Corps Cmdr. inspected Bde on the march. C.O. went with other officers of the DIV. to watch a practice [illegible] new method of attack by the French. 32 O.R. and 5 O.R. returned from a course of Lewis Gun instruction and Stokes mortar respectively.	APP II

769a

Instructions regarding War Diaries and Intelligence Summaries are contained in F. S. Regs., Part II. and the Staff Manual respectively. Title Pages will be prepared in manuscript.

WAR DIARY or INTELLIGENCE SUMMARY

(Erase heading not required.)

Army Form C. 2118

Place	Date	Hour	Summary of Events and Information	Remarks and references to Appendices
	6th		1 Officer per coy and 2nd in cmd and 1 N.C.O per platoon went to trenches to stay with French for 24 hours before Battn arrived. Cold intense	APP. ~~III~~
	7th		Bn relieved 2me Bataillon 108me Regiment 12th Corps 24me DIVISION in support about 2 miles E of ASSEVILLERS. Relief went off very quietly and satisfactorily in a great measure due to the great trouble taken by the French. Capt. K. B HILL arrived from 1st Battn K.R.R. in exchange with Capt. W.C SMITH who left the Battn	" IV " IV A " V R/35282 Cpl. C.G. MILLMAN died of pneumonia in F. Amb.
	8th		C.O. and 2nd in cmd went to reconnoitre front line occupied by French third batt & is to occupy on night of 11th/12th Quiet day	
	9th		Quiet day. C.O and 2nd in cmd went up again to reconnoitre new line.	
	10th		1 Officer 4 N.C.Os and 4 Riflemen per coy and 2nd in cmd. went up to ~~stay~~ with French for 24 hours before relief took place on 11th. Quiet day Capt. E.G.G. Gibb to hospital 2/Lt E.A. WARNER to 4th Army School. Capt T.R. FORSYTH FORREST rejoined from 4th Army school	
	11th	6pm to 8pm	Battn relieved ~~1st B~~ 1re Bataillon 123me Regiment in the front line, the brigade this side slipping to the right ~~a~~ by 1 battn front. Very quiet and French arrangements very good. The Adjutant and 1 French officer ~~per coy~~ ~~[illegible]~~ with each of our coys for 24 hours	APP. V A

TWC

K. [illegible] Capt

Army Form C. 2118

Instructions regarding War Diaries and Intelligence Summaries are contained in F. S. Regs., Part II. and the Staff Manual respectively. Title Pages will be prepared in manuscript.

WAR DIARY or INTELLIGENCE SUMMARY

(Erase heading not required.)

Place	Date	Hour	Summary of Events and Information	Remarks and references to Appendices
			Position of Coys. D on Right, B on left C in support and A in reserve. Very cold	APP VI
	12th		Shelling of our back communication trenches with 5.9 and 4.2 fairly heavy from 8.30 – 11 p.m. Looked as if Germans suspected a relief. Also a 2 minute bombardment at 1.30 a.m. on B Coy front and support lines Very quiet on the whole. Freezing at night but warmer during the day.	R 15837 Rfn. Gould Rd. Rfn. A/2430 JONES Killed 1 O.R. wounded
	13th	6pm. –7pm.	Very quiet day. A Coy. relieved a Coy. of the 7th Bn NORTHUMBERLAND FUSILEERS who had relieved the French Coy of the 249me Regiment the previous day. The Battn. thus side slipped to the right by 1 coy front and the L.N. LANCS on our left took over about 300 yds of our left front. Position of Coys A on right C on left D in support B in reserve. Quiet day. Our 2 Battalion observation posts were shelled during day with result of one being completely demolished by a direct hit of a large minenwerfer killing 1 observer and wounding another.	Rfn. R/15644 FAULKNER killed 1 O.R. Wd. APP VI A

771C

1875 Wt. W593/826 1,000,000 4/15 J.B.C. & A. A.D.S.S./Forms/C. 2118.

Army Form C. 2118

Instructions regarding War Diaries and Intelligence Summaries are contained in F. S. Regs., Part II. and the Staff Manual respectively. Title Pages will be prepared in manuscript.

WAR DIARY
or
INTELLIGENCE SUMMARY
(Erase heading not required.)

Place	Date	Hour	Summary of Events and Information	Remarks and references to Appendices
	14th	7.30pm–10pm	Relieved by Black Watch of 3rd Bde. Marched back to billets at CHOIGNOLLES about 7 miles in rear. Brigade in reserve for 8 days. Warmer during day but froze at night	1 O.R. W1. APP VI B
	15th		Day spent in cleaning up	
	16th		Bombing raid by German Aeroplanes during night at about 12 midnight and 6 a.m. No damage here. Coy Training during morning 2/Lt L.R. Vickers to 9th Bn K.R.R.C.	
	17		Col. ABADIE D.S.O. went to HAVRE to pay visit to No 1 Inf. BASE DEPOT. 2nd in command and 1 Officer met Brigadier to reconnoitre approaches to the Corps front in case of Reserve Bde being required to reinforce. Weather breaks and a heavy Thaw sets in.	
	18		Training in the attack on a double objective out of trenches	
	19		Batt. route march. LT. GOTT to IV Army sniping school CAPT. FORSYTH HOSPITAL to Hpl.	

772e

HQRS. C. No

1875 Wt. W593/826 1,000,000 4/15 J.B.C. & A. A.D.S.S./Forms/C. 2118.

Army Form C. 2118

Instructions regarding War Diaries and Intelligence Summaries are contained in F. S. Regs., Part II. and the Staff Manual respectively. Title Pages will be prepared in manuscript.

WAR DIARY
or
INTELLIGENCE SUMMARY
(Erase heading not required.)

Place	Date	Hour	Summary of Events and Information	Remarks and references to Appendices
	20		Rain all day. Training indoors. Conference of C.Os at BDE HQ.	
	21		C.O and O.C. Coys visit line to be taken on relief of 3rd BDE	
			2/Lt J.P. Macdowell to Rgt.	
			2/Lt A.C HEBERDEN joined Bn.	
	22		Col. ABADIE D.S.O. returns from HAVRE. Coy training.	
			Draft of 116 O.R. arrive	
			LIEUT. F RoBarts, 2/Lt R. MADELEY, 2/Lt E.M. Pollard joined	
	23		2/Lt A.L. GRACIE to IV Army Signal school. 2/Lt D H Taylor joined	1. O R. wd
			Battn relieved 1/S.W.B in left sector as support Battn	APP VII
	24		Quiet day	APP. VII A
	25		Quiet day 12 O.R. joined. Col ABADIE D.S.O left to go to the IVth	APP. VIII
	26		Army School for a 10 days conference. CAPT H F E SMITH joined HQ. to do 2nd in Command to MAJ: A.C. OPPENHEIM who took over the command of the Batt:	
	27		Batt. relieved the 1st Northamptonshire Rgt in the front line	

772c

1875 Wt. W593/826 1,000,000 4/15 J.B.C. & A. A.D.S.S./Forms/C. 2118.

Army Form C. 2118

WAR DIARY
or
INTELLIGENCE SUMMARY
(Erase heading not required.)

Instructions regarding War Diaries and Intelligence Summaries are contained in F. S. Regs., Part II. and the Staff Manual respectively. Title Pages will be prepared in manuscript.

Place	Date	Hour	Summary of Events and Information	Remarks and references to Appendices
			Position of Coys A on left B on the right, D in support C in reserve	No A203366 Rfn Mitchell B Coy killed
	27.		Germans reported to be retiring on the Ancre front. Lt Gott returned from IVth Army sniping school & joined HQ as intelligence officer. Quiet day. Advanced party of 5 officers & 13 ORs of 1/10th Manchesters joined.	App IX, IXA, IXB
	28.		At 5.25 am the left Coy liberated smoke to assist troops further North, accompanied by 5 minutes intense bombardment. Enemy retaliation slight. Internal relief. Position of Coys. C on the left D on the right. B in support A in reserve.	1 Cpl X, 1 Rfn wounded.

H. S. E. Smith Capt

7764C

SECRET.

1st Div. No. G. 247/13.   2nd Bde. No. G. 38/1.

INSTRUCTIONS REGARDING THE RELIEF OF THE 24th FRENCH DIVISION.

---

1. A depot of Bombs will be established at the MEUDON QUARRY (Left Brigade H.Q.) on the night of the 4th/5th February.

2. In addition to the above each man will carry at least 2 bombs into the line with him.

3. Brigades in the line will be responsible for the upkeep of the Communication Trenches in front and including Tranchee de CROUSAZ and the GRAND BOIS. The 6th Welch will be responsible for their upkeep West of this line. The main ones that will be kept up by the 6th Welch are shown in green on the attached sketch. The Communication Trenches in this sector are in very good condition and the Major-General directs that steps shall be taken to ensure this condition being maintained. Instructions regarding the Communication trenches to be maintained when the Division sidesteps will be issued later.

4. As soon as the troops of the 1st Division move into the Reserve area i.e. CHUIGNES - MARLY - OLYMPE etc. and until G.O.C. 1st Division assumes command on the 8th, they will be under the tactical command of the G.O.C. 24th French Division.

Brigadiers will therefore report their arrival in the Reserve area to G.O.C. 24th French Division (H.Q., BOISVERT - G.36.b.) as well as to Headquarters 1st Division. They and their Battalion Commanders must know the lines of approach to both sectors of the French 24th Division front.

5. It is important that the enemy should be kept in ignorance of the relief for as long as possible. It is therefore necessary that there should be no movement in the open, East of the line ASSEVILLERS - BOIS DE VIROFLAY. The communication trenches will be used by all ranks east of this line. This order is to be brought to the notice of all troops and rigidly enforced. The line beyond which vehicles may not go in daylight is shown on the attached sketch.

6. It is also necessary that there shall be no increase of activity after relief. This includes Artillery fire, T.M. fire, Rifle grenades and sniping. When increased activity is to be shown, orders will be issued from Divisional Headquarters. The D.A. should not fire salvoes.

7. There are many dugouts and shelters in various parts of the new area. Some of these may be unoccupied from time to time.

Troops are forbidden to damage or tamper with any dugouts or shelters even though they are unoccupied.

This order will be read out on three consecutive parades and carefully explained to the men. Certificates to the effect that every man has had his attention drawn to this order will be forwarded to Divisional Headquarters by noon on Monday 5th February by the following:-

G.O's.C. Brigades.   G.O.C. R.A.
C.R.E.   O.C. 6th Welch.   A.D.M.S.

(sd) W.G. DOBBIE, Lieut-Colonel,

30th January, 1917.   General Staff, 1st Division.

APP.I

COPY NO.....9.. 776c

S E C R E T.

Battalion Order No. .6. by Lieutenant-Colonel R.N.Abadie, D.S.O.
Commanding, In the Field.
2nd February, 1917.

Reference Maps:-
1/100,000 Sheets. AMIENS & LENS.

....

1......... 2nd Infantry Brigade and attached troops will march on February 3rd 1917 and go into huts.

2.... ....Order of March of Brigade.
Brigade Headquarters.
1st Northamptonshire Regiment.
1st Loyal North Lancs Regiment.
2nd Bn King's Royal Rifle Corps.
1/6th Welch Regiment.
etc.,
Intervals of 10 minutes between battalions.

3..........ROUTE. RIBEMONT - MERICOURT L'ABBE - SAILLY-LE-SEC - SAILLY LAURETTE - CERISSY - MORCOURT - MERICOURT-SUR-SOMME.

4..........BRIGADE BILLETING PARTIES. on bicycles will rendezvous at the Church, RIBEMONT at 9-50 a.m. and will proceed in one body under command of the senior officer; reporting to the ~~senior~~ Staff Captain at the Church MERICOURT-SUR-SOMME.
Companies will detail the usual billeting parties under command of Captain. E.J.G.Gibb.

5..........2nd Bn K.R.R.C. with 1st and 2nd Line transport will march at 9-50 a.m.

6..........Starting Point. The BREWERY at BRESLE.

7..........Order of March.
Hd Qrs, B.Coy, Band, C.Coy, D.Coy, Buglers, A.Coy, 1st Line Transport, 2nd Line Transport, one horsed Ambulance wagon.

8..........HALTS. there will be no longer halts than the usual 10 minutes halt before each clock hour.

9..........ACKNOWLEDGE.
BREAKFASTS............. 7.AM.
10 —— OFFICERS KITS. at Q M STORES. 9.AM.
BLANKETS. ON SQUARE at 7.15 a.m.

C. Amb[illegible]
2nd Lieutenant.
A/Adjutant, 2nd Bn King's Royal Rifles....

Issued by orderly at 7.30 p.m.

Copy No. 1....Bn Headquarters.
No. 2....A. Coy.
No. 3....B.Coy.
No. 4....C.Coy.
No. 5....D.Coy.

Copy No. 6.....Hd Qr Coy.
No. 7.....Quarter Master.
No. 8.....Transport Officer.
No. 9.....War Diary.
No. 10....R.S.M.

APP II

COPY NO.......9.......

S E C R E T.

Battalion Order No, 7. by Lieutenant-Colonel R. N. Abadie, D.S.O.
Commanding, In the Field.
4th February, 1917.

777c

Reference Maps :-
1/40,000 Sheets, 62c & 62d.

....

1.......... 2nd Infantry Brigade and attached troops will move to fresh area tomorrow.

2.......... Company Billeting parties as usual, under command of Lieut: W.H.E.Gott, will meet the Staff Captain, 2nd Infantry Brigade at the Church, Mericourt, at 9 a.m. tomorrow.

3..........Order of March of Column.

23rd Field Coy R.E.
* Brigade Hd Qrs.
1st Bn Loyal North Lancs.
2nd Bn King's Royal Rifle Corps.
2nd Machine Gun Coy.
etc.,

4..........2nd Bn King's Royal Rifles will go into Camp No. 2. CHUIGNES.

5..........Starting Point of Battn:- Road Junction, R. 4. C. 2. 3.

6..........ORDER OF MARCH OF BATTN.
The Battn will move off in the following order at 11.15 a.m.
Headquarters.
C. Company.
D. Company.
A. Company.
B. Company.
1st Line Transport.
2nd Line Transport.

7..........The Band will receive separate instructions.

8..........Blankets will be rolled in bundles of ten and placed ~~outside~~ on edge of road by Cookers ~~huts~~ by....9....a.m.

9..........Officers Kits and Mess Stores will be ready for loading by....10.......a.m. by the Horse Trough.

10..........Acknowledge.

C. Ambler.
2nd Lieutenant.
A/Adjutant. 2nd Bn King's Royal Rifles.

Issued by Orderly at.....1.30.....p.m.

Copy No. 1..........Bn Headquarters.
No. 2..........A. Coy.
No. 3..........B. Coy.
No. 4..........C. Coy.
No. 5..........D. Coy.
Copy No. 6..........Hd Qr Coy.
No. 7..........Quarter Master.
No. 8..........Transport Off'r
No. 9..........War Diary.
No. 10..........R. S. M.

* By an after order the order of march was changed and the battn led the column.

APP III

S E C R E T.

BATTALION ORDER NO. 8.

COPY NO. 2

6th February. 1917.

778C

Reference Maps:-.
AMIENS. No. 17. 1/100,000
62.C. s.w. 1/40,000

1......... The 2nd Bn K.R.R.C. will relieve "E" Battalion of the 108th French Regiment in the support area tomorrow night (Feb: 7/8th).

2......... B. Coy will relieve "E.2" Coy.
C. " " " "E.3" "
D. " " " "E.4" "
A. Coy will go into unoccupied shelters.

3......... The Battalion will parade in fighting order wearing jerkins with greatcoats folded on the back, carrying rations for the 8th on the man, and will move off at 5-30 p.m. in the following order from the CHUIGNES CROSS ROADS.

Headquarters.
2 Hd Qr Limbers.
B. Coy.
Hd Qr Water Limber.
C. Coy.
D. Coy.
A. Coy.

Lewis Gun Limbers will follow immediately behind Companies. 32 Magazines per Gun will be taken in - The balance will be left in charge of one Lewis Gunner per Coy.

4......... Blankets (in bundles of ten), packs and officers' kits will be ready by 2 p.m. outside huts.

5......... ROUTE. DOMPIERRE. - ASSEVILLERS.

6.........GUIDES. French guides will be furnished for Headquarters and each platoon at the Road Junction on the DOMPIERRE - ASSEVILLERS Road at point M.6.d.1.1.

7.........S.A.A. 120 rounds per man will be carried on the man. There is a Brigade Reserve at Brigade Hd Qrs.

8.........BOMBS. Each Coy will take in 17 boxes of Mills No.5. These will be fuzed under Coy arrangements tomorrow morning and on arrival will be kept at Company Hd Qrs.

There is a Brigade Bomb Store at the Brigade Hd Qrs which are in the Quarry at N.16.a.8.4.

9.........Sergt Ravenscroft, one signaller and one stretcher bearer will be guided up to 108th Battn Hd Qrs at 10 a.m. tomorrow by 2nd Lieut F.A.Gill.

10........Pioneers. Four with Headquarters and one with each Coy. The latter will parade with their Companies.

11........WATER. 20 full tins per Coy can be drawn from Battn Dump on arrival. Battn Dump at N.15.b.3.2. Water is obtained from N.15,d.t.e. and must be chlorinated before use.

12......... Command of the sector will remain with Colonel ODRY Commanding the French Brigade until 10 a.m. on the 8th February, at which

779 c

hour Brigadier General Commanding 2nd Infantry Brigade will take over. command of the Right sub-sector.

The Brigade will be covered by the French Artillery until 10 a.m. on the 10th inst., after which hour the by the 1st Divisional Artillery.

Each front Battalion is in direct communication by telephone with the French Artillery Group covering the front.

Corpl Waite, A.Coy will remain with Hd Qr Signallers on completion of the relief until 10 a.m. on the 10th inst., when he will rejoin his Company.

13....... Battn Hd Qrs will open in the wood about N.15.d.6.5.on arrival.

14.........Completion of relief will be reported immediately by runner.

15...... Acknowledge.

C. Ambler.

2nd Lieutenant.

A/Adjutant, 2nd Bn King's Royal Rifles....

Issued by Orderly at ...10.15... p.m.

Copy. No. 1.....War Diary.
No. 2.....C.O.
No. 3.....Major Oppenheim for 108th Regiment.
No. 4.....A. Coy.
No. 5.....B. Coy.
No. 6.....C. Coy.
No. 7....D. Coy.
No. 8.....Signalling Sergeant.
No. 9.....Quarter Master.
No.10.....Transport Officer.
No.11.....Medical Officer.
No.12......Hd Qr Coy.
No.13......R.S.M.
No.14.....Office Copy.
No. 15....Office Copy.

APP IV

780c

Copy of letter from General HIRSCHAUER, K.C.B. to H.Q. III Corps.

Sir,

Allow me to thank you this very evening for the great honour bestowed upon me by ordering a Brigade of your 1st Division to march before me.

I was struck by the splendid appearance, fitness and carriage of these men who come from all parts of England, Will you be so kind as to convey my sincere congratulations to the General of the 1st Division and to the General of the Brigade.

Believe me to remain,

Yours very sincerely,

HIRSCHAUER. K.C.B.

APP IV

1st Div. No. G. 247/16. Rna. 2nd Bde. No. G. 38/19.

781c

Sir.

Allow me to thank you this very evening for the great honour bestowed upon men by ordering a brigade of your 1st Division to march before me.

I was struck by the splendid appearance, fitness and carriage of those menwho come from all parts of England. Will you be so kind as to convey my sincere congratulations to the General of the 1st Division and to the General of the Brigade.

Believe me to remain,

Yours very sincerely,

HIRSCHAUER. K.C.B.

\- 2 -

1st Division.

The attached letter from General HIRSCHAUER is forwarded.

(sd) H.T.Lewis, Captain,
for Brigadier General,
General Staff,
III Corps.

H.Q., III Corps.
6th February, 1917.

\- 3 -

~~O.C. Royal Sussex.~~
~~O.C. Loyal N. Lancs.~~
~~O.C. Northamptons.~~
O.C. K. R. R. C.
~~O.C. No. 2 M.G. Coy.~~
~~O.C. 2nd T.M. Batty.~~

For information.

Copy to each Coy (5) ~~1 to~~ original to War Diary

1 Copy also for War Diary

[signature]

Bt. Major, Brigade Major,
2nd Infantry Brigade.

8th February, 1917.

War Diary

APP IV(A)

SECRET.

Copy.No. 4.

RMA

2nd Infantry Brigade Order No. 121.

2nd February, 1917.

782c

Reference Maps :-
1/40,000 Sheets 62.C., and 62.D.
Attached Tracing.

1. The 2nd Infantry Brigade, with 1/6th Welch Regiment, 23rd Field Company R.E., No. 141 Field Ambulance and No. 3 Company, 1st Division Train. attached, will move to a forward area on February 5th in accordance with the attached March Table.

2. Units will march complete with their 1st Line Transport and baggage wagons.

3. Billeting Parties with bicycles will report to the Staff Captain at the Church, MERICOURT at 9 a.m. on the 5th instant.

4. 2nd Infantry Brigade will relieve the 108th French Regiment in the line on the night 7/8th instant.
Machine Guns will go into the line on the night of the 6/7th instant and will overlap for 24 hours with the French guns. Detailed orders for the relief will be issued later.

5. Brigade Headquarters will close at MERICOURT SUR SOMME at 10 a.m. on 5th February and re-open at CHUIGNES at 2 p.m. on the same date.

6. Acknowledge.

A.G.F. Isaac

Bt. Major, Brigade Major,
2nd Infantry Brigade.

Issued at 4 p.m.

Copies to :-

1. Royal Sussex.
2. Loyal N. Lancs.
3. Northamptons.
4. K. R. R. C.
5. No. 2 M.G. Coy.
6. 2nd T.M. Battery.
7. 1/6th Welch Regt.
8. 23rd Field Coy. R.E.
9. 141 Field Ambulance.
10. No. 3 Coy. Div. Train.
11. 1st Division.
12. 1st Brigade.
13. 3rd Brigade.
14. G.O.C.
15. Staff Captain.
16. Bde Signal Officer.
17. Bde Transport Officer.
18. War Diary.
19.) Office.
20.)

March Table to accompany 2nd Infantry Brigade Order No. 121. Dated 2nd February, 1917.

UNIT.	FROM	TO	ROUTE.	STARTING POINT.	TIME.	REMARKS.
23rd Field Coy. R.E.	Camp 5. MERICOURT.	MILL M.6.d.5.0.	CHUIGNOLLES - CHUIGNES - DOMPIERRE.	Cross Roads R.2.c.2.1.	11.14 a.m.	Horses to Eastern part of Chateau grounds FONTAINE-LE-CAPPY.
Brigade Headquarters.	MERICOURT.	CHUIGNES.	CHUIGNOLLES - Cross Roads R.17.a.	-do-	11.19 a.m.	
1st Loyal N. Lancs.	Camp 6. MERICOURT.	CHUIGNES "A".	-do-	-do-	11.20 a.m.	
2nd K. R. R. C.	Camp 6. MERICOURT.	CHUIGNES. "B".	-do-	-do-	11.27 a.m.	
No. 2 M.G. Coy.	MERICOURT.	CHUIGNES.	-do-	-do-	11.33 a.m.	
2nd T.M.Battery.	MERICOURT.	CHUIGNES.	-do-	-do-	11.36 a.m.	
No. 3 Coy. Div.Train.	MERICOURT.	CHUIGNES.	-do-	-do-	11.37 a.m.	
1st Northamptons.	Camp 5. MERICOURT.	CHUIGNOLLES "A".	CHUIGNOLLES.	-do-	11.40 a.m.	
2nd Royal Sussex.	MERICOURT.	CHUIGNOLLES "B".	-do-	-do-	11.47 a.m.	
No. 141 Field Ambulance.	MERICOURT.	MARLY.	CHUIGNOLLES - Cross Roads R.4.d.	-do-	12.3 p.m.	Will billet with No. 2 F.A. in the 6 Southern-most Huts in Camp, MARLY.
1/6th Welch Regt.	Camp 5. MERICOURT.	Camp 52.A.	CHUIGNOLLES Road as far as road junction R.8.a.7.9. thence direct.	-do-	12.6 p.m.	

787c

SECRET. War Diary

APP. V

COPY NO........1

BATTALION ORDERS NO. 8.

6th February, 1917.

784C

Reference Maps:-
AMIENS. No.17..1/100,000
62 C. s.w. 1/40,000.

1......... The 2nd Bn K.R.R.C. will relieve "E" Battalion of the 108th French Regiment in the support area tomorrow night (Feb: 7/8th)

2.........
B.Coy will relieve "E.2" Coy.
C. " " " "E.3" "
D. " " " "E.4" "
A.Coy will go into unoccupied shelters.

3......... The Battalion will parade in fighting order wearing jerkins with greatcoats folded on the back, carrying rations for the 8th on the man, and will move off at 5-30 p.m. in the following order from the CHUIGNES CROSS ROADS.

Headquarters.
2 Hd Qr Limbers.
B, Coy.
Hd Qr Water Limber.
C.Coy.
D. Coy.
A. Coy.

Lewis Gun Limbers will follow immediately behind Companies. 32 Magazines per gun will be taken in - The balance will be left in charge of one Lewis Gunner per Company.

4......... Blankets (in bundles of ten), packs and officers' kits will be ready by 2 p.m. outside huts.

5.........ROUTE. DOMPIERRE - ASSEVILLERS.

6.........GUIDES. French guides will be furnished for Headquarters and each platoon at the Road Junction on the DOMPIERRE - ASSEVILLERS Road at point M.6.d.1.1.

7.........S.A.A. 120 rounds per man will be carried on the man. There is a Brigade Reserve at Brigade Hd Qrs.

8.........BOMBS. Each Coy will take in 17 boxes of Mills No. 5. These will be fuzed under Coy arrangements tomorrow morning and on arrival will be kept at Company Hd Qrs.

There is a Brigade Bomb Store at the Brigade Hd Qrs which are in the Quarry at N.16.a.8.4.

9.........Sergt Ravenscroft, one signaller and one stretcher bearer will be guided up to 108th Battn Hd Qrs at 10 a.m. tomorrow by 2nd Lieut: F.A.Gill.

10.........Pioneers. Four with Headquarters and one with each Coy. The latter will parade with their Companies.

11.........WATER. 20 full tins per Coy can be drawn from Battn Dump on arrival. Battn Dump at N.15.b.3.2. Water is obtained from N.15.d.5.9. and must be chlorinated before use.

12......... Command of the sector will remain with Colonel ODRY Commanding the French Brigade until 10 a.m. on the 8th February, at which hour Brigadier General Commanding 2nd Infantry Brigade will take over

785c

command of the Right sub-sector.

The Brigade will be covered by the French Artillery until 10 a.m. on the 10th inst., after which hour by the 1st Divisional Artillery.

Each front Battalion is in direct communication by telephone with the French Artillery Group covering their front.

Cpl Waite, A.Coy, will remain with Hd Qr Signallers on completion of the relief until 10 a.m. on the 10th inst., when he will rejoin his Company.

13......Battn Hd Qrs will open in the wood about N. 15. d. 6. 5. on arrival.

14......Completion of relief will be reported immediately by runner.

15......Acknowledge.

C Andrews

2nd Lieutenant.

A/Adjutant, 2nd Bn King's Royal Rifles.....

Issued by Orderly at 10. 15 P.M.

Copy No. 1..........War Diary.
No. 2..........O.C.
No. 3..........Major Oppenheim for 108th Regiment.
No. 4..........A. Coy.
No. 5..........B. Coy.
No. 6..........C. Coy.
No. 7..........D. Coy.
No. 8..........Signalling Sergeant.
No. 9..........Quarter Master.
No. 10.........Transport Officer.
No. 11.........Medical Officer.
No. 12.........Hd. Qr. Coy.
No. 13.........R.S.M.
No. 14.........Office Copy.
No. 15.........Office Copy.

SECRET

BOULOGN'S Sector.

G 38/12

786c

PROPOSAES for the relieve of the 7th February.

The british bataillons shall come up to the initial point (road from Dompierre to Assevillers, to the Moulin de Becquincourt) in the following order :

5.30 p.m. : Brigade staff,
5.45 p.m. : Z Bataillon (Z I, Z 2, Z 3, Z 4)
6.I5 p.m : A Bataillon (A 2, A I, A 3, A 4)
6.45 p.m : E Bataillon (E I, E 2, E 3, E 4)

The guides of the IO8th Regt :

I guide for the Brigade's staff,
I guide for each Bataillon's staff,
I nom.com.Officer and 4 guides for each company.

Will be up to the initial point with the british nom.com.Officers who came already in the regiment's sector, half an hour before the fixed time.

Itinerary :

Z Bataillon - Road from Assevillers/Barleux "Martinique" communication's trench;

A Bataillon - Road from Assevillers/Barleux and Roumanie and Genie, communication's trench;

Brigade and Bataillon E staff : Road Assevillers/Dompierre

The Major Comg the IO8th Inf.Regt.

O C KRRC

Passed to you for information & retention

Albaac[?] B^de Major
Bde Maj
2^d Bde

Move Table

SECRET.

Copy No. 4.

787C

2nd Infantry Brigade Order No. 123.

5th February, 1917.

Reference Maps :-
1/40,000 62.C., 62.D.
1/10,000 62.C.SW.1., 62.C.SW.2.
Trench Maps already issued.

1. 2nd Infantry Brigade will relieve the 108th French Regiment in the line on the night of the 7/8th instant.

2. Following preliminary moves will take place on the 6th instant:-

i. One Officer and 4 N.C.Os. per Company from 2nd Royal Sussex Regiment, 1st Northamptonshire Regiment, 2nd K.R.R.C. will go into the line on this date for reconnaissance duties.
2nd Royal Sussex Regiment to the Right French Battalion.
1st Northamptonshire Regt. to the Left French Battalion.
2nd K.R.R.C. to French Reserve Battalion.
These Officers and N.C.Os. will be at the Western entrance to ASSEVILLERS at 2.30 p.m. on the 6th instant where guides from the French will meet them and lead them in. They will take two day's rations with them.

ii. Machine Guns will move into the line on the 6th instant and will overlap for 24 hours with French Machine Guns. For the purposes of relief 8 Lewis Guns complete with teams will be attached to No. 2 Machine Gun Company. Four Lewis Guns to be furnished by O.C. 2nd Royal Sussex Regiment and four to be furnished by O.C. 1st Northamptonshire Regiment.
Lewis Guns as above in limbers and teams with two day's rations will report to O.C. No. 2 Machine Gun Company at his Headquarters CHUIGNOLLES at 1.30 p.m. on the 6th instant.
No. 2 Machine Gun Company with the Lewis Guns mentioned above will be at the Western entrance to ASSEVILLERS at 3 p.m. on the 6th instant where guides from the French will meet them and lead them in.

iii. Brigade Signalling Officer with one N.C.O. will accompany the Officers mentioned in sub-para. 1. and will proceed to the Headquarters, 108th French Regiment, BOIS DE BOULOGNE, N.16 central on the 6th instant and will reconnoitre all lines of communication.

3. The remainder of the Brigade, less 1st Loyal N. Lancs. Regt., No. 2 Machine Gun Company, 2nd Trench Mortar Battery and South African Sharpshooters, will move up and relieve the 108th French Regiment in the line on the 7th instant in accordance with the attached Move Table.

4. O.C. No. 2 Machine Gun Company will assume command of all Machine Guns in the line at 6 p.m. on the 7th instant.

5. 1st Loyal N. Lancs. Regiment, 2nd Trench Mortar Battery and South African Sharpshooters will be in Brigade Reserve at CHUIGNES. A.

6. All 1st Line Transport will move to the vicinity of FONTAINE-LES-CAPPY on the 7th instant in accordance with instructions to be issued by the Staff Captain.

7. ....

788c

11 7. Each man will go into the line with two MILLS Bombs and 120 rounds of S.A.A. on him.

8. Command of the Sector will remain with Colonel ODRY Commanding the French Brigade until 10 a.m. on the 8th February, at which hour Brigadier General Commanding 2nd Infantry Brigade will take over command of the Right Sub-sector.

9. The Brigade will be covered by the French Artillery until 10 a.m. on the 10th instant after which hour by the 1st Divisional Artillery.
Each Front Battalion is in direct communication by telephone with the French Artillery Group covering their front.

10. Administrative Instructions will be issued later.

11. Brigade Headquarters will close at CHUIGNES at 2 p.m. on the 7th instant and will open at the BOIS DE BOULOGNE N.16 central at 7 p.m. on the same date.

12. Acknowledge.

A.G.? Isaac

Bt. Major, Brigade Major,
2nd Infantry Brigade.

Issued at :- 9 p.m.

Copies to.

1. Royal Sussex.
2. Loyal N. Lancs.
3. Northamptons.
4. K. R. R. C.
5. No. 2 M.G. Coy.
6. 2nd T.M. Battery.
7. No. 3 Coy. A.S.C.
8. 1st Division "G".
9. 1st Division "Q".
10. 1st Brigade.
11. 3rd Brigade.
12. G.O.C.
13. Staff Captain.
14.) Brigade Signal Officer.
15.)
16. Brigade Transport Officer.
17. Brigade Scout Officer.
18. 24th French Division.
19. Colonel ODRY, through 24th French Division.
20. 108th French Regiment, through 24th French Div.
21. War Diary.
22.) Office.
23.)

Move Table to accompany 2nd Infantry Brigade Order No. 123. Dated 5th February, 1917.

Date.	Unit.	Starting Point.	Time.	Route.	Guides from the French will meet Units :- Place.	Time.	Remarks.
7th Feb'y.	2nd Brigade Headquarters.	Cross-roads 800 yards E. of CHUIGNES M.8.c.8.3.	4.30 p.m.	DOMPIERRE ASSEVILLERS.	Road junction on the DOMPIERRE ASSEVILLERS Road Point M.6.d.1.1.	5.30 p.m.	
7th Feb'y.	2nd Royal Sussex Regiment. Right Battalion to take over Sector Z.	- do -	4.45 p.m.	-do-	-do-	5.45 p.m.	Coys. to march in the following order. Right Front Coy., Left Front Coy., Support Company, Reserve Company.
7th Feb'y.	1st Northampton Regiment. Left Battalion to take over Sector A.	- do -	5.15 p.m.	-do-	-do-	6.15 p.m.	Coys. to march in the following order Left Front Coy., Right Front Coy., Support Company, Reserve Company.
7th Feb'y.	2nd K.R.R.C. Support Battn. to take over from French Reserve Battn. in Sector E.	- do -	5.45 p.m.	-do-	-do-	6.45 p.m.	Companies to march in the following order :- E.1., E.2., E.3., E.4.

789c

War Diary ✓ Rua APP V A

SECRET. Copy No. 4

7900

2nd Infantry Brigade Order No. 124.

10th February, 1917.

Reference Maps.
1/10,000 Sheets 62.D.SW.1. and 62.C.SW.2.
Trench Maps already issued.

1. The following reliefs will take place on the night 11/12th February :-
(1). 2nd Battalion K.R.R.C. will relieve the 1st Battalion 123rd French Regiment in the line.
Guides from the French will be at the CEMETRY N.21.a. on the BELLOY - FLAUCOURT Road at 6 p.m.
All details to be arranged direct between Battalion Commanders concerned.
(2). 1st Battalion Northamptonshire Regiment will be relieved in the line by 1st Battalion S.W. Borderers (less 1 Company). Relief to be complete by 10 p.m. All details to be arranged direct between Battalion Commanders concerned.
On relief 1st Northamptonshire Regiment will move back into Support at GREAT WOOD.

2. The following preliminary moves will take place on the 10th instant :-
(1). Advanced parties of 2nd Battalion K.R.R.C. will go into the line and remain in the line for reconnaissance duties. Guides from the French will be at the CEMETRY N.21.a. at 2 p.m.
(2). Advanced parties of 1st Battalion S.W. Borders will go into the line and remain in the line for reconnaissance duties. Guides from 1st Battalion Northamptonshire Regiment will be at Brigade Headquarters N.16.a.8.2. at 2 p.m.

3. Machine Gun Reliefs.
(1). One section No. 2 Machine Gun Company with 4 Lewis Guns and teams to be furnished by O.C. 2nd K.R.R.C. attached will move into the line on the 10th instant and will overlap for 24 hours with the French Machine Guns.
Guides from the French will be at the CEMETRY N.21.a. at 2 p.m.

(2). The guns of No. 2 Machine Gun Company now in the section of the line held by 1st Battalion Northamptonshire Regiment will be relieved by No. 3 Machine Gun Company on the 10th instant. All details to be arranged direct between Company Commanders concerned.

4. On the 12th instant the following moves will take place :-
(1). 1st Battalion Loyal N. Lancs. Regiment will move to ASSEVILLERS with Battalion Headquarters at N.13.d.6.9. to be clear of CHUIGNES by 11.45 a.m.
(2). 2nd Battalion Royal Sussex Regiment will be relieved in the line by 1st Battalion Loyal N. Lancs. Regiment. Relief not to start before 5 p.m. All details to be arranged direct between Battalion Commanders concerned.

5. Completion of reliefs to be reported by wire to Brigade Headquarters.

6. Acknowledge.

A G F Isaac.

Bt. Major, Brigade Major,
2nd Infantry Brigade.

Issued at 9 a.m.

Copies to :- P.T.O.

SECRET. War Diary RHA APP V A

Copy No. 4

790C

2nd Infantry Brigade Order No. 124.

10th February, 1917.

Reference Maps.
1/10,000 Sheets 62.D.SW.1. and 62.C.SW.2.
Trench Maps already issued.

1. The following reliefs will take place on the night 11/12th February :-

(1). 2nd Battalion K.R.R.C. will relieve the 1st Battalion 123rd French Regiment in the line.
Guides from the French will be at the CEMETRY N.21.a. on the BELLOY - FLAUCOURT Road at 6 p.m.
All details to be arranged direct between Battalion Commanders concerned.

(2). 1st Battalion Northamptonshire Regiment will be relieved in the line by 1st Battalion S.W. Borderers (less 1 Company). Relief to be complete by 10 p.m. All details to be arranged direct between Battalion Commanders concerned.
On relief 1st Northamptonshire Regiment will move back into Support at GREAT WOOD.

2. The following preliminary moves will take place on the 10th instant :-

(1). Advanced parties of 2nd Battalion K.R.R.C. will go into the line and remain in the line for reconnaissance duties. Guides from the French will be at the CEMETRY N.21.a. at 2 p.m.

(2). Advanced parties of 1st Battalion S.W. Borders will go into the line and remain in the line for reconnaissance duties. Guides from 1st Battalion Northamptonshire Regiment will be at Brigade Headquarters N.16.a.8.2. at 2 p.m.

3. Machine Gun Reliefs.

(1). One section No. 2 Machine Gun Company with 4 Lewis Guns and teams, to be furnished by O.C. 2nd K.R.R.C., attached will move into the line on the 10th instant and will overlap for 24 hours with the French Machine Guns.
Guides from the French will be at the CEMETRY N.21.a. at 2 p.m.

(2). The guns of No. 2 Machine Gun Company now in the section of the line held by 1st Battalion Northamptonshire Regiment will be relieved by No. 3 Machine Gun Company on the 10th instant. All details to be arranged direct between Company Commanders concerned.

4. On the 12th instant the following moves will take place :-

(1). 1st Battalion Loyal N. Lancs. Regiment will move to ASSEVILLERS with Battalion Headquarters at N.13.d.6.9. to be clear of CHUIGNES by 11.45 a.m.

(2). 2nd Battalion Royal Sussex Regiment will be relieved in the line by 1st Battalion Loyal N. Lancs. Regiment.
On relief 2nd Battalion Royal Sussex Regiment will move back into Relief at ASSEVILLERS.

5. Completion of reliefs to be reported by wire to Brigade Headquarters.

6. Acknowledge.

A G I Isaac.

Bt. Major, Brigade Major,
2nd Infantry Brigade.

Issued at 9 a.m.

Copies to :- P.T.O.

791

Copies to :-

No. 1. 2nd Royal Sussex.
2. 1st Loyal N. Lancs.
3. 1st Northamptons.
4. 2nd K. R. R. C.
5. No. 2 M.G. Coy.
6. 2nd T.M. Battery.
7. No. 3 Coy. A.S.C.
8. 1st Division (for information).
9. 1st Brigade.
10. 3rd Brigade.
11. G.O.C.
12. Staff Captain.
13. Brigade Scout Officer.
14.) Brigade Signal Officer.
15.)
16. Brigade Transport Officer.
17. 249th French Regiment.
18. War Diary.
19.) Office.
20.)

APP VI Copy No. 1

Battalion Order No 4

Reference French Maps 1/20,000 62c. S.W. 9 · 2 · 17

1. The Battalion will relieve a Battalion of the 123rd French Reg on the night of the 11/12th February.
Our Companies for the purpose of the relief will be known by numerals not by letters.
   B. Coy (No 2 Coy) will go in on the right.
   D. " (No 4 ") " " " " " left. 792c
   A " (No 1 ") less two platoons will relieve the French Reserve Coy
   C " (No 3 ") will go into support in an unoccupied area.
Two platoons of A Coy will go into dug-outs Nos. 1. to 13.
2. B & D Coy will each detail 2 L.G. teams each of four complete with 16 magazines per gun to be attached to No 2. M.G. Coy. They will report at Battn: Hd. Qrs. at 1·45 p.m. to-day when they will go into the front line and remain there.
3. One Officer, 4 N.C.O's and 4 Riflemen (1 from each platoon) will be attached to the French Companies to be relieved from 2 p.m. to-day With this party will proceed 2 Signallers for Battn. Hd. Qrs. and each Company who will stay with the French. Sgt Ravenscroft will arrange to lay a line to-morrow to the new Hd. Qrs chosen for C Coy.
4. O's C. B & D Coy will each detail an Officer to report at Bn. Hd. Qrs at 10 a.m. to-day to reconnoitre the route which they will guide for carrying parties to-night & which will be supplied by A Coy. The carrying party will draw the following stores from Bde Hd. Qrs. dumps at N. 16. a. 8. 4 and will dispose of them as under.

			Bn.H.Q	R. Coy	L. Coy
Mill's No 5	boxes	100	50	25	25
S.A.A.	"	16	8	4	4
Very Lights 1"	"	5	3	1.	1.
do 1½"	"	3	1.	1.	1.

5. On the night of the 11/12th Feb: the relief will take place in the following order.
   (B Coy) No 2 Coy
   (D ") " 4 "
   (A ") " 1. "
   (C ") " 3 "
Guides will be at the Cemetery at 6 p.m. . 5 guides per Coy will be supplied except for A Coy which will only require 3.
6 Two listening patrols per Coy in front line will be established about 75 yards in front of our wire as soon as the relief is complete. Smocks will be drawn from Bn. H.Q.
7. Completion of relief will be reported by runner to Bn. H.Q
8. The ration dump will be at N. 21. a. 6. 1.

9 A Coy will carry rations & R.E. material for the front line Coys.

10. Acknowledge.

Issued at 9.30 am

Distribution.
Copy No 1 & 2 War Diary
3 A. Coy
4 B. "
5 C "
6 D "

79 3c

Lt Colonel
Comdg 2nd F.I.

War Diary

RUA

APP. VI A

SECRET.

Copy No. 4

794 C

2nd Infantry Brigade Order No. 125.

11th February, 1917.

Reference Maps.
1/10,000 36.C.SW.1., 36.C.SW.2.
Trench maps already issued.

1. On the night [illegible] 14th instant the following moves will take place :-

(1). The 1st Battalion Loyal N. Lancs. Regiment will extend its right taking over the line from 2nd K.R.R.C. as far as a point midway between the boyaux BERRY and CAYENNE point N.22.d.6.3. All details to be arranged direct between Battalion Commanders concerned. Relief to be complete by 10 p.m.

(2). 2nd K.R.R.C. will extend its right taking over line from 7th Northumberland Fusiliers as far as VILLERS - CARBONNEL - ESTREES Road exclusive (N.29.c.1.4.) All details to be arranged direct between Battalion Commanders concerned. Relief to be complete by 10 p.m. (Headquarters of 7th Northumberland Fusiliers are at P.C. NANCY N.28.c.7.4.)

2. On completion of these moves the Right Section of the 1st Divisional Sector will be held by 2nd Infantry Brigade as under:-

1st Loyal N. Lancs.) Left Sub-section)	From N.17.c.4.3. to N.22.d.6.3.
2nd K. R. R. C.) Right Sub-section.)	From N.22.d.6.3. to N.29.c.1.4.

3. The 2nd Infantry Brigade front will be covered by the Right Group, 1st Divisional Artillery.

4. Completion of reliefs to be reported by wire to Brigade Headquarters.

5. Acknowledge.

A. G. Isaac

Bt. Major, Brigade Major,
2nd Infantry Brigade.

Issued at 10 a.m.

Copies to :-

1. Royal Sussex.
2. Loyal N. Lancs.
3. Northamptons.
4. K. R. R. C.
5. No. 2 M.G. Coy.
6. 2nd T.M. Battery.
7. No. 3 Coy. A.S. C.
8. 1st Division (for information).
9. 1st Brigade.
10. 3rd Brigade.
11. 149th Brigade.
12. G.O.C.
13. Staff Captain.
14. Brigade Scout Officer.
15.) Brigade Signal Officer.
16.)
17. Brigade Transport Officer.
18. Right Group, 1st Div. Artillery.
19. War Diary.
20.)
21.) Office.

APP VI B

War Diary

Relief

SECRET.

Copy No. 4

2nd Infantry Brigade Order No.126.

13th February,1917.

791c

Reference Maps.
1/10,000 36 C. SW.1.& 2.
Trench maps already issued.

1. 2nd Infantry Brigade will be relieved by 1st Infantry Brigade on the night 14/15th instant.

2. Reliefs will be carried out in accordance with the attached table. All details to be arranged direct between Battalion Commanders concerned.

3. No.2.M.G.Company, 2nd Trench Mortar Battery will be relieved by No.1. M.G.Company and 1st Trench Mortar Battery on the night 13/14th instant.

4. Billeting parties will meet the Staff Captain at the CHURCH, CHUIGNES at 12 noon on the 14th instant.

5. Completion of reliefs will be reported to Brigade Headquarters by wire.

6. Brigade Headquarters will close at BOIS de BOULOGNE at 5 p.m. on the 14th instant, and reopen at CHUIGNES at 10 p.m. on the same date.

7. Acknowledge.

A G F Isaac

Bt Major,Brigade Major,
2nd Infantry Brigade.

Issued at 10. a.m.

Copies to :-

1. Royal Sussex.
2. Loyal N.Lancs.
3. Northamptons.
4. K. R. R. C.
5. No.2. M.G.Company.
6. 2nd T.M.Battery.
7. No.3.Coy A.S.C.
8. 1st Division (for information).
9. 1st Brigade.
10. 3rd Brigade.
11. 149th Brigade.
12. G.O.C.
13. Staff Captain.
14. Brigade Scout Officer.
15.) Brigade Signal Officer.
16.)
17. Brigade Transport Officer.
18. Right Group,1st Div. Artillery.
19. War Diary.
20.) Office.
21.)

196

Table to accompany 2nd Infantry Brigade Order No.126. dated 13th February,1917.

Unit 2nd Brigade to be relieved.	Relieving Unit 1st Brigade.	Platoon guides 2nd Bde. PLACE & TIME.	Destination Units 2nd Brigade.	ROUTE.	Remarks.
2nd K.R.R.C. and One platoon 1st L.N.Lancs Regt.	1st Bn Black Watch.	Western entrance to ASSEVILLERS N.7.c.9.3. 5.30 p.m.	CHUIGNES.	ASSEVILLERS — DOMPIERRE.	From N.29.c.1.4. to N.22.d.8.7.
1st L.N.Lancs. less one platoon.	8th Royal Berks. Regt.	ditto. 6.30 p.m.	CHUIGNES.	ditto.	From N.22.d.8.7. to N.17.c.4.3.
1st Battalion Northamptonshire Regiment.	1st Cameron Highlanders.	ditto. 3 p.m.	CHUIGNOLLES.	ditto.	To use communication trenches EAST of ASSEVILLERS.
2nd R.Sussex Regt.	10th Glosters.	ditto. 1 p.m.	CHUIGNOLLES.	ditto.	
No.2. M.G.Company. 2nd T.M.Battery.	No.1.M.G.Company. 1st T.M.Battery.	ditto. 5 p.m.	CHUIGNES.	ditto.	On 13th February. To take over billets vacated by 1st Bde units.

SECRET. Rma. Copy No. 4 APP. VII A

2nd Infantry Brigade Order No. 127.

21st February, 1917.

798c

Reference Maps.
1/20,000 Sheets 62.c.N.W. and 62.c.S.W.
1st Division SECRET Map No.4 and 4A. 1/10,000.

1. The 2nd Infantry Brigade will relieve the 3rd Infantry Brigade in the Left Sector on the night 23rd/24th February, 1917, with the exception of No. 2 Machine Gun Company and 2nd Trench Mortar Battery who will relieve corresponding Units of the 3rd Brigade during the early morning of the 23rd February, Vide Table attached.

2. Parties consisting of 1 Officer per Company, 1 N.C.O. per Platoon and 2 Lewis Gunners per team will be sent in advance. Guides will meet these parties at Support Battalion Headquarters N.4.c.2.1. at 10.30 a.m. 23rd February.

3. Battalions moving into the line will break the journey for Teas on the open ground to the West of DOMPIERRE.
Times of arrival at Cross Roads M.10.b.3.7. will be as under:-

1st Northamptonshire Regiment........	4.00 p.m.	23rd Feb.
1st Loyal N. Lancs. Regiment.........	4.45 p.m.	"
2nd King's Royal Rifle Corps.........	5.30 p.m.	"

4. Battalions will move from CHUIGNES with 50 yards between platoons, after leaving DOMPIERRE this will be increased to 100 yards between platoons. There will be no movement East of DOMPIERRE before 5 p.m.

5. The Dugout Sections of the 2nd Royal Sussex and 2nd K.R.R.C. will join the 1st Loyal N. Lancs. and 1st Northamptons. respectively on the evening of 24th February under orders to be made between Commanding Officers concerned. The O.C. 1st Loyal N. Lancs. and the O.C. 1st Northamptons. will arrange accommodation.

6. Lewis Gun drums will not be taken over on relief. Twenty drums per gun will be taken into the line, the remainder being left with Battalion Reserve S.A.A.

7. 2nd Brigade Headquarters will close at CHUIGNES at 3 p.m. on 23rd February and re-open at H.31.d.8.8. at 6 p.m. 23rd February.

E.E. Calthrop

Captain, Brigade Major,
2nd Infantry Brigade.

Issued at 8.30 p.m.
Copies to :-

1. 2nd R. Sussex.
2. 1st L.N.Lancs.
3. 1st Northants.
4. 2nd K.R.R.C.
5. No. 2 M.G. Coy.
6. 2nd T.M.Battery.
7. G.O.C.
8. Staff Captain.
9. Brigade Signal Officer.
10. -do-
11. Brigade Transport Officer.
12. Brigade Intelligence Offr.
13. Supply Officer, 2nd Brigade.
14. No. 3 Coy. Div. Train.
15. 141st Field Ambulance.
16. 1st Division "G".
17. 1st Division "Q".
18. 1st Infantry Brigade.
19. 3rd Infantry Brigade.
20. 144th Infantry Brigade.
21. Left Sub-Group. Artillery.
22. A.D.M.S.
23. C.R.E.
24. Lowland Field Coy. R.E.
25.) War Diary.
26.)
27.) Office.
28.)

Table to accompany 2nd Infantry Brigade Order No. 127. Dated 21st February, 1917.

Date.	Unit of 2nd Brigade.	Unit of 3rd Brigade.	Destination.	Route.	Guides. Number.	Guides. Place.	Guides. Time.	Remarks.
Early morning 23rd.	No.2 M.G.Coy.	No.3 M.G.Coy.	Line.	CHUIGNES.- DOMPIERRE - ASSEVILLERS BOULOGNE QUARRY.-	Details to be arranged direct between Commanding Officers.			One Section to be in Reserve at TELEGRAPH CAMP M.3.b.8.8. To take over No.3 M.G. Coy. H.Q. about N.11.c.9.6½
Early morning 23rd.	2nd T.M.Batty.	3rd T.M.Batty.	Line.	CHUIGNES - DOMPIERRE - HERBECOURT - FLAUCOURT QUARRY N.11.a.6.9.	Details to be arranged direct between Commanding Officers.			Reserve Teams to be accommodated in bank near QUARRY N.11.a.4.8. H.Q. to be at old 3rd M.G.Coy. H.Q. at N.10.d.3.2. temporary.
Afternoon 23rd.	2nd R.Sussex.	2nd R.M.F.	Reserve. TELEGRAPH CAMP.	CHUIGNES - Cross roads M.10.b.3.7.	Details to be arranged direct between Commanding Officers.			Column must be clear of Cross roads M10.b. 3.7. by 3.30 p.m.
Night 23/24th.	1st Northants.	1st Glosters.	Right Battalion.	CHUIGNES - DOMPIERRE - ASSEVILLERS BOIS DE BOULOGNE.	Details to be arranged direct between Commanding Officers - but to be clear of cross roads M.6.c.5.8. by 5.30 p.m.			May not move East of DOMPIERRE before 5 p.m. Battalion Headquarters N.10.d.9½.9.
Night 23/24th.	1st L.N.Lancs.	2nd Welch.	Left Battalion.	CHUIGNES - DOMPIERRE - HERBECOURT - FLAUCOURT QUARRY N.11.a.6.9.	1 per platoon 1 for H.Q.	West Entrance to HERBECOURT H.31.a.1½9½.	6.15 p.m.	Will move by road as far as the QUARRY N.11.a.6.9. Battalion Headquarters N.11.a.6.9.
Night 23/24th.	2nd K. R. R. C.	1st S.W.B.	Support.	CHUIGNES - DOMPIERRE - HERBECOURT - FLAUCOURT.	-do-	-do-	7 p.m.	Battalion Headquarters N.4.c.2.1.

APP. VII

SECRET.

COPY NO. 1

BATTALION ORDER NO. 9.

22nd February, 1917.

197c

Reference Maps:- 1/20,000, 62 C.N.W. and 62.C.S.W.
1st Divl Secret Map No.4. and No. 4 A. 1/10,000.

1....... The Battalion will relieve the 1st S.W.B. on the night of the 23/24th Feb: 1917, in support.

2....... Advanced parties consisting of one Officer per Coy, one signaller per Coy, one N.C.O. per Platoon and two Lewis Gunners per team, Sergt Francis, one policeman and two scouts for Hd Qrs, will parade at the Orderly Room at 7-30 a.m. on the 23rd.

Dress:- Fighting Order and next day's rations.

Guide will meet this party at support Bn Hd Qrs. N.4.c.2.1. at 10-30 a.m.

3....... The Battalion will march via CHUIGNES - DOMPIERRE - HERBECOURT - FLAUCOURT.

One guide per platoon and one for Hd Qrs will meet the Battn at the W. entrance of HERBECOURT. H.31.a.1½.9½. at 7.p.m. and will lead platoons as they arrive.

4....... The Battn will break the journey for tea on the open ground W. of DOMPIERRE(M.10.b.3.7.) and will move from CHUIGNES with 50 yds between platoons. After leaving DOMPIERRE this will be increased to 100 yards.

5....... Companies will leave the starting point (road opposite C. Coy's billets) at the following times :-

Headquarters...... 3-25 p.m.
C. Coy............ 3-30 p.m.
A. Coy............ 3-35 p.m.
D. Coy............ 3-40 p.m.
B. Coy............ 3-45 p.m.

Dress:- Fighting Order with next day's rations.

Companies will leave M.10.b.3.7. after tea in the same order following each other at correct distance. Hd Qrs will ~~stop~~ start at 6 p.m.

6....... Each Coy will march with its own Lewis Gun Limber and Cooker with the exception of C. Coy who will share a cooker with A. Coy.

Hd Qrs will march with its own Limber.

7....... Lewis Gun Drums will not be taken over on relief. 20 Drums per Gun will be taken into the line, the remainder being left with Battn Reserve S.A.A.

8....... O.C. Coys will arrange with the Quarter Master to draw 50 pairs of Trench Boots and Hd Qrs ~~will~~ 20 pairs. These will be taken by Companies on their transport for use in the trenches and will be looked on as Trench Stores.

9....... All blankets, packs and Officers' valises to be stacked in barn at entrance to Bn H.Q. by 10 a.m. on the 23rd inst..

C Ambler. 2nd Lieutenant.
A/Adjutant 2nd Bn King's Royal Rifles...

Issued by Orderly at 10.45 a.m.

Copies to:-. 1. War Diary. 2. War Diary. 3. O.C. A.Coy. 4. O.C. B.Coy.
5. O.C. Coy. 6. O.C. D. Coy. 7. Hd Qr Coy. 8. R.S.M.
9. 1st S.W.B. 10. Q.M. 11. T.O. 12. Sniping Sgt.

Battalion Order No. 9. [illegible] Copy No. #2

SECRET.   25.2.17.

Ref No. 4. A Secret Map (dated 19.2.17)   800c

1. The Battn will relieve the 1st Northamptonshire Regt on the night of the 26/27th Feb as follows:—

(a) B. Coy will relieve Northants B. Coy from Sap 23 inclusive to Sap B. inclusive.

(b) A. Coy will relieve Northants D. Coy from Sap B. inclusive to junction of MEUDON ALLEY with Front line inclusive.

(c) D. Coy will relieve Northants C. Coy in Support with 2 platoons in dug-outs from N.17.c.3.7. to N.17.a.6.3. 1 platoon in dug-outs along same trench but about 100 yards further N. and 1 platoon in dug-outs in ROUMANIA SUPPORT Trench just N. of Sap B.

(d) C. Coy will relieve Northants A. Coy in reserve in GIGAREL Trench astride of GUADELOUPE Trench.

2. Platoon guides will be at the following places and times:—

(a) MEUDON QUARRY at 5 p.m. from Northants D. Coy for our A. Coy.

(b) N.16.a.7.5. (on road leading into QUARRY Old Bde Hd Qrs) at 6.30 p.m. from Northants B. Coy for our B. Coy.

(c) N.16.a.7.5. at 7 p.m. from Northants C. Coy for our D. Coy.

(d) Junction of BOULOGNE ALLEY with BOULOGNE RESERVE at 7.15 p.m from Northants A. Coy for our C. Coy.

2 guides per Coy will meet the advance

parties of the Northamptons at the following places and times :—

(a) B & D Coys for Northamptons A & B Coys respectively N.16.a.7.5 at 12 noon.

C & A Coys for Northamptons C & D Coys respectively MEUDON QUARRY at 12 noon.

4. Ration dump will be at ASSEVILLERS-BARLEUX road in cutting about N.15.a.6.2.
Water will be drawn in petrol tins from water-carts at well in N.15.a.4.7. All empty water-tins after relief to be taken to reserve Coy Hd Qrs (C Coy)
All carrying will be done by the RESERVE Coy.
Rations will be drawn at the dump to-morrow at 11 p.m., and 7 p.m. nightly afterwards.

5. Relief complete to be reported by code to Batt'n Hd Qrs in BOULOGNE RESERVE at N.11.c.0.9.

Issued at

Camblin 2nd Lt a/adjt

Copy No 1 War Diary
2 "
3 A. Coy
4 B. "
5 C "
6 D. "
7 Q.M.
8 1/ Northants.

801c

War Diary

IX

SECRET.

2nd Bde. No. G. 38/29.

O.C. Royal Sussex.
O.C. Loyal N. Lancs.
O.C. Northamptons.
O.C. K. R. R. C.
O.C. No. 2 M.G. Coy.
O.C. 2nd T.M. Battery.
H.Q. 1st Division.)
1st Brigade.)
145th Brigade.) for information.
Left Sub-Group Artillery.)
Lowland Field Coy. R.E.)
X/1 T.M. Battery.)

---

1. In order to assist the operations of Troops further North the 1st Division will discharge Smoke from its line, should the wind be favourable, at Zero on the 28th instant.

2. The 2nd Brigade will liberate smoke on a front of 400 yards - 200 yards on each side of the junction of MEUDON AVENUE with the front line. i.e. from N.17.b.5.7. to N.11.d.7.4.

3. The Staff Captain will arrange to draw 100 Smoke Candles from the Grenade Supply Coy. and send up 50 to each of the 2nd Royal Sussex and 2nd K.R.R.C. with the Transport tonight.

4. The artillery is arranging to barrage the enemy's front line opposite the front from which Smoke will be discharged from Zero to 0.5 minutes.

5. No. 2 M.G. Company will arrange to fire short bursts from Zero to 0.5 minutes on all approached to the enemy lines.

6. The O.C. 2nd Royal Sussex and O.C. 2nd K.R.R.C. will arrange to hold their front line with Lewis Guns only; all men possible being put into dugouts in the Support lines or lines further back.

7. The hour of Zero will be sent later.

Captain, Brigade Major,
2nd Infantry Brigade.

27th February, 1917.

ALL Coys IXA Secret 803 War Diary

1. In order to assist the operations of troops further North, the 1st [illegible] will discharge smoke from its lines, should the wind be favourable at Zero on the 28th inst.

2. The 2nd Brigade will [illegible] to smoke 400 yds / 200 yds on each on a front of 400 yds of MEUDON AVENUE side of the junction of [illegible] with the front line - i.e. from N.17 b.5.7 to N.11.d.7.4.

3. A Coy will draw 50 smoke candles from Batt. HQ. before 10 pm tonight and will make the following arrangements to light them at ZERO time which will be communicated in BAB code :-
Coys [illegible] 1 man with 5 candles covering 20 yds = 10 men covering 200 yds and one + 1 NCO to every 2 men, the whole officer superintending
Total 1 officer 5 NCOs 10 men.

4. A & B Coys will arrange to hold the front line with L Guns only, each team to consist of 1 NCO & 3 men [illegible]

804c

one sentry only up at a time, remaining men to be put into dugouts in the support lines or lines further back – O.C. A & B Coys will resume their original positions when they think the situation is quiet, reporting to Batt HQ by wire (or orderly if wire is broken) when they have done so. The following code will be sent to denote this:– "BACK."

5. The Artillery is arranging to barrage the enemy's front line opposite the front from which smoke is discharged from Zero to 0.5 minutes.

6. No 2 M.G. Coy will arrange to fire short bursts from Zero to 0.5 minutes on all approaches to the enemy lines.

7. The internal relief as ordered by B.O. No 10 will not take place

till this operation has been carried out, unless it is postponed till the following day, when the relief will take place according to B.O. No 10 and arrangements made accordingly by O.C. Coys concerned.

27/2/17.

[illegible signature] O.C. F.T.

Ref. O.1.

Acknowledge by bin

War Diary   IX B   AW7

SECRET.   2nd Bde. No. G. 38/29.

O.C. Royal Sussex.
O.C. Northamptons.
O.C. K. R. R. C.
O.C. No. 2 M.G. Coy.
O.C. 2nd T.M. Battery.
Left Sub-Group Artillery.
Lowland Field Coy. R.E.
X/1 T.M. Battery.

805c

Reference this office No. G. 38/29 and B.M. 279 of today's date.

1. ZERO hour on the 28th will be 5.25 a.m.

This hour is only to be communicated to those whom it immediately concerns. In no case should it be communicated by telephone.

2. Correct time will be sent over the telephone between 10 p.m. and 11 p.m. tonight.

3. To throw the 50 Smoke Candles each Battalion will employ 25 men i.e. 2 Candles per man, to be thrown at ZERO.

4. ACKNOWLEDGE BY WIRE.

E.E. Calthrop
Captain, Brigade Major,
2nd Infantry Brigade.

27th February, 1917.

27th Div[illegible] Battalion Order No 10 X [illegible]

SECRET 27-2-17 Copy No 1

806c

Ref: No 4A SECRET MAP (dated 22-2-17.)

1. An internal relief will take place on the night of the 28th/1st March as follows:—
   C. Coy will relieve A. Coy.
   D. Coy will relieve B. Coy.

   4 L. Guns to be taken in the front line by each Coy.

   All arrangements to be made by O's C. Coys concerned.

2. Dump for all Coys and H.Q same as to-day viz: N. 10. b. 6.4.

3. A. Coy will carry for D. and C. Coys
   B. " " " itself.
   H.Q " " " " "
   Water dump as before.

3. Relief complete to be reported by code to Battn. H.Q.

Issued at,

[signature] Major.
Comdg.

Copy No 1 War Diary
2 " "
3 A. Coy
4 B. "
5 C. "
6 D. "

WAR DIARY.

(WITH APPENDICES).

2nd.Bn. THE KING'S ROYAL RIFLE CORPS.

2nd. INFANTRY BRIGADE.

1st.DIVISION.

MARCH. 1917.

Instructions regarding War Diaries and Intelligence Summaries are contained in F. S. Regs., Part II. and the Staff Manual respectively. Title Pages will be prepared in manuscript.

WAR DIARY
or
INTELLIGENCE SUMMARY
(Erase heading not required.)

2nd Bn. K. R. R. Corps

Army Form C. 2118

Vol 30

Place	Date	Hour	Summary of Events and Information	Remarks and references to Appendices
	Mar 1		Very clear day. Slight increase in hostile shelling.	
	2		2nd in Command left the line to go to witness demonstration of attack at III Corps School. Batt: was relieved in the front line by 1st Northamptonshire Rgt and moved to the reserve area at BECQUINCOURT.	APP I
	3		Batt marched by Coys to ~~[illegible]~~ CHUIGNES for baths and feet washing.	
	4		Whole Batt on fatigue for road mending and wiring the Corps line.	
	5		Whole Batt on fatigue for road mending and wiring the Corps line. 2nd Lieut BURTON (4th NORTHANTS) to hospital sick.	2Lt. BURTON to hosp. sick
	6		Batt relieved 1st NORTHAMPTONSHIRE REGT in the front line. Relief went off quietly. Position of Coys: A left front Coy, B right front Coy, D Coy ~~reserve~~ support coy, and C Coy reserve coy	
	7	4.15am.	Raid by Batt on our left (N. LANCS REGT). A and B Coys evacuated the front line with the exception of Lewis guns, until enemy retaliation had ceased. Retaliation was slight. Intermittent shelling all day.	
	8.	12.15pm.	Whilst they were going round the trenches a 5.9. shell fell amongst a party and severely wounded the a/Adjt (2/Lt C. AMBLER) and an orderly and	2/Lt Ambler wounded 3 O.R. killed & 1 O.R. wounded

Army Form C. 2118

Instructions regarding War Diaries and Intelligence Summaries are contained in F. S. Regs., Part II. and the Staff Manual respectively. Title Pages will be prepared in manuscript.

WAR DIARY
or
INTELLIGENCE SUMMARY
(Erase heading not required.)

Place	Date	Hour	Summary of Events and Information	Remarks and references to Appendices
	8		killed the C.O.s orderly. MAJOR OPPENHEIM D.S.O also suffered from concussion. Internal relief C relieved A and D relieved B. LT. COL. ABADIE D.S.O. returned from the conference at the 4th ARMY SCHOOL and resumed command of the Batt. 2nd LIEUT BLACKETT (transferred from 7th Batt) rejoined the Batt & took over command of C COY. Slight fall of snow.	MAJ. OPPENHEIM D.S.O to hosp sick APP II
	9.		Quiet day. Fall of snow. MAJOR OPPENHEIM to hospital suffering from concussion.	
	10.		Misty day. Advanced party 8th R. BERKS. REGT. came round trenches.	APP III
		11pm	Front line thinned in anticipation of enemy artillery retaliation for an attack NORTH. Retaliation very slight.	
			2nd LIEUTS V.B. CHERRY and H.B. DAWSON left for 1st DIV. SCHOOL.	
	11.		Batt relieved by 8th R. BERKS. REGT. Relief went off slowly. Batt moved into Bde in RESERVE in dug-outs at BECQUINCOURT During the afternoon left COY (C) fairly heavily shelled. One man killed	1 O.R. killed

1875 Wt. W593/826 1,000,000 4/15 J.B.C. & A. A.D.S.S./Forms/C. 2118.

Army Form C. 2118

Instructions regarding War Diaries and Intelligence Summaries are contained in F. S. Regs., Part II. and the Staff Manual respectively. Title Pages will be prepared in manuscript.

WAR DIARY
or
INTELLIGENCE SUMMARY
(Erase heading not required.)

Place	Date	Hour	Summary of Events and Information	Remarks and references to Appendices
	12	10am	Batt marched to huts at CHUIGNES. Rain in the afternoon. Capt. DIMMER V.C., LIEUTS MILLS and CULL, and 2nd LIEUT ROBBINS joined the Batt with a draft of 28 O.R.s	
	13.		All coys. Baths, & fitting clothing. Box gas respirators issued and tested in gas chamber. MAJOR OPPENHEIM D.S.O. returned from hospital. Trench board tracks laid in the camp.	
	14.		Training all day. Lecture on attack to Officers and N.C.O.s in the evening by the G.O.C. 2nd Inf Bde. MAJOR OPPENHEIM D.S.O. ~~returned~~ to hospital suffering from concussion. Rain most of the day. Road fatigues near the camp.	Maj. OPPENHEIM to hosp. sick
	15.		G.O.C. inspects coys in new formation of attack. Training all day. 2nd LIEUT BOUCHIER arrived with a draft of 70 O.R.	
	16.		Misty morning — slight frost. Training all day.	

1875 Wt. W593/826 1,000,000 4/15 J.B.C. & A. A.D.S.S./Forms/C. 2118.

Army Form C. 2118

Instructions regarding War Diaries and Intelligence Summaries are contained in F. S. Regs., Part II. and the Staff Manual respectively. Title Pages will be prepared in manuscript.

WAR DIARY
or
INTELLIGENCE SUMMARY
(Erase heading not required.)

Place	Date	Hour	Summary of Events and Information	Remarks and references to Appendices
	17.		Morning G.O.C. 1st Div inspected A & C Coys in the new formation of attack. News received of German retirement in front of 1st and 3rd Brigades. 2nd LIEUT CHEVIS leaves for IV ARMY MUSKETRY SCHOOL. CAPT H.W. BUTLER. M.C. arrives from VIIth CORPS HQRS to take up the duties of Adjutant.	
	18.	10.30am	Church Parade at CHUIGNES. In the afternoon Batt. inter-platoon cross country race (2 miles). Won by 4 Platoon. News received that patrols of 1st & 3rd Bdes have crossed the SOMME, and that PERONNE has fallen. 2nd LIEUT A.C. HEBERDEN rejoins from L-G. Course.	
	19.		B and D coys practise new attack formation	
			Work as usual.	

1875 Wt. W593/826 1,000,000 4/15 J.B.C. & A. A.D.S.S./Forms/C. 2118.

Instructions regarding War Diaries and Intelligence Summaries are contained in F. S. Regs., Part II. and the Staff Manual respectively. Title Pages will be prepared in manuscript.

WAR DIARY
or
INTELLIGENCE SUMMARY
(Erase heading not required.)

Army Form C. 2118.

Place	Date	Hour	Summary of Events and Information ½ mile E of BELLOY	Remarks and references to Appendices
	20.		Bn relieved 2nd Bn WELCH REGT in support line (O.B.1 + 2) Relief complete by 1.30 pm. Salvage in afternoon by all coys.	APP IV
			CAPT. L. G. MOORE D.S.O. to 184th INF. BDE, to take up the duties of BDE. MAJOR.	
	21.		Bn work on ESTREES — VILLERS-CARBONNEL road.	
			2nd LIEUT T.P. McDOWELL rejoined from Hospital.	
	22.		Bn work on road.	
	23.		Bn work on road.	
	24.		Bn work on road. Part of the 5th CAV. DIVISION go through.	1 O.R. accidently wounded.
			LIEUT F. ROBARTS rejoined from Hospital. Draft of 21 O.Ranks.	
	25.		Bn work on road. 2nd LIEUT SIMPSON joined Bn. Summer Time began.	1 O.R. accidently wounded.
	26		Bn work on road. Rain	

Instructions regarding War Diaries and Intelligence Summaries are contained in F. S. Regs., Part II. and the Staff Manual respectively. Title Pages will be prepared in manuscript.

WAR DIARY
or
INTELLIGENCE SUMMARY
(Erase heading not required.)

Army Form C. 2118

Place	Date	Hour	Summary of Events and Information	Remarks and references to Appendices
	27.		BN work on road. Rain and snow.	
			CAPT. V.B. HILL to IVth ARMY. INF. SCHOOL.	
			2nd LIEUT A.L. GRACIE from IVth ARMY. SIGNAL. SCHOOL.	
	28.		BN work on road. Rain.	
	29.		BN work on road. Heavy rain.	
			CAPT. E.F. CAMPBELL joins BN & takes command of B Coy.	
	30.		BN work on road. Rain.	
			2nd LIEUT H.C. CHEVIS rejoined from IVth ARMY. MUSKETRY CAMP.	
	31.		Work on road. Slight showers.	

[illegible] Lt.
2nd Bn. K.R.R.C.

R. [illegible] Lt Col
Cmdg 2nd Bn K.R.R.C.

1875 Wt. W593/826 1,000,000 4/15 J.B.C. & A. A.D.S.S./Forms/C. 2118.

W. Diary

APP I

SECRET

Copy No. 1

Battn Order No 11

1-3-1917.

1. The Battn will be relieved by the 1/Northants on the night of the 2nd/3rd. and will go into Bde Reserve taking over the billets occupied by the 1st L. N. Lancs in BECQUINCOURT, whilst in Reserve the Battn will be at 1 hour's notice.

2. Advance parties. Each Coy will send back by daylight 1 N.C.O per platoon and HQ 1 rifleman per section i/c of 1 N.C.O to take over the new billets.
O.C. Companies will arrange to be met by guides from their advance parties who will lead them to their billets These parties will report at HQ at 11AM tomorrow

3. Coys will go back independently when relieved.

4. D. B & A Coys' limbers & Maltese Cart will be in cutting on ASSEVILLERS–BARLEUX road at about N. 15. a. 5. 1½. from 7.30. p.m.
C. Coy limber and the Mess Cart will be at the ordinary ration dump ~~at 7.30~~ from 8.0 p.m.
A limber for petrol tins will be at water dump as soon after dark as possible.

5. O.C. Companies will report to the present B.H.Q by code when relief is complete and verbally at the new B.H.Q. when the Coys arrive.

Issued at 9 PM

Copy No 1 War Diary
2 " "
3 A. Coy
4 B "
5 C "
6 D "
7 T. O

[illegible] Capt & Adjt
for Major
Cmdg
1-3-17.

Copy No 2.

Batt'n Order No 13

SECRET  7-3-17

1. There will be an internal relief on the night of the 8th/9th.

2. C. Coy will relieve A. Coy as left front Coy.
D. " " " B. " " right " "
B. Coy will go into support with one platoon (the strongest) in dug-outs at junction of PIERSON TRENCH and MEUDON ALLEY in close support to C. Coy and 1 platoon in dug-out just West of ROUMANIA SUPPORT in 22 ALLEY in close support to D. Coy. Both front line Coys will have 4 L.G's in the line.

3. B. Coy will arrange to have an anti-aircraft L.G. in the HOLLOW ROAD.

4. All arrangements for relief to be made by O's C. Coys concerned

5. Relief complete to be reported by code or by orderly to Bn. Hd. Qrs.
C. Coy will include platoon of B. in their report.

6. Rations at 10 p.m.

Issued at p.m.

A. C. Offerton Major
Comdg

Copy No 1 War Diary
2 " "
3 A. Coy
4 B. "
5 C. "
6 D. "
7 T. O.

SECRET. War Diary Copy No 1 APP III

Battn Order No 14.

Ref: Map 1/10,000 62.c. S.W. 2. 8-3-17.

1. In order to assist operations on our left and to do as much damage as possible to the enemy defences a feint raid and bombardment will take place against BARLEUX QUARRY on the night of the 9/10th March.

2. The O.C. Royal Sussex Regt was to arrange to entirely vacate the front line by 6. am. this morning. D. and C. Coy 2nd K.R.R.C will hold the line with L.Guns and will withdraw the remainder from the front line to under cover as near to the front line as possible. One Officer and one N.C.O. of each Coy will remain in the front line. This will be carried out after dark

3. Artillery Action. Zero to plus 2 minutes concentrated bombardment on enemy wire from N.12.c.10.30 to N.12.c. 15.65. to N.12.c.35.65. and the enemy front line from N.12.c.15.35. to N.12.c.17.57. to N.12.c.40.59. At plus 2 minutes all guns will creep forward at 50 yards a minute on to a line N.12.c.35.13 to N.12.c.50.43. to N.12.c.40.60. At plus 5 minutes all guns will jump back on to original zero target. Plus 5 minutes to plus 8 minutes concentrated bombardment on original target.

4. X/1 Medium T.M. Batty will be co-operating on wire and trenches in N.12.c.

5. No 2. M.G.Coy will fire bursts into BARLEUX and sweep front line trenches in N.12.a. N.17.b

6. No.2. T.M. Batty will co-operate in N.12.c.

7. Zero will be communicated later.

8. Lt Gott will synchronise watches at each Coy H.Q commencing at 9.45 p.m. with C.Coy.

9. O's.C. C and D. Coys will arrange to re-occupy their front line on the cessation of enemy's probable retaliation. When this has been done the word "AGAIN" will be wired to Bn. H.Q.

10. Acknowledge.

Issued at

R Brodie Lt-Col Comdg.

Copy No 1 & 2 War Diary
3 A. Coy
4 B. "
5 C. "
6 D. Coy
7 M.O.
8 T.O.
9 I.O.

APP IV

SECRET.

Copy No. 1

2nd Bn. K.R.R.C. Order No. 15. 18th March 1917.

Reference Map 62. C. S.W. 1/20000

1. 2nd Brigade is relieving 3rd Brigade on 19th and 20th March in Right Sector of Divisional Front.

2. One Officer and one N.C.O. from H.Q. and from each of the Coys, will report to the 1st Bn. S.W.B.(Support Battn) on the afternoon of March 19th to take over all papers and stores, and will await arrival of Battn on 20th.

3. On moving up, two sandbags will be worn on the braces.

4. 32 Drums per Lewis Gun will be taken into the line. The remaining 12 per gun will be handed over to the Q.M. tomorrow. None will be taken over from the 3rd Brigade.

5. All trench stores, trench maps, aeroplane photos, work programmes, defense schemes will be taken over on the 20th March.

6 On 20th march :—

~~6.~~ Packs will be stacked at ~~Band Hut by~~ Bde Store 7.30 a.m. ~~on 20th~~
Blankets rolled in bundles of ten will be stacked at ~~Band~~ Bde Store ~~Hut~~ by 7.30 a.m.
Officers' valises will be stacked at the ~~1~~.Q.M. stores by 7.30 a.m.
Officers' Coy Mess Stores will be loaded on Lewis Gun limber ....
Hd. Quarters limber will be loaded by 8.30 a.m.

7. Battalion will march off at 8.45 a.m., 50 yards between platoons, in the following order :-

Bn.Hd. Qrs.
A.Coy.
Band.
B.Coy.
C.Coy.
Buglers.
D.Coy.

Route. ~~DOMPIERRE Cross Roads, M.6.c.57, ASSEVILLERS.~~ FOUCAUCOURT, ESTREES & N 27 d 4.4

Starting Point. ~~2nd Brigade Hd. Qrs.~~ Band Hut

8. Guides will meet the Battn at ~~ASSEVILLERS Cross Roads~~ ~~N.13.b.27.~~ N 27 d 4.4

9. Acknowledge.

H E Smith Capt
~~Lieutenant-Colonel.~~
~~Cmdg. 2nd Bn.~~ King's Royal Rifles.
Adjutant 2nd Battn.

Issued at 8 PM

Copy No. 1......War Diary.
No. 2......War Diary.
No. 3......A.Coy.
No. 4......B.Coy.
No. 5......C.Coy.
Copy No. 6......D.Coy.
No. 7......T.O.
No. 8......Q.M.
No. 9......M.O.
No. 10......R.S.M.

W A R D I A R Y.

2nd. Bn. THE KING'S ROYAL RIFLE CORPS.

2nd. INFANTRY BRIGADE.

1st. DIVISION.

APRIL. 1917.

Instructions regarding War Diaries and Intelligence Summaries are contained in F. S. Regs., Part II. and the Staff Manual respectively. Title Pages will be prepared in manuscript.

Army Form C. 2118

I DIVN.

2nd KRRC **WAR DIARY** for April

or

~~INTELLIGENCE~~ **SUMMARY**

(Erase heading not required.)

Vol 31

Place	Date	Hour	Summary of Events and Information	Remarks and references to Appendices
	APRIL.			
	1		Bn work on ESTREES–VILLERS.CARBONNEL road. Coys have baths.	
	2		Bn work on road. Draft of 14 O.R.s joined the BN.	
	3.		Bn work on road. 1 Coy & Hqrs have baths. Fine day.	
	4.		Bn work on road. Very wet & some snow. The news arrived that the U.S.A. had joined the Allies.	
	5.		Bn work on road. Very wet.	
	6.		Bn work on road. The departure of the Bn from BELLOY arranged for the 7th was postponed.	
	7.		Bn work on road. Very wet.	

1875 Wt. W593/826 1,000,000 4/15 J.B.C. & A. A.D.S.S./Forms/C. 2118.

Instructions regarding War Diaries and Intelligence Summaries are contained in F. S. Regs., Part II. and the Staff Manual respectively. Title Pages will be prepared in manuscript.

WAR DIARY
or
INTELLIGENCE SUMMARY
(Erase heading not required.)

Army Form C. 2118

Place	Date	Hour	Summary of Events and Information	Remarks and references to Appendices
	APRIL			
	8.	10 a.m.	Bn marched to huts at CHUIGNES, & in the afternoon cleaned up.	1. O.R. accidentally wounded.
	9.		Cleaning up & fitting clothing. A few showers of rain.	
	10.		Platoons train sections in the use of their different arms	
	11.		Innoculation. Specialist training for sections. Work done on making a 30 yds range. Capt. J.H.S. DIMMER V.C. M.C. to Hosp.	
	12.		Specialist training for sections. Work done on 30 yds range which was completed. Capt. T.R. FORSYTH FORREST rejoined from Hosp. LIEUT. J.L. MUSCAT to Hosp. 2nd LIEUT. E.M. POLLARD " "	
	13.		Specialist training for sections. 1st round of 2nd Bde Football Competition (association) 2nd K.R.R.C. beat 2nd R. SUSSEX by 7 — nil. 1st L.N. LANCS drew with 1st NORTHAMPTONS. 2nd Bde M.G. COY beat 2nd Bde TR. MORTAR BATTERY. LIEUT. F. ROBARTS to T.O.W. COY.	

1875 Wt. W593/826 1,000,000 4/15 J.B.C. & A. A.D.S.S./Forms/C. 2118.

Instructions regarding War Diaries and Intelligence Summaries are contained in F. S. Regs., Part II. and the Staff Manual respectively. Title Pages will be prepared in manuscript.

WAR DIARY
or
INTELLIGENCE SUMMARY
(Erase heading not required.)

Army Form C. 2118.

Place	Date	Hour	Summary of Events and Information	Remarks and references to Appendices
	14.		Fine day. Attack practised by Bn in the morning. In a replay 1st L. N. LANCS beat 1st NORTHAMPTONS 5–2 goals.	
	15.	10.15	Church Parade in a hut at CHUIGNES. Rain all the day. Football match v 1st L. N. LANCS postponed. Heard that 28 5.9 guns were captured by our forces in the ARRAS offensive. 24 O.R.s joined the BN. 2nd LIEUT H. D. WILLIAMS to hosp	
	16.	11.15am	Bn marched to billets at MORCOURT. Fine day. In the afternoon the C.O. inspected all coys in fighting order.	
	17.		Open warfare attack practised in the morning. Very wet.	

2449 Wt. W14957/M90 750,000 1/16 J.B.C. & A. Forms/C.2118/12.

Army Form C. 2118.

Instructions regarding War Diaries and Intelligence Summaries are contained in F. S. Regs., Part II. and the Staff Manual respectively. Title Pages will be prepared in manuscript.

WAR DIARY
or
INTELLIGENCE SUMMARY
(Erase heading not required.)

Place	Date	Hour	Summary of Events and Information	Remarks and references to Appendices
	18.		Wet. Indoor parades, 2nd LIEUT. N.F.E. ANSON. M.C. rejoined Bn	
	19.		OPEN warfare attack practised. Draft of 4 O.Rs joined Bn. 2nd LIEUT. W.J.C. GARRARD to Hosp.	
	20.		Attack practised. Semi-Final of 2nd Bde ASSOCIATION FOOTBALL COMPETITION. 2nd K.R.R.C. beat 1st L.N.LANCS 2 goals – nil. 2nd Bde M.G. COY drew a bye.	
	21.		Coys train.	
	22.	10.15	Church parade and baths. Fine day. Officers 2nd K.R.R.C beat Officers 2nd R.SUSSEX by 18 points to 8. at Rugby Football.	
	23.		Bn do an advanced guard scheme between MORLANCOURT and CHIPPILLY. In the afternoon inter-communication in battle was practised.	

2449 Wt. W14957/M90 750,000 1/16 J.B.C. & A. Forms/C.2118/12.

Army Form C. 2118.

WAR DIARY
or
INTELLIGENCE SUMMARY.
(Erase heading not required.)

Instructions regarding War Diaries and Intelligence Summaries are contained in F. S. Regs., Part II. and the Staff Manual respectively. Title pages will be prepared in manuscript.

Place	Date	Hour	Summary of Events and Information	Remarks and references to Appendices
	24.	7.50.	Fine day. Bn parade for a practise attack by 2nd Bde. 34th SQUADRON R.F.C & ~~BATTY~~ Bde R.F.A. took part. The attack was over ground between PROYART and MORCOURT. CAPT. W.L. CLINTON joined Bn. ~~& was appointed~~ Rea. ~~TEMPY MAJ & 2ND in COMMAND.~~ Rea Lt Col	
	25.		Coys train in the morning. In the afternoon there was an inter-coy Tug-of-war to see which coy should represent the Bn in the 2nd Bde SPORTS. B Coy were the winners. LIEUT. A.PINNOCK & 2ND LIEUT. E.W. BARNES (S.A.M.Rifles) & 11 O.Rs joined the BN.	
	26.		BN. march to MORLANCOURT AERODROME for drill. Afternoon – musketry & football, lecture on sanitation. 2nd LIEUT. A.L.KELLY to 3RD ARMY H.Q. St POL.	
	27.		Coys train in morning. 1st round of Bde OFFICERS TUG-OF-WAR 2nd K.R.R.C. beat 1st L.N. LANCS.	
	28.		Coys train at CHIPPILLY. Afternoon Bde SPORTS. 1st L.N.LANCS points, 33 2nd K.R.R.C. points. 25 (Second)	

2353 Wt. W2544/1454 700,000 5/15 D. D. & L. A.D.S.S./Forms/C. 2118.

Army Form C. 2118.

Instructions regarding War Diaries and Intelligence Summaries are contained in F. S. Regs., Part II. and the Staff Manual respectively. Title pages will be prepared in manuscript.

WAR DIARY
or
INTELLIGENCE SUMMARY.
(*Erase heading not required.*)

Place	Date	Hour	Summary of Events and Information	Remarks and references to Appendices
	28		2Lt GILL 4th Northamptonshire Regt posted to Flying Corps. Attached to Battn. Had been with battalion since Oct 1916 and like 2Lt GARRARD (vide 19/4/17) has rendered very useful service to the battalion during this last winter	T. Abadie
	29		11 O.R.s rejoined the Battalion. Capt. Butler M.C. adjt. went to Hospital. 2nd Lt Ravenscroft took on acting adjt. Battn. were warned that they would move to Peronne Area for working on railways. Orders received late at night that we should move by train to ROISEL (East of PERONNE) on the next day for repairing the railway. Lt. GOTT admitted to hospital.	P. Ravenscroft
	30.		Battn. moved off at 8·30 AM & marched to BRAY s. SOMME. Dinners at the Station. Entrained about 2·15 PM Arrived ROISEL about 10 P.M. where tents had been pitched for us. Glorious weather.	

2353 Wt. W2544/1454 700,000 5/15 D. D. & L. A.D.S.S./Forms/C. 2118.

W A R   D I A R Y.

(WITH APPENDICES).

2nd.Bn. THE KING'S ROYAL RIFLE CORPS.

2nd. INFANTRY BRIGADE.

1st.DIVISION.

MAY.1917.

Instructions regarding War Diaries and Intelligence Summaries are contained in F. S. Regs., Part II. and the Staff Manual respectively. Title pages will be prepared in manuscript.

4 KRRC

Army Form C. 2118.

WAR DIARY
or
INTELLIGENCE SUMMARY.

(Erase heading not required.)

Vol 32

Place	Date	Hour	Summary of Events and Information	Remarks and references to Appendices
	May.			
ROISEL	1.		BN. settle into camp.	
	2.		BN work on railway.	
	3.		BN work on railway. CAPT. V.B. HILL ~~rejd~~ rejoined from IVth ARMY INF. SCH. Fine day.	
	4.		BN work on railway.	

2/KRR C

Army Form C. 2118.

Instructions regarding War Diaries and Intelligence Summaries are contained in F. S. Regs., Part II. and the Staff Manual respectively. Title pages will be prepared in manuscript.

WAR DIARY
or
INTELLIGENCE SUMMARY.
(Erase heading not required.)

Place	Date	Hour	Summary of Events and Information	Remarks and references to Appendices
ROISEL	5.		Bn work on railway. Training for one company.	
	6.		Fine day. No fatigues. Bn play 6th Welch & won 6 — nil. 14 O.R.s & CAPT. SIR J.V.E. LEES joined the BN.	
	7.		Bn work on railway. CAPT. L.A. BLACKETT to IVth ARMY SCHOOL.	
	8.		BN work on railway. Very wet.	
	9.		BN work on railway & played 1st GRENADIER GUARDS at MARQUAIX. Draw — no score after a close game.	
	10.		BN work on railway. One coy train. Play 1st GREN. GDS. at football & win 2 goals to 1. CAPT BUTLER M.C. from hosp. Slight shelling in evening.	1 O.R. wounded.
	11.		BN work on railway & play 6th WELCH at Rugby Football, & lost 14 — nil. LIEUT H.J.F. MILLS ~~rejd~~ rejoined BN. from L-G. Course.	

2353 Wt. W2544/1454 700,000 5/15 D. D. & L. A.D.S.S./Forms/C. 2118.

2/KRRC

Army Form C. 2118.

Instructions regarding War Diaries and Intelligence Summaries are contained in F. S. Regs., Part II. and the Staff Manual respectively. Title pages will be prepared in manuscript.

WAR DIARY
or
INTELLIGENCE SUMMARY.
(Erase heading not required.)

Place	Date	Hour	Summary of Events and Information	Remarks and references to Appendices
	12.		BN work on railway	
	13		Fine day. No fatigue. BN Rifle Meeting in the afternoon. Inter-section rapid won by A Coy.	
	14.		BN. work on railway.	
	15.		BN work on railway. Fine day. 2nd CAV. DIV. come to ROISEL area	
			LT H. PINNOCK & 2ND LIEUT H. ROBINS to hosp.	
	16.		BN moved to MORCOURT by train from ROISEL to MERIGNOLLES.	
			CAPT. T.B.J. MAHAR & 2/LT. C. SAVIN joined the BN. Rained all day	
	17.		Clean up. Night Operations.	
			Draft of 9 ORs joined the BN.	
	18.		Baths. BN rifle meeting at CHIPPILLY. Inter Coy Section Rapid won by B Coy	

2353 Wt. W2544/1454 700,000 5/15 D. D. & L. A.D.S.S./Forms/C. 2118.

Instructions regarding War Diaries and Intelligence Summaries are contained in F. S. Regs., Part II. and the Staff Manual respectively. Title pages will be prepared in manuscript.

WAR DIARY
or
INTELLIGENCE SUMMARY.
(Erase heading not required.)

Army Form C. 2118.

Place	Date	Hour	Summary of Events and Information	Remarks and references to Appendices
	19.		BN. march to VILLERS-BRETONNEUX. Very hot. Poor billets.	
	20.		Cleaned up & change some billets.	M.P.I
	21.		Fine day. BN route march.	
	22.		Rain. Bde heats of DIV. Sports. Draft of 11 ORs joined the BN.	
	23		Bn route march & bathe. DIV. Boxing in afternoon.	
	24.		Training. DIV. Sports. Won by 2nd Bde The BN had 2 firsts & 2 seconds. 2nd LIEUTS A.E. BOUCHER & A. SIMPSON rejd the BN from DIV. Training Sch.	
	25.		Coys train & fit clothing. Final of Bde Football. v M.G. COY. BN win 8 goals — nil.	1 O.R. accidentally drowned.

Instructions regarding War Diaries and Intelligence Summaries are contained in F. S. Regs., Part II. and the Staff Manual respectively. Title Pages will be prepared in manuscript.

WAR DIARY
or
INTELLIGENCE SUMMARY
(Erase heading not required.)

Army Form C. 2118

Place	Date	Hour	Summary of Events and Information	Remarks and references to Appendices
	26.		BN scheme in wood fighting. Fine day.	
	27.		BN move by train from VILLERS BRETONNEUX to BAILLEUL to METEREN. Arrived 8 p.m. Fine day. Draft of 11. ORs. joined the BN.	
	28.		Clean up. Fine day.	
	29.		BN Route March in morning.	
	30.		Coys train. Two coys on range.	
	31.		Fine day. BN route march & Staff Ride for officers. G.O.C.s (Brigade) inspection in afternoon. 2ND LIEUT. CHAMBERS joined BN. (Formerly served 9 months with 8th Bn in France until wounded 15/9/16.)	

R. Abadie Lieut. Colonel
2/6/17 King's Royal Rifles
Comdg. 2nd Bn.

A.P.I

Fourth Army No. G.S.697.

1st Division.

It is now 10 months since the 1st Division joined the Fourth Army, and I cannot allow them to leave without expressing my gratitude for all the excellent services they have rendered during that time.

The conspicuous part played by the Division in the heavy fighting around CONTALMAISON, POZIERES, HIGH WOOD and EAUCOURT L'ABBAYE was beyond praise and reflects the highest credit on all concerned. Though they lost over 10,000 officers and men, and have suffered much during an exceptionally cold and trying winter, yet they are today, if possible, in a higher state of fighting efficiency than they were last July. The result is in the highest degree satisfactory.

There is no Division in the British Army which holds a finer record than the 1st Division, and I can never forget the conspicuous gallantry they displayed at the Battle of LOOS when in the IV Corps. It is a matter of deep regret to me that they are now leaving the Fourth Army.

In thanking all ranks for what they have done, and in wishing them the best of good fortune in the future, I shall hope that at no distant date I may again have the good fortune to find them under my Command.

H Rawlinson

General,
Commanding Fourth Army.

H.Q., Fourth Army,
20th May, 1917.

WAR DIARY.

(WITH APPENDICES).

2nd.Bn. THE KING'S ROYAL RIFLE CORPS.

2nd. INFANTRY BRIGADE.

1st.DIVISION.

JUNE.1917.

Instructions regarding War Diaries and Intelligence Summaries are contained in F. S. Regs., Part II. and the Staff Manual respectively. Title pages will be prepared in manuscript.

WAR DIARY
or
INTELLIGENCE SUMMARY.
(*Erase heading not required.*)

2 KRRC Vol 33 2/1

Army Form C. 2118.

Place	Date	Hour	Summary of Events and Information	Remarks and references to Appendices
JUNE				
METEREN	1.		Fine day. Coys train. 2/LT W.F.A. CHAMBERS joined the BN.	
	2.		Fine day. Range in use. 2/LT. H.B. DAWSON rejoined from 1st DIV. School.	
	3.		Fine day. C.O. lectures Officers & N.C.Os on Musketry.	
	4.		Fine day. Coy train. 1 O.R. to L-G Course LE TOUQUET	
	5.		Fine day. Coys train.	
	6.		2 O.Rs to Bayonet Fighting Course. 1st DIV. School. 2 sections (B & D Coys) Rifle Grenade " 1 " (A Coy) Lewis Gun "	
	6.		Route march to the FORET DE NIEPPE near HAZEBROUCK & bathe in the canal. Fine day with thunderstorm in evening. News arrived that B.M.3 & Hon. CAPTAIN. A.E. ROBINSON had received the M.C.	

(A7092). Wt W12839/M1293. 75,0 0. 1/17. D. D. & L., Ltd. Forms/C.2118/14.

Instructions regarding War Diaries and Intelligence Summaries are contained in F. S. Regs., Part II. and the Staff Manual respectively. Title pages will be prepared in manuscript.

WAR DIARY
or
INTELLIGENCE SUMMARY.
(Erase heading not required.)

Army Form C. 2118.

Place	Date	Hour	Summary of Events and Information	Remarks and references to Appendices
V.	7		Fine day. News arrived of the victory at Messines of II ARMY. Work near billets. C.O. addresses the BN. The 1st DIV. was in Reserve to X CORPS but was not required.	
B.	8		Fine day. Work near billets. News of more successes near MESSINES. Draft of 12 O.Rs joined the BN. CAPT. T.R. FORSYTH FORREST rejoined BN from 1st DIV. Training School. C.S.M. W.F. WILSON promoted to commissioned rank of 2/LIEUT. & posted to 2nd Bn. K.R.R.C.	
	9		Fine day. 2nd Bde Rifle Meeting won by the BN. by 7 points. News arrived that CAPTAIN. H.E. SMITH had been awarded the LEGION D'HONNEUR (CROIX de CHEVALIER).	
	10.		CAPT. J.H.S. DIMMER. V.C. M.C. invalided to England. Church Parade. Officers 2nd K.R.R.C. XI play Officers XI 2nd Bde & lose by 4 wickets.	

(A7092). Wt W12839/M1293. 75,0.0. 1/17. D. D. & L., Ltd. Forms/C.2118/14.

Instructions regarding War Diaries and Intelligence Summaries are contained in F. S. Regs., Part II. and the Staff Manual respectively. Title pages will be prepared in manuscript.

WAR DIARY
or
INTELLIGENCE SUMMARY.
(Erase heading not required.)

Army Form C. 2118.

Place	Date	Hour	Summary of Events and Information	Remarks and references to Appendices
	11		BN march to billets at and around ST MARIE CHAPPEL.	
	12.		Fine day Coys train. Draft of 11 O.Rs joined the BN.	
	13.		Fine day. Coys train. CAPT. L.A. BLACKETT M.C. rejoined from IVth ARMY SCHOOL. LIEUT. HON. L.M. S[T] AUBYN to TRANSPORT COURSE. ABBEVILLE. 2/LT. E.M. POLLARD transferred to 12th Bn. K.R.R.C. 8 O.Rs to L-G. Course, 17 O.Rs to Rifle Grenade Course, & 3 O.Rs to BAYONET FIGHTING Course — all at 1st DIV. SCHOOL.	[illegible]
	14.		Fine day. Coys train.	
	15.		Fine day. Coys train.	

Army Form C. 2118.

WAR DIARY
or
INTELLIGENCE SUMMARY.
(Erase heading not required.)

Instructions regarding War Diaries and Intelligence Summaries are contained in F. S. Regs., Part II. and the Staff Manual respectively. Title pages will be prepared in manuscript.

Place	Date	Hour	Summary of Events and Information	Remarks and references to Appendices
16.			BN marched to FORET DE NIEPPE near HAZEBROUCK & bathed. Very hot day. Distance 20 miles in full marching order.	
17.			Fine day. Church parade.	
18.			Bayonet Fighting Competition won by 14 Section B Coy.	
19.			Fine day. Coys train. Billeting parties leave.	
20.			BN. marched to WORMHOUDT & arrived 8.30 am & went into billets. Distance 15 miles	App I
21.			BN. marched to TETERGHEM near DUNKERQUE, arrived 8.0 am & went into billets. Distance 12 miles.	

(A7092). Wt W12839/M1293. 75,0 0. 1/17. D. D. & L., Ltd. Forms/C.2118/14.

Army Form C. 2118.

Instructions regarding War Diaries and Intelligence Summaries are contained in F. S. Regs., Part II. and the Staff Manual respectively. Title pages will be prepared in manuscript.

WAR DIARY
or
INTELLIGENCE SUMMARY.
(Erase heading not required.)

Place	Date	Hour	Summary of Events and Information	Remarks and references to Appendices
22.			BN rest & clean up. LT. A. PINNOCK rejoined from L-G. course. 2/LT. B.C. MUNRO M.C. rejoined from 12th Bn K.R.R.C.	
23.			BN. entrain for COXYDE & then march to huts ½ mile EAST of COXYDE BAINS.	
24.			Fine day. Church parade.	
25.			Fine day. Coys train & bathe.	
26.			Fine day. Coys train & bathe. 7 O.Rs to L-G. Course 17 O.Rs to Rifle Grenade Course, 3 O.Rs. to Bayonet Fighting Course — all at 1st Div. School.	

(A7092). Wt W12839/M1293. 750,000. 1/17. D. D. & L., Ltd. Forms/C.2118/14.

Army Form C. 2118.

Instructions regarding War Diaries and Intelligence Summaries are contained in F. S. Regs., Part II. and the Staff Manual respectively. Title pages will be prepared in manuscript.

WAR DIARY
or
INTELLIGENCE SUMMARY.

(Erase heading not required.)

Place	Date	Hour	Summary of Events and Information	Remarks and references to Appendices
	27.		Fine day. Coys train & bathe. Brigadier and C.O. reconnoitred front at present held by 1st Bde. Enemy bombardment most of the day.	
	28.		Fine day. Coys train & bathe. The sea was full of Jelly-Fish & numbers of men were stung, especially amongst the L.N. LANCS. REGT.	
	29.		Fine day. Coys train & bathe. Bn concert in the evening.	
	30.		Wet & windy. Coys train.	

30/6/17.

R. Abadie Lt Col
KRRC
Cmdg 2nd Bn

App I

Battalion Order No.108.........Copy No. 2.

19th June 1917.

Reference HAZEBROUCK 5a.
& DUNKERQUE.1.A. 1/100,000.

1...The 2nd Bde and attached units will march brigaded tomorrow morning, as under:-

	Destination.
Bde Hd Qrs...........	Chateau, just N. of M. in WORMHOUDT.
L.N.Lancs.	
2/K.R.R.C............	An area about T. of WORMHOUDT.
etc.	

2...<u>Starting point</u>. Road junction 250 yards N.N.W. of L. of LE HAUT en BAS. Time 4.45 a.m.

3...<u>ROUTE.</u> RYVELD-LE TEMPLE-Z of OUDEZEELE-WORMHOUDT.

4...<u>ORDER of MARCH.</u> Hd Qrs. B. C. Band & buglers. D. A., water carts-maltese cart, rear guard.

5...<u>REARGUARD</u>. Consisting of all Nos. 1 & 2 of Lewis Gun Sections and stretcher bearers of A. Coy under an officer.

6...Transport (less water carts and Maltese cart) will be brigaded under Brigade Tpt Officer.
Starting point.....As for Battalion.
Time...............5-45 a.m.
Route..............As for Battalion.
Companies will have guides for cookers at Windmill Road junction ¼ mile SOUTH of first O. in WORMHOUDT.

7...All water-bottles will be filled before 9 p.m. tonight. No water will be available after that hour.

8...The 2nd Brigade will continue march on 21st.

<u>Order of march.</u>	<u>Destination.</u>
Bde Hd Qrs.	COUDEKERQUE-BRANCHE.
2/K.R.R.C.	Cross Roads. S. of N. in ROSENDAEL.
etc.	

9...<u>Starting point.</u> (21-6-17). Windmill 1 mile S.S.E. of R. in WYLDER.
Time......4-15 a.m.

10...<u>ROUTE. 21-6-17.</u> GALGHOEK.

11...<u>ORDER of MARCH.</u> 21-6-17. H.Q. C., D. Band & buglers. A. B. Coys. Water cart Maltese cart. Rear guard as detailed in para. 5 will be found by B. Coy.

12...<u>TRANSPORT.</u> 21-6-17. (less water-carts, Maltese cart) will be brigaded under Bde Tpt Officer.
Starting point......As for Battalion.
Starting time.......5-[illegible] a.m.
Route...............As for Battalion.
Guide from Companies will meet Cookers at GALGHOEK.

13...<u>HALTS.</u> 10 minutes before each clock hour.

14...All ~~units~~ must have breakfasts before starting.

15...Companies will send an Officer to Battn: Hd Qrs at 7 p.m. on 19th and 20/June. with a watch

16...Drinking of water from water-bottles on the march will be restr-

16..continued.
regulated by Company Commanders.

17...The Transport Officer will arrange to draw packs carried by the Supply wagon, from Bde Hd Qrs at COUDEKERQUE-BRANCHE on the afternoon of the 21st June.

18...Acknowledge.

2nd Lieut.
A/Adjutant.

King's Royal Rifle Corps..........
for Comdg 2nd Battalion.....

Issued at 1 p.m. by orderly.

Copy No.1 & 2.War Diary.
3.4.5.6....Companies.
7...2nd in Command.
8...Intelligence Officer.
9... Adjutant.
10....Quartermaster.
11....Transport Officer.
12....Medical Officer.

WAR DIARY.

(WITH APPENDICES).

2nd.Bn. THE KING'S ROYAL RIFLE CORPS.

2nd. INFANTRY BRIGADE.

1st.DIVISION.

JULY.1917.

2
1

Army Form C. 2118.

WAR DIARY
or
~~INTELLIGENCE SUMMARY.~~
(Erase heading not required.)

Instructions regarding War Diaries and Intelligence Summaries are contained in F. S. Regs., Part II. and the Staff Manual respectively. Title pages will be prepared in manuscript.

2nd K.R.R.C. JULY 1917

Vol 34

Place	Date	Hour	Summary of Events and Information	Remarks and references to Appendices
In the Field	1st July		Church Parade in the Theatre at 9.30AM. Brig. Gen. A.B. Hubback CMG + Brigade Major E.E Calthorp MC wounded while going round the line. ~~Capt. …~~ Lt Col. R.N. Abadie DSO assumed temp. command of 2nd Inf Bde.	
	2nd		Company Training on the sand dunes.	
	3rd		The Battalion took over Support Battalion Left Sector in cellars in NIEUPORT BAINS. The Battalion went up in "Battle Strength" only. The Remainder moved to RINK CAMP just West of OOST-DUNKERQUE BAINS.	
	4th		The Battalion took over the Left Sector of the whole Western Front. "A" coy on Left "D" in centre and "B" on Right with "C" coy in Support. Lt F.C. Gill relieved 2nd Lt W.F.A. Chambers at the 2nd Australian Tunnelling Coy.	
	5th		Capt. T.R. Forsyth Forrest left the Battalion for Senior Officers Course Aldershot. Draft of 11 O.R.s joined. Casualties 1 or. K. 15 or. W.	
	6th		Brig. Gen G.C KEMP. C.B. R.E. assumed command of 2nd Inf. Bde. 2nd Lt Nigel Anson MC slightly wounded by Minenwerfer He came back to RINK CAMP for a rest. Casualties 4 O.R. K 8 O.R. W.	
	7th		Much shelling especially on the Left. "C" company relieved "A" company. Lt Col R.N Abadie DSO took command of the Battalion in the Line. Major Sir J.V. Lees Bart. returned to RINK CAMP. Casualties 2 O.R. K. 4 O.R. W.	
	8th		2nd Lt Nigel Anson M.C. went up the line again. Casualties 1 O.R. Killed 8 O.R. Wounded.	
	9th		A raiding party of Rhodesians under 2nd Lt T.P. McDowell raided the enemy trenches by "BLACK DUNE" at 11.30P.M. They only found one marine whom they brought back. He was killed by an enemy shell on our wire. The same shell wounded 2nd Lt T.P. McDowell and seven O.R.s + killed Rfn DUNCAN.	[illegible]

Army Form C. 2118.

Instructions regarding War Diaries and Intelligence Summaries are contained in F. S. Regs., Part II. and the Staff Manual respectively. Title pages will be prepared in manuscript.

WAR DIARY
or
~~INTELLIGENCE SUMMARY.~~
(*Erase heading not required.*)

Place	Date	Hour	Summary of Events and Information	Remarks and references to Appendices
	10th		Intense enemy shelling on front & back areas all day. Enemy attacked at 7.10 AM when about 70% of the Battalion were casualties. Total casualties 17 officers and 478 O.R. Detailed account is issued separately. Officers killed 2nd Lt H A C Heberden 2nd Lt F. C. Smith (Northants) attached to the Regt & to the T.M.B. Officers Missing Lt Col R.N. Abadie DSO Capt. W L Clinton, Lt J H Mills, Lt A. Pinnock, 2nd Lts. B C Munro M.C, N.F. Anson M.C, W. Sheepshanks, A. Simpson, H.C. Chevis, E.W. Barnes, A.G. Boncher, H.J. Lindsay, R. Madeley, Officers Wounded & believed Prisoners of War. Lt W H E Gott, 2nd Lt D.H. Taylor, Capt H.K. Ward MC M.B. RAMC	
	11th		Capt H F E Smith, Capt H.W. Butler MC & 2nd Lt A.L. Gracie with about 20 men arrived at RINK Camp having swum the River YSER. They arrived in the early morning. In the evening about 15 men of B coy also swam the river & rejoined the Battn. Capt. Pallant MC RAMC attached to the 1st Loyal North Lancs. was the means of saving several of these men's lives in the water.	
	12th		The Brigadier addressed the Battalion at 5.30 PM. Lt F.C. Cull rejoined from Aust. Tunnelling Coy.	
	12th		Lt the Hon L.M. St. Aubyn left the Battn for Intelligence Duties at G.H.Q.	
	13th		Major Gen. E.P. Strickland CB DSO addressed the Battn & the 1st Battn Northamptonshire Regt. He expressed great satisfaction at the way both Battns had behaved and said ~~that~~ if he had ever wished two Battalions to carry out a particularly dangerous job ourselves & the Northants would not have been very far off the top of the list. ~~Lt F.C. Cull rejoined from 2nd Australian Tunnelling Coy~~ Draft of 10 O.R. arrived.	

235. Wt. W2544/1454 700,000 5/15 D. D. & L. A.D.S.S./Forms/C. 2118.

Instructions regarding War Diaries and Intelligence Summaries are contained in F. S. Regs., Part II. and the Staff Manual respectively. Title pages will be prepared in manuscript.

WAR DIARY
or
~~INTELLIGENCE SUMMARY.~~
(Erase heading not required.)

Army Form C. 2118.

Place	Date	Hour	Summary of Events and Information	Remarks and references to Appendices
	14th		2nd Lt. C.T. Mason + Capt W.L. Webster RAMC joined the Battalion	
	15th		Battn moved to GHYVELDE south of BRAY DUNES at 9.30 AM. Relieved by Manchesters 2/8 Battn 66th Div. Battn was encamped in a pleasant meadow. Battn moved under 3rd Bde orders.	
	16th		Battn moved to CAPELLE S.W. of DUNKERQUE. Battn was rather scattered in farm buildings. Corps Commander, Lt. Gen Du Cane, addressed officers on the march and the Battn then marched past. Very good draft of 236 other ranks arrived composed of various London Regts + ASC.	
	17th		2nd Lt L.J. Barnes M.C rejoined the Battn. Draft of 161 O.R arrived.	
	18th		Battn prepared to move to LE CLIPON but orders were cancelled at the last moment. Draft of 29 O.R. joined the Battn.	
	19th		Battn moved to ST POL s. MER. and encamped on grassy parts of the sand dunes. 2nd Lt C.G. Reed joined the Battn. Draft of 38 O.R. arrived. Rejoined 2nd Bde.	
	20th		2 Instructors from Div. School were attached to Battn. for training purposes	
	21st		Lt. Col. F.G. WILLAN D.S.O. took over command of the Battn. Capt. A. Cook M.C., Lt D.H Buckland, Lt P.C umming 2nd Lt E.H. Braybrooke joined the Battn.	
	22nd		Brigade Church Parade (less 1st L North Lancs) 10AM	

Army Form C. 2118.

Instructions regarding War Diaries and Intelligence Summaries are contained in F. S. Regs., Part II. and the Staff Manual respectively. Title pages will be prepared in manuscript.

WAR DIARY
or
~~INTELLIGENCE SUMMARY.~~
(Erase heading not required.)

Place	Date	Hour	Summary of Events and Information	Remarks and references to Appendices
	22nd	(contd)	Major F. Bryce & Capt. M.S. Ormrod arrived.	
	23rd		Company Training.	
	24th		Company Training.	
	25th		2nd Lts F.R. Harman, D.R. Willmott & J.J. Shaw joined Battn. Draft of 24 O.R. joined.	
	26th		Major F. Bryce transferred to 8th Battn. K.R.R.C.	
	27th		Company Training	
	28th		2nd Bde. Horse Show 2 P.M.	
	29th		Wet. Church Parade cancelled. 2nd Lt H. Grundy joined the Battn. Water Polo V. R. Sussex won 4-0. Association V. R. Sussex lost 2-3.	
	30th		Battn moved at 2.20 P.M. to LE CLIPON Camp on the Dunes where the whole Division is concentrated. 2nd Lt J.J. Shaw to Hospital.	
	31st		Dull day with rain. Company Training	

[signature]
Lt. Colonel
King's Royal Rifles
Comdg 2nd Bn

2353 Wt. W2544/1454 700,000 5/15 D. D. & L. A.D.S.S./Forms/C. 2118.

2nd Brigade No. G. 3/1/1.

REPORT ON THE OPERATIONS OF JULY, 10TH, 1917.

Reference Map - ~~Secret Map attached.~~

1. PERIOD PREVIOUS TO THE ATTACK.

For some day previous to the attack the enemy had subjected our line to intermittent bombardments, shelling the whole area East of the River YSER, particularly local Headquarters and Communication Trenches.

On the West of the River he shelled NIEUPORT BAINS heavily at times, and hit or knocked out the majority of O.Ps. The trenches on the Western bank were also shelled; the three bridges at the mouth of the River were rather heavily shelled on the 9th - some damage being done.

There was a considerable amount of hostile Counter-Battery fire, and back areas were shelled.

The hostile infantry activity was below normal, very little movement being seen, and the nights were particularly quiet, both as regards artillery and infantry. There was the normal amount of hostile machine gun fire at night.

Hostile aircraft was active during the days of the 5th, 6th and 7th, flying considerably over our lines, but on the 8th and 9th it was less in evidence.

2. HOSTILE ARTILLERY PROGRAMME UNTIL 7.10 p.m. on the 10th inst.

5.30 a.m. Enemy heavy artillery started a casual shelling of the Reserve line, the bridges, and NIEUPORT BAINS.
6.45 a.m. Shelling much increased, heavy barrage on front line for an hour.
7.45 a.m. Barrage lifted to Support and Reserve lines.
8.45 a.m. Barrage lifted to S.W. side of the YSER.
9.45 a.m. to 9.50 a.m. Lull.
9.50 a.m. Barrage on Support lines.
10.50 a.m. Barrage lifted to S.W. side of the YSER.
11.50 a.m. Barrage dropped on to front line.
11.55 a.m. Barrage on S.W. side of the YSER.
11.50 a.m. to 11.55 a.m. Lull.
12.55 p.m. Barrage dropped to Support line.
1.55 p.m. Barrage dropped to front line.
1.55 pm. to 2.10 p.m. Lull.
2.10 p.m. to 7 o'clock. The front and support lines and S.W. bank of the YSER and the bridge-head were continuously barrage.
There was a distinct lull of about 10 minutes at 6.10 p.m.

From 1.15 p.m. a continuous barrage was maintained on the bridges and Western bridge-heads. Shells of at least 8" calibre were falling at a rate of 4 a minute.

Another distinct barrage was also put across the houses at the Eastern end of NIEUPORT BAINS.

The times given above are only approximate and while a barrage is reported in one place it means that the shelling was heaviest here.

The Battalion Headquarters were apparently maintained under a continuous barrage except during the lulls.

The bridges were destroyed at the following times :-

By 8.30 a.m. MORTLAKE BRIDGE WAS CUT IN TWO.
By 12.55 p.m. KEW BRIDGE WAS DESTROYED.
By 4.55 p.m. RICHMOND BRIDGE WAS SMASHED.

The tunnels and covered trenches on the Western side of the YSER were blown in before 4 p.m. and there was no covered means of approach to the bridge-heads.

Throughout the day all back areas, Headquarters, Battery positions and ways of approach to the front area were kept under a steady fire, and the frequency with which all lines and means of communication were cut by this bombardment added extraordinarily to the difficulties of control of the situation.

3. COMMUNICATION AND REPORTS.

The situation was reported by continual messages from Observation posts of the Support Battalions, and retaliation was asked for by the Brigade on numerous occasions. Touch was maintained with the Divisional Artillery throughout, but it was found best to control the fire from artillery O.Ps.

Reports of the situation were received from Battalions East of the YSER by pigeon; all telephone and wireless communication was cut by 10.15 a.m.

Message Timed.	Extracts from Messages.
11. 7 a.m.	O.C. 2nd K.R.R.C. reported that Right Company H.Q. was blown in, Battalion Headquarters was being heavily shelled, he was reinforcing Right with one platoon. (Pigeon message).
5.15 p.m.	O.C. 2nd K.R.R.C. estimated casualties at 35% (Pigeon message).
6.30 p.m.	O.C. 1st Loyal North Lancashire Regt. reported C.R.E. had gone forward to investigate repairs necessary to No.1.Bridge and that he was trying to send two orderlies over the River in tubs.
7.10 p.m.	O.C. 2nd K.R.R.C. reported that he had two companies with no officers; that Battalion H.Q. had been moved into tunnel in BEACH ALLEY; that he was endeavouring to reinforce, enemy planes were flying low. (Pigeon message).
7.10 p.m.	White rockets bursting into two white lights.- Bombardment heavy. (Note. This was taken to be the S.O.S. signal and acted on as such, but the green light appeared as a perfect white).
7.18 p.m.	Movement can be seen about German Reserve line.
7.25 p.m.	Golden rain rockets opposite both Battalions.
7.44 p.m.	A lot of movement over our line. Right Battalion. Groups of men.
7.45 p.m.	Enemy attacking.
7.52 p.m.	Enemy have overrun Right Battalion, probably also Left.
7.50 p.m.	Telephone message from O.C. 1st Loyal North Lancashire Regt. that he was holding West of canal as front line.
7.55 p.m.	O.C. 1st Loyal North Lancashire Regt. reported by telephone that a few of the 2nd K.R.R.C. had swum across the River and report they are absolutely overrun.
Untimed.	Enemy have reached BARE SUPPORT and SISTON LANE roughly. Dugouts burning, prisoners going back. Enemy apparently waiting.
Telephone message.	Small party of 2nd K.R.R.C. putting up a fight close to Battalion Headquarters.
8.15 p.m.	Enemy advancing in extended order to water at M.15.c.
8.20 p.m.	Enemy working round our left at M.14.b.5.5.
8.50 p.m.	Small group of our men behind River barricade about Eastern end of No.1.Bridge.
8.55 p.m.	Dugout near Right Battalion H.Q. burning.
8.57 p.m.	Golden rain rockets opposite Left Battalion.

9.10 p.m. Enemy at M.14.b.5.5. Advancing slightly and reinforcing firing line.
9.13 p.m. Enemy crossed BACK WALK on our extreme left making for BEACH AVENUE. Think trying to surround Battalion H.Q.
9.30 p.m. Field guns appear to have been brought into position behind the sand dunes.
11.10 p.m. About 40 "MOAN" are holding Eastern end of No.1.Bridge. Enemy holding Right Bank of Canal between No.2 & 3 Bridges.
1.25 a.m. Captains BUTLER & SMITH and Lieut. GRACIE and Artillery Liaison Officer have come back. They report enemy digging hard by BLUE RESERVE. They think this will be his main line of resistance. Could artillery get on please. Enemy also active round KITCHENS.

The extracts given above are only on points of particular interest.

4. INFANTRY.

The hostile infantry attacked in three waves, each wave consisting of a line of groups of men. Each group estimated at between 6 & 8 men strong. They are reported by survivors from the Right Battalion to have debouched from their lines at the junction of the Battalion front, i.e., about M.15.b.20.25, and to have split into two, one half going to their left and working down EAST TRENCH and the other half to their right towards Right Battalion Headquarters at M.15.d.25.65. The enemy is believed to have reached the Battalion Headquarters in about an hour. The enemy infantry carried out their assault under a creeping barrage.

Against the Left Battalion the enemy is believed to have attacked in groups over the top and to have had a particularly large working party along the coast.

As will be seen in the messages given in para. 3 the first rear observers saw of the enemy was groups of men on the whole front simultaneously. These groups were in three waves and after the first creeping barrage of the assault there was a distinct lull in the hostile artillery fire, though a slow barrage was maintained on the bridges and NIEUPORT BAINS.

Parties of the enemy carried small flammenwerfer which were used for firing dugouts. Smoke bombs are reported to have been used, and also "stick handle" bombs. They wore grey uniforms with steel helmets and either wore white or yellow armlets according as to whether they were bombers or flammenwerfer carriers.

The enemy is believed to have used light machine guns as he swept the whole length of the N.W. bank of the YSER from the dunes whilst another machine gun near the left Battalion Headquarters took a large party of "C" Coy. 1st Northamptonshire Regt. in the rear. The machine gun reported by observer at M.14.b.5.5. had a heavy mounting resembling our Vickers Gun tripod; the mounting being carried separately by one man.

Officers who succeeded in getting back estimated our casualties in killed and wounded at the moment of attack as being from 70% to 80% of the effectives. The majority of the dugouts were blown in and their occupants either killed, wounded or imprisoned. The trenches were in most places nearly levelled and the communication trenches hopelessly blocked. That there was considerable resistance offered was evident from the fact that many of the enemy groups extended, stopped or proceeded cautiously from time to time, but actual fighting was impossible to observe from O.Os. owing to smoke.

Survivors of "C" Company of the 1st Northamptonshire Regt. state that their company resisted until practically all of them were knock out, and the remnant almost surrounded. A few of these managed to escape across the river. Ther are no survivors from the other companies. The enemy pentrated into NOSE TRENCH and NOSE SUPPORT on the right. The Battalion Scout Sergeant escaped by making his way round to the Battalion by making his way round to the Battalion Headquarters of the Border Regt. (Left Battn. 32nd Div.). informed them of the situation and told them the enemy were working their way round behind them.

The Officer Commanding this Battalion at once formed a defensive flank and strong point, therefore stopping a further advance on the enemy's part.

At about 8.30 p.m. a party, apparently officers, were seen near Right Battalion Headquarters fighting at close quarters till the last.

On the Left front the enemy appeared to be seriously held up about SISTON LANE as there was another short artillery preparation (directed by very lights from aeroplanes) and another distinct attack where the reserve company of the 2nd K.R.R.Corps appeared to make their stand.

Survivors who passed close by here report seeing many dead Germans andaconsiderable number of our men killed in the open. They report that at the Regimental Aid Post of the 2nd K.R.R.Corps the enemy bombed stretcher bearers and wounded.

The signal for lifting the hostile barrage appeared to be golden rain rockets.

The Machine Gun Officer who collected a party of 30 men at the River barricade threw his gun into the River before crossing to prevent it falling into the hands of the enemy.

A party of about 16 men of the 2nd K.R.R.Corps who were unable to get out of their dugout on the 10th had two smoke bombs thrown in amongst them by the enemy who molested them no further. On the 11th they got out of the dugout and succeeded in making their way back across the river.

5. CASUALTIES. The following numbers of all ranks were East of the River, not including Machine Gun Company, Trench Mortar Batteries, and Tunnelling Company.

	East of YSER.		Rejoined.		Casualties.	
	OFF.	O.R.	OFF.	O.R.	OFF.	O.R.
1st Northamptonshire Regt.	20	508	0	9	20	499.
2nd K.R.R.Corps.	20	~~501.~~ 524	3	46	17	~~455.~~ 478
TOTAL.	40	~~1009~~ 1032	3	55	37	~~954.~~ 977

6. AIRCRAFT. Hostile aircraft flew over our lines during the lulls in the bombardment, and when the enemy infantry attacked they flew very low over the whole area firing machine guns. The bridges over the YSER were barraged by them with machine gun fire. They directed Artillery fire by very lights and they are reported to have opened machine gun fire on slightest movement East of the River during the preliminary bombardment.

7. OUR ARTILLERY. The Divisional Artillery was firing continuously throughout the day. Counter Preparation was ordered at 10.45 a.m. and was continued more or less throughout the day, though later some of the heavy artillery was employed on neutralising fire, but without causing much diminution of enemy's fire.

There can be little doubt that the enemy has adopted the same tactics as have been so successfully employed by us in attack lately, but with the extra advantage that we were provided with dugouts which ~~xxxxxx~~ were not shell-proof, with trenches never very good and much damage, and that our aeroplane~~s~~ arrangements were so incomplete that the enemy were at entire liberty in the air, and we obtained no information of any value from our own Air Service.

For the same reason the Counter-Battery work appeared far less effective than is generally the case.

(sd). G.C.~~KEMP~~ KELLY,
Brigadier General,
Commanding 2nd Infantry Brigade.

14th July,1917.

3rd Brigade No. B.M.522.

Officer Commanding:-
1st South Wales Borderers,
2nd Welch Regt.
1st Northants Regt.
2nd K.R.R.Corps,
2nd Machine Gun Coy,
3rd Machine Gun Coy,
3rd T,M.Battery.
Sec. 1. Field Ambulance.
No 4 Coy Train.

The present 3rd Brigade Group less 1st Northants.Regt. 2nd K.R.R.Corps and No. 2 MachineGun Coy will be prepared to continue the march tomorrow. In which case 1st Northants. Regt. 2ndK.R.R.Corps and No 2 Machine Gun Coy will come under orders of G.O.C. 2nd Brigade and will probably move into the 2nd Brigade Area (ST. POL).

Captain,
Brigade Major,
3rd Infantry Brigade

18/7/17.

SECRET

Copy No 1

Addendum and Corrigendum to March Table issued with 3rd Infantry Brigade Order No 118

-*-*-*-*-*-*-*-*-*-*-*-*-*-*-*-*-*-*-

1. No 4 Company Train will move as ordered in 3rd Brigade Order No 118 less Supply Wagons. Further orders for these will be issued by the Staff Captain.

2. All baggage wagons will precede the main column under orders to be issued by Staff Captain.

3. All personnel detailed to remain at the Transport Lines will march with the Transport of their respective Unit.

R. Wingate. Captain,

17/7/17. Brigade Major, 3rd Infantry Brigade.,

-*-*-*-*-*-*-*-*-*-*-*-*-*-*-*-*-*-

Issued to:-

Copy No	
1/6.	6 Units (3rd Bde)
7.	2/K.R.R.Corps
8.	1/North'n Regt
9.	No 2 M.G.Coy
10.	Qr Mr. 1/S.W.B.
11.	Qr.Mr. 2/Welch Regt
12.	Qr.Mr. 2/K.R.R.Corps
13.	Qr.Mr. 1/North'n Regt
14.	No 1 Field Ambulance
15.	No. 4 Coy Train.
16.	Supply Officer, 3rd Bde.
17.	Staff Captain.
18.	Bde Transport Officer
19.	Bde Signal Officer
20.	Bde Intelligence Officer
21.	1st Division "G"
22.	1st Division "Q"
23.	1st Inf. Brigade
24.	2nd Inf. Brigade
25/26.	War Diary
27.	Office

SECRET

Copy No 5

3RD INFANTRY BRIGADE ORDER NO 117

1. The Brigade will move on the 18th instant remaining in present area tomorrow.

2. Strong advanced parties, strength as already arranged, will rendezvous at PTE SYNTHE Church at 1.p.m. tomorrow, 17th instant, whence they will march under Staff Captain's orders to LE C IPON Camp via BOOMSTREATE - MARDICK - Road Junction just South of last S in HAU DES DUNES.

3. The Company of 1st South Wales Borderers for duty under A.P.M. will proceed as already ordered.

4. All rations, Camp kettles, Officers kits, etc., for the advanced parties and for the Company 1st South Wales Borderers will be brought to PTE SYNTHE Church at 12.30.p.m. whence they will proceed by lorry under Brigade arrangements.

5. Para 5 of Administrative Order No 14 is cancelled. Para 6 will hold good for 18th inst. refilling tomorrow being normal at 11.a.m.

6. ACKNOWLEDGE.

R. Wingate Captain,

16/7/17.

Brigade Major, 3rd Infantry Brigade.

Issued to:-

Copy No	
1/4.	4 Units, 3rd Bde
5/7	3 Units, 2nd Bde
8/11	4 Quartermasters.
12.	No 1 Field Ambulance.
13.	No 4 Coy Train
14.	Supply Officer, 3rd Bde.
15.	Staff Captain.
16.	Bde Signalling Officer
17.	1st Division "G"
18.	1st Division "Q"
19/20.	War Diary.
21.	Office.

S E C R E T

3RD INFANTRY BRIGADE ADMINISTRATIVE ORDERS NO 14

1. A rigid censorship of all letters will be enforced as soon as the Brigade moves into LE CLIPON Camp. All Censor stamps will therefore be returned to Bde Headquarters by 12 noon tomorrow, accompanied by a Certificate that all envelopes already stamped have been withdrawn.
   From 12 noon onwards all letters will be put through the ordinary post, franked but unstamped, and will be opened at the Base. Correspondence to be cut down to a minimum. Officers letters will be franked in Battalions by Commanding Officers and on the Staff by Brigadiers.
   Letters containing information that they should not will be destroyed and not returned to the individuals. Cases of direct disobedience of Censorship orders will be dealt with by Court Martial

2. No Officer or man who once enters LE CHIPON Camp will be allowed out again.
   Every Unit will therefore have to detach certain people to remain with the Transport Lines in addition to ordinary Transport, as under taking care that any doubtful cases should be left with Transport

   In Camp. Fighting Troops. Battns 2 Riders, other Units 1 Rider.
   Company Cookers.
   Company Water Carts.
   Chaplains.

   With Transport. Transport (less Cookers and Water Carts) 1st & 2nd Line including all loaders.
   Interpreters.
   All Officers for whom applications have been submitted for transfer or for other employment of any sort.
   All N.C.Os and men who have been selected for Commissions.
   Personnel who will buy for Officers Messes or Canteens.
   Veterinary Officers and Sergeants, Bde Post Office and personnel.
   Quartermasters representatives in charge of Supply loaders.
   At least one reliable policeman.

   Units will send to this office by 9.a.m. tomorrow lists by Officers, Warrant Officers and other ranks of parties to go into Camp and to remain with Transport.

   N.B.:- Horses will draw in Cookers and Water Carts into the Camp and then will return at once to Transport Lines, being escorted out of the Camp by an Officer.

3. TENTAGE.
   Tents will be allotted on following basis:-
   Field Officers....... 1 per tent.
   Other " .... 2 " "
   Other ranks ....14 " "
   Extra Tents:-
   Per Coy for Wt Os.... 1 tent
   Each Coy Office...... 1 "
   Each Coy Store....... 1 "
   Each Bn Guard........ 1 "
   Each Bn Orderly Room. 2 "
   Each Bn Q.M.Stores... 2 "

   Tentage indents for both parties to be rendered to this office by 9.a.m. tomorrow based on present strengths of Units.
   It is hoped that each Unit will eventually have 1 Nissen Hut and 1 Marquee in addition.
   Tents will be drawn from Ordnance at the Camp on arrival.

4. GUIDES
   Transport will march to LE CLIPON massed by Brigades (less, in every case Cookers and Water Carts).
   3rd Brigade Transport under the Senior Officer.
   2nd " " " 2/Lieut DOULLAS, 1st Northampton Regt.
   One guide for each Transport will report at Bde Hd Qrs 1.p.m. and will be sent to respective starting points.

5. ADVANCE PARTIES each with at least 1 Officer to report to Staff Captain at Ordnance Store, LE CLIPON Camp at 11.a.m. tomorrow to draw tents and pitch camps.

6. SUPPLIES
For consumption 17th to be carried on Cookers or on the man.
For consumption 18th to be drawn from Refilling Point at G.12.d.7.2 at 11.a.m. tomorrow and to be divided up BEFORE MOVING OFF. into (a) those going into the Camp
(b) Those remaining with Transport Lines.
The former will be met by a guide at MARDICK SQUARE and conducted to TRAMHEAD not to arrive there before 3.p.m.
The latter will be met by a guide at GRAND-SYNTHE CHURCH to proceed direct to Transport lines.
O.C. No 4 Coy Train will be responsible for both columns and will not start until dividing up is complete.

7. BAGGAGE will go direct to Transport lines and there be divided up. Baggage for the Camp will be repacked and taken up to Tram base to be there by 5.p.m. Respective Brigade Transport Officers will superintend.

8. WATER CARTS will be filled before going into Camp. There will be Water lorries at MARDICK SQUARE for this purpose.
They will afterwards be filled from wells in the Camp. These require chlorination.

9. 3rd Brigade details will be organised for administrative purposes into a Battalion. Captain Somerset will, 2nd Welch Regt, will Command until further orders. Quartermaster, Major Thomas, 1st South Wales Borderers, Adjutant to be detailed by Captain Somerset from Officers left behind.

10. These orders so far as they concern the troops are to be read out to all ranks on arrival.

11. ACKNOWLEDGE

[signature] Captain,
Staff Captain, 3rd Infantry Brigade

16/7/17.

Copies to:-
4 Units, 3rd Brigade
3 Units, 2nd Brigade
No 4 Coy Train
Bde Supply Officer
Section No 1 Field Ambulance
Signals, 3rd Brigade
Office - 3 copies

SECRET.

1ST DIVISION ADMINISTRATIVE INSTRUCTIONS NO.10.

MOVE OF 1ST DIVISION TO LE CLIPON CAMP.

1. RAILHEADS.
3rd Brigade Group from 16th instant inclusive) DUNKERQUE.
Remainder of Division (less Divnl.Artillery))
from the 17th instant inclusive)

2. SUPPLIES. Table attached.
Supply arrangements after the 18th instant will be notified later.

3. ORDNANCE. Will move to LE CLIPON Camp on the 17th instant. Stores will be issued to 3rd Brigade Group on 17th inst, at LE CLIPON Camp, to the remainder of the Division in this area up to the 16th inst, and in LE CLIPON Camp from the 18th instant inclusive.
The Divisional Artillery remaining in this area will be transferred to 66th Division for Ordnance Services from the 17th inst, inclusive.

4. LAUNDRY. Will move to 64 RUE DE JEAN BART. ST POL under orders to be issued separately. The Advanced Laundry at ST. IDESBALDE will close on the 16th instant.
All dirty clothes must be returned by evening of the 16th instant.

5. LORRIES. 6 Lorries per Brigade Group will be available and will travel straight through to LE CLIPON Camp, except 1 for Brigade H.Q. which will be available until the completion of move.
Lorries going straight through will be met by a guide at GRANDSYNTHE Church and directed to the Transport Lines. A guard with 3 day's rations will travel with each Brigade Group of lorries.
Lorries will report at 9.0 a.m on first day of move.

6. GRENADE SUPPLY COY.
will break up on evening of the 16th inst, and personnel will rejoin their units by 6.p.m. From the 17th instant inclusive they will be rationed by their units. The D.A.C. Wagons will return to their sections. List of all stores handed over to the 66th Division will be sent to this office by Officer Commanding as soon as possible.

7. AREA STORES.
All tents and camp and area stores (including Chaff cutters which are not private property) will be handed over on relief.
Lists of all stores handed over will be forwarded to Divisional Headquarters by the 20th instant. Yukon packs and meat safes are to be taken to the new area.
No latrines, ablution benches or cook-houses in this area are to be dismantled or removed.

8. PETROL TINS.
Petrol Tins in excess of Battalion and other units' establishment will be handed over on relief.

9. CANTEENS.
Arrangements are being made for wet and dry Divisional Canteens at LE CLIPON Camp.

(Cont'd)

10. AREA COMMANDANTS.
The Area Commandants, ST IDESBALDE, COXYDE BAINS and OOST DUNKERQUE BAINS each with his clerk and servant will remain at their present duties until relieved by officers detailed by 66th Division who will ration them for consumption 18th instant and following days. All other personnel attached to them will rejoin their units on the 16th instant. When relieved Area Commandants will rejoin their units at LE CLIPON Camp.

11. BILLETS. The certificate referred to in Divisional Routine Order 624 will be rendered with least possible delay, after vacating billets in this area.

12. Salvage Coy. Will march under the orders of the General Officer Commanding 1st Infantry Brigade.

13. Acknowledge.

A.P. Holbrook Lieut.Colonel.
A.A. & Q.M.G., 1st Division.

15th July 1917.

1st. DIVISION. No. 5410/123.

DISTRIBUTION :-

1st Infantry Brigade.
2nd Infantry Brigade.
3rd Infantry Brigade.
1st Divnl.Artillery.
1st Divnl.Engineers.
1/6th Welsh Regiment.
1st Divnl. Signals.
1st Divn. Train.
1st Div.Supply Column.
A. D. M. S.
A. D. V. S.
A. P. M.
D. A. D. O. S.
O.C. Div.Employment Coy.
1st Divisional School.
1st Divnl.Gas Officer.
O.i/c Reinforcement Camp.
Fourth Army, H.Q.
XV Corps, H.Q.
Camp Commandant.
Area Commandant, ST.IDESBALDE.
-do- COXYDE-BAINS.
-do- OOST-DUNKERQUE-BAINS.
O.i/c 1st Divnl.Store.
O.i/c 1st Divnl.Laundry.
O.C. 1st Div. Salvage Coy.
W.O. i/c Railhead Post Office.
"G".
66th Division H.Q.

SUPPLY ARRANGEMENTS.

-0-0-0-0-0-0-0-0-0-0-0-

Date.	Group.	Supply Column Dump.	Refilling Point.	Time.	Remarks.
15th	3rd Brigade.	GHYVELDE.	as usual.	before moving.	
16th.	-do-	ST. POL.	GHYVELDE.	before moving.	
17th.	-do-	ST. POL.	ST. POL.	Time to be notified later.	
	2nd Brigade.	GHYVELDE.	as usual.	as usual.	
	1st Brigade.	ST. POL.	as usual.	before moving.	
18th.	3rd Brigade.	as for 17th.			
	2nd Brigade.	GHYVELDE @	GHYVELDE.	on arrival.	
	1st Brigade.	ST. POL.	ST. POL.	on arrival.	

NOTE :- 1. Exact places for Refilling will be notified later.

2. Rations for Divisional Headquarters for consumption on 18th inst, will be delivered direct to Divisional Headquarters by lorry on afternoon of 17th inst.

@ This may be changed to ST. POL. Area.

C.O. 1st S.Wales Bord.	C.O.Section No 1 Fd Amb.
" 2nd Welch Regt.	" No 4 Coy Train.
" 1st North'n Regt.	Supply Officer, 3rd Bde.
" 2nd K.R.Rif.Corps	Bde Transport Officer
" 2nd M.Gun Coy.	Bde Major.
" 3rd M.Gun Coy	Post Office.
" 3rd T.M.Battery	

-.-.-.-.-.-.-.-.-.-.-.-.-.-.-.-.-

Reference 3rd Brigade Order No. 116.

1. Billeting parties of 1st S.Wales Borderers, 2nd Welch Regt, No 4 Coy Train and Section, No 1 Field Ambulance will meet the Staff Captain or his representative at 7.30.a.m. 16th instant at H.9.a.9.9 (Sheet 19, 1/40,000) at Junction of PTE SYNTHE - DUNKERQUE and KROMBEKE[illegible] - DUNKERQUE Roads.

1. Billeting parties of 2nd K.R.R.Corps, 1st Northants, 2nd M.G. Coy, 3rd T.M.Battery and Bde Headquarters will meet the Staff Captain or his representative at 7.30.a.m. 16th instant at the bridge H.28.b.0½.8 (Sheet 19, 1/40,000) - the first Canal Bridge SOUTH OF FORT LOUIS.

2. Brigade Field Post Office will be attached to No 4 Coy Train.

3. Units will unload their Supply wagons at their new billets as quickly as possible and return them to No 4 Company Train without delay.

4. Refilling for consumption 18th - time and place will be notified later.

A.H.M. Wedderburn.

Captain,

15/7/17. for Staff Captain, 3rd Infantry Brigade.

Recd 5AM 16

23

SECRET

CORRIGENDUM TO 1ST DIVISION R.A.M.C. ORDER NO 107.

Last paragraph concerning move of No.2.Field Ambulance is cancelled, and the following substituted :-

> So as to leave maximum accommodation available for incoming Unit, Officer Commanding No.2.Field Ambulance will arrange that all personnel not actually required move to billets in COXYDE BAINS on afternoon of 16th.
>
> The whole Unit will concentrate in this place on morning of 17th, and will move on 18th under orders to be issued by 2nd Brigade.

OFFICE OF A.D.M.S. will close at ST. IDESBALDE at 10.a.m. on 17th instant and move to COUDEKERQUE BRANCHE.

Jno. C. Stubbs
Capt for/ Colonel,
A.D.M.S., 1st Division.

Issued at 4.0.p.m. on 15th July 1917.

Copies to :-

No.1.	No. 1. Field Ambulance.
No.2.	No. 2. Field Ambulance.
No.3.	No.141.Field Ambulance.
No.4.	"Q", 1st Division.
No.5.	"G.S.", 1st Division.
No.5.	D.D.M.S., XVth Corps.
No.7-9.	A.D.M.S., 66th Division.
No.10-14.	1st Brigade.
No.15-19.	2nd Brigade.
No.20-24.	3rd Brigade.
No.25.	1st Div. Train.
No.26.	1st D.E.
No.27.	A.D.V.S.
No.28-30.	Office.

SECRET. 2nd Brigade No. G. 3/100/1.

ADDENDA AND CORRIGENDA No.2. TO 2ND INFANTRY BRIGADE ORDER No. 148.

The destination of units of 2nd Brigade on relief will now be as follows, and not as previously stated.

2nd Brigade Headquarters.	COXYDE BAINS (old Div.H.Q.)
1st Loyal N. Lancs.Regt.	COXYDE BAINS.
2nd Royal Sussex Regt.	OOST DUNKIRK.
2nd T.M.Battery.	COXYDE BAINS.
216th Machine Gun Coy.	CAMP JEANNIOT.

A. C. Chichester-Constable

Captain, Brigade Major,
2nd Infantry Brigade.

15th July,1917.

Issued to all recipients of 2nd Brigade Order No. 148.

3RD INFANTRY BRIGADE ADMINISTRATIVE ORDERS NO 13

-*-*-*-*-*-*-*-*-*-*-*-*-

1. All Camp and Area Stores will be handed over to relieving units including ~~Government Chaff cutters~~, latrine seats, practice bombs and wiring stores. Yukon Pack Carriers and Meat safes will however not be handed over. Receipts to be obtained in duplicate, one copy being forwarded to this office.

2. Lorries allotted as follows:-
   1 for 2nd K.R.R.Corps.
   1 for 1st Northants Regt.
   To be at RINCK CAMP at 9.a.m. tomorrow (15th). 2nd M.Gun Company being short of guns and belt boxes must move on its own Transport.
   1 for 2nd Welch Regiment
   1 for 1st South Wales Borderers
   1 for 3rd M.Gun Coy & 3rd T.M.Battery.
   1 for 3rd Bde Hd Qrs.
   To be at X Roads W.6.a.9.6 COXYDE BAINS at 9.a.m. where Unit guides will meet and convey to Q.M.Stores. Lorries with the exception of Bde Hd Qrs lorry will go direct to final destination, where they will await arrival of Brigade. Each Unit, except 2nd Welch Regt, will detail guard of 1 N.C.O. and 2 men, and 2nd Welch Regt 1 Officer and 2 men, to accompany lorries, parties rationed for consumption 17th. Officer detailed by 2nd Welch Regiment will be in charge of all parties and will conduct lorries in convoy, meeting guide at GRAND SYNTHE Church 12 noon. Full lorries rendezvous X Roads W.6.a.9.6 at 10.30.a.m.
   Bde Hd Qr lorry will proceed independently with Bde Hd Qrs.
   2nd Welch Regiment to wire name of Officer selected.

KRB 685

KRB 688

3. Billeting parties all Units will meet Staff Captain at Area Commandant's Office GHYVELDE at 12.45.p.m. tomorrow.

4. Baggage wagons will return to Units tonight. Supply wagons will march with No 4 Coy Train full. Refilling for consumption 17th instant at GHYVELDE - times later.

5. Section No 1 Field Ambulance accompanying Bde will arrange for collection and disposal of sick.

6. Cycle orderlies from No 4 Coy Train, Section No 1 Fd Amblce, 2/K.R.R. 1/Northants & No 2 M.G.Coy will report to Signals 3rd Bde at 8.a.m. tomorrow, rationed for consumption 15th after which Bde Hd Qrs will ration. KRB 684

7. Brigade Post Office will move with Supply Section No 4 Coy Train.

8. Any men of 2nd Welch Regt or 1st S.W.Borderers who may be left behind to hand over revolver guns, etc., will be left rationed for consumption 16th and will report to 1st Gloucester Regt when relieved, being moved and rationed by them.

9. Refilling tomorrow at 9.a.m.

10. Usual certificates re cleanliness of billets vacated to be forwarded to Brigade Headquarters.

11. ACKNOWLEDGE.

R. C. Arnold Captain,
Staff Captain, 3rd Infantry Brigade.

14/7/17.

Copies to:-
6 Units, 3rd Bde.
2nd K.R.R.Corps
1st Northants
2nd M.Gun Coy
2nd Bde - for information.
No 4 Coy Train

Supply Officer, 3rd Bde.
No 1 Field Ambulance
Signals, 3rd Brigade
Office (2)

SECRET

Copy No 4

3RD INFANTRY BRIGADE ORDER NO 113

Reference Map, Sheets 11 & 19. 1/40,000

1. The 3rd Infantry Brigade Group will be relieved by the 199th Infantry Brigade on the 15th July 1917.
   On relief the 3rd Infantry Brigade will move to GHYVELDE in accordance with attached table.

2. For purpose of the move the 3rd Infantry Brigade Group will consist of
   1st S.Wales Bord.
   1/North'n Regiment
   2/Welch Regiment.
   2/K.R.Rif.Corps.
   No 2 M.G.Company
   No 3 M.G.Company
   3rd T.M.Battery.
   1 Sec. No 1 Field Ambulance.
   No 4 Company Train.

3. The guides as stated in table will be at W.6.d.8.8. at 8.30.a.m. with written instructions stating which Unit they are meeting.

4. All Defence Schemes, papers re Defence, Secret maps, COXYDE Maps 1/20,000 and LOMBARTZYDE 1/20,000 will be handed over.

5. Brigade Headquarters will close on completion of relief and open on arrival at GHYVELDE.

6. ACKNOWLEDGE.

R Wingate Captain,

14th July 1917. Brigade Major, 3rd Infantry Brigade.,

Issued to:-
- 1/6 6 Units, (3rd Bde)
- 7 2/K.R.Rif.Corps
- 8. 1/North'n Regt.
- 9. No 2 M.G.Company
- 10/13. 4 Quartermasters.
- 14. No 1 Field Ambulance.
- 15. No 4 Coy Train.
- 16. Supply Officer, 3rd Bde.
- 17. Staff Captain.
- 18. Bde Transport Officer.
- 19. Bde Signal Officer.
- 20. Bde Intelligence Officer.
- 21. 1st Division "G"
- 22. 1st Division "Q"
- 23. 1st Infantry Brigade
- 24. 2nd Infantry Brigade
- 25) War Diary.
- 26)
- 27. Office.

MARCH TABLE TO ACCOMPANY 3rd BRIGADE ORDER No. 113.

No.	Unit.	To	Starting Pt.	Time	Route
1.	1/North'n Regt.	ARMBOUTS CAPPEL	D.21.d.0.2	7.15.a.m.	UKEM - BOOMKENS - I.29.a.0.7.
2.	2/M.G.Coy.	PONT DU PTE SYNTHE	-do-	7.25.a.m.	" " "
3.	2/K.R.Rif Corps	CAPPELLE	-do-	7.30.a.m.	" " "
4.	3rd Inf Bde H.Q.	CAPPELLE	-do-	7.40.a.m.	" " "
5.	3/M.G.Coy (less 2 Sections)	CAPPELLE	-do-	7.43.a.m.	" " "
6.	3rd T.M.Bty.	CAPPELLE	-do-	7.48.a.m.	" " "
7.	2/Welch Regt. (less 2 Coys)	PTE SYNTHE	D.14.b.9.5.	7.15.a.m.	Main Road - DUNKERQUE - H.9.a.9.9.
8.	1/S.Wales Bord.	" "	-do-	7.25.a.m.	" " "
9.	No 4 Coy Train	" "	-do-	7.40.a.m.	" " "
10.	1 Sec.No 1 Fd Amb.	" "	-do-	7.45.a.m.	" " "
11.	2 Secs 3/M.G.Coy	CAPPELLE	Under Divisional arrangements		

NOTE:- Transport will accompany Units.
1-6 to constitute a column under Major J.ANGELL, M.C.
7-10 to constitute a column under Lieut-Colonel C.T.TAYLOR, 1st S.Wales Borderers.
Regulation halts will be observed unless otherwise ordered by Column Commanders.
The Brigade Group will continue the march on 17th instant.

Parade 7.15.
Breakfast 6
Rev. 5.
Sick 5.30

SECRET. 2nd Brigade No. G. 3/10A/4.

ADDENDA AND CORRIGENDA No.1. TO 2ND INFANTRY BRIGADE ORDER NO. 148.

---

1. The 1st Gloucester Regt.(less 2 Coys.) and the 2nd Royal Munster Fusiliers will not be relieved on 16th inst., but will remain in their present camp.

2. The Brigade will not now move on the 17th inst., but will march to the BRAY DUNES area on 18th inst. under orders to be issued later.

3. The destination of units after relief on 16th/17th will be as follows :-

1st L.N.Lancs.Regt.	Camp LEFEVRE
2nd R. Sussex Regt.	OOST DUNKIRK
2nd T.M.Battery.	Camp LEFEVRE.

4. All details from RINCK CAMP will move to the camps/or billets allotted to their respective units on the afternoon of the 16th inst.

5. After relief on the night of the 17th/18th inst. the 216th Machine Gun Company will move to Camp LEFEVRE.

6. Brigade Headquarters will move to COXYDE BAINS on completion of relief on the morning of 17th inst.

F. C. Chichester-Constable

Captain, Brigade Major,
2nd Infantry Brigade.

14th July,1917.

Issued to all recipients of 2nd Infantry Brigade Order No.148.

SECRET

Copy No 11

3RD INFANTRY BRIGADE ORDER NO 115

Reference Map, Sheets 11 & 19. 1/40,000

1. The 3rd Infantry Brigade Group will be relieved by the 199th Infantry Brigade on the 15th July 1917.
   On relief the 3rd Infantry Brigade will move to GHYVELDE in accordance with attached table.

2. For purpose of the move the 3rd Infantry Brigade Group will consist of

   1st S.Wales Bord.
   1/North'n Regiment
   2/Welch Regiment.
   2/K.R.Rif.Corps.
   No 2 M.G.Company
   No 3 M.G.Company
   3rd T.M.Battery.
   1 Sec. No 1 Field Ambulance.
   No 4 Company Train.

3. The guides as stated in table will be at W.8.d.6.6. at 8.30.a.m. with written instructions stating which Unit they are meeting.

4. All Defence Schemes, papers re Defence, Secret maps, COXYDE Maps 1/20,000 and LOMBARTZYDE 1/20,000 will be handed over.

5. Brigade Headquarters will close on completion of relief and open on arrival at GHYVELDE.

6. ACKNOWLEDGE.

R Wingate Captain,

14th July 1917.

Brigade Major, 3rd Infantry Brigade.,

Issued to:-

1/6 6 Units, (3rd Bde)
7 2/K.R.Rif.Corps
8. 1/North'n Regt.
9. No 2 M.G.Company
10/13. 4 Quartermasters.
14. No 1 Field Ambulance.
15. No 4 Coy Train.
16. Supply Officer, 3rd Bde.
17. Staff Captain.
18. Bde Transport Officer.
19. Bde Signal Officer.
20. Bde Intelligence Officer.
21. 1st Division "G"
22. 1st Division "Q"
23. 1st Infantry Brigade
24. 2nd Infantry Brigade
25) War Diary.
26)
27. Office.

MARCH TABLE TO ACCOMPANY 3RD BRIGADE ORDER No. 115
-*-*-*-*-*-*-*-*-*-*-

No.	Unit.	Relieving Unit.	Starting Point.	Time	Route	Guides	Remarks
1.	No.4 Coy Train.	No 4 Coy, 66th Div. Train	Camp.	10.15.a.m.	SEE REVERSE SIDE	-	
2.	1/North'n Regt. (less Transport))						
3.	2/K.R.Rif Corps (less Transport))	2/8th Manch:Regt.	W.6.d.6.6	10.20.a.m.		1 to be provided by 1/North'n Regt.	
4.	No 2 M.G.Coy (less Transport))						
5.	3rd Infy Bde H.Qrs party (less Trpt)	199th Infy Bde H.Q.	W.6.d.6.6	10.48.a.m.		2	
6.	Transport of 2, 3 4 & 5	-	W.6.d.6.6	11.0.a.m.		-	To march in above order brigaded under 3rd Infy Bde Transport Officer.
7.	3rd T.M.Battery	199/T.M.Battery	W.6.d.6.6.	11.30.a.m.		1	To follow 6.
8.	1 Sec No 1 Fd Ambce	-	W.6.d.6.6	11.35.a.m.		-	
9.	2nd Welch Regt	2/7th Manch: Regt	ST.IDESBALDE	After relief		(1 Bn Hd Qrs (1 per Coy	To join column on COXYDE-LA PANNE Rd so as to follow 1 Sec. No 1 Fd Ambce
10.	1/S.Wales Bord.	2/6th Manch:Regt	W.6.d.6.6.	After relief		(1 Bn Hd Qrs (1 per Coy	To follow 2/Welch Regt.
11.	No 3 M.G.Coy.	No 199 M.G.Coy.	W.6.d.6.6.	After relief		1	To follow 1/S.Wales Bord. May move in 2 portions, if relief of 2 sections is delayed.

A distance of 200 yards between Company and Sections of Transport of equivalent Road space will be observed to allow circulation of normal traffic.

TURN OVER

ROUTES

Unit No	
1.	Road Junction W.22.b. - X roads W.23.c.8.2 - E.5.b. - ADINKERKE-X Roads D.15.b. - GHYVELDE.
2,3,4,& 5,6,) 7,8,10 & 11.)	OOXYDE - Road junction W.22.b. - X Roads W.23.c.8.2 - E.5.b. - ADINKERKE - X roads D.15.b.- GHYVELDE
9.	ST IDESBALDE - X Roads W.18.c. - Road Junction W.22.b. - Cross Roads W.23.c.8.2 - E.5.b. - ADINKERKE - X Roads D.15.b. - GHYVELDE.

SECRET

2nd INFANTRY BRIGADE. No. a11/120

Reference :- HAZEBROUCK & DUNKERQUE SHEETS, 1/100,000. COPY NO. 19

1st Division R.A.M.C. Order No. 107.

14th July, 1917.

1st Division R.A.M.C. Order No.106 is cancelled.

The 1st Division (less D.A.) will be relieved by the 66th Division on the 15th, 16th and 17th instant, and will move to LE CLIPON area.

Date.	Formation.	Relieved by	Destination.
15th.	3rd Brigade.	199th Brigade.	GHYVELDE AREA.
16th.	3rd Brigade.		CAPPELLE AREA.
Night) 16/17.)	2nd Brigade.	197th Brigade.	OOST DUNKERKE AREA.
17th.	3rd Brigade.		LE CLIPON AREA.
17th.	2nd Brigade.		GHYVELDE AREA.
17th.	1st Brigade.	198th Brigade.	BRAY DUNES.area.
17th.	Div H.Q.	66th Division.	ROSENDAEL.
18th.	1st Brigade.) 2nd Brigade.) Div.H.Q.)		LE CLIPON AREA.

The following moves of Medical Units will take place :-

NO.1.FIELD AMBULANCE.

One Section of No.1. Field Ambulance will be attached to 3rd Brigade and will move on 15th instant under orders to be issued by 3rd Brigade.

Remainder of No.1. Field Ambulance will be attached to 1st Brigade and will move on 17th instant under orders to be issued by 1st Brigade.

Present Camp will be taken over by 2/2nd East Lan. Field Ambulance, at 9.a.m. on 17th.

NO.2.FIELD AMBULANCE.

An advance party from 2/1st East Lancs Field Ambulance, consisting of 2 Officers and 10 Other Ranks, will report by 3.p.m. on 15th instant at No.2.Field Ambulance Headquarters for instruction in the method of evacuating casualties.

The Advanced Dressing Stationsat NIEUPORT BAINS and LAITERIE ROYALE will be taken over by 2/1st East Lancs Field Ambulance on the 16th instant, and all personnel and Cars of No. 2 Field Ambulance will be concentrated at OOST DUNKERKE BAINS by midnight 16/17th.

Field Ambulance Headquarters OOST DUNKERKE BAINS will be handed over on morning of 17th.

All blankets, stretchers, aid post stores, and equipment held surplus to moblization table will be handed over, and receipts forwarded to this Office vide A.D.M.S. No.1650 dated 7/1/17.

All details of relief and exchange of equipment to be arranged between field Ambulance Commanders concerned.

No.2. Field Ambulance will be attached to 2nd Brigade and will move on 17th instant under orders to be issued by 2nd Brigade.

NO.141.FIELD AMBULANCE.

No.141.Field Ambulance will remain at BRAY DUNES and continue to operate as XVth Corps Rest Station.

OFFICE OF A.D.M.S.

The Office of A.D.M.S. will move to ROSENDAEL on 17th instant and will open in LE CLIPON area on 18th at a time and place to be notified later.

MEDICAL ARRANGEMENTS.

During the move Medical Units will collect the sick of their Brigade Group transferring them to Corps Main Dressing Station or Corps Rest Station as convenient.

Medical arrangements for new area will be issued later.

Jno. C. Stubbs
Capt for/
Colonel,
A.D.M.S., 1st Division.

Issued at 8.0.p.m. on 14th July,1917.

Copies to :-
No.1. No. 1. Field Ambulance.
No.2. No. 2. Field Ambulance.
No.3. No.141.Field Ambulance.
No.4. "Q" 1st Division.
No.5. "G.S." 1st Division.
No.6. D.D.M.S., XVth Corps.
No.7-9. A.D.M.S., 66th Division.
No.10-14. 1st Brigade.
No.15-19. 2nd Brigade.
No.20-24. 3rd Brigade.
No.25. 1st Div.Train.
No.26. 1st D.E.
No.27. A.D.V.S.
No.28-30. Office.

"A" Form.

Army Form C.2121 (in pads of 100).

MESSAGES AND SIGNALS.

No. of Message ....

Prefix .... Code .... m. Office of Origin and Service Instructions.	Words	Charge	This message is on a/c of:	Recd. at .... m.
	Sent At .... m. To .... By		.... Service. (Signature of "Franking Officer.")	Date .... From .... By ....

TO A B C D } Coys.

Sender's Number.	Day of Month.	In reply to Number.	AAA
HB 127	10		

It is very probable that the enemy may attack with Infantry after or under cover of this bombardment AAA It is imperative to hold the front line trench at all costs AAA You will therefore reinforce the front line as follows.

B coy 3 platoons in front line, one in BLUE & BARE Support

D coy 3 platoons in front line, one in support

C coy 2 platoons front line
1 in support
1 in reserve to watch sea shore

"A" Form.
MESSAGES AND SIGNALS.

Army Form C.2121
(in pads of 100).
No. of Message..................

Prefix .... Code .... m. Office of Origin and Service Instructions.	Words	Charge	This message is on a/c of:	Recd. at .... m.
	Sent		.... Service.	Date ....
	At .... m.			From ....
	To			
	By		(Signature of "Franking Officer.")	By ....

TO A B C D } Coys

Sender's Number.	Day of Month.	In reply to Number.	AAA
HB 127	10	Continued	

A coy will be disposed as follows

One platoon will be at
dugout at junction of BEACH
ALLEY and BOYAU DRESCH
and will be at the disposal of
O.C. D coy who will inform me
as soon as he makes use of
it.

By	(Signature of "Franking Officer.")	By

TO A Coy
B
C
D

Sender's Number.	Day of Month.	In reply to Number.	AAA
* HB 127	10		

The remainder of A coy will remain in their present position by Battn Hd Quarters

You will endeavour to take up these dispositions unseen AAA

It is vital for the Allies that we maintain our hold on our present trench system.

Report compliance as soon as possible

Acknowledge by runner —

From

Place

Time 2.42 pm

The above may be forwarded as now corrected.

(Z) R. Abadie Lt Col

Censor. Signature of Addressor or person authorised to telegraph in his name.

* This line should be erased if not required.

750,000. W 2183 M169. H. W & V., Ld. 6/16.

SECRET. Copy No. 6

~~2nd Infantry Brigade Order No. 147.~~

2nd Battalion King's Royal Rifle Corps.

Reference Sunprint Trench Map, 1/5,000.

1. A Raid will be carried out by "B" Company on the night of 9th/10th July, 1917.

(The 1st Battalion Northamptonshire Regiment are carrying out a raid about M.16.a.7.0. at the same hour.)

2. Party. 2/Lieut. McDOWELL and 20 O.R.

3. Point of entry M.15.a.83.76. on South side of GRAND DUNE.

4. Object. To kill Germans and to secure prisoner for identification.

5. Point of exit from our line M.15.a.73.68.

6. Plan.

AT ZERO - 3 minutes.

Two Stokes guns to open fire 5 rounds per gun for one minute on enemy post on GRAND DUNE. To cause enemy to take to dugout.

Three guns (25th Bde.R.F.A.) fire 1 round a minute up to Zero, away from point to be raided. Noise to cover Stokes and exit of party.

Two guns of No.2.M.G.Coy. fire bursts up to Zero, away from point to be raided. Noise to cover Stokes and exit of party.

AT ZERO - 2 minutes.

Infantry leave our trench and enter that of enemy as quickly and silently as possible.

"Raid" consists of three parties :-

Assault party - moves to left on entering and disposes of garrison of post securing a prisoner.

Blocking party - moves 20 yards down to right along trench.

Overland party - crosses trench to Northern entrance of GRAND DUNE dugout to cut off enemy retreating to North along trench. The O.C. Raiding Party will arrange his own signal for return. The raid will be carried out as quickly as possible.

7. ZERO. Will be at 10.45 p.m.

8. AT ZERO.

25th Brigade R.F.A.)
2" Trench Mortars.)
2nd T.M.Battery.)
No.2.M.G.Coy.)
Will open fire as shown on attached map.

216th M.G.Coy. On back areas according to harassing fire scheme.

Rate of fire.	Howitzers.	18 Pdrs.	2" T.M.
ZERO to plus 10	2 rounds per gun per minute.	3 rounds per gun per minute.	1 round per gun per minute.
Plus 10 to plus 15	1 -do-	2 -do-	1 round per 2 mins.
Plus 15 onwards	1 -do-	1 -do-	1 round per 3 mins.

9. Signal. As soon as the raiding party is back in our own trenches, a gold and silver rain rocket will be fired from in rear of GRAND DUNE as a signal for the barrage to cease. It will be repeated from near Left Battalion Headquarters.

10. Raiding party.

Dress. Canvas suits with badges of rank and universal buttons.

Faces. Blacked.

Identification. All maps, papers, letters etc., and any other means by which any member of the raiding party might be identified by the enemy will be removed.
The Company Commander will personally inspect each member of the party.

Arms & Equipment. Assault party - Knob kerries, revolvers and Mills and P. bombs.

Overland party. Rifles, bayonets, Mills and P. bombs.

Blocking party. Rifles, bayonets, bombs (two men with revolvers instead of rifles).

11. Headquarters. Battalion Headquarters will move to Centre Company Headquarters at 10 p.m. 9/7/17 until raid is complete.

12. Communication. The Battalion Signalling Officer will arrange for Visual communication with O.C. 25th Brigade R.F.A.

Code. "All in Cease Fire" - McDOWELL

by phone and M by Visual.

13. <u>Synchronisation of watches.</u>

Watches will be synchronised at Left Support Battalion Headquarters at 5 p.m. and 8 p.m. on 9/7/17 by representative of:-

25th Brigade R.F.A.
D.T.M.O.
2nd T.M.Battery.
No.2.M.G.Coy.
2nd Battn. K.R.R.Corps.

14. <u>Medical.</u> The M.O. will arrange for a Medical Aid Post at the Centre Company Headquarters.

7th July,1917.

Copies to :-

1. O.C. "B" Coy.(K.R.R.C.)
2. 2/Lieut. McDOWELL "
3. 25th Brigade R.F.A.
4. D.T.M.O.
5. 2nd T.M.Battery.
6. No.2.M.G.Coy.
7. 1st Northants.
8. G.O.C.
9. 216th M.G.Coy.
10 & 11. War Diary.
12 & 13. Office.

SQUARES M { 9 C AND D
15 a AND B

Hows
2"TM
Stokes

9

DUNE AVENUE
DUNE ALLEY
DUNE TRENCH
WHITE DUNE
BRITISH FRONT LINE
POLDER TRENCH

15

SCALE 1/5,000

50
YARDS 100 0 100 200 300 400 500 YARDS

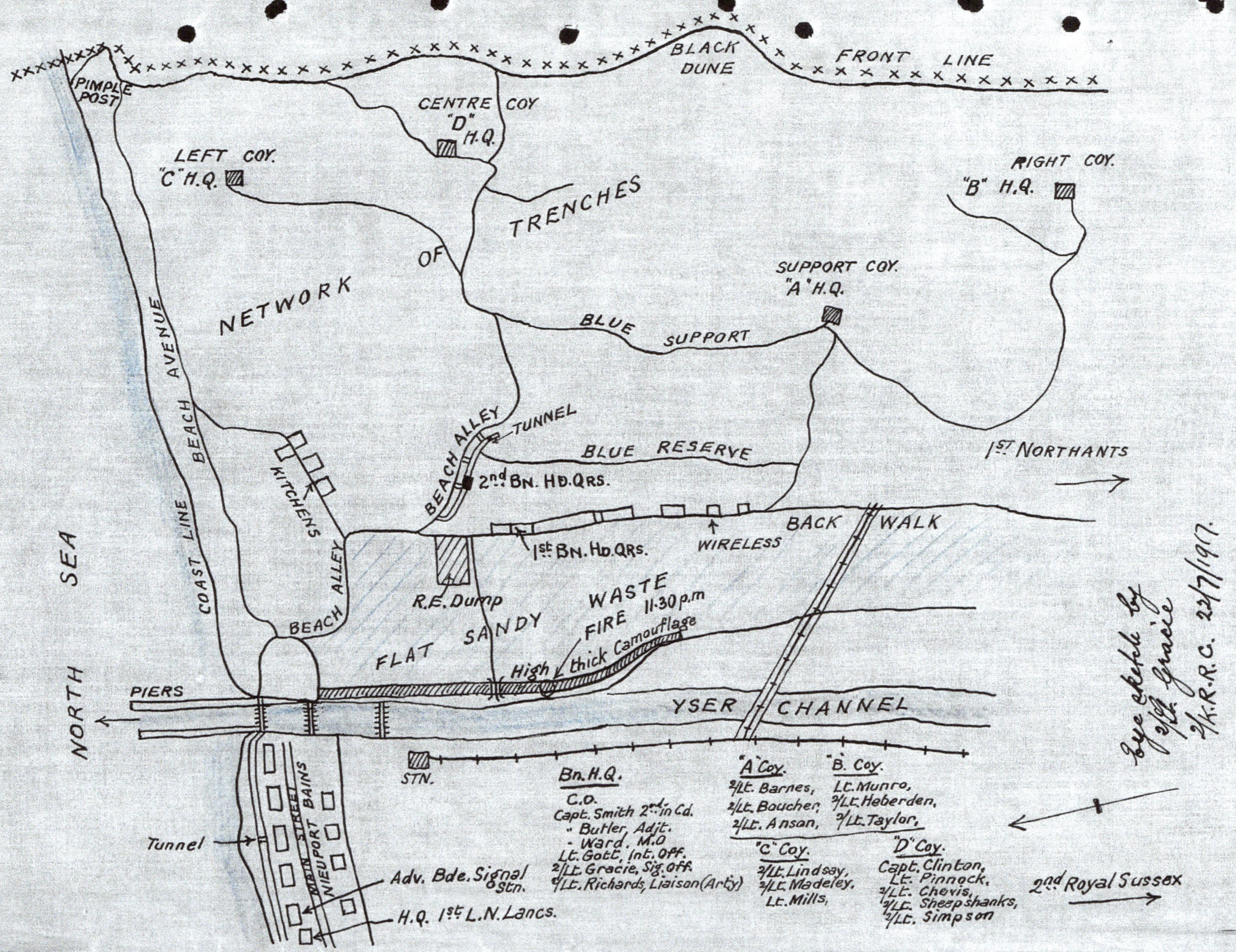

BLACK DUNE

FRONT LINE

PIMPLE POST

CENTRE COY "D" H.Q.

LEFT COY. "C" H.Q.

RIGHT COY. "B" H.Q.

NETWORK OF TRENCHES

SUPPORT COY. "A" H.Q.

BLUE SUPPORT

TUNNEL

BEACH ALLEY

BLUE RESERVE

2nd BN. HD.QRS.

KITCHENS

1st NORTHANTS

BACK WALK

WIRELESS

1st BN. HD.QRS.

COAST LINE

BEACH AVENUE

SEA

BEACH ALLEY

R.E. Dump

FLAT SANDY WASTE

FIRE 11.30 p.m

High thick Camouflage

NORTH

PIERS

YSER CHANNEL

STN.

MAIN STREET NIEUPORT BAINS

Tunnel

Adv. Bde. Signal Stn.

H.Q. 1st L.N. Lancs.

Bn. H.Q.

C.O.
Capt. Smith 2nd in Cd.
" Butler, Adjt.
" Ward, M.O.
Lt. Gott, Int. Off.
2/Lt. Gracie, Sig. Off.
2/Lt. Richards, Liaison (Arty)

"A" Coy.
2/Lt. Barnes,
2/Lt. Boucher,
2/Lt. Ansan,

"B" Coy.
Lt. Munro,
2/Lt. Heberden,
2/Lt. Taylor,

"C" Coy.
2/Lt. Lindsay,
2/Lt. Madeley,
Lt. Mills,

"D" Coy.
Capt. Clinton,
Lt. Pinnock,
2/Lt. Chevis,
2/Lt. Sheepshanks,
2/Lt. Simpson

2nd Royal Sussex

Eye sketch by
2/Lt. Gracie
2/K.R.R.C. 22/7/1917.

WAR DIARY.

2nd. BN. THE KING'S ROYAL RIFLE CORPS.

2nd. INFANTRY BRIGADE.

1st. DIVISION.

AUGUST. 1917.

Army Form C. 2118.

Instructions regarding War Diaries and Intelligence Summaries are contained in F. S. Regs., Part II. and the Staff Manual respectively. Title pages will be prepared in manuscript.

WAR DIARY
or
~~INTELLIGENCE SUMMARY.~~

(*Erase heading not required.*)

2nd K.R.R.C. AUGUST 1917

Hour, Date, Place	Summary of Events and Information	Remarks and references to Appendices
In the Field		
1st	Draft of 17 ORs joined the Battn. Band Sgt HOARE arrived. Rain all day.	
2nd	Draft of 24 ORs arrived. Association football H.Q. v. A coy on the sands. H.Q. won 2-1. Rain on & off all day.	
3rd	More rain. Company training.	
4th	Battn. route march through LOON PLAGE & MARDICK.	
5th	Bde. Church Parade with Major General commdg 1st Div. presented Ribbons afterwards. Bishop of KHARTOUM preached	
6th	Company training.	
7th	Collective training W. of the Camp.	
8th	Training. Weather improving.	
9th	Training.	

(9 26 6) W 257—976 100,000 4/12 H W V 79/3298

Instructions regarding War Diaries and Intelligence Summaries are contained in F. S. Regs., Part II. and the Staff Manual respectively. Title Pages will be prepared in manuscript.

WAR DIARY
or
INTELLIGENCE SUMMARY
(Erase heading not required.)

Army Form C. 2118.

Place	Date	Hour	Summary of Events and Information	Remarks and references to Appendices
	August 1917			
	10th		2nd Lts. D.W.T. GURNEY, H.W. NUGENT HEAD, J.N. CHENEY, E.J.G. PALMER, R.J. TRINDER, A. WINTER, F.V. HANCOCK, J.C. WHITE, S. JOHNSON. and 29 O.Rs joined the Battalion. Association Football against 2nd R. Sussex Regt. We won 5-2.	
	11th		The Whole Battalion practised landing & unloading from a practise pontoon.	
	12th		Bde. Church Parade 10 AM. Officers played Officers of 2nd R. Sussex Regt. at Rugby football and beat them 41-3. Battn. practised climbing the Sea Wall. Bde. hired a piano which was put in our camp.	
	13th		Battn route march through MARDICK, GDE SYNTHE, PTE SYNTHE & FORT MARDICK	
	14th		Crate of Books from Padre for use of the Battn.	
	15th		Lt F.C. CULL joined 2nd Trench Mortar Battery (Stokes) Draft of 22 O.Rs arrived. 2nd Bde. Boxing Competition on the sands. No 5696 Rfn J McMAHON won the Welter weight.	
	16th		Field day on the Dunes with live shells & Stokes mortars. Concert at 8 P.M. in Church Army Tent. G.O.C. 2nd Bde was present.	[signature]

2449 Wt. W14957/M90 750,000 1/16 J.B.C. & A. Forms/C.2118/12.

Army Form C. 2118.

Instructions regarding War Diaries and Intelligence Summaries are contained in F. S. Regs., Part II. and the Staff Manual respectively. Title Pages will be prepared in manuscript.

WAR DIARY

or

INTELLIGENCE SUMMARY

(Erase heading not required.)

Place	Date	Hour	Summary of Events and Information	Remarks and references to Appendices
	17th		Training.	
	18th		Platoon competition throughout 2nd Bde over the Obstacle Course.	
	19th		Draft of 19 ORs joined the Batt. League Association match against 2nd Bde HQ. We Won 4-0. Bde. Church Parade 10 AM.	
	20th		Training. Practise game of Rugby on the sands. 2nd Lt L. J. BARNES M.C. granted acting rank of Captain.	
	21st		League Rugby against 1st Northamptonshire Regt. We won 47-4. A+B coys. made rafts of canvas & brushwood.	
	22nd		Lt. D. H. BUCKLAND granted acting rank of Capt. League association match against 2nd R. Sussex. Draw 3 all.	
	23rd		Concert 8.15 PM in Church Army Tent.	
	24th		Rehearsal on the beach for Inspection & March Past. Showers of Rain.	

2449 Wt. W14957/M90 750,000 1/16 J.B.C. & A. Forms/C.2118/12.

Instructions regarding War Diaries and Intelligence Summaries are contained in F. S. Regs., Part II. and the Staff Manual respectively. Title Pages will be prepared in manuscript.

WAR DIARY
or
INTELLIGENCE SUMMARY
(Erase heading not required.)

Army Form C. 2118.

Place	Date	Hour	Summary of Events and Information	Remarks and references to Appendices
	25th		Inspection & March Past on the Beach. General Sir Henry Rawlinson Bart, G.C.V.O. K.C.B. commdg 4th Army presented Ribbons. G.O.C. 4th Army expressed great satisfaction at discipline of the 1st Division. Lt. F. ROBARTS struck off strength with 11th Prisoner of War Coy.	
	26th		Church Parade with 1st Northants on the beach. League Rugby against 2nd R. Sussex Regt. We won 37–0. This was the final of the 2nd Bde matches.	
	27th		Rain all day.	
	28th		Rain & Wind all day. Cinema & Church Army Tent both blown down.	
	29th		Route March. Rain most of the day.	
	30th		Rain	
	31st		A+B coys were enemy force to a 2nd Bde attack. C+D coys did Night Operations. Party of Sailors landed on the beach to be entertained by the Division.	[illegible]

[illegible] Lieut. Colonel
KINGS ROYAL RIFLES,
COMDG. 2nd BN.

2449 Wt. W14957/M90 750,000 1/16 J.B.C. & A. Forms/C.2118/12.

WAR DIARY.

2nd.BN.THE KING'S ROYAL RIFLE CORPS.

2nd. INFANTRY BRIGADE.

1st. DIVISION.

SEPTEMBER.1917.

Instructions regarding War Diaries and Intelligence Summaries are contained in F. S. Regs., Part II. and the Staff Manual respectively. Title pages will be prepared in manuscript.

WAR DIARY
or
~~INTELLIGENCE SUMMARY.~~
(Erase heading not required.)

Army Form C. 2118.

2nd K.R.R.C. September 1917

Place	Date	Hour	Summary of Events and Information	Remarks and references to Appendices
[illegible] Field	1.		23 Other Ranks joined. 2nd Bde. Association Semi Final. We drew again with the R. Sussex 2 all. 2nd Lt Gracie broke a small bone in his hand which put him out of action for the remainder of the month.	
	2.		Bde. Church Parade on the sands 10 AM.	
	3.		10 other ranks joined.	
	4.		2nd Bde association semi final. We beat the Sussex 1-0.	
	5.		Bde. Field Day round about Moulin Spycker with Engineers, Cyclists & M.M. Guns. Beautiful day.	
	6.		Lt. Col F.G. Willan DSO left the Battalion to command the 56th Inf. Bde	
	7		The Battalion acted as "enemy" to the remainder of the 2nd Bde on a scheme round about Moulin Spycker.	
	8.		2nd Bde association final. We lost to the 1st L. North Lancs. Score 3.0.	
	9.		Church Parade on the Beach 10.30 AM. Lt. Col G.C Kelly arrived and too[k]	

(A7092). Wt. W12839/M1293. 75,000. 1/17. D. D. & L., Ltd. Forms/C.2118/14.

Army Form C. 2118.

Instructions regarding War Diaries and Intelligence Summaries are contained in F. S. Regs., Part II. and the Staff Manual respectively. Title pages will be prepared in manuscript.

WAR DIARY
or
~~INTELLIGENCE SUMMARY.~~
(Erase heading not required.)

2 R.M.L.I. September 1917

Place	Date	Hour	Summary of Events and Information	Remarks and references to Appendices
	9 (continued)		over command of the Battalion. 10 other ranks joined the Battn.	
	10.		Company Training.	
	11.		Demonstration of the Message Carrying Rocket in the morning. Party of Sailors 5 officers and about 40 other ratings landed from the monitor H.M.S. General Wolfe as guests of the Battalion. 4 officers and 20 other ratings went to see the Messines Ridge. Major Sir J.V.B. Lees Bart accompanied them. Regt. Concert in the evening at 8.30 p.m.	
	12.		Sailors returned from Messines. 2nd Bde. Tug o' War Semi final. We pulled the 1st Northants over after 6 exciting minutes.	
	13.		Sailors left in 'busses for Dunkerque at 2 p.m. Tug o' War Final. We were pulled over by the 2nd R. Sussex.	
	14.		Battalion Sports in the afternoon.	
	15		Two platoons of "C" coy with T.M.B. gave a spectacular demonstration	

(A7092). Wt W12839/M1293. 750,000. 1/17. D. D. & L., Ltd. Forms/C.2118/14.

Army Form C. 2118.

Instructions regarding War Diaries and Intelligence Summaries are contained in F. S. Regs., Part II. and the Staff Manual respectively. Title pages will be prepared in manuscript.

WAR DIARY
or
~~INTELLIGENCE SUMMARY.~~
(Erase heading not required.)

2 KRRC September 1917

Place	Date	Hour	Summary of Events and Information	Remarks and references to Appendices
	15th	continued	of attacking a "strong point" for the benefit of the sailors who were guests of other regiments. This was unavoidably held over when the sailors were with this Battn.	
			Several officers & men of the Battn. visited HMS "General Wolfe".	
	16		Church Parade 9.30am	
	17		Monitors weighed anchor & departed.	
	18		Company training	
	19		Field Day on the Sand Dunes.	
	20		Company Training 2nd Lt EA Warner to Hospital	
	21		Adjutant's Parade on the beach.	
	22		Staff Ride in motor busses for all officers in the morning.	
	23		2nd Bde. Race Meeting on the Sands 2PM. The Regt. secured 1 first place 1 second place 1 third place. Church parade in morning	

(A7092). Wt. W12839/M1293. 75 ,0 o. 1/17. D. D. & L., Ltd. Forms/C.2118/14.

Army Form C. 2118.

WAR DIARY
or
INTELLIGENCE SUMMARY.
(*Erase heading not required.*)

Instructions regarding War Diaries and Intelligence Summaries are contained in F. S. Regs., Part II. and the Staff Manual respectively. Title pages will be prepared in manuscript.

2 KRRC — September 1917

Place	Date	Hour	Summary of Events and Information	Remarks and references to Appendices
	24		Cloudless day. Practise game of rugby football against the 1st South Wales Borders (3rd Bde) We lost 8 - 0.	
	25		Battalion Field Day round about Moulin Spycker Lovely day	
	26		Dull day. Practise game of rugby on the sands. 2nd Lt. H. J. FLETCHER, 1st R Wells Yeomanry, joined Battn as Transport Officer	
	27		Brigade Field Day round Moulin Spycker The Battn was in support.	
	28.		Quiet & easy day	
	29		Practised boarding the "monitor" (marked out on the grass)	
	30.		Bde. Church parade on sands at 10 a.m. Maj. Gen. Montgomery MGGS. 4th Army lectured to all officers of the Division at 2.30pm on the War generally.	

[signature] Lt. Col. commdg 2 KRRC

(A7092). Wt W12839/M1293 75,000 1/17. D. D. & L., Ltd. Forms/C.2118/14.

WAR DIARY.

2nd.Bn. THE KING'S ROYAL RIFLE CORPS.

2nd. INFANTRY BRIGADE.

1st.DIVISION.

OCTOBER.1917.

Army Form C. 2118.

Vol 37

Instructions regarding War Diaries and Intelligence Summaries are contained in F. S. Regs., Part II. and the Staff Manual respectively. Title pages will be prepared in manuscript.

WAR DIARY
or
~~INTELLIGENCE SUMMARY.~~
(Erase heading not required.)

2 K.R.R.C. October 1917

Place	Date	Hour	Summary of Events and Information	Remarks and references to Appendices
	1st		Major Sir J. V. E. Lees Bart left for Senior Officers Course Aldershot. Div. Semi Final Rugby Football 3 p.m. We lost to the South Wales Borderers 3rd Bde. 13-0.	
	2nd		Capt. T. R. Forsyth-Forrest rejoined from Senior Officers Course Aldershot. 1 O.R. joined. Bde. Field Day. O.C. 2 KRRC commanded Advanced Guard.	
	3rd		2nd Lt C. T. E. Birks attached to Battn from 1st Northants for instruction. Windy day; Battn watched demonstration of S.O.S. of Red Smoke. 2nd Bde. Cross Country Race 3 miles. Battn. was 4th.	
	4		Wet day.	
	5		6 Signallers left for 1st Battalion. 2nd Lt Trinder & 2 O.R. left for P.T. & B.F. Course at St. Pol.	
	6.		Wet day. } Lectures & Coy. Training under cover where possible.	
	7.		Wet day }	
	8.		Wet day } 2nd Lt E. A. Warner returned from Hospital.	
	9.		Bde. Field Day round about Fort Mardyck	
	10.		Company Training.	[signature]

(A7092). Wt. W12839/M1293. 750,000. 1/17. D. D. & L., Ltd. Forms/C.2118/14.

Army Form C. 2118.

Instructions regarding War Diaries and Intelligence Summaries are contained in F. S. Regs., Part II. and the Staff Manual respectively. Title pages will be prepared in manuscript.

WAR DIARY
or
~~INTELLIGENCE SUMMARY.~~
(*Erase heading not required.*)

2 KRRC — October 1917

Place	Date	Hour	Summary of Events and Information	Remarks and references to Appendices
	11.		2nd Lt White & 1 OR left for XV Corps Training School. Lecture for Officers by Capt. Smythe 4 Army Staff on Aeroplane Photos with lantern slides.	
	12.		Gen. Sir Henry Rawlinson commdg 4th Army lectured to Officers at 2.30 pm after which 2 platoons of C coy did an attack on a strong post which the General watched. Draft of 12 ORs joined the Battalion.	
	13.		Wet all day.	
	14.		Major Gen. inspected all drafts that joined during the past month. Brig. Gen. presented Rfn Bradley with parchment from Royal Humane Society for saving a man from drowning in the Somme Canal.	
	15.		2nd Lt A.C. Hubbard joined the Battalion.	
	16.		Riding Lessons & Cavalry Drill for Officers on the Beach.	
	17.		Battalion practised an attack for ~~the~~ a party of Americans to watch.	
	18.		An American Major Gen., Brig. Gen. & staff; G.O.C. 4th Army; Maj. Gen. and many other people including Brig. Gen. Sercold, who lunched with the Battalion afterwards, watched demonstrations by the Battn. & other Bns in the Division.	R Wace ? Lt Col

(A7092). Wt W12839/M1293. 75,0.0. 1/17. D. D. & L., Ltd. Forms/C.2118/14.

Army Form C. 2118.

Instructions regarding War Diaries and Intelligence Summaries are contained in F. S. Regs., Part II. and the Staff Manual respectively. Title pages will be prepared in manuscript.

WAR DIARY

or

~~INTELLIGENCE SUMMARY.~~

(Erase heading not required.)

2 KRRC October 1917

Place	Date	Hour	Summary of Events and Information	Remarks and references to Appendices
	19		2nd Lt Winter & 2 O.Rs left for 4th Army Musketry Camp at Pont Remy. Battalion watched M.G. Coy. fire barrage over their heads into the sea. Lt. Col Clarke XV Corps M.G. Officer lectured to Officers.	
	20.		M.G. Coy. fired barrage with lifts along the beach. Battalion watched from the Sand Dunes. Regt. Concert in Cinema Hangar at 8.30 P.M.	
	21		Interpreter F. Cools (Belgian Mission) attached to the Battalion. Capt. T.R. Forsyth Forrest left the Battn. to take over 2nd in Command of the 1st Northants.	
	22		Battn. moved at 8.15 AM for ETTINGHEM, N.W. of WORMHOUDT. Arrived about 4.45 PM. Drums on the march. The Battn. covered an area of about 6 sq. miles.	
	23		Wet day. Coys. rested.	
	24.		Left at 8 AM for an area about a mile W. of HERZEELE and 2 miles E. of WORMHOUDT. Arrived about 1 P.M. Coys. just as far apart as at Ettinghem.	
	25		Left at 8.20 AM for a camp about 2 miles W. of POPERINGHE. Arrived about 12 Noon. Very Muddy & Windy.	[signature illegible]

(A7092). Wt. W12839/M1293. 75,0.0. 1/17. D. D. & L., Ltd. Forms/C.2118/14.

Army Form C. 2118.

Instructions regarding War Diaries and Intelligence Summaries are contained in F. S. Regs., Part II. and the Staff Manual respectively. Title pages will be prepared in manuscript.

2 KRRC

WAR DIARY
or
~~INTELLIGENCE SUMMARY.~~
(Erase heading not required.)

October 1917

Place	Date	Hour	Summary of Events and Information	Remarks and references to Appendices
	26.		Draft of 11 O.R. arrived. 2nd Lt. W. J. D. Sneddon rejoined the Battn. Very wet.	
	27		Lt. Col. G. C. Kelly went forward to see the line.	
	28		Church Parade. Company training in the morning.	
	29		Lieut D. H. Buckland left to join 2nd Inf. Bde. ~~[illegible] Company Training~~ Route marching + Night operations.	
	30		Company Training in the morning. Very wet in the afternoon.	
	31		Company Training + Musketry - Bayonet Fighting + Physical Training.	

(A7092). Wt. W12839/M1293. 75,0.0. 1/17. D. D. & L., Ltd. Forms/C.2118/14.

WAR DIARY.

2nd. Bn. THE KING'S ROYAL RIFLE CORPS.

2nd. INFANTRY BRIGADE.

1st. DIVISION.

NOVEMBER. 1917.

Army Form C. 2118.

Instructions regarding War Diaries and Intelligence Summaries are contained in F. S. Regs., Part II. and the Staff Manual respectively. Title pages will be prepared in manuscript.

WAR DIARY
or
~~INTELLIGENCE SUMMARY.~~
(Erase heading not required.)

2 K.R.R.C.

2 KRR

November 1917.

Vol 38

Place	Date	Hour	Summary of Events and Information	Remarks and references to Appendices
	1		Company training + Night Operations.	
	2		Company training + Night Operations – Lieut W. F. A. Chambers rejoined from leave to England – Dull weather –	
	3.		Company route marches – Regimental concert at 5.30 p.m. – Brig-Gen G. C. Kemp C.B. came to dinner – 2Lt H. C. B. Dawson left on leave to England –	
	4.		Lt-Col. F. C. Kelly, Capt Hill, Lieuts Barnes M.C, Warner, Blackett M.C + 2Lt Gracie M.C went forward to reconnoitre the line – Church Parade – ~~Lt Col~~ Brig-Gen G. Rennie + ~~Capt P. ...~~ + Capt P. Llewellyn Davis visited the battalion.	
	5.		Preparations for move to the line carried out. Advanced party of 1st Black Watch arrive.	
	6.		The battalion moved off as per appendix I. Advanced party consisting of 5 officers + 160 O.Rs of "A" Echelon reconnoitred the line in the evening.	
	7.		The battalion left IRISH FM + took over the line of the PADDEBEEK S.W. of WESTROOSEBEKE from the 1st RMLI on the left + the Anson battalion on the right. The relief was carried out without mishap. Battalion headquarters was in a "pill box" at BURNS HOUSE + owing to the isolation of the right + support companies an auxiliary headquarters was established at another "pill box" near ALBATROSS FM under the supervision of Capt: Armrod. Conditions in the front line were very bad owing to the marshy state of the ground. Our own + hostile artilleries very active throughout	

(A7092). Wt W12839/M1293 75,0.0. 1/17. D. D. & L., Ltd. Forms/C.2118/14.

Army Form C. 2118.

WAR DIARY
or
~~INTELLIGENCE SUMMARY.~~

(Erase heading not required.)

Instructions regarding War Diaries and Intelligence Summaries are contained in F. S. Regs., Part II. and the Staff Manual respectively. Title pages will be prepared in manuscript.

2 KRRC

November 1917

Place	Date	Hour	Summary of Events and Information	Remarks and references to Appendices
	7.		His tour – The battalion was temporarily attached to the 3rd Imperial Inf: Bde.	
	8.		2 Lt A.C. Hubbard + 4 other ranks killed by shellfire. 8 other ranks wounded.	
	9.		17 Other ranks wounded. 1st NORTHAMPTONS relieved the battalion in the evening, which then returned to HILLTOP ~~FM~~ CAMP + IRISH FM.	
	10.		Coys. marched to REIGERSBURG for baths. Wet day. 1 O.R. wounded.	
	11.		Went back to same part of the line. Relieved 1st Northants. Good relief.	
	12.		No rain + fairly quiet day. 1 O.R. Killed in action 4 O.R. wounded.	
	13.		Lt. L.A. Blackett MC. wounded. Battalion relieved by 1st Northants. Very quick relief. Battn. returned to HILLTOP FARM. 6 O.R. wounded	
	14.		Battn. moved back to DAMPRÉ CAMP near BRIELAN. N.N.E. of VLAMERTINGHE. 1 O.R. wounded.	
	15.		Baths for Battalion. Shelled slightly by H.V. Gun in the evening.	
	16.		10 O.R. joined the Battn. Shelled by H.V. Gun. Close, but no casualties in the Battalion	

(A7092). Wt. W12839/M1293. 75,0.0. 1/17. D. D. & L., Ltd. Forms/C.2118/14.

Instructions regarding War Diaries and Intelligence Summaries are contained in F. S. Regs., Part II. and the Staff Manual respectively. Title pages will be prepared in manuscript.

Army Form C. 2118.

WAR DIARY
or
~~INTELLIGENCE SUMMARY~~.
(*Erase heading not required.*)

2 KRRC — November 1917

Place	Date	Hour	Summary of Events and Information	Remarks and references to Appendices
In the Field	17		Day spent in cleaning up & reorganising. Shelled at 8 PM & 12 Midnight. No casualties	
	18		Moved at 1.30 PM to ~~HILL TOP~~ & IRISH FARM. Details moved to REIGERSBURG ~~Camp~~ Camp.	
	19		Battn relieved 10th Glosters in the line just to the Right of the former sector. The ground was a little higher & therefore a little less damp. Just before moving off at 3 PM. 2 O.R. killed & 22 wounded at IRISH FARM.	
	20		2nd Lt R.J. TRINDER wounded. O.R. 5 wounded. Alarm that enemy were going to attack.	
	21		Enemy did not attack. 2 OR killed 2 OR wounded. Battn relieved by 1st Northants and returned to HILL TOP FARM.	
	22		Moved back to DAMPRÉ CAMP. Quiet night. Lt.Col. KELLY went on leave.	
	23		Quiet day spent in cleaning up.	
	24		Moved at 11 AM to POPERINGHE. Arrived about 2 PM. Very comfortable billets. Lt. C.R. FRYER, J.R.P. MAXWELL 2/Lts. E.J. BEST, L. CARTWRIGHT, A.P. CUNNINGHAM, S.A. CROSS & 7 O.R. joined the Battn.	
	25.		Lt Chambers & Echelon "B" rejoined the Battn from HOUDEKERQUE.	

A6945 Wt. W11422/M1160 350,000 12/16 D. D. & L. Forms/C./2118/14.

Instructions regarding War Diaries and Intelligence Summaries are contained in F. S. Regs., Part II. and the Staff Manual respectively. Title pages will be prepared in manuscript.

WAR DIARY
or
~~INTELLIGENCE SUMMARY.~~
(Erase heading not required.)

Army Form C. 2118.

2 KRRC — November 1917

Place	Date	Hour	Summary of Events and Information	Remarks and references to Appendices
In the Field	26		Seats were taken at two Concert Parties in Poperinghe for the Battn.	
	27		Battn. moved from Poperinghe to HERZEELE at 8.25 am. Arrived about 1 P.M. H.Q. billeted in a convent. A & B coys in the village. C & D in neighbouring farms. Rather scattered but quite comfortable.	
	28		Company training. } Fine weather	
	29		Company training & baths }	
	30		Company training & baths }	

H. L. E. Smith Major
commdg 2 KRRC

A6945 Wt. W11422/M1160 350,000 12/16 D. D. & L. Forms/C./2118/14.

W A R   D I A R Y.

2nd. Bn. THE KING'S ROYAL RIFLE CORPS.

2nd. INFANTRY BRIGADE.

1st. DIVISION.

DECEMBER. 1917.

Instructions regarding War Diaries and Intelligence Summaries are contained in F. S. Regs., Part II, and the Staff Manual respectively. Title pages will be prepared in manuscript.

WAR DIARY
or
~~INTELLIGENCE~~ SUMMARY.
(*Erase heading not required.*)

Army Form C. 2118.

2 KRRC — December 1917

Vol 39

Place	Date	Hour	Summary of Events and Information	Remarks and references to Appendices
FRANCE HERZEELE	1		Company Training. Cold but fine day.	
	2		Voluntary Church Service.	
	3.		Company Training	
	4.		Company Training	
	5.		Prepared to move.	
BELGIUM CROMBEKE	6.		Battalion moved by march route to NOYEN camp CROMBEKE Belgium. The back area for HOUTHOULST FORREST sector. Some French cavalry were still in the Camp & the Colonel did everything he could to help us.	
	7.		Companies carried out training. Ground was not very spacious. V. Cold.	
	8.		Lt Col Kelly returned from leave	
	9.		Wet day. The French moved out of the camp	
	10.		Quiet day spent in company training	
	11		Association match V. 1st L. N. Lancs. Score one all.	
WOESTEN	12		The Battn moved to a camp well camouflaged in a wood E. of WOESTEN. Men comfortable but rather crowded in elephant shelters &c	

A6945 Wt. W11422/M1160 350,000 12/16 D. D. & L. Forms/C./2118/14.

Army Form C. 2118.

WAR DIARY
or
INTELLIGENCE SUMMARY.
(Erase heading not required.)

Instructions regarding War Diaries and Intelligence Summaries are contained in F. S. Regs., Part II, and the Staff Manual respectively. Title pages will be prepared in manuscript.

2 KRRC — December 1917

Place	Date	Hour	Summary of Events and Information	Remarks and references to Appendices
	13		Day spent in improving camp. 3 officers + 210 O.R. on a working party (laying cables)	
	14		Major Ormond & Capt Hill reconnoitred forward area. Very quiet.	
			5 officers + 3 coys on a working party (building a railway)	
	15		5 officers & 3 coys continued building the Railway. 2nd Lt Braybrooke went to England for M.G. course.	
	16		Voluntary Church Service	
	17		Major Ormond left to assume 2nd in command of 11th Battn.	
			4 officers & 200 O.R.s carried R.E. material for R.E. in forward area.	
	18		4 officers + 200 ORs buried cable for Signal Section. Very cold.	
IN THE LINE	19		Very cold. The Battn relieved 1st S.W. Borderers in Support area. Moved off 2-30 am	
	20		Battn relieved 2nd Welch in Right Sector of Division. Very quiet. Relief complete about 8 P.M. Very cold. Overcoats were brought up for men who were not under cover.	
	21		Very quiet & misty. Wire was put out in part of outpost line at night.	
	22		Capt V.B. HILL & 2 ORs wounded. Bright day with increased artillery & air activity. S.O.S. signal on our Right in the evening. Our line remained quiet.	
	23		1 OR wounded. Quiet day. Frost & wiring continued	
	24		Relieved by 1st Northamptonshire Regt. Moved back to Support area.	

A6945 Wt. W11422/M1160 350,000 12/16 D. D. & L. Forms/C./2118/14.

Army Form C. 2118.

WAR DIARY
or
~~INTELLIGENCE SUMMARY.~~
(Erase heading not required.)

Instructions regarding War Diaries and Intelligence Summaries are contained in F. S. Regs., Part II. and the Staff Manual respectively. Title pages will be prepared in manuscript.

2 KRRC — December 1917

Place	Date	Hour	Summary of Events and Information	Remarks and references to Appendices
	25.		Every available man was out at night carrying or wiring. Snow fell & lay.	
	26		3 OR joined the Battn. Carrying & wiring as for 25th Dec.	
WOESTEN	27.		Relieved by 1st Camerons & moved back to the Camp at WOESTEN	
CROMBEKE	28.		Relieved by 10th Gloucesters & moved back to CROMBEKE.	
	29.		Cleaned up. Still very cold	
	30		Continued cleaning up. Company training.	
	31.		Company training 2nd Lt. D. McCLURE & 2nd Lt. R.B. KIRKLAND & 32 O.R. joined the Battn. Major Sir J.V. LEES Bart. rejoined from Senior Officers Course Aldershot.	

[signature] Lt Col
Comdg 2 KRRC

A6945 Wt. W11422/M1160 350,000 12/16 D. D. & L. Forms/C./2118/14.

1st Division

2nd Brigade

2nd BTN. Kings Royal Rifle Corps

From 1st January 1918 To ~~31st December 1918~~ 1919 JUNE

Instructions regarding War Diaries and Intelligence Summaries are contained in F. S. Regs., Part II, and the Staff Manual respectively. Title pages will be prepared in manuscript.

WAR DIARY
or
~~INTELLIGENCE SUMMARY.~~
(Erase heading not required.)

Army Form C. 2118.

2 KRRC — January 1918 — Vol 40

Place	Date	Hour	Summary of Events and Information	Remarks and references to Appendices
CROMBEKE	1		Celebrated Christmas Day. Fine sunny day with frost. Sports were held in the morning. Christmas Dinner. Concerts in evening. Sergts Mess Concert Vocal from 8th Royal Berks Concert Party gave two performances which were much appreciated. ~~2nd Lt D McClure & R.B. Kirkbright and 32 other ranks joined the Battn~~	
	2.		A little warmer but still cold. Company & Specialist Training.	
	3.		Two Regimental Concerts. One for A & B coys & the other for C & D coys.	
	4.	–	Company Training.	
WOESTEN	5.	–	Battn moved to LA BERGERIE CAMP near WOESTEN. The same camp as mentioned last month on the 12th.	
	6.		Battn provided working parties of 7 officers + 250 O.Rs. Carrying stores to Front Line.	
	7.		8 ORs joined the Battn. Working Parties 8 officers + 250 O.R. ditto.	
	8.		Working Parties 7 officers 250 ORs. A few shells were put round about us. No damage and the only occasion the Germans paid us any attention.	
	9.		Company Training.	
	10.		Working Parties 7 officers + ~~250~~ 300 men	
	11.		Working Parties 6 officers + 300 men. Thawed.	

A6945 Wt. W11422/M1160 350,000 12/16 D. D. & L. Forms/C./2118/14.

Instructions regarding War Diaries and Intelligence Summaries are contained in F. S. Regs., Part II, and the Staff Manual respectively. Title pages will be prepared in manuscript.

Army Form C. 2118.

WAR DIARY
or
INTELLIGENCE SUMMARY.
(Erase heading not required.)

2 KRRC — January 1918

Place	Date	Hour	Summary of Events and Information	Remarks and references to Appendices
In the Line	12		Thaw. Battn relieved 1st S.W.B. in Battn in Support Area. Same as before.	
	13		2nd Lt EJG Palmer left Battn for M.G. Corps Grantham.	
			Battn relieved 2nd Welch in Front Line Right sector of Div. Front as before.	
			Started freezing again	
	14		More Snow. 2nd Lt S.A. CROSS Missing believed killed. 2 OR wounded	
			They were out on patrol and ORs state 2nd Lt Cross shot through throat.	
			Search party failed to find body.	
	15		1 OR wounded. Terrific storm during the night. Wind + Rain. All dug	
			outs flooded. Carrying parties did 500 yds in 3½ hrs. All the "Beeks" swollen	
	16		1 OR missing 4 OR wounded	
	17		Battn relieved by 1st Northants. + came back into Support. Provided	
			large carrying parties	
	18		News arrived that Capt. V.B. HILL had died of septic pneumonia.	
	19		Carrying Parties. Concert in WOESTEN for details + transport.	
	20		18 Fijians left Battn for 1st Battn.	
	20 (cont.)		Battn relieved by 1st Camerons. Moved back to LA BERGERIE Camp.	
			1 OR rejoined from Wounded.	

A6945 Wt. W11422/M1160 350,000 12/16 D. D. & L. Forms/C./2118/14.

Instructions regarding War Diaries and Intelligence Summaries are contained in F. S. Regs., Part II. and the Staff Manual respectively. Title pages will be prepared in manuscript.

WAR DIARY
or
~~INTELLIGENCE SUMMARY.~~
(Erase heading not required.)

Army Form C. 2118.

2 KRRC — January 1918

Place	Date	Hour	Summary of Events and Information	Remarks and references to Appendices
CROMBEKE	21st		Battn. moved back to NOYON camp.	
	22		Day spent in cleaning up. Fine & sunny. Mud plentiful.	
	23		Company Training.	
	24		Capt. C.H. HORDERN joined the Battn. Company Training.	
	25.		2nd Lt H.J. SHAW + 3 ORs joined the Battn. Working Party of 3 + 164.	
	26		1 OR joined from wounded. Concert in YMCA Marquee 5.30 PM.	
WOESTEN	27		Battn moved into Bde in Support, 32nd Div being in Front Line,	
			to DEKORT Camp between WOESTEN & ELVERDINGHE. Camp formally occupied	
			by 2nd R. Sussex when in this area. 1 OR accidentally wounded.	
	28		Lt Col G.C. Kelly temporarily commanded 2nd Inf. Bde. Major Sir J.V.E.	
			Lees Bart commanded Battn.	
	29.		Company training. Improvements to Camp. Misty weather	
	30.		B. Gen G.C. Kemp (temp. commanding 1st Div) came round camp	
	31.		Weather became colder. Company Training.	
			The late Capt V.B. Hill granted Military Cross by His Majesty the King	

G.C. Kelly Lt-Col
Commdg 2 KRRC

A6945 Wt. W11422/M1160 350,000 12/16 D. D. & L. Forms/C./2118/14.

Instructions regarding War Diaries and Intelligence Summaries are contained in F. S. Regs., Part II. and the Staff Manual respectively. Title pages will be prepared in manuscript.

WAR DIARY
or
~~INTELLIGENCE SUMMARY~~.
(Erase heading not required.)

Army Form C. 2118.

2 K.R.R.C. Feb. 1918

Vol 41

Place	Date	Hour	Summary of Events and Information	Remarks and references to Appendices
WOESTEN	1		Company training in morning and recreational training in afternoon.	
	2		Lt-Col G.C. KELLY rejoined BN. from temporarily commanding 2nd Infantry Bde.	
	3		Company training. At the request of Division the BN started to form a STRING BAND	
	4		The Major General inspected the Camp. Training as usual	
	5		Lt-Col G.C. KELLY proceeded to take temporary command of 1st Inf. Bde. Major Sir J.V.E Lees Bart.	
	~~8~~		took over command of the BN. 1 O.R. joined the BN.	
	~~8~~ 6		All coys were bathed. Competition in drill + turnout between ~~a~~ Platoon from BN HQRS and best platoon in D Coy. Former won	
	7		All coys were "pedicured"	
IN THE LINE	8		Afternoon ~~[illegible]~~ of 8th Battn marched to ELVERDINGHE and entraining proceeded ~~[illegible]~~ by light railway to KEMPTON PARK. Detrained here, had tea and ~~[illegible]~~ when dusk moved up to FRONT LINE relieving 4th N. Staffs of 35th Div in left sector of DIVISION. Battn front approx. from about 1000 yds N of POELCAPPELLE to line of LEKKERBOTERBEEK about 1000 yds S.E. of POELCAPPELLE. 2Lt H.B. DAWSON proceeded to England for 6 months tour of duty. Capt H F E Smith D.S.O. admitted to hospital.	
	9		Very cold but visibility excellent. 2 ORs joined BN.	
	10		Frosty and misty. Very quiet. Little wiring of main line of resistance at night	
	11		Enemy Artillery a little more active. 2 O.Rs wounded	

A6945 Wt W11422/M1160 350,000 12/16 D. D. & L. Forms/C./2118/14.

Instructions regarding War Diaries and Intelligence Summaries are contained in F. S. Regs., Part II. and the Staff Manual respectively. Title pages will be prepared in manuscript.

WAR DIARY
or
~~INTELLIGENCE~~ SUMMARY.
(Erase heading not required.)

Army Form C. 2118.

2 KRRC Feb. 1918

Place	Date	Hour	Summary of Events and Information	Remarks and references to Appendices
	12	8.30 pm	Relieved by 1st Northamptonshire Regt. Marched down to Support Area at HUGEL HOLLOW. 1 O.R. wounded and 8 ORs joined BN.	
	13		Companies to "pedicurium". Numerous working parties at night on Corps line of resistance. Warmer weather.	
	14		BN moved up to right Sector of DIVISION and relieved 2nd BN Royal Sussex Regt, BN front from LEKKERBOTERBEEK along the line of the PADDEBEEK in all about 1500 yds. 2/Lt W. T. D. SNEDDON proceeded to England for 6 months tour of Duty.	
	15		Bright clear day with moon at night. Very quiet. Wiring in front of outpost line at night also working parties from support coy on line of resistance.	
	16		Another clear day. Enemy artillery more active also E. aircraft. Wiring + work as before.	
	17		At about 6 AM on the 17th, in the half light, a party of the enemy attempted to raid one of 'A' Coy's posts. The party, 40 strong, was led by 2 officers and included two light machine guns to cover its withdrawal. We accounted for 19 KILLED, 1 WOUNDED PRISONER, and 1 M.G. captured. Our only loss was 2/Lieut R.D. WILLMOT, who was in command of the post, killed; it was chiefly owing to his gallant conduct and that of Sgt Hinstridge, Rfn Jones and Rfn Green that the	

Instructions regarding War Diaries and Intelligence Summaries are contained in F. S. Regs., Part II. and the Staff Manual respectively. Title pages will be prepared in manuscript.

WAR DIARY
or
~~INTELLIGENCE SUMMARY.~~
(Erase heading not required.)

Army Form C. 2118.

2 K.R.R.C. Feb. 1918.

Place	Date	Hour	Summary of Events and Information	Remarks and references to Appendices
			enemy was so successfully dealt with.	
	18		BN was relieved again by the 1st Northamptonshire Regt and then moved down to the support area at HUGEL HOLLOW. Working parties during night.	
	19		Coys to the "pedicurium".	
	20		Relieved by the 1st BN The Black Watch. Bn entrained at Kempton Park and detrained at ELVERDINGHE and then marched to CARIBOU CAMP.	
	21		General cleaning up of equipment etc:-	
	22		Company training. 5 O.Rs joined BN.	
	23		Company training.	
	24.		The Commanding Officer reconnoitred ARMY LINE and lunched with Lt. Col KELLY whose Bde was in the line at the time. Voluntary Church Service	
	~~25~~		~~Voluntary Church Service~~ 3 ORs joined BN. Lt D.H. Buckland rejoined BN from 2nd Inf Bde	
	25		Lecture by Brigadier General Kemp CMG to Officers. Company training in morning.	
	26		Coy Commanders reconnoitred ARMY LINE in forward zone. Night operations.	
	27		Snow - very cold. Work done in huts - short lectures by Platoon commanders.	
	28		Company training. Night operations.	

H Butler
Capt. Cmdg 2 K.R.R.C.

A6945 Wt. W11422/M1160 350,000 12/16 D. D. & L. Forms/C./2118/14.

Army Form C. 2118.

Instructions regarding War Diaries and Intelligence Summaries are contained in F. S. Regs., Part II. and the Staff Manual respectively. Title pages will be prepared in manuscript.

WAR DIARY
or
INTELLIGENCE SUMMARY.
(Erase heading not required.)

2 K.R.R.C. March 1918

Vol 42

Place	Date	Hour	Summary of Events and Information	Remarks and references to Appendices
CARIBOU CAMP	1		Company training. Divisional cinema in Recreation hut in evening.	
	2		Maj. Sir J.V.E. Lees Bart, Capt. C.H. HORDEN and 2nd LT G.E. McCABE wounded while reconnoitring Army Battle Zone. Capt H. BUTLER M.C. took over command of BN. Concert in evening partly regimental and partly performance of the "PEDLARS" (32nd Div. Concert Party).	
KEMPTON PARK.	3		At 4.30 AM BN marched to ELVERDINGHE and entraining proceeded to WIELTJE (Nr St. JULIEN) where they detrained and then marched to KEMPTON PARK. Cookers met BN here and all ranks had breakfast after which most of the BN went out on working parties principally on the ARMY LINE. Later in evening we relieved the 1st BN GLOUCESTERSHIRE REGT and took over their billets at KEMPTON PARK. 2nd BDE was now in Support.	
	4		Large working parties employed on ARMY LINE and on one or two English PILL BOXES in course of construction. 'C' Coy sent up to PHEASANT TRENCH to mann positions in the support system in the FORWARD ZONE.	
	5.		Working parties as before. 9 OR's joined BN.	
	6.		At 4.30 am. BN "stood to" for SOS on RT DIV front but "Stood down"	

A6945 Wt. W11422/M1160 350,000 12/16 D. D. & L. Forms/C./2118/14.

Army Form C. 2118.

WAR DIARY
or
2 KRRC INTELLIGENCE SUMMARY. March 1918
(*Erase heading not required.*)

Instructions regarding War Diaries and Intelligence Summaries are contained in F. S. Regs., Part II. and the Staff Manual respectively. Title pages will be prepared in manuscript.

Place	Date	Hour	Summary of Events and Information	Remarks and references to Appendices
			again within 30 mins. Working parties again. 33 OR's joined BN. "D" Coy relieved	C' at PHEASANT TRENCH
	7		Working parties as usual.	
	8		Day free from working parties. News received that 2/LT D. McLURE had died suddenly at 4th ARMY Musketry School at NORTEBECOURT apparently from Fulminating Pneumonia as was discovered from a POST MORTEM. "A" Coy relieved "C" at	PHEASANT TR.
	9		Working parties again on same tasks as before.	
	10		Working parties as usual. 1 OR wounded. "B" Coy relieved "A" at PHEASANT TR.	
	11		Working parties. 1 OR wounded.	
	12		Working Parties. Divisional Band played to us in the afternoon	
	13		Stood to for S.O.S. on Left at 2.30 am. Stood down 3.30 am. Stood to again at 8 PM for a few minutes. 2nd Lt McCabe rejoined from wounded.	
	14		Working Parties as usual. Much gunfire at night but no S.O.S.	
	15.		25 OR joined the Battn. S.O.S. on Left at 9.30 PM. Working Parties as usual	
FRONT LINE	16		Relieved 1st S.W.B. in Left Sector of Bde. POELCAPELLE. Relief Complete by 11 PM 1.O.R. accidentally wounded. 42 O.R. joined Battn. 2nd Lts F.W. COTTON J.M. HUNTER & G.P. KINNEAR joined Battn.	

A6945 Wt. W11422/M1160 350,000 12/16 D. D. & L. Forms/C./2118/14.

Army Form C. 2118.

WAR DIARY
or
~~INTELLIGENCE~~ SUMMARY.
(*Erase heading not required.*)

Instructions regarding War Diaries and Intelligence Summaries are contained in F. S. Regs., Part II, and the Staff Manual respectively. Title pages will be prepared in manuscript.

2 KRRC March 1918

Place	Date	Hour	Summary of Events and Information	Remarks and references to Appendices
	17.		Fine Day. B coy on the left ~~[illegible]~~ ~~[illegible]~~ much worried by T.M. A raid on one of their posts expected an precautionary measures taken.	
	18.		Brig. Gen KAY wounded. Lt Col BELLAMY (R. Sussex) temp. commanded Bde. B coy repulsed raid that was expected. 2nd Lt WINTER brought his patrol back through both the enemy barrage & our own without loss. 1 OR joined Battn.	
	19.		Rain. Enemy artillery active on our front. 8 O.R. wounded 20 joined Battn.	
	20		Enemy attempted raids on our posts. Repulsed. We caught 3 prisoners & killed many. Sgt. WOODHOUSE C coy distinguished himself also 2nd Lt HARMON at 2.20 am. Relieved by 2nd R Sussex. Battn went into support at HUGAL HALLOWS (Battn HQ) MARINE VIEW & PHEASANT TR. Much shelling in early evening. 2 OR Killed in action 1 OR joined Battn.	
	21		Fine Sunny Day. Coys Battled. Battn HQ gassed in evening. 1 OR Killed in action 13 O.R. wounded.	
	22		Sunny Day. Relieved 1st Northants in Right Sector of Bde. Relief complete 10.15 pm. 3 ORs wounded 1 OR Killed in action	
	23		A quiet warm spring day.	

A6945 Wt. W11422/M1160 350,000 12/16 D. D. & L. Forms/C./2118/14.

Army Form C. 2118.

WAR DIARY
or
~~INTELLIGENCE SUMMARY~~.
(Erase heading not required.)

Instructions regarding War Diaries and Intelligence Summaries are contained in F. S. Regs., Part II. and the Staff Manual respectively. Title pages will be prepared in manuscript.

2 KRRC — March 1918

Place	Date	Hour	Summary of Events and Information	Remarks and references to Appendices
	24		Lt Col. G.C. KELLY returned from leave and appointed G.O.C. 2nd Inf Bde.	
			1 O.R. killed in action.	
	25		1 O.R. wounded	
	26		Relieved by 2nd Royal Sussex. Battn again went into Support at Same Places	
	27		6 O.R. joined Battn.	
CALIFORNIA DUG OUTS	28		Bde relieved by 3rd Bde. Battn relieved by 1st Glosters and went to CALIFORNIA	
			DUGOUTS. C coy remaining in Support System of Forward Zone. 2 O.R.	
			joined Battn. 3 O.R. wounded	
	29		Working Party on Army Battle Zone. 11 O.R. of A coy killed in sleep	
			by one shell landing on their dug out.	
	30		Moved some companies to Army Battle Zone for better protection.	
			Capt H.K. WARD M.C. RAMC rejoined Battn having been exchanged from	
			Germany. 1 O.R. rejoined from wounded	
CANAL BANK + BATTLE ZONE	31		Battn HQ + A coy moved to CANAL BANK for better accomodation	
			Major Sir J.V. LEES Bart rejoined from leave after being wounded + took	
			command of Battn. 2nd Lt WINTER received M.C.	

[illegible signature]
Major commdg 2 KRRC

A6945 Wt. W11422/M1160 350,000 12/16 D. D. & L. Forms/C./2118/14.

2nd Brigade.

1st Division.

2nd BATTALION

KING'S ROYAL RIFLE CORPS

APRIL 1918.

Instructions regarding War Diaries and Intelligence Summaries are contained in F. S. Regs., Part II, and the Staff Manual respectively. Title pages will be prepared in manuscript.

WAR DIARY
or
INTELLIGENCE SUMMARY.
(Erase heading not required.)

2nd Bn KRRC

April 1918.

Army Form C. 2118.

Q T Vol 4

Place	Date	Hour	Summary of Events and Information	Remarks and references to Appendices
CANAL BANK	1		Warm Spring Day. C coy. joined the Battn. from Battle Zone. 1 OR wounded	
	2		Provided usual working parties.	
	3		4 OR joined the Battlion. D coy joined Battn at CANAL Bank from Battle Zone. HQ played HQ 2nd R. Sussex at Association and beat them 6.1.	
	4		19 OR. joined including CSM Cooper wounded Nov 1917. Warning Orders came in that we were to move either that night or early in the morning.	
	5		Moved at 8.40 AM to entrain at BOESINGHE for MERVILLE. Orders cancelled while we were in the train and eventually we detrained at CHOCQUES Nr BETHUNE. Marched to LAPUGNOY arrived about 6 PM. Billeting Party only just arrived ahead of us via MERVILLE.	
LAPUGNOY	6		Old members of the Battn. visited many friends of 2 years ago. Inhabitants very pleased to see the "Premier Division".	
	7		Battn. moved by busses to take over front line S. of BETHUNE-LA BASSEE road.	
IN THE LINE			Details marched to LE PREOL N.E. of BEUVRY. Gas shells at night.	
	8		Quiet day in the line. 5 OR joined the Battn.	
	9		4.15 AM. The most terrific bombardment started N of the Canal. The enemy	

Instructions regarding War Diaries and Intelligence Summaries are contained in F. S. Regs., Part II, and the Staff Manual respectively. Title pages will be prepared in manuscript.

WAR DIARY
or
~~INTELLIGENCE~~ SUMMARY.
(Erase heading not required.)

Army Form C. 2118.

2 KRRC — April 1918

Place	Date	Hour	Summary of Events and Information	Remarks and references to Appendices
	9 (cont.)		attacked 7 AM in thick mist. Our sector in the line fairly quiet. The Details & Transport at Le PREOL came in for a considerable amount of shelling. 2nd Lt. F.D. GOLDING & H.J. SHAW, 2 OR & 6 horses wounded. 3 OR wounded in the line.	
	10		Heavy shelling on the left. 1 OR wounded. Details moved to BURBURE S. of LILLERS. Transport to ANNEZIN.	
	11.		Fairly quiet in the line & Battn occupied in making fire bays for defensive left flank. 2Lt J.H. CHENEY & 1 OR wounded. 2nd Lts HEAN, BASSOM, CARTON and HARVIE joined the Battn.	
	12		Usual day & work in the line. Details moved to MARLES les MINES.	
	13		1 OR killed in action. Cold & misty day. Usual day in the line.	
	14		Lt. Col. E.G. St AUBYN assumed command of the Battn.	
	15		1 OR wounded. Usual work in the line. Details moved to GOSNAY. Major Sir J.V.E. LEES Bart handed over command and joined details.	
	16		1 OR killed & 4 wounded. Details moved to VERQUIN where the transport also moved. Enemy put up S.O.S. Barrage on our front.	

A6945 Wt. W11422/M1160 350,000 12/16 D. D. & L. Forms/C./2118/14.

Instructions regarding War Diaries and Intelligence Summaries are contained in F. S. Regs., Part II. and the Staff Manual respectively. Title pages will be prepared in manuscript.

WAR DIARY
or
~~INTELLIGENCE SUMMARY.~~
(*Erase heading not required.*)

Army Form C. 2118.

2 KRRC

April 1918

Place	Date	Hour	Summary of Events and Information	Remarks and references to Appendices
	17		1 OR wounded. Quiet day, drill.	
	18		The enemy attacked GIVENCHY. Heavy shelling on our left. 1 OR killed, 1 OR died of wounds 7 OR wounded. Details stood to all day.	
	19		2 OR wounded. 14 OR joined the Battn. Quiet day.	
	20		1st Northamptonshire Regt. lent to 1st Bde and took back posts captured the day before. Fairly quiet on our front. 2 OR wounded. Details moved by bus to RAIMBERT.	
	21		1 OR wounded	
	22		7 OR wounded.	
	23		Enemy raid our left coy (B coy) 6 OR wounded. We accounted for 7 Germans killed and several wounded. Major Sir J.V. ELLES Bart left to assume command of the 18th Battn.	
	24		Quiet day. Details moved to MAISNIL les RUITZ.	[illegible]
	25		Quiet day. Details moved to a Nissen Hut Camp in BOIS de TROISSART near COUPIGNY. Very hot day. Thunderstorm.	
	26		Quiet & misty day.	

A6945 Wt. W11422/M1160 350,000 12/16 D. D. & L. Forms/C./2118/14.

Instructions regarding War Diaries and Intelligence Summaries are contained in F. S. Regs., Part II. and the Staff Manual respectively. Title pages will be prepared in manuscript.

WAR DIARY

or

~~INTELLIGENCE~~ SUMMARY.

(Erase heading not required.)

Army Form C. 2118.

2 KRRC — April 1918

Place	Date	Hour	Summary of Events and Information	Remarks and references to Appendices
	27		17 OR joined the Battn. Details moved to COUPIGNY Huts.	
	~~28~~		~~[illegible]~~ Battn relieved by 1st Northants during the day. Battn moved to support in CAMBRIN village.	
	28		5 OR wounded. Very noisy night on the left.	
	29		Quiet day. Wiring in early morning.	
	30		Quiet day.	
			During the long period the Battn held the front line men received a bath and the canteen was open, thus lessening to a slight degree the weariness of this abnormal period of trench warfare. The division was congratulated by the C in C [illegible] for the magnificent defence it put up.	

May 1st 1918

Geoffrey St Aubyn
Lt Col
Comdg 2nd Battn KRRC

A6945 Wt. W11422/M1160 350,000 12/16 D. D. & L. Forms/C./2118/14.

Army Form C. 2118.

Instructions regarding War Diaries and Intelligence Summaries are contained in F. S. Regs., Part II. and the Staff Manual respectively. Title pages will be prepared in manuscript.

WAR DIARY
or
~~INTELLIGENCE~~ SUMMARY.
(Erase heading not required.)

2nd Bn KRRC — May 1918 — Vol 44

Place	Date	Hour	Summary of Events and Information	Remarks and references to Appendices
CAMBRIN	1		Since 24th ulto owing to losses in first brigade, 1st BLACK WATCH lent its two remaining Coys to the CAMERON HIGHLANDERS, necessitating the retention of A B + C Coys remaining in support under command of OC 1st BLACK WATCH. Also owing to 1st ~~NORTHAMPTONS~~ LOYAL NORTH LANCS being too weak to fully man front, D Coy was in VILLAGE LINE as reserve coy. to them. Whilst at CAMBRIN much wiring was done to improve defence of localities – also large carrying parties provided. Fine day. 2 OR joined Batt. Quiet.	
	2		Fine day. Quiet.	
	3		Fine day. 2nd Lts. S.C.F. De Salis, E.V. DAVIES, F.W. KIDDLE, J.A.C. LEITH + J.T. ELDRIDGE joined Batt.	
	4		Wet. Quiet. Lt CHAMBERS + 2nd Lt CUNNINGHAM left CAMBRIN + joined Details + Headquarters at NOEUX-LES-MINES. 2 OR wounded by shell. 1 OR previously shell wounded, now reported died of wounds 29/4/18	
	5		Fine day, quiet.	
	6		3 Coys in CAMBRIN relieved by 1st NORTHAMPTONS + D Coy by 1st LOYAL NORTH LANCS + joined Headquarters at NOEUX-LES-MINES.	
	7		General cleaning up + inspections etc.	
	8		Owing to information gained from prisoners, attack on our front expected + Batt were under	

Army Form C. 2118.

Instructions regarding War Diaries and Intelligence Summaries are contained in F. S. Regs., Part II. and the Staff Manual respectively. Title pages will be prepared in manuscript.

WAR DIARY
or
~~INTELLIGENCE SUMMARY.~~
(Erase heading not required.)

2 KRRC

MAY 1918

Place	Date	Hour	Summary of Events and Information	Remarks and references to Appendices
NOEUX-LES	8		orders to move at quick notice. This continued during remainder of day at NOEUX.	
MINES	9.		Company training. Fine day. 2 OR joined Batt.	
	10.		" " " " 1 OR " "	
	11.		" " " " 1 OR " "	
HOHENZOLLERN	12.		Batt. relieved the 1st SOUTH WALES BORDERERS in left Batt sector. frontage BURBURE ALLEY	
SECTOR			to RAILWAY ALLEY A27b to Gun - GORRE MAP. Fine day. Details (ECHELON B) at BOIS D'OHLAIN	
	13		Gas successfully discharged at 10.30 pm (Cylinders) + 12.30 am (Projectors) on our front.	
	13		Fine but cold day. Quiet. Considerable work on improvement of defences.	
	14.		Fine. Quiet. Work continued.	
	15.		Fine. Quiet. Work continues. 7 OR joined Battalion.	
ANNEQUIN	16.		Batt. relieved by 1st NORTHAMPTONS, less 1½ Companies left in VILLAGE LINE under command of OC. 1st NORTHAMPTONS, and proceeded to ANNEQUIN in support. 6 OR joined Batt.	
	17.		2½ Coys on working parties. Fine day.	
	18		2½ " " " " " Patrols of NO MANS LAND on frontage of proposed raid made by officers + sergeants concerned - see under date 23rd.	
	19		Work continued. D Coy commence practice for raid: tapes laid out 1000x west SAILLY LABOURSE	

A6945 Wt. W11422/M1160 350,000 12/16 D. D. & L. Forms/C./2118/14.

Army Form C. 2118.

WAR DIARY
or
~~INTELLIGENCE SUMMARY~~.
(Erase heading not required.)

Instructions regarding War Diaries and Intelligence Summaries are contained in F. S. Regs., Part II. and the Staff Manual respectively. Title pages will be prepared in manuscript.

2 K.R.R.C. MAY 1918.

Place	Date	Hour	Summary of Events and Information	Remarks and references to Appendices
HOHENZOLLERN	20		Batt, less D Coy, who remained at ANNEQUIN practising for forthcoming operation, relieve	
SECTOR			2nd ROYAL SUSSEX on right sub-sector HOHENZOLLERN, from RAILWAY ALLEY G.4.a to	
			SAVILLE ROW G.4.b (CORRE MAP). 1 Coy ROYAL SUSSEX under orders OC 2KRRC as	
			reserve coy. MAJOR H.E.F. SMITH DSO in command in the line. 7 OR joined BATTN. 2 OR wounded.	
	21		Fine day, quiet. 1 OR wounded. Echelon B at BOIS D'OHLAIN.	
	22		Fine day, quiet, 1 OR wounded. Work continued, wiring & general improvement of	
			trenches. Reconnaisance patrol in front of said sector found wire badly cut & easily	
			negotiable. 1 OR wounded.	
	23		Quiet, fine day, full moon.	
	24	12.30	midnight. "D" Coy, under command Capt FRYER raided front line & second line (FOSSE TR)	
			on frontage 125x to depth of 315x from our front line. Area CORRE map A28.c.58.22 to	
			A28.c.95.55 (left) and A28.c.68.03 to A28.d.22.30 (right). 4 Off. 110 other ranks, with 1 RE	
			officer & 8 sappers, total 123 participated. Preparations - previous wire cutting by	
			Medium TMs & 18 pounders on sector & to right & left, and gas projected by TMs for one or	
			two nights previously. Zero at 12.30, box barrage very effective. 1st wave started from our front	
			line Zero plus 2, objective enemy's front line, second wave 40x behind, objective FOSSE TRENCH	

A6945 Wt. W11422/M1160 350,000 12/16 D. D. & L. Forms/C./2118/14.

Instructions regarding War Diaries and Intelligence Summaries are contained in F. S. Regs., Part II. and the Staff Manual respectively. Title pages will be prepared in manuscript.

WAR DIARY
or
~~INTELLIGENCE SUMMARY~~.
(Erase heading not required.)

2K RRC

MAY 1918

Army Form C. 2118.

Place	Date	Hour	Summary of Events and Information	Remarks and references to Appendices
HOHENZOLLERN SECTOR	24		Creeping barrage preceded infantry. 4 prisoners brought back, estimated casualties inflicted 70. Considerable damage inflicted on dugouts in second trench, where most casualties caused. Dugouts dealt with by smoke bombs + "mobile charges". 2nd Lts HARVIE + COTTON wounded, 15 OR. wounded, 1 OR. (Cpl ROWLEY) died of wounds. RE Officer, LT COWLEY + 3 Sappers also wounded. All ranks got back + no identification left behind.	Operation orders (2) No. 8 and sketch map enclosed.
			BATT HQ. in QUARRY TUNNEL (Lt COL ST AUBYN who had superintended arrangements) RAP also in QUARRY TUNNEL. Communication by wire maintained from Batt HQ. + D Coy's HQ. in enemy's front line. Recall sounded from Coy HQ. by two buglers Regtl + Coy's calls.	
			2Lt J R N GARTON wounded at CENTRAL KEEP, 2 OR. included. Artillery (hostile) slightly more active.	
	25		Fine day, special feature exceptional British aerial activity + considerable movement of small parties enemy in vicinity of AUCHY + HAISNES. Lt COL ST AUBYN joins details at D'OHLAIN	
	26		Fine day, quiet. 1 OR. died of wounds (wounded 24th) RFMN FERRER 1 OR. wounded	
	27		Fine day, quiet, enemy sent over exceptional quantity gas shells. 1 OR killed in action: RFMN SMART (Adjt's orderly)	

Army Form C. 2118.

Instructions regarding War Diaries and Intelligence Summaries are contained in F. S. Regs., Part II, and the Staff Manual respectively. Title pages will be prepared in manuscript.

WAR DIARY
or
INTELLIGENCE SUMMARY.
(Erase heading not required.)

2 K.R.R.C. MAY 1918

Place	Date	Hour	Summary of Events and Information	Remarks and references to Appendices
NOEUX-LES-MINES	28		Batt. relieved by 1st BATT BLACK WATCH & proceeded to NOEUX-LES-MINES.	
	29		Fine day. "cleaning up" & inspections. 1 OR. rejoined Batt. Officers' riding school started	
	30		Fine day. Company training, tactical work. Officers riding school continued. 1 OR rejoined, 1 OR. wounded.	
	31		Fine day. Company training, tactical work. Officers' riding school continued.	

June 2nd 1918

G. St Aubyn Lieut Colonel
Comdg 2nd Bn K.R.R.C.

A6945 Wt. W11422/M1160 350,000 12/16 D. D. & L. Forms/C./2118/14.

S E C R E T. 2nd Battn. King's Royal Rifle Corps. Copy No. 8.

Order No. 33.C.

---

1. Today is "Y" Day.

2. Zero is at 12.30 aM "Y.Z". Night.

3. The services of a searchlight have now been secured as a guiding light. It will be situated in L.4.d. Its beam will be aligned on the Head of RAILWAY ALLEY pointing up in the air. It will open at Zero plus 33 and will show its light and obscure its light for equal periods of 10 seconds.

4. Rum issue will be drunk at Zero minus 10.

Lieut Colonel.
King's Royal Rifle Corps.
Commdg 2nd Battalion.

23/5/18.

Copies No. 1 to 5. D.Coy.
6. C.O.
7. Office.
8. War Diary.
9. R.E.
10. 1/Northamptonshire Regt.
11.)
12.)Retained.

SECRET. FORMATIONS. Copy No. 8

1D^{x}

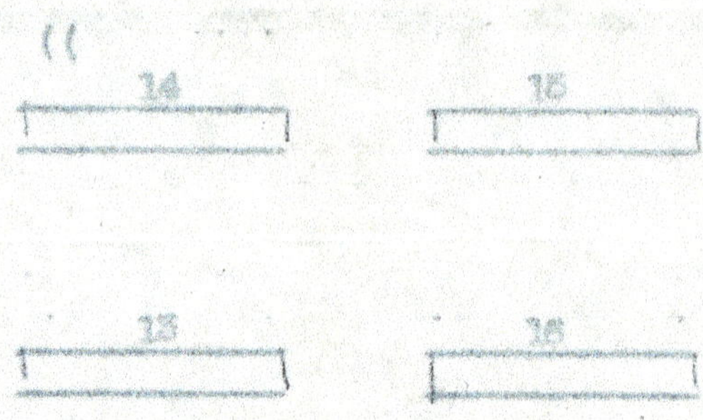

BOCHE FRONT LINE.

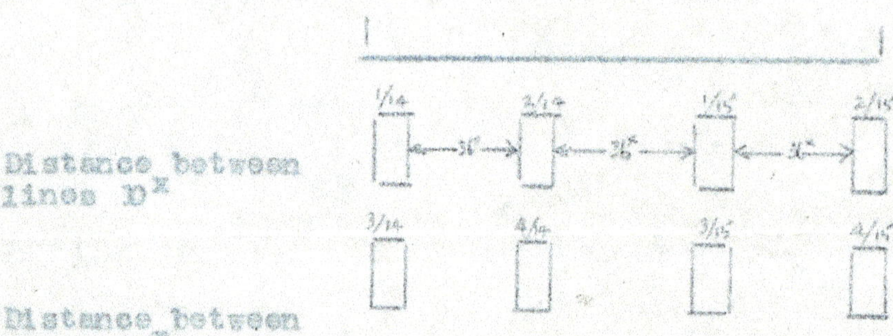

1st Wave.

DUTIES. 1/14 to seize junction of FRONT and LEFT trench and push down LEFT TRENCH 10^{x} so deal with dug-out if met with and block it.
Required 1 Stokes bomb for block.
3/14 to picket dug-out shewn 20^{x} to left of LEFT TRENCH and block trench - deal with occupants of dug-out.
6 P. Bombs for dug-out.
2/14 occupy trench at 8 Post.
4/14 mops up trench from 8 Post to left.
1/15 Occupy trench at 7 Post.
3/15 mop up trench to left.
2/15 seize junction of FRONT and RIGHT TRENCH and block FRONT line 30^{x} to right of junction.
4/15 to mop up to left.

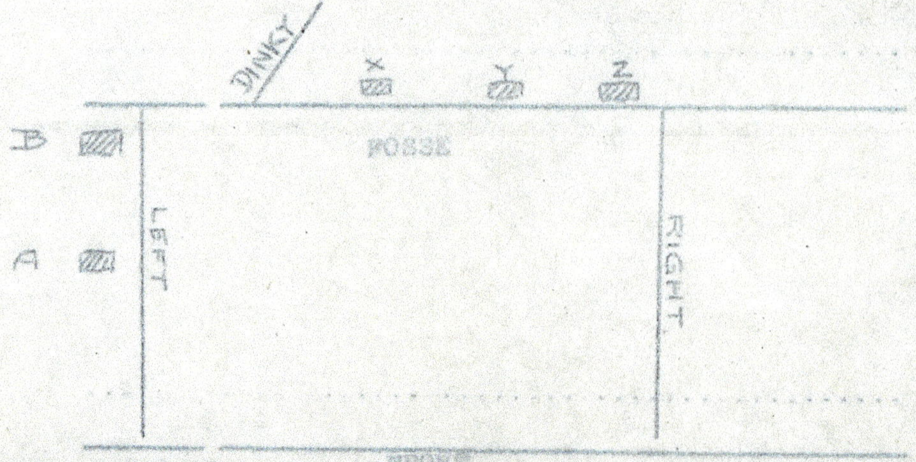

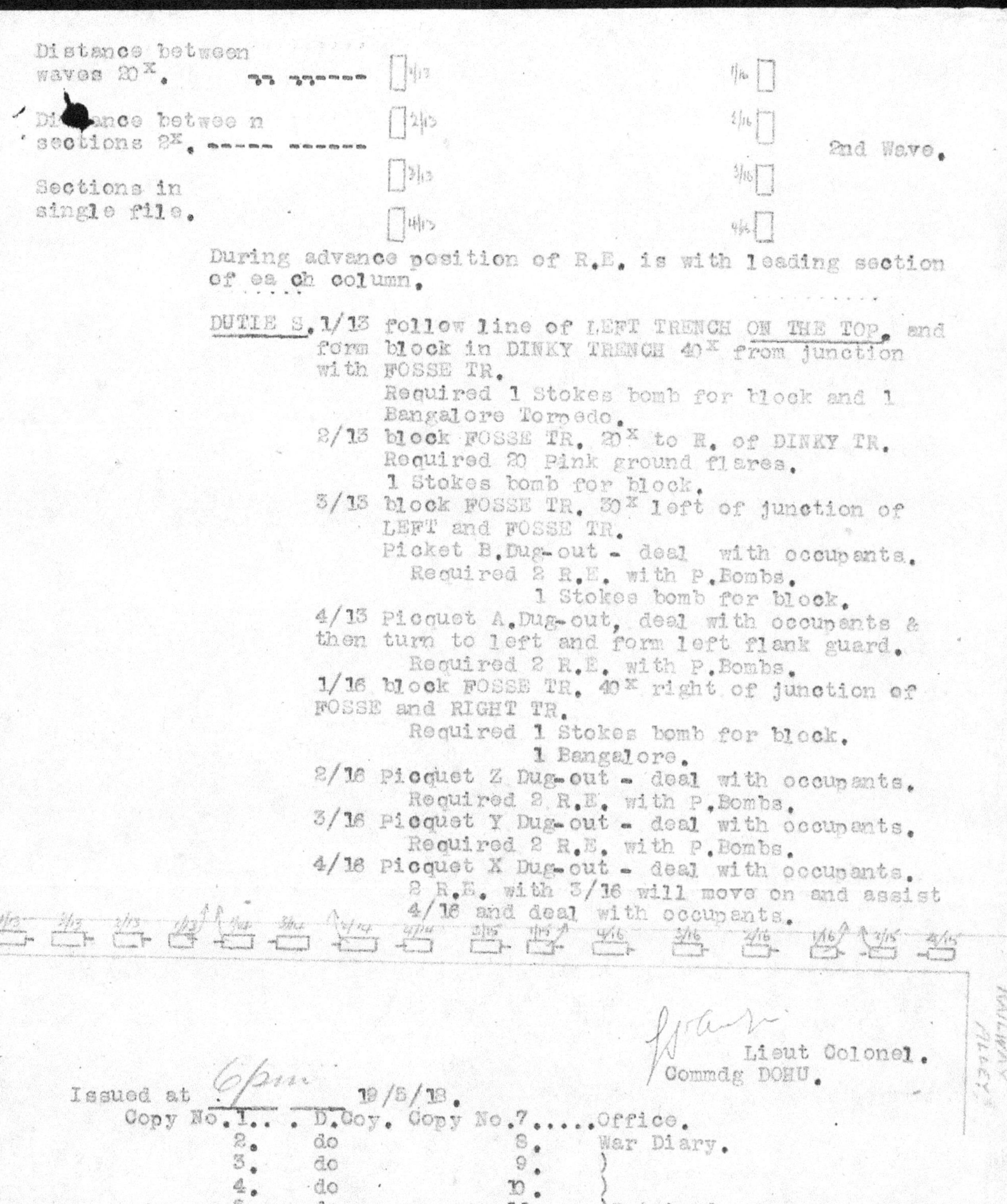

Distance between
waves 20ˣ. -- ------ 1/13 1/16

Distance between
sections 2ˣ. ----- ------ 2/13 2/16 2nd Wave.

Sections in
single file. 3/13 3/16

4/13 4/16

During advance position of R.E. is with leading section of each column.

DUTIE S. 1/13 follow line of LEFT TRENCH ON THE TOP, and form block in DINKY TRENCH 40ˣ from junction with FOSSE TR.
Required 1 Stokes bomb for block and 1 Bangalore Torpedo.
2/13 block FOSSE TR. 20ˣ to R. of DINKY TR.
Required 20 Pink ground flares.
1 Stokes bomb for block.
3/13 block FOSSE TR. 30ˣ left of junction of LEFT and FOSSE TR.
Picket B.Dug-out - deal with occupants.
Required 2 R.E. with P.Bombs.
1 Stokes bomb for block.
4/13 Picquet A.Dug-out, deal with occupants & then turn to left and form left flank guard.
Required 2 R.E. with P.Bombs.
1/16 block FOSSE TR. 40ˣ right of junction of FOSSE and RIGHT TR.
Required 1 Stokes bomb for block.
1 Bangalore.
2/16 Picquet Z Dug-out - deal with occupants.
Required 2 R.E. with P.Bombs.
3/16 Picquet Y Dug-out - deal with occupants.
Required 2 R.E. with P.Bombs.
4/16 Picquet X Dug-out - deal with occupants.
2 R.E. with 3/16 will move on and assist 4/16 and deal with occupants.

RAILWAY ALLEY.

Lieut Colonel.
Commdg DOHU.

Issued at 6pm 19/8/18.

Copy No.1.. . D.Coy. Copy No.7.....Office.
2. do 8. War Diary.
3. do 9.)
4. do 10.)
5. do 11.)Retained.
6. C.O. 12.)

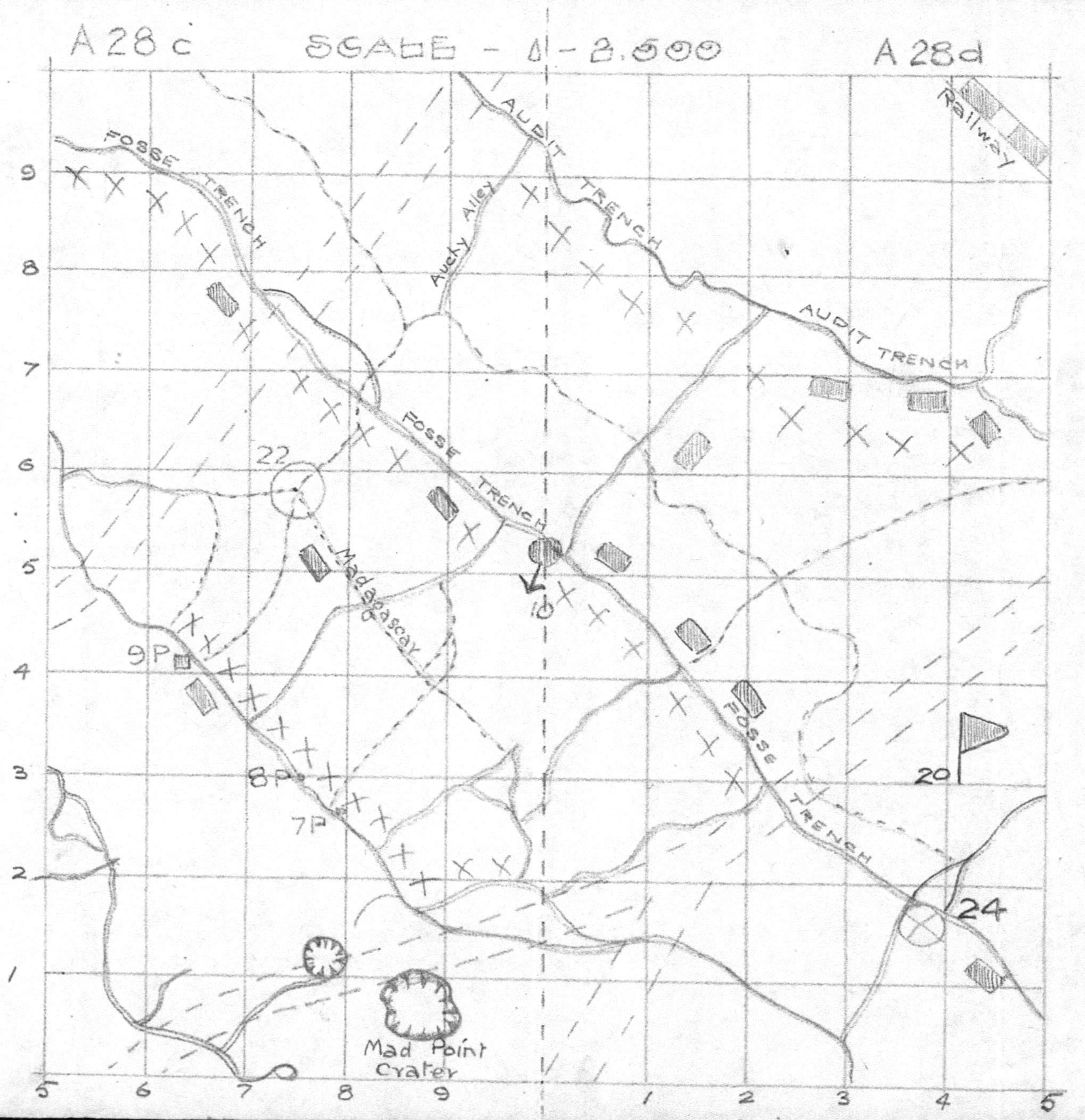
A 28 c
SCALE - 1-2,500
A 28 d
Railway
FOSSE TRENCH
AUDIT TRENCH
Aucky Alley
FOSSE TRENCH
AUDIT TRENCH
22
FOSSE TRENCH
Madagascay
10
9P
8P
7P
20
FOSSE TRENCH
24
Mad Point Crater
9
8
7
6
5
4
3
2
1
5
6
7
8
9
1
2
3
4
5

S E C R E T. 2nd K.R.R.C. Copy No....... 8
Order No. 33.
Reference Sketch Map attached.

Intention. 1. The Battalion will raid an area in the German line boundaries as follows :-

FRONT TRENCH.
FOSSE TRENCH.
RIGHT TRENCH.
LEFT TRENCH.

all inclusive.

Detail. 2.(a) D.Co y plus 8 men R.E. will carry out this raid under orders of Capt; FRYER.

(b) Time and date will be notified later.

(c) Stre ngth :- 4 Officer and 1[illegible] Other Ranks.

(d) Dress. Rifle and sword without equipment. 50 rounds S.A.A. will be carried in the right bottom pocket of jacket.
Bombs will be issued only to sections which have suitable tasks for bombing.
1st Wave will ~~[illegible]~~ wear white arm-band 4" wide on right arm.
Seco nd wave will wear white arm-ba nd 4" wide on both arms.
Wire cutters will be carried slung round the neck by whit e tape. In the second wave the leading section of each platoon will carry the wire cutters of the platoon.

(e) Formation. The Coy will attack under a barrage in two waves - each of two platoons.
Sepa rate instructions as to (1) the tasks allotted each section - (2) the barrage - (3) co-operation by gas mortar bombs and projectors are being issued.

(f) Signalling Sgt will arrange that a telephone with necessary operators accompanies O.C. Raid to his Hd Qrs in the enemy line.

(g) The Signal to withdraw on completion of raid is :-
1. Regimental Call and D.Coy's Call on Bugle.
2. Rocket - Red over Green over Red.

(h) The Signal to artillery to stop firing is a succession of white parachute lights.

(i) Ther e will be a guiding light in rear of our lines to direct stragglers.

(j) Sgt Bgr BROWN and 1 Rfn will establ ish a checking in post at the sentry post in RAILWAY ALLEY. Section Cdrs will report present or otherwise to Sgt BROWN and the R fn will count the men passing him.

(k) Sgt BROOKSBANK and 6 Rfn will establish a police post at Head of RAILWAY ALLEY to receive and conduct prisoners to Bn. Raid Hd.Qrs.

(l) C.Q. M.Sgt D.Coy, is responsible for collecting on the afternoon of Y. day from all men taking part in the raid :-
1. Identity Discs.
2. K.R.B's.
3. Pay Books and all papers.

(m) O.C. D.Coy is responsible for handing to the Adjutant on Y. day all copies of orders, instructions and maps issued to his Coy.

(n) Orders for synchronisation of watches will be issued later and attention is drawn to the necessity for abso lute accuracy.

Reports. 3. To Battn Raid Hd.Qrs. which will be established at Hd. Qrs Right Front Coy Left Battalion at Zero -45.

[signature]
Lieut Colonel.
Commdg [illegible].

Copies 1 to 5. D.Coy. Copy No.8 War Diary.
6. C.O. 9 to 12 Retained.
7. Office.

Issued at ____________

20/5/18

War Diary

SECRET. 2nd Bn. K.R.R.C. Copy No........

Order No. 33A.

References to the Sketch Map.

1. Password for the raid is "DON".

2. Special identity discs will be issued for the raid and a record will be made showing to whom each disc is issued.

3. Time of Parade for raiding party....Zero -95. Leading Section will pass Starting Point, which is "D" Coy's Headquarters, at that hour.
Route. Railway Line to FACTORY, thence via RAILWAY ALLEY.

4. Parties to conduct prisoners across No Man's Land will be detailed from 14 and 15 Platoons. Prisoners will be handed to Sgt Brooksbank at the head of RAILWAY ALLEY.

5. "P" Bombs will be carried by the Sections, King's Royal Rifle Corps detailed to clear dug-outs and not as previously stated by the R.E. The R.E. will be in charge of Bangalore Torpedoes and will carry mobile charges for the destruction of dug-outs.

6. All ranks are reminded that ;.
   1. Specimens of enemy clothing and food are required.
   2. German soldiers usually carry documents in the tail pockets of their tunics.
   3. A careful search should be made for any signs of gas installation.

7. TIMETABLE.

~~Zero minus 4 False S.O.S. on another front.~~
Zero minus 2 to Zero plus 2. Feint barrage North.
Zero plus 2 Raiders leave trenches. Barrage opens on enemy Front and Support Line.
Zero plus 4 Barrage lifts 50x.
Zero plus 6 Barrage lifts 50x. Raiders enter enemy front line.
Zero plus 7 Barrage on to enemy Support Line.
Zero plus 9 Barrage lifts 50x.
Zero plus 11 Barrage lifts 50x and raiders enter enemy Support line.
Zero plus 13 Barrage lifts to AUDIT TRENCH.
Zero plus 33 Recall signal by O.C.Raid.

In addition to above there will be a Box Barrage by the Artillery; Stokes Mortars firing on selected targets and M.G's firing on vulnerable spots.

E. St Aubyn

Issued at 5pm 21st May 1918. Lieut.Colonel,
King's Royal Rifle Corps...
Commdg 2nd Battn.

Copies No.1 to 5. D.Coy. Copy No
6. C.O.
7. ~~Adjutant~~ War Dy. 9. Lieut Cowley. R.E.
8. Office. 10. 1/Northamptonshire Regt.
11 & 12. Retained
~~11 2/Bde~~

DIAGRAM of BARRAGE (not to scale)

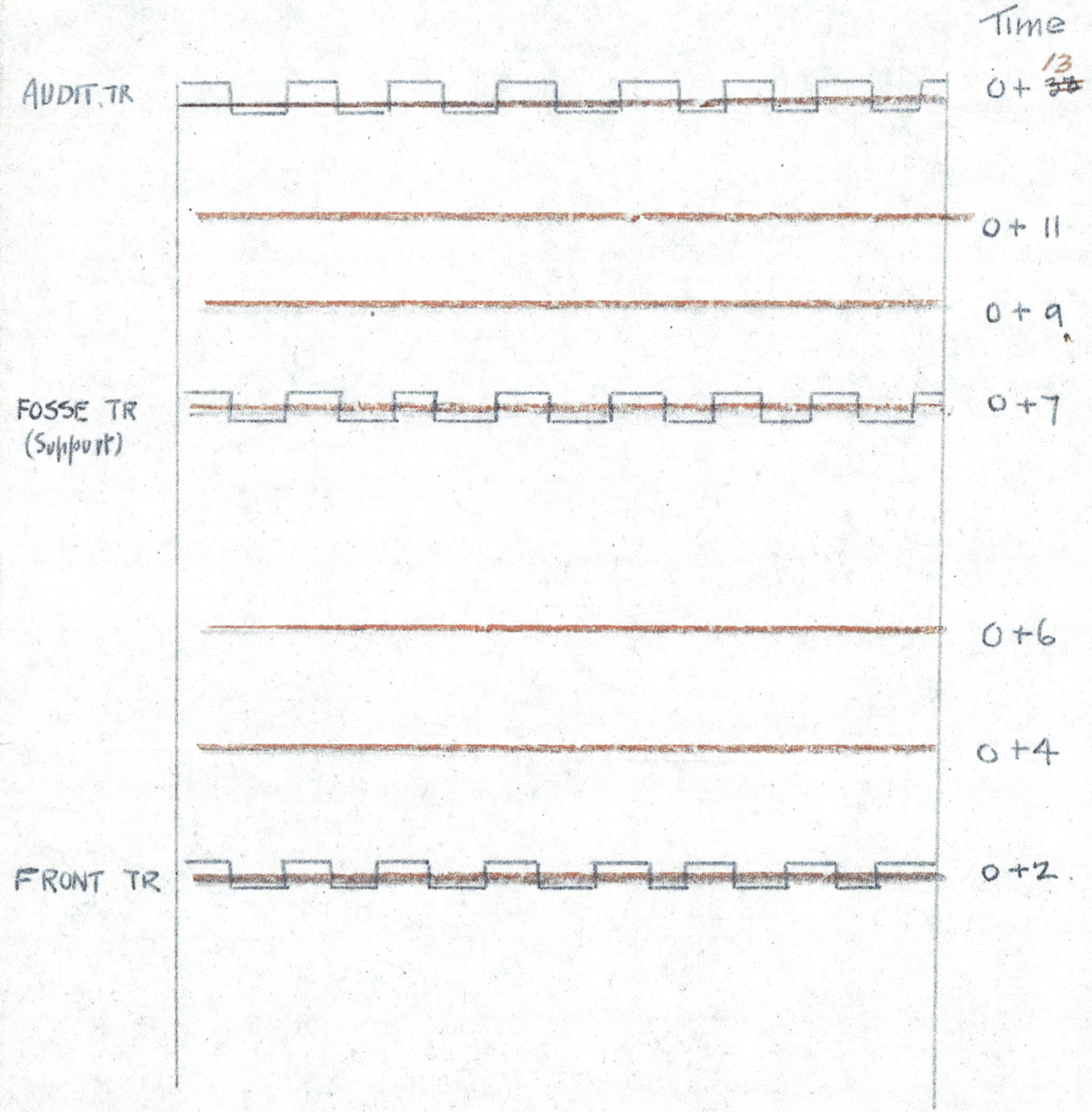

S E C R E T. 2 nd Bn. King's Royal Rifle Corp s. Copy No......8
Order No.33.B.

....

1. The Route by which raiding party will withdraw after the raid is along the Front Line to QUARRY TUNNEL.
Sgt. Brooksbank will prevent men going down RAILWAY ALLEY and "C" Coy's Post w ill show them the entrance to QUARRY TUNNEL at L.16.
2. Sgt.Bgr. Bro wn will "check in" in QUARRY TUNNEL and not as previously a rranged.
3. R.A.P.....QUARRY TUNNEL.
Battn Raid Headquarters. QUARRY TUNNEL at the entrance in rear of L.16 Post and not as previously stated.
4. The Guiding light referred to in Order No.33, para 2, sub para "i". will be a bo nfire lit under Brigade arrang ements half way up ANNEQUIN FOS SE.

[signature]
Lie ut Colonel.
Commdg. 2nd Bn. K.R.R.C.

22/5/18.

Issued at 5.30pm....
Copies No. 1 t o 5. D.Coy.
6. C.O.
7. Office.
8. War Diary.
9. R.E.
10. 1/Northampton Regt.
11.)
12.)Retained.

Army Form C. 2118.

Instructions regarding War Diaries and Intelligence Summaries are contained in F. S. Regs., Part II. and the Staff Manual respectively. Title pages will be prepared in manuscript.

WAR DIARY
or
INTELLIGENCE SUMMARY.
(Erase heading not required.)

2nd Bn KRRC — June 1918. — Vol 47

Place	Date	Hour	Summary of Events and Information	Remarks and references to Appendices
Noeux les Mines	1st		Continuation of Company training – fine and hot day –	
	2nd		Church parade. After the service the Battalion marched past General Morland, Cmdg XIII Corps. He expressed himself pleased with the turn out. In the afternoon the 2nd Brigade held a Gymkana on the polo ground – Noeux. The Batt secured 5 firsts and 4 2nds. Another fine and hot day. 6 other ranks joined the Battalion	1 OR from wd
	3rd		The Batt went to the Bois d'Ohlain for an outpost scheme. Still fine	
	4th		Company Training – cloudy but hot.	
Cambrin	5th		The Batt relieved the 2nd Welsh at Cambrin. One Coy went into Pont Fixe and the Village Line. Details returned to Ohlain. A hostile attack was expected on our front. Cloudy and close. 3 OR & 9 OR rejoined the Batt. Lt Dawson was slightly wounded	1
	6th		Hostile attack still feared. Cloudy and hot. 2 OR wounded.	
	7th		No change in the situation. Heavy shelling by enemy with a certain amount of gas – Fine day – 2 ORs ~~of company~~ killed 1 OR died of wds 2 ORs wd (gas)	WFA Chambers
	8th		Situation more normal but hostile shelling still above ordinary. Fine. 10 ORs rejoined Batt.	

A6945 Wt. W11422/M1160 350,000 12/16 D. D. & L. Forms/C./2118/14.

Instructions regarding War Diaries and Intelligence Summaries are contained in F. S. Regs., Part II. and the Staff Manual respectively. Title pages will be prepared in manuscript.

WAR DIARY
or
INTELLIGENCE SUMMARY.
(Erase heading not required.)

Army Form C. 2118.

Place	Date	Hour	Summary of Events and Information	Remarks and references to Appendices
Cambrin	9th		B Coy relieved A Coy at Pont Fixe. This place was somewhat heavily gas-shelled	
			– Slight rain –	
	10th		A Quiet day. Colder and more rain 2 ORs wd (gas)	
	11th		Another quiet day, but fine and warmer 3 ORs wd (gas)	
	12th		Third quiet day – fine and warm 1 OR wd.	
Cuinchy	13th		The Batt relieved the Royal Sussex in the Left Sub-Sector of the Left Bde	WPA Chambers Lt
			Fine – 7 ORs joined the Battalion.	
	14th		Some activity of hostile artillery and Trench Mortars – Fine – 2 ORs killed	
	15th		Quiet day, usual trench routine. Fine. 1 OR died of wounds.	
	16th		Quiet day. Capt Warner leaves the line for a course and 2nd Lt Gracie for leave	
			2nd Lt Cunningham takes over B Coy. Our snipers claim one hit upon enemy.	
			Slight rain in the morning but fine afterwards 2 ORs wounded (gas).	
	17th		Activity on the part of hostile artillery. Retaliation was asked for several	
			times. Lt Ravenscroft went down to take over adjutantcy of 1st Bn. Reception	
			Camp. 1 OR rejoined from wd.	
	18th		Comparatively quiet until the evening, when 11th Bn on our right discharged	

A6945. Wt. W11422/M1160 350,000 12/16 D. D. & L. Forms/C./2118/14.

Army Form C. 2118.

Instructions regarding War Diaries and Intelligence Summaries are contained in F. S. Regs., Part II, and the Staff Manual respectively. Title pages will be prepared in manuscript.

WAR DIARY
or
INTELLIGENCE SUMMARY.
(Erase heading not required.)

Place	Date	Hour	Summary of Events and Information	Remarks and references to Appendices
Cuinchy	18th		gas projectors, and on our left the 55th Div made a small attack. A five minutes intense barrage by 6ins guns and 18 pdr shrapnel was arranged to deal with the Trench Mortars which had caused trouble previously. Capt Cook came up from Details to act as Works Officer.	
	19th		During the night 18/19 very heavy hostile artillery activity smashed up our trenches in several places. Rain in the morning. 2 ORs joined Batt.	Lt
	20th		Another intensive fire on hostile T.Ms by 6ins guns and 18 pdr shrapnel lasting 15 mins. Fine day. 4 ORs wounded.	
Noeux les Mines	21st		Continuous rain in the evening. The Batt is relieved by the 1st Camerons at 9pm and returns to Noeux-les-Mines. The Details rejoin from Bois d' Ohlain	W.A. Chambers
	22nd		Dull and chilly. Day spent at Baths and upon general cleaning up. Batt Mess at the Mairie. Capt Hale MC joined Battalion; 2nd Lt Cotton from Wd and 2nd Lt Best from sick leave.	
	23rd		Church Parade.	
	24th		Company training — showery.	

A6945 Wt. W11422/M1160 350,000 12/16 D. D. & L. Forms/C./2118/14.

Instructions regarding War Diaries and Intelligence Summaries are contained in F. S. Regs., Part II, and the Staff Manual respectively. Title pages will be prepared in manuscript.

Army Form C. 2118.

WAR DIARY
or
INTELLIGENCE SUMMARY.
(Erase heading not required.)

Place	Date	Hour	Summary of Events and Information	Remarks and references to Appendices
Nœux les Mines	25th		Company training - showery -	
	26th		Company training continued. fine - Lt HB Dawson rejoined from wd	
	27th		Batt Scheme at the Bois d' Ohlain - fine	
	28th		Company training - fine 1 OR rejoined from wd.	
	29th		Batt marches out to Labuissière to rehearse for inspection by HRH Duke of Connaught on Monday. Major General Strickland inspected the 2nd Brigade. Fine. The Batt was brought back by motor bus.	
	30th		Voluntary Church Parade - cleaning up for next day's inspection. Fine.	
			During this tour at Nœux an epidemic of, so called, Spanish influenza swept through the Batt: the fever generally lasted three days. Capt Ward made a temporary hospital of the School buildings in Rue Hugette. The officers were also affected.	
			G St Aubyn Lieut. Colonel Comdg 2nd Bn Kings Royal Rifle Corps	

A6945 Wt. W11422/M1160 350,000 12/16 D. D. & L. Forms/C./2118/14.

Instructions regarding War Diaries and Intelligence Summaries are contained in F. S. Regs., Part II, and the Staff Manual respectively. Title pages will be prepared in manuscript.

WAR DIARY
or
~~INTELLIGENCE SUMMARY.~~
(Erase heading not required.)

2nd Bn. K.R.R.Corps.

Army Form C. 2118.

July 1918

Place	Date	Hour	Summary of Events and Information	Remarks and references to Appendices
Noeux Les Mines.	July 1st		The Battalion went to La Buissière by motor lorry for the inspection of the 2nd Brigade by H.R.H. Duke of Connaught. The following members of the Battalion were presented with the honours they had gained: 2nd Lt Winter with the MC, Sgt Hinchridge with D.C.M., Sgt Couch with M.M. His Royal Highness expressed himself extremely pleased with the appearance and turn out of the Brigade. The Battalion was taken home by lorry as many were still feeling the effects of fever. Capt H.W. Butler MC took over duties of 2nd in command. A draft of 16 ORs arrived.	
Hohenzollern Section	July 2nd		The Battalion relieved the 2nd Welch Regiment in the left subsector of the Hohenzollern Section. The Details went to the Bois D'Ohlain. This tour of duty in the trenches was one of the quietest which the Battalion has ever had. It was chiefly spent in work, improving the wire and defences. A certain amount of training was also done.	
	July 3rd		A quiet day. Capt Harden returned to the Battalion, also a draft of 11 ORs.	
	4th		Another quiet day.	
	5th		Fine. A quiet day. L/cpl Oldham of the Rhodesian platoon was killed by shell.	W.A. Chamberlin [signature]

A6945 Wt. W11422/M1160 350,000 12/16 D. D. & L. Forms/C./2118/14.

Instructions regarding War Diaries and Intelligence Summaries are contained in F. S. Regs., Part II. and the Staff Manual respectively. Title pages will be prepared in manuscript.

WAR DIARY
or
INTELLIGENCE SUMMARY.
(Erase heading not required.)

July 1918

Army Form C. 2118.

Place	Date	Hour	Summary of Events and Information	Remarks and references to Appendices
Hohenzollern Sector	July 6th		A fine day. 2 ORs wounded and 1 OR died of wounds. A draft of 17 ORs arrived.	
Annequin	7th		The Battalion was relieved by the 1st Northamptonshire Regt and went back to Annequin. ~~Captain~~ Major Butler went down to Echelon B. A draft of 1 OR joined us.	
	8th		Very hot. A heavy thunderstorm in the evening. A draft of 8 ORs arrived.	
	9th		Very fine. Much aerial activity by both sides. One EA was driven down. The Germans shelled Annequin Fosse more than usual. The CO, Company Commanders & Lt Gracie reconnoitred the Cambrin Sector. 1 OR wounded. A draft of 41 came.	
	10th		Quiet. 1 O.R. wounded. A draft of 3 ORs came.	
	11th		Quiet. 1 O.R. wounded. A draft of 3 ORs came. While in Annequin working parties of 100 men were provided every night to the two front Battalions. All companies went to the Baths and had one day on the range each.	
Cambrin Sector	12th		The Battalion relieved the 2nd Royal Sussex Regt in the Right subsector of the Cambrin Sector. A draft of 7 ORs arrived.	
	13th		One of our aeroplanes demonstrated with a new kind of S.O.S rocket used to show the flanks of an enemy attack. The Germans put down a barrage for	

[illegible signature] NA

A6945 Wt. W11422/M1160 350,000 12/16 D. D. & L. Forms/C./2118/14.

Instructions regarding War Diaries and Intelligence Summaries are contained in F. S. Regs., Part II, and the Staff Manual respectively. Title pages will be prepared in manuscript.

WAR DIARY
or
INTELLIGENCE SUMMARY.
(Erase heading not required.)

Army Form C. 2118.

July 1918

Place	Date	Hour	Summary of Events and Information	Remarks and references to Appendices
Cambrai Sector	July 13th		ten minutes on our Reserve and support line. In retaliation we gave them twenty minutes with all calibres. 1 O.R. wounded. A draft of 35 arrived.	
	14th		Intermittent showers: cold. Towards night it rained heavily. Lt Col E.G. St Aubyn went to Hospital and Major H.W. Butler MC assumed temporary command. A draft of 6 ORs arrived.	
	15th		Quiet. Lt P.D. Ravenscroft rejoined from Divisional Reception Camp. A draft of 8 ORs arrived.	
	16th		Very hot and sunny. Quiet. Signallers communicated with the Bois D'Ohlain by Helio. A draft of 3 ORs came up.	
	17th		Very hot. Three Italians escaped from the Germans and entered our front line. The Blues came up as our Machine Gunners. A draft of 6 ORs came up	
	18th		Quiet. Lt Col F. Badham of the Worcester Regt, from E. Africa was attached to the Battalion for instruction. 2nd Lt Cartwright left for Machine Gun School at Grantham. A draft of 18 ORs arrived.	
	19th		Quiet. 1 O.R. wounded.	
	20th		Quiet. 1 O.R. wounded. A draft of 10 ORs arrived.	

A6945 Wt. W11422/M1160 350,000 12/16 D. D. & L. Forms/C./2118/14.

Instructions regarding War Diaries and Intelligence Summaries are contained in F. S. Regs., Part II. and the Staff Manual respectively. Title pages will be prepared in manuscript.

WAR DIARY
or
INTELLIGENCE SUMMARY.
(Erase heading not required.)

July 1918

Army Form C. 2118.

Place	Date	Hour	Summary of Events and Information	Remarks and references to Appendices
Cambrin Sector	July 20.		All this week our heavy artillery and Trench Mortars were cutting the Enemy's wire along the whole Corps Front. Our patrols were active, one or two going out every night. Some got into the Boche line and walked along it without encountering anyone.	
			At midnight 20-21st the Royal Sussex carried out a raid.	
	21st		A company from a new Division, the 59th came in for instruction. In the afternoon the 1st Bn The Black Watch relieved the Battalion. The Relief was complete by 6 pm and the Battalion moved to Noeux les Mines via Vermelles & Noyelles. A draft of 5 ORs arrived.	
Noeux les Mines			The Commanding Officer of the 12th Batt paid the Batt. a visit.	
	22nd		Baths and clothes fitting. This week the whole Batt was inoculated. A draft of 7 ORs arrived.	
	23rd		Very wet. A draft of 2 ORs arrived.	
	24th		Half the Battalion went to the Bois D'ohlain for a scheme. A draft of 7 ORs arrived.	[illegible] NPA
	25th		A draft of 1 OR arrived.	
	26th		A draft of 8 ORs arrived.	

A6945 Wt. W11422/M1160 350,000 12/16 D. D. & L. Forms/C./2118/14.

Instructions regarding War Diaries and Intelligence Summaries are contained in F. S. Regs., Part II. and the Staff Manual respectively. Title pages will be prepared in manuscript.

WAR DIARY
or
INTELLIGENCE SUMMARY.
(Erase heading not required.)

Army Form C. 2118.

July 1918

Place	Date	Hour	Summary of Events and Information	Remarks and references to Appendices
Noeux les Mines.	July 27th.		Wet. A draft of 2 ORs arrived.	
	28th.		The Brigade held their eliminating competition for the Divisional Horse Show. The Battalion won the Infantry Officers Chargers Event. A draft of 1 OR came	
	29th.		~~The Battalion played the 1st Corps at Cricket.~~ There was a Lewis Gun Competition, in rapid Stripping won by D Coy. A draft of 1 OR came.	
	30th.		The Batt played the 1st Corps at Cricket. In the evening there was a Battalion Concert.	
	31st.		The Battalion relieved the 1st Bn the South Wales Borderers in the Cambrin Sector. Two platoons were attached to the Royal Sussex, & went to Port Pixe & Horsham Posts	

August 5th. 1918.

H. Wilson. Major
Comdg 2nd Bn K.R.R.C.

A6945 Wt. W11422/M1160 350,000 12/16 D. D. & L. Forms/C./2118/14.

2/KRRC

Instructions regarding War Diaries and Intelligence Summaries are contained in F. S. Regs., Part II. and the Staff Manual respectively. Title pages will be prepared in manuscript.

WAR DIARY
or
INTELLIGENCE SUMMARY.
(Erase heading not required.)

Army Form C. 2118.

August 1918

WO 41

Place	Date	Hour	Summary of Events and Information	Remarks and references to Appendices
Cambrin	1st		Lt. Col. Badham was in command of the Battalion. A quiet day. 12 ORs joined the Battalion	
	2nd		Occasional shelling of Ponte Lixe. This was normal for every day. Quiet. 1 OR joined the Battalion. 1 OR wounded	
	3rd		C.O. and Company Commanders reconnoitred the Left Subsector. 3 OR joined Batt	
Left Subsector	4th		The Batt relieved the 2nd Royal Sussex Regt in the Left Subsector.	
	5th		Rain set in and continued through the night. 2 ORs joined Batt.	
	6th		Quiet.	
	7th		Sunny. Col St Aubyn rejoined from Hospital. An enemy low flying aeroplane was brought down by a Stokes Mortar. The 1st Cameron Highlanders made a successful raid on our right. There was no retaliation on our Sector. 2 ORs joined the Batt.	
Cambrin.	8th		Bright day. The 2nd Royal Sussex relieved us. The relief was complete by 7 pm. We went to Cambrin as Support Batt. Batt HQ was shelled during the night. German maps which were issued to the Battalion showed the exact position of a signal station opposite Batt H.Q. 1 OR wounded. 1 OR joined Batt.	

A6945 Wt. W11422/M1160 350,000 12/16 D. D. & L. Forms/C./2118/14.

Instructions regarding War Diaries and Intelligence Summaries are contained in F. S. Regs., Part II. and the Staff Manual respectively. Title pages will be prepared in manuscript.

WAR DIARY
or
INTELLIGENCE SUMMARY.
(*Erase heading not required.*)

Army Form C. 2118.

Place	Date	Hour	Summary of Events and Information	Remarks and references to Appendices
CAMBRIN.	9th.		During this period all companies went to the Baths. Training of Scouts and Tactical schemes for Officers were also carried out.	
	10th.		Very Hot. 1 OR joined the Batt.	
	11th.		Very Hot. Considerable shelling by Germans. NOEUX LES MINES was also shelled. 1 OR wounded. 3 ORs joined the Battalion.	
Right Subsector	12th		The Battalion relieved 1st Northamptonshire Regt as Right Battalion of Left Brigade. 1 O.R. accidentally wounded. 1 OR joined Batt.	
	13th		In this sector there was great patrolling activity on our part. Patrols went into the German front line by night and by day and brought back notice-boards and other trophies. 2nd Lt Cotton and 2nd Lt Liddle brought in a trench mortar. The Germans had evacuated their front line system. Wire cutting by our artillery commenced along the whole front. Gas projectors were let off and continual harassing fire was maintained by our side. 4 O.R. joined the Battalion.	
	14th.		Quiet. 1 OR wounded. Lt Fryer rejoined. 2nd Lts BELL, R. JACOMB-HOOD, H. GOSS & P J Smith joined.	

A6945 Wt. W11422/M1160 350,000 12/16 D. D. & L. Forms/C./2118/14.

Instructions regarding War Diaries and Intelligence Summaries are contained in F. S. Regs., Part II. and the Staff Manual respectively. Title pages will be prepared in manuscript.

Army Form C. 2118.

WAR DIARY
or
INTELLIGENCE SUMMARY.
(Erase heading not required.)

Place	Date	Hour	Summary of Events and Information	Remarks and references to Appendices
CAMBRIN Right Subsector	15th		Normal activity. 2nd Lts M.D.B. Lister & O.L. Marlow and 1 O.R. joined Batt.	
	16th		A patrol went out to reconnoitre the German support line. 2nd Lt HANCOCK and 2nd Lt GURNEY went on in front with two sergeants. They walked up the communication trench; on turning into the main trench they were fired upon. 2nd Lt HANCOCK who could not be got away, was killed. 2nd Lt GURNEY was badly wounded.	
			2nd Lt S. BURROUGHES joined the Batt. 3 O.Rs wounded, 1 accidentally wd.	
	17th		The two front line companies were relieved by the other two companies.	
			1 O.R. joined the Batt.	
	18th		Lt Col Badham went to command the 2nd Royal Sussex Regt.	
			2nd Lt R.F. KING and 1 OR joined the Batt.	
	19th		Normal. 2 OR joined the Batt.	
	20th		Normal	
	21st		Normal	
	22nd		The Batt was relieved by the 6th Somerset Light Infantry and proceeded to BEUGIN near HOUDAIN. It embussed outside NOEUX LES MINES	

A6945 Wt. W11422/M1160 350,000 12/16 D. D. & L. Forms/C./2118/14.

Instructions regarding War Diaries and Intelligence Summaries are contained in F. S. Regs., Part II. and the Staff Manual respectively. Title pages will be prepared in manuscript.

WAR DIARY
or
INTELLIGENCE SUMMARY.
(Erase heading not required.)

Army Form C. 2118.

Place	Date	Hour	Summary of Events and Information	Remarks and references to Appendices
BEUGIN	22nd		and reached BEUGIN about midnight. 1 OR wounded, 1 off. acc. wounded.	
	23rd		Was spent cleaning up. During the stay at BEUGIN a complete scheme of training drawn up by the Division was to be carried out beginning with Platoon training. A long and a short range was also available. This was carried out as far as company schemes. see attached papers. 3 ORs joined Batt.	
	24th		2nd Lts. A Robinson and J.C. Butler joined the Batt.	
	25th		Church Services. Baths for companies.	
	26th		Training	
	27th		Training	
	28th		Training	
	29th		Training	
	30th		Training	
	31st		The Batt received sudden orders to move South. It marched to DIEVAL entrained and reached ARRAS at 6 AM the next morning	WA Chambers Lt

G. St Aubyn Lt Colonel
Cmdg 2nd Batt
The Kings Royal Rifle Corps

A6945 Wt. W11422/M1160 350,000 12/16 D. D. & L. Forms/C./2118/14.

2nd Bn K.R.R.C.

Instructions regarding War Diaries and Intelligence Summaries are contained in F. S. Regs., Part II. and the Staff Manual respectively. Title pages will be prepared in manuscript.

WAR DIARY
or
INTELLIGENCE SUMMARY.
(*Erase heading not required.*)

Army Form C. 2118.

September 1918

Place	Date	Hour	Summary of Events and Information	Remarks and references to Appendices
ARRAS	Sept 1.		The Batt reached ARRAS. at 6 A.M. It passed the day in billets and proceeded into the line in the evening into reserve for the attack carried out by the Canadian Division. At 12 midnight they moved up to GOUEAPPE. The transport came by road to ARRAS. it split into Echelon A and Echelon B. the former proceeded with the Bn After GOUEAPPE Echelon A followed the Batt at 100 yds distance along road & and across country; and followed the Batt at the same distance during the operations of the succeeding days.	
	2		The Batt. then went in artillery formation of platoons the attack by the Canadians began at dawn. The Bn followed up the advance about four miles behind. Towards evening halted about 1000 yds in front of VIS-EN-ARTOIS. S. of main ARRAS. CAMBRAI Roads left of the Bn was on the road. The Bn bivouaked in shell holes for the night. Harassing fire round Bn area one Lewis Gun team was knocked out completely.	
	3		Orders to stand by at 1.a.m. Commanding Officer and Coy Commanders reconnoitred area North of CAMBRAI road occupied by a Bn of Essex Regt who was holding the SENSEE River the left flank of the attack.	

A6945 Wt. W11422/M1160 350,000 12/16 D. D. & L. Forms/C./2118/14.

Army Form C. 2118.

Instructions regarding War Diaries and Intelligence Summaries are contained in F. S. Regs., Part II, and the Staff Manual respectively. Title pages will be prepared in manuscript.

WAR DIARY
or
INTELLIGENCE SUMMARY.
(Erase heading not required.)

Place	Date	Hour	Summary of Events and Information	Remarks and references to Appendices
	3 (contd)		Meanwhile BN began to advance with the intention of wheeling to the left in the valley in front of DRURY. Orders came to return to original positions. At dusk Bn. moved forward again in column of route down the CAMBRAI road for about 1000x. The road was heavily bombed and all the surrounding countrysides – no casualties were sustained. We wheeled to the left and marched through ETERPIGNY where we picked up our guides: From this point Coys went off to relieve the ESSEX RGT. in area S.E. of ETAING proceeding in artillery formation.	
	4		At 3AM we began to advance again: while doing so came under heavy H.E. barrage from field guns (we were apparently shown up by an incendiary shell which burst in the midst of the Bn). We lay down and then went on again and were lucky to have only 2 casualties – one killed and one wounded. Wheeling slightly to the E. we took up our main position just before dawn on the main DRURY– road throwing out sentry groups on the forward slopes of the hill to the SENSÉE river. 'B' Coy and 2 platoons of 'D' moved forward to the village of L'ÉCLUSE and the remaining 2 pltns of D together with 2 pltns of C occupied a maze of trenches S.W. of L'ÉCLUSE. Remainder of Bn distributed in depth and was settled by dawn on the 4th. Echelon 'A' of the transport	

A6945 Wt. W11422/M1160 350,000 12/16 D. D. & L. Forms/C./2118/14.

Instructions regarding War Diaries and Intelligence Summaries are contained in F. S. Regs., Part II, and the Staff Manual respectively. Title pages will be prepared in manuscript.

WAR DIARY
or
INTELLIGENCE SUMMARY.
(Erase heading not required.)

Army Form C. 2118.

Place	Date	Hour	Summary of Events and Information	Remarks and references to Appendices
			halted at the X roads 200x behind Bn Hqrs (which was 400x SW of MAZE) and had the horses put in RECOURT wood.	
	5.		Fairly quiet. Sunny & delightful. A Coy holding road was shelled with 5.9's and suffered a few casualties. Night quiet – patrols went over 2 main bridge heads leading from L'ECLUSE and reached first houses of TORQUENILLES meeting with no opposition.	
	6		During the day accommodating parties from the relieving Bn came up. Deluge of rain & hail for two hours afterwards it was clear. During the morning the 10th Bde Gas Officer patrolled the valley now in front of our front line to see if it was clear of gas, it was mustard gas & something else mixed with it – the village was clear. N.B. The village was shelled in the square the men were all forward. Roads were shelled heavily near Bn HQ Qrs. on account of a 6" and Field Guns being close. Night Boche harassing fire very severe.	[illegible]
	7		13th London Regt relieved us arriving 9-30 P.m Relief complete 11-50 P.m During the day enemy shelling on our positions. The Bn then moved in column of route 100x between P'toons down the main Road to DURY and then along a track to the CAMBRAI Rd. and picked up cookers at PICHARTS factory. Shelled at 4 a.m. Bn had hot tea	

A6945 Wt. W11422/M1160 350,000 12/16 D. D. & L. Forms/C./2118/14.

Instructions regarding War Diaries and Intelligence Summaries are contained in F. S. Regs., Part II, and the Staff Manual respectively. Title pages will be prepared in manuscript.

WAR DIARY
or
INTELLIGENCE SUMMARY.
(*Erase heading not required.*)

Army Form C. 2118.

Place	Date	Hour	Summary of Events and Information	Remarks and references to Appendices
	7.		moved to embussing point and went into HERMAVILLE arriving at 6 a m on the	
	8		8th. The day was spent cleaning up and refitting.	
	9		Rest reorganizing of Batt. into one full Coy. A. B & C Coys two Platoons. D Coy two Platoons. Two Officers of the 16th Bn visited us.	
	10		Bn moved off by 9. a m marched four miles to ACQ and entrained at 12 noon with transport. Moving off eventually about 2.15 P.m we spent the night in Train and arrived at GUILLANCOURT from which we marched four miles to PROYART.	
	11		The Batt spent the day in cleaning up.	
	12		It rained all day a few parades was attempted but it proved too wet	
	13		The Batt. moved in motor busses to ATHIES where it was billeted in old cellars & nissen huts.	
	14.		The Batt moved by road to FOX COPSE N. of the road at N. 4. central. The remainder of day was spent in making shelters, in the evening Commanding Officer showed us scheme of attack	
	15		Sunday, Church services, inspection of fighting order in the morning, C.O. Adjt. and Coy Commanders went to VERMAND to reconnoitre	[signature]

A6945 Wt. W11422/M1160 350,000 12/16 D. D. & L. Forms/C./2118/14.

Instructions regarding War Diaries and Intelligence Summaries are contained in F. S. Regs., Part II, and the Staff Manual respectively. Title pages will be prepared in manuscript.

WAR DIARY
or
INTELLIGENCE SUMMARY.
(Erase heading not required.)

Army Form C. 2118.

Place	Date	Hour	Summary of Events and Information	Remarks and references to Appendices
	15		very fine day. At 8-30 P.m. we moved out across country through TERTARY to a wood E. of COURLANCOURT where the Batt spent the night in dug-outs. Very slight shelling.	
	16		The morning was spent in preparations. Orders for the attack was read out. the Batt moved up at 8 P.m. A storm during the night.	
	17		2nd Lt DRAPKIN joined Batt. 2 O.R. wounded. Batt occupied in making final arrangements for to-morrows attack. Bn HQrs moved up soon after dusk to MAISSEMY.	
	18		By 4-30 AM. the Bn was formed up ready for the attack. The Bn was attacking on a front of about 800 yds which gradually narrowed down to about 500 yds at the final objective. area extended from the impassable marsh ground of the R. OMIGNON on the left to the road running N.E. from MAISSEMY to BERTHACOURT. The 2nd R. Sussex Regt were on our left and the 1st Cameron Highlanders on our Right. our first objective was an enemy trench system along the high ground in M.18.a (half way between MAISSEMY and BERTHACOURT). The second and final objective was BERTHACOURT - there	[signature]

A6945 Wt. W11422/M1160 350,000 12/16 D. D. & L. Forms/C./2118/14.

Army Form C. 2118.

Instructions regarding War Diaries and Intelligence Summaries are contained in F. S. Regs., Part II. and the Staff Manual respectively. Title pages will be prepared in manuscript.

WAR DIARY
or
INTELLIGENCE SUMMARY.
(Erase heading not required.)

Place	Date	Hour	Summary of Events and Information	Remarks and references to Appendices
	18		and sure enough much movement in the shape of small groups of men was observed working forward from that village at about 4.45 P.M. we had a telephone line back to Brigade which was laid as we advanced and our Artillery liaison officer was able to get back to his Brigade and within a few minutes an excellent barrage of shrapnel and H.E. was put down in the area where movement was seen with the result that the counter attack failed to develop.	
			The Colonel had been hit in the foot earlier in the day and was eventually evacuated Major BUTLER taking his place.	
			2Lt F.A. SIMONDS joined Bn. one O.R. joined Bn. 2Lt J. ELDRIDGE Killed	
			" J. ELMHURST " " " E.H. BEST "	
			Capt. L.J. BARNES. M.C. Wd. 23 O.R. Killed 6 missing 95 O.R. Wd	
			Lt. W.F.O. CHAMBERS "	
			2Lt. A. WINTER	
			" M.D.B. LISTER "	

A6945 Wt. W11422/M1160 350,000 12/16 D. D. & L. Forms/C./2118/14.

Instructions regarding War Diaries and Intelligence Summaries are contained in F. S. Regs., Part II. and the Staff Manual respectively. Title pages will be prepared in manuscript.

WAR DIARY
or
INTELLIGENCE SUMMARY.
(Erase heading not required.)

Army Form C. 2118.

Place	Date	Hour	Summary of Events and Information	Remarks and references to Appendices
	18		there was a further objective for the exploiting of success but this was not attempted on account of the Bns on our right being held up. Zero was at 5-20. a. m. and the Bn moved forward A. Coy under Capt Barnes M.C. in front with B Coy under 2Lt Cunningham M.M. supporting the rt half of A Coy and C. Coy under Capt Cook M.C. supporting lt half of A. D Coy under 2Lt Corner was in Bt reserve the morning was very wet and unpleasant but the weather cleared up towards noon. Prisoners soon began to come in but news was difficult to get on account of the heavy Scotch mist which hung thickly in the valleys and thus prevented any visual signalling or direct observation of the attack. The Colonel went forward and got in touch with the Coy Comdrs of C and B Coys and learnt that the Bn was held up by M.Gs on the left and right flanks.	
			C. Coy was ordered to work round the left flank and B Coy together with a portion of the left Coy of the Camerons were to work round the right while A Coy held the M.Gs in front. This worked very well and it was mostly through the splendid leadership	

A6945 Wt. W11422/M1160 350,000 12/16 D. D. & L. Forms/C./2118/14.

Instructions regarding War Diaries and Intelligence Summaries are contained in F. S. Regs., Part II. and the Staff Manual respectively. Title pages will be prepared in manuscript.

WAR DIARY
or
INTELLIGENCE SUMMARY.
(Erase heading not required.)

Army Form C. 2118.

Place	Date	Hour	Summary of Events and Information	Remarks and references to Appendices
	18		of 2 Lt CUNNINGHAM that the position was turned. He took charge of the whole situation on our right and himself dealt with the crew of one enemy gun. All this caused considerable delay and as it was not till about 9.45 a.m. that the position was turned it was discovered that our barrage had gone [illegible] far ahead. However without the aid of the barrage the Bn pushed forward quickly C on the left, A (now commanded by 2 Lt NUGENT HEAD - Capt BARNES having been seriously wounded) in the centre and B on the right. D was still in full strength and in reserve. They fought their way right through the village of BERTHAUCOURT to the eastern outskirts and finally consolidated there throwing out sentry groups in front of the main line of resistance. Throughout the operations enemy shelling was practically negligible and most of the opposition was from M.Gs. Bn Hd Qrs took up a position in a half dug trench just short of the village from which an extensive view could be obtained of the country beyond. We had been told to expect a counter attack from PONTRUET a village 500 yds to E of BERTHAUCOURT	[illegible]

Instructions regarding War Diaries and Intelligence Summaries are contained in F. S. Regs., Part II, and the Staff Manual respectively. Title pages will be prepared in manuscript.

WAR DIARY
or
INTELLIGENCE SUMMARY.
(Erase heading not required.)

Army Form C. 2118.

Place	Date	Hour	Summary of Events and Information	Remarks and references to Appendices
	20		Counter preparation in morning. Bosch artillery active again on position	
			in front left. Bn was relieved by the 6th SHERWOOD FORESTERS [illegible] Div.	
			and marched back to bivouacs in COUPLAINCOURT WOOD.	
			2Lt C. B. D. WAKE joined Bn. 2Lt [illegible] WHITE [illegible]	
	21		Baths for whole Bn. remainder of day spent in cleaning up. [illegible] joined Bn.	
	22		The Bn. cleaned up and remainder of the day rested.	
	23		Preparation for the attack on the morrow. Bn moved off at [illegible]	
			And at different points along the road came under heavy [illegible] fire	
			but suffered no casualties. ~~The enemy [illegible] had [illegible]~~	
			2Lt W. S. GIBBS, 2Lt R. E. POLLETT, [illegible] joined Bn.	
	24		The enemy had [illegible] of the attack [illegible] at 5 a.m. [illegible] they	
			were [illegible] the valleys with gas & shelling the roads. The Royal Sussex	
			were attacking on our left again with the 3rd Bde on our right. The Bn	
			was to clear the valley running through M 20 and 21 and was allotted two	

A6945 Wt. W11422/M1160 350,000 12/16 D. D. & L. Forms/C./2118/14.

Instructions regarding War Diaries and Intelligence Summaries are contained in F. S. Regs., Part II. and the Staff Manual respectively. Title pages will be prepared in manuscript.

WAR DIARY
or
INTELLIGENCE SUMMARY.
(Erase heading not required.)

Army Form C. 2118.

Place	Date	Hour	Summary of Events and Information	Remarks and references to Appendices
	19		We had a counter preparation Barrage put before dawn Lt. CHAMBERS	
			came up. The enemy attempted at 3. P.m to bomb down a communication	
			trench on our extreme right but was stopped by counter bombing.	
			Unfortunately both Lt CHAMBERS and 2Lt CUNNINGHAM were wounded during	
			this minor operation and the latter afterwards died of wounds. 2Lt [illegible]	
			took over B Coy temporarily. A small fighting patrol went out from	
			D Coy that night and proceeded down the main road towards [illegible].	
			They bumped into strongly held enemy post and 2Lt MARLOW who was	
			leading was never seen again. Enemy artillery did a considerable amount	
			of harassing fire round Bn HQrs and left the front line alone. We had	
			a counter preparation barrage that evening so [illegible] that [illegible] Bn	[illegible]
			HQrs moved back about 300 yds to the [illegible] which formed our 2nd	
			objective as they had suffered several casualties in their forward	
			position. 2Lt A. CUNNINGHAM M.M. died of wounds, 2Lt Marlow missing	
			2 O.Rs killed 13 O.R. wounded.	

Instructions regarding War Diaries and Intelligence Summaries are contained in F. S. Regs. Part II. and the Staff Manual respectively. Title pages will be prepared in manuscript.

WAR DIARY
or
INTELLIGENCE SUMMARY.
(Erase heading not required.)

Army Form C. 2118.

Place	Date	Hour	Summary of Events and Information	Remarks and references to Appendices
	24		Tanks which however were never seen after zero with the final objective of LEDUC TRENCH between M.15.d 75.10 to corner of CORNOUILLERS wood. (exclusive) C. Coy was on the left D on the right B. in support and A. in reserve. C. Coy worked along ESSLING alley and had to block the two sunken roads in M.21.a. while 'B.' cleared ARBOUSIERS road.	
			The attack progressed well from the very beginning except on our right where a party of about 200 of the enemy held out till dusk when they were mopped up. Many prisoners and much booty was taken and objectives taken by [illegible] A.M. Towards dusk the Bn moved up to SAMSON and CHEVILLARD Trench and took over part of the front held by R. Sussex at 8. P.m. We had a shrapnel barrage and A and C. Coys. bounded forward to a sunken road on the important ridge running through M.16.B. Bn. Hd Qrs. moved to CHEVILLARD trench. Little opposition was met with.	
			Lt. H.B. DAWSON. Wd. 2Lt S.T. BOLTIN. wd. 2Lt. T.W. COTTON. Wd. 2Lt. E.V. DAVIES. wd. 2Lt. P.J. SMITH wd. 8. O.R. Killed. 1. O.R. missing. 31. O.R. wd.	

A6945 Wt. W11422/M1160 350,000 12/16 D. D. & L. Forms/C./2118/14.

Instructions regarding War Diaries and Intelligence Summaries are contained in F. S. Regs., Part II. and the Staff Manual respectively. Title pages will be prepared in manuscript.

WAR DIARY
or
INTELLIGENCE SUMMARY.
(*Erase heading not required.*)

Army Form C. 2118.

Place	Date	Hour	Summary of Events and Information	Remarks and references to Appendices
	25		The enemy shelled our positions fairly heavily and at 2.P.m attempted a counter attack which was bloodily repulsed by rifle and Lewis gun fire and also by the splendid barrage so promptly by our Divisional Artillery. Enemy shelling remained very heavy throughout the day both on the sunken road and on the trench systems. Many casualties were sustained	
	2		2 Lt. C.B.D WOKE. Killed, Lt. P.D. RAVENSCROFT. Wd. 2nd Lt. A.C. MEE. Hos. Lt. Colonel. E.C. ST. AUBYN. Wd. 13. O.R. Killed. 80. O.R. wd. 2. O.R. missing 85. O.R. joined Bn.	
	26		Early in the morning the enemy recommenced his shelling but stopped at about 7.30. a.m. The last shell bursting just outside Bn Hd Qrs shelter and wounded the Colonel in the head. Major BUTLER. M.C. again came up and took command of Bn. The Coys in front had been having a bad time and arrangement were made for D. Coy to relieve A. Coy while C. Coy while C. Coy came back 300 yds to a hedgerow after being relieved by B. Coy. A Coy and Bn Hd Qrs went back to a sunken road in MUGUET WOOD. and so one was in the trench system which the	

A6945 Wt. W11422/M1160 350,000 12/16 D. D. & L. Forms/C./2118/14.

Instructions regarding War Diaries and Intelligence Summaries are contained in F. S. Regs., Part II, and the Staff Manual respectively. Title pages will be prepared in manuscript.

WAR DIARY
or
INTELLIGENCE SUMMARY.
(*Erase heading not required.*)

Army Form C. 2118.

Place	Date	Hour	Summary of Events and Information	Remarks and references to Appendices
			the enemy were at liberty to shell on.	
	27.		A quiet day altogether both from shelling and Enemy operations. The sunken road in front and the high ground in which it was situated was of the greatest importance as it prevented the enemy of observing the preparations being made for the big attack on the 29th when the canal was forced and it was held at all costs.	
	28		Another quiet day. The Bn was relieved by the 1st GLOSTER REGT. and Bn marched down by Coys to VERMAND and were billeted in bivouacs.	
	29		Bn rested all men had baths cleaned up. Lt P. D. RAVENSCROFT rejoined.	
	30		Bn rested cleaned up. Lt Colonel E. G. ST. AUBYN rejoined. 1. U R fd Bn.	
			Sgd [illegible] Capt for Lt Colonel Comdg 2nd Bn KRRC	

A6945 Wt. W11422/M1160 350,000 12/16 D. D. & L. Forms/C./2118/14.

11

WAR DIARY
or
INTELLIGENCE SUMMARY.
(Erase heading not required.)

Army Form C. 2118.

Instructions regarding War Diaries and Intelligence Summaries are contained in F. S. Regs., Part II. and the Staff Manual respectively. Title pages will be prepared in manuscript.

2nd Bn K. R. R. Corps
for October 1918
Vol 49

Place	Date	Hour	Summary of Events and Information	Remarks and references to Appendices
	1.		The Bn in bivouack at VERMAND. boys training and cleaning up. a very nice day.	
	2		A fine day boys did training and improved bivouacs [illegible]	
	3		Bn received orders to move to PONTRUET marched off at 6.30 a.m reached its destination by 9-30 a.m. as ~~morning~~. We only remained for about an hour when we received orders to march back to CAULINCOURT. We had dinners on the way back arriving at our destination by 2-30. p.m. a fine day. Bn all in bivouacs [illegible]	
	4		Bn rested cleaned up and improved bivouacs a fine day.	
	5		Bn cleaned up and [illegible] carried out.	
	6		Bn had Church parade afterwards Br Gen KELLY addressed the Bn. Afterwards Bn paraded and ~~the~~ Major Gen STRICKLAND addressed the Bn on the good work carried out on the 18th and 24th of Sept. of the splendid performance of the Bn during the Battles of the 18th and 24th of Sept. [illegible] joined Bn.	
			Major H. E. SMITH. D.S.O. joined and took over Command of the Bn	

A6945 Wt. W11422/M1160 350,000 12/16 D. D. & L. Forms/C./2118/14.

Instructions regarding War Diaries and Intelligence Summaries are contained in F. S. Regs., Part II, and the Staff Manual respectively. Title pages will be prepared in manuscript.

WAR DIARY
or
~~INTELLIGENCE SUMMARY.~~
(*Erase heading not required.*)

Army Form C. 2118.

October 1914

Place	Date	Hour	Summary of Events and Information	Remarks and references to Appendices
	6		The Bn was put under orders to move at two hours notice.	
			Colonel St. AUBYN left us to command 3rd Bde.	
	7		Bn still under orders to move at two hours notice in Motor Buses.	
			orders to stand down at 5.45 P.m. Bn resumed the normal	
	do		2Lt. A.F. STEPHEN joined Bn. 20 O.R. joined.	
	8		Bn received orders to move to bivouac N.E. of BELLENGLISE arriving	
			about 1-30 P.m. a very fine day everyone enjoyed the march. [illegible]	
	9		Coys cleaned up and did Coy drill in the morning in the	
			afternoon Coys improved bivouacs.	
	10		Bn did Coy training a fine day. Lieut T. C. STEPHEN joined Bn.	
	11		Coy Training a fine day. Brig. Gen. St. AUBYN visited Bn.	
			one O.R. joined.	
	12		Coys carried on with Coy training. Showery did not interfere with the	
			work	
	13		Coy training ~~[illegible]~~. Showery.	
			Lt. G. C. ARGENTON. 2Lt. J. H. JONES PARRY. 2Lt. J. H. NENTER. joined Bn.	

A6945 Wt. W11422/M1160 350,000 12/16 D. D. & L. Forms/C./2118/14.

Instructions regarding War Diaries and Intelligence Summaries are contained in F. S. Regs., Part II. and the Staff Manual respectively. Title pages will be prepared in manuscript.

WAR DIARY
or
INTELLIGENCE SUMMARY.
(*Erase heading not required.*)

Army Form C. 2118.

October 1918

Place	Date	Hour	Summary of Events and Information	Remarks and references to Appendices
	14		Coys carried on with training A fine day 20 O.R. joined Bn	
	15		Bn had a field day. A fine day.	
	16		Bn received orders to march to BECQUIGNETTE FARM. E. Side of BOHAIN everything went well. on arrival Bn Bivouacked in a wood. C.O. Officers Coy Comdrs. went forward to reconnoitre. Final preparations made for the Battle of to-morrow. A fine wet day.	
	17		Bn moved off at 1.30 a.m. to assembly positions in the BOIS de BUSIGNY. The Bn. in conjunction with the 1st Northamptons on the right and an American Bn. on the left was to follow close behind the attack of 6th DIV. and when they latter had gained their objective was to leap frog through and carry on with the attack. The morning mist and the thick smoke from the smoke barrage made things very difficult and Coys temporarily were disconnected from one another. They however all got in touch again before we were due to pass through the 6th Div. and the Bn pushed forward in section artillery formation A on the left B on the right, D in support and C in Reserve — Bn Hqrs moving in rear of D Coy. When passing through the 6th Div. we found that they were digging in some 800–1000 yds	[illegible]

D. D. & L., London, E.C. (A8004) Wt. W1771/M2731 750,000 5/17 Sch. 52 Forms/C2118/14

Instructions regarding War Diaries and Intelligence Summaries are contained in F. S. Regs., Part II. and the Staff Manual respectively. Title pages will be prepared in manuscript.

WAR DIARY
or
INTELLIGENCE SUMMARY.
(Erase heading not required.)

Army Form C. 2118.

October 1918

Place	Date	Hour	Summary of Events and Information	Remarks and references to Appendices
	17th		short of their objective. Little opposition was met with at first from Enemy infantry + M.G's. but enemy shelling was fairly heavy. Everything went smoothly till the enclosed country N. of LA VALLEE MULÂTRE was reached. It was here that the enemy had a great number of well concealed nests of MG's in hedges etc: which kept up a big volume of fire. Two of these guns were successfully outflanked by one of D Coy platoons but the remainder held up the attack. Consequently B+C Coys were ordered to work right round the left flank. While doing this they had to deal with a sunken road to the left rear which was still strongly held by the enemy as the Americans were a little late. However this was done 30 prisoners being taken and later these two Coys together with one platoon of the Americans successfully rushed 5 Enemy MG's which were firing from a railway embankment. However this did not ease the situation on the right but the 2 Coys (A+D) made another attempt to move forward with the help of 3 whippet tanks but were frustrated once more on account the heavy enfilade fire still directed on them and because the tanks were all quickly knocked out by anti-tank guns. Unable to get on the Bn held on to the ground already won and during the night the 2nd Royal Sussex Regt. pushed through us but could only make little headway as they discovered that both their flanks were in the air	Casualties:– 2/Lt J.M. Hunter " H.C. Grant " W.S. Gibbs } Killed 2/Lt A.J. Stephens Died of Wounds Capt R.P. Maxwell Lt B.V. Cherry 2/Lt T.O.S. White " T. Spatter " F. Tallman } Wounded 1/Lt Graves O Ranks. 16 Killed 6 Died of Wounds 185 Wounded 2 " (Gas) 16 Missing

D. D. & L., London, E.C.
(A8004) Wt. W1771/M2-31 750,000 5/17 Sch. 52 Forms/C2118/14

Instructions regarding War Diaries and Intelligence Summaries are contained in F. S. Regs., Part II. and the Staff Manual respectively. Title pages will be prepared in manuscript.

WAR DIARY

or

~~INTELLIGENCE SUMMARY.~~

(Erase heading not required.)

Army Form C. 2118.

October 1918

Place	Date	Hour	Summary of Events and Information	Remarks and references to Appendices
	18th		Bn rested in same position while 3rd Bde attacked through us.	
	19th		At dusk the Bn marched to positions just W. of MAZINGHIEN and took up positions as reserve Bn to Bde which relieved front held by one American division.	
	20th		Bn remained in present positions. 4 OR wounded 2 OR Killed 1 OR died of wounds.	
	21st		Lt. Col. H.F.E. Smith D.S.O. wounded. Maj. H. Butler M.C. assumed command. Bn relieved 2nd Royal Sussex Regt. on the left sector of Bde front and held a front of about 800 yds facing CATILLON. 6 OR's wounded. 2/Lt J.A. Draphin M.M. wounded.	
	22nd		Capt. E. Rogerson RAMC wounded. Lt H.G. Oxley, Lt. J.M. Sladen, Lt. A.E. Ashrop, 2/Lt. A.A. le M. Simpson, 2/Lt E.W.E.J. Erskine, 2/Lt J. Gourdie, ~~2/Lt J. Gourdie~~, 2/Lt. J.A. Ralph + 1 OR joined Bn. 23rd Capt. E. Forbes RAMC joined as M.O. Bn prepared for minor operation due to come off on morning of 23rd.	
	23rd		At 1.30 AM in the moonlight Bn acting as reserve Bn. to Bde participated in the minor operation the object of which was to push our line 1000 yds further forward. The enemy put down a heavy barrage 1½ mins. after Zero and although in reserve and unused the Bn suffered heavy casualties. 2/Lt. A.C. Dick wounded + died of wounds, CSM Burt killed, 13 OR. Killed, 2 OR's Died of Wounds, 4 OR's gassed and 36 OR's wounded. That evening Bn was relieved by 1st Bn. The Black Watch Regt. and marched down to MOLAIN to good billets.	
	24th		15 OR's Band + Buglers injured by bomb. During afternoon Bn marched to WASSIGNY and took over billets of 1st S.W.B.	
	25th		49 OR's joined.	
	26th		Bn had baths.	
	27th		Bn relieved the 1st Bn L.N.L. in the right Bn sector of the right Bde in the line along the OISE CANAL from the LOCK (2 miles S. of CATILLON) to just S. of the main road running through PETIT CAMBESIS where we had the FRENCH on our right flank. The relief was late because the French had chosen to do a minor operation which brought down the enemy S.O.S. barrage on our front and caused us some casualties. 3 OR killed and 1 wounded. Lt W.J.D. Sneddon [?] + 20 OR's joined Bn.	
	28th		In attempting to dislodge a strong post of the enemy this side of canal which formed a bridge-head we incurred several casualties. 2/Lt. R.E. Pallett [?] wounded and 3 OR's killed 3 OR's wounded.	

D. D. & L., London, E.C. (A8004) Wt. W1771/M2-31 750,000 5/17 Sch. 52 Forms/C2118/14

Instructions regarding War Diaries and Intelligence Summaries are contained in F. S. Regs., Part II. and the Staff Manual respectively. Title pages will be prepared in manuscript.

WAR DIARY
or
INTELLIGENCE SUMMARY.
(Erase heading not required.)

Army Form C. 2118.

October, 1918

Place	Date	Hour	Summary of Events and Information	Remarks and references to Appendices
	29th		Bn held the line of the canal by means of small posts arranged in depth and the patrols sent out at night reported that there were no enemy this side of canal except at the bridge head in PETIT CAMBRESIS. 2 OR's killed and 13 wounded. Enemy harassing fire (especially in the early hours of the morning when it assumed the proportions of a heavy counter preparation) was exceptionally heavy throughout the tour.	
	30th		In the evening Bn was relieved by the 2nd Bn Welsh Regt. and marched to VAUX ANDIGNY into very good billets. 1 OR wounded during relief. Lt Col H.E.E. Smith DSO and 1 OR rejoined Bn.	
	31st		The Commanding Officer reconnoitred for assembly positions for forthcoming operations during morning and the Bn. reorganised and refitted. 2/Lt R.L. Booth and 30 OR joined Bn.	HLGrace Lt

H E E Smith
Lieut. Colonel
Comdg 2nd Bn K R R Corps

D. D. & L., London, E.C.
(A8004) Wt. W1771/M2 31 750,000 5/17 Sch. 52 Forms/C2118/14

Instructions regarding War Diaries and Intelligence Summaries are contained in F. S. Regs., Part II. and the Staff Manual respectively. Title pages will be prepared in manuscript.

WAR DIARY
or
INTELLIGENCE SUMMARY.
(Erase heading not required.)

Army Form C. 2118.

9/K.R.R.C. November 1918

Place	Date	Hour	Summary of Events and Information	Remarks and references to Appendices
VAUX-ANDIGNY	1.		Bn rested and reorganised. The Divisional Concert party aided by the Regimental String Orchestra gave an entertainment every afternoon.	
"	2.		Coy Cmdrs reconnoitred assembly positions for operations of the 4th.	
"	3.		At dusk - about 16.30hrs - Bn marched off to a staging posn. - about half way to assembly positions - where they rested in bivouacs and had a hot meal. It was very dark and rained fairly heavily but luckily stopped at about 2000hrs. At 2300hrs Bn moved forward again and reached assembly positions which were about 200yds W of SAMBRE CANAL and opposite the LOCK East of the village of REJET DE BEAUVIEUE at about 02.45hrs. 14 O.R's joined Bn prior to marching off.	
	4.		At Zero (05.45 hrs) on the 4th the 1st DIV. was to force the passage of the OISE CANAL between PETIT CAMBRÉSIS and CATILLON. The 2nd Bde were attacking on the right with the 2/60th on the right and the 2nd Royal Sussex Regt. on the left. The Bn. less one Coy was to cross the Canal after the Sussex by means of the LOCK in S.1d. and a subsidiary crossing was to be attempted by 'A' Coy 100yds South of Lock. At Zero + 6 the Bn. moved forward but did not get across according to programme. There was considerable delay in getting the bridges across and the confusion great on account of the smoke. However the Bn eventually got across after sustaining a few casualties at the LOCK and advanced to the 1st objective without any appreciable resistance from the enemy. The barrage was protective for 1½hrs after capture of 1st objective which was the Road from S3c52 to junction of road and CANAL. The right Coy was relieved by the 1st Northamptons and the remaining three Coys advanced to the 2nd objective echeloned in depth and formed a right defensive flank for the 2nd Royal Sussex Regt. The enemy surrendered freely and put up a poor fight. Before dusk we advanced our line a little further and side slipped a bit to the right to gain touch with the 1st Northamptons. Lt. H.G. Oxley & 2Lt Burroughes Killed, 2Lt W.E. Booth Wounded. There were no counter attacks and enemy shelling except in the initial stages of the attack was practically negligible. Bn. was not relieved but were eventually squeezed out and at 1600hrs marched back to billets at WASSIGNY.	Ref. Map. OISE CANAL 1/40000 10 OR's Killed 3 " Missing 59 " Wounded
	5.			

P.T.O.

D. D. & L., London, E.C. (A8004) Wt. W1771/M2731 750,000 5/17 Sch. 52 Forms/C2118/14

Instructions regarding War Diaries and Intelligence Summaries are contained in F. S. Regs., Part II. and the Staff Manual respectively. Title pages will be prepared in manuscript.

WAR DIARY
or
INTELLIGENCE SUMMARY.
(Erase heading not required.)

Army Form C. 2118.

November 1918.

Place	Date	Hour	Summary of Events and Information	Remarks and references to Appendices
	6.		Bn marched in the pouring rain to good billets in FRESNOY-LE-GRAND where the whole DIV. came out to rest.	
FRESNOY LE GRAND	7.		Bn bathed and rested. There was a Cinema and the Div. Concert Party to occupy the evenings.	
	8.		Bn. refitted and cleaned up - everybody paying special attention to smartness of turnout. A couple of hours per day was spent on parade. C.O inspected Bn	
"	9.			
	10.			
"	11.		The Armistice Signed. Commanding Officer addressed the Bn.	
"	12.		2/Lt J. Goundie, Lt C.H. Freshwater, Lt A. Leslie, 2/Lt. A.V. Standen, 2/Lt. H. Beaumont, Lt. D.H. Buckland, 2/Lt. J.A. Drapkin M.M., and 135 O.R's joined Bn.	
	13.		The Bn. moved to FAVRIL by bus. Transport was brigaded and moved separately.	
FAVRIL	14.		The whole Bn. was inspected by Comdg. Officer.	
DOMPIERRE	15		Bn marched to DOMPIERRE. Route through GRAND FAYT - MARBAIX.	
SARS-POTERIES	16.		Bn marched to SARS-POTERIES. Route - ST AUBIN - DOURLERS - LA SAVATE. Capt. H.K. Ward	RAMC M.O. rejoined a Bn.
"	17.		Sunday - Church Parade for all.	
THIRIMONT	18.		Bn. marched to THIRIMONT. Route - SOLRÉ-LE-CHATEAU - GRANDRIEU - BEAUMONT.	
WALCOURT	19		Bn marched to WALCOURT. Route - MARZELLE - STRÉE - CLEREMONT - MERTENNE -	
"	20		Rested in WALCOURT. Did short route marches in the morning and a little training under company arrangements. Inhabitants were most hospitable.	A.L. Grain? Lt
"	21			
"	22			
MORIALMÉ	23		Bn Marched to MORIALMÉ - Route CHASTRES - FRAIRE: Bn in very good billets.	
FALAEN	24		Bn marched to FALAEN - Route. FLORENNES - CORENNE - FLAVION.	
"	25		Bn rested and held equipment inspections.	
"	26		From 0900 hrs till 1300 hrs. Bn did Platoon - Company + Bn Drill with a little Ceremonial Drill.	
"	27		Lt. H. d'Argenton rejoined Bn. from hospital.	
"	28		Bathed most of Bn. in improvised baths.	
"	29			
"	30		Played the 2nd Field Ambulance at Association. Won 3-1.	

H. S. E. Smith
Lieut. Colonel
Comdg 2nd Battn
Kings Royal Rifles

D. D. & L., London, E.C. (A8004) Wt. W1771/M2-31 750,000 5/17 Sch. 52 Forms/C2118/14

Instructions regarding War Diaries and Intelligence Summaries are contained in F. S. Regs., Part II. and the Staff Manual respectively. Title pages will be prepared in manuscript.

WAR DIARY
or
INTELLIGENCE SUMMARY.
(Erase heading not required.)

2 NRR

Army Form C. 2118.

December 1918.

Vol 57

Place	Date	Hour	Summary of Events and Information	Remarks and references to Appendices
CHESTRUVIN	1.		Bn marched to CHESTRUVIN area. Companies were rather scattered but had quite good billets. A short march – route through WEILLEN.	
FOY N'DAME	2.		Bn marched to FOY N'DAME. Route DINANT – BOISSELLES. We marched past DIV. General on Bridge over MEUSE and then again past the Corps Commander Lt. Gen. BRAITHWAITE a couple of miles further on. Billets were very poor – both for horses and men – as the village is very small (only 200 inhabitants).	
CIERGNON	3.		Bn marched to CIERGNON. Route [illegible]CELLES:- A small village with very good stables for horses but not too wonderful men's billets.	
"	4.		Rained the whole day. Coys held inspections.	
"	5.		Coys at disposal of Coy Cmdrs from 0900 – 1200 hrs.	
"	6 } 7 }		Battalion drill on a fine Parade Ground by the side of the river.	
"	8 }			
HAVERSIN	9		Bn marched to HAVERSIN. Route BOIS des ANGES — BOIS de MONT GAUTHIER. Good billets. Headquarters lived as guests of the Baron in the Château.	
MELREUX	10		Bn marched to MELREUX. Route NETTINE – HEURE – NOISEUX — DEVLIN. A long march, about 16 miles, but roads were good and we were going down hill all the way.	
EREZEE	11		Bn marched to EREZEE. Route NY – SOY. A very hilly march. Billets fair.	
	12 } 13 }		Bn rested and cleaned up. It rained hard both days.	
ODEIGNE	14		Bn marched to ODEIGNE. Route GRANDMENIL — MANHAY. It rained at the start, but after a long and steep climb, we came out above the clouds. Fine scenery. Billets very inadequate and dirty.	
OTTRE	15		Bn marched to OTTRE. Route BELLE HAIE – REGNE. Two Coys and H.Q. were in OTTRE; remaining Coys were in JOUBIEVAL, a mile further on. Billets good.	

(A8004) D. D. & L., London, E.C. Wt. W1771/M2·31 750,000 5/17 Sch. 52 Forms/C2118/14

Instructions regarding War Diaries and Intelligence Summaries are contained in F. S. Regs., Part II. and the Staff Manual respectively. Title pages will be prepared in manuscript.

WAR DIARY
or
INTELLIGENCE SUMMARY.
(Erase heading not required.)

Army Form C. 2118.

Place	Date	Hour	Summary of Events and Information December 1918.	Remarks and references to Appendices
COURTIL	16		Bn marched to COURTIL. Route SALMCHATEAU – BOVIGNY. A short march. Billets fair.	
KROMBACH	17		Bn marched to KROMBACH crossing the frontier into GERMANY on the way. At the frontier we marched past the Div: General. Bad roads.	
MANDERFELD	18		Bn marched to MANDERFELD. Route NEUNDORF — ST VITH. H.Q. and 2 Coys in MANDERFELD and 2 Coys in BERTHERATH 2½ miles further on. This was the longest march of the whole journey at least 20 miles for the two further Coys. Beautiful country.	
DAHLEM.	19		Bn marched to DAHLEM. Route KRONENBURG. Some snow during the march. Billets fair.	
	20		Some of the Bn had baths.	
BLANKENHEIM	21		Bn marched to BLANKENHEIM. a very pretty village. Billets very good for all ranks.	
MUNSTEREIFEL	22		Bn marched to MUNSTEREIFEL. Route TONDORF — EICHERSHEID. A splendid march over the hills with views over RHINE valley. Billets excellent.	
PALMERSHEIM	23		Bn marched to PALMERSHEIM. Route KIRSPENICH – FLAMERSHEIM.	
LENGSDORF	24		Bn marched to LENGSDORF. Route MIEL – BUSCHOVEN – DUISDORF. This was, as we thought, our final destination. Accomodation very fair.	
	25		Men rested and cleaned up. Voluntary church parade.	
	26		Resting and settling down.	
	27		Officers Christmas Dinner.	
	28		Mens' Christmas Dinner at midday. C.O. went round dinners. Sergeants dinner in evening.	

D. D. & L., London, E.C.
(A8004) Wt. W1771/M2731 750,000 5/17 Sch. 52 Forms/C2118/14

Army Form C. 2118.

Instructions regarding War Diaries and Intelligence Summaries are contained in F. S. Regs., Part II. and the Staff Manual respectively. Title pages will be prepared in manuscript.

WAR DIARY
or
INTELLIGENCE SUMMARY.

(Erase heading not required.)

December 1918.

Place	Date	Hour	Summary of Events and Information	Remarks and references to Appendices
LENGSDORF	29		Sports during the morning, held indoors on account of rain. Five officers and 130 O.R. joined Bn from Reception Camp.	
ALFTER	30		Bn marched to ALFTER, about 3 miles. It had been found that LENGSDORF was outside the billeting area. ALFTER a considerable improvement on LENGSDORF. It is a bigger and cleaner village. Each Coy is self-contained in one big hall apiece. Officers billets scattered.	
"	31.		Demobilization and Education Schemes rivalling each other in prolixity and intricacy.	

H. J. E. Smith
Lieut-Colonel
Comdg 2nd Battn
The King's Royal Rifle Corps

D. D. & L., London, E.C.
(A8004) Wt. W1771/M2 31 750,000 5/17 Sch. 52 Forms/C2118/14

2 KRRC

Army Form C. 2118.

Instructions regarding War Diaries and Intelligence Summaries are contained in F. S. Regs., Part II. and the Staff Manual respectively. Title pages will be prepared in manuscript.

WAR DIARY
or
INTELLIGENCE SUMMARY.
(Erase heading not required.)

January 1919.

Vol 52

Place	Date	Hour	Summary of Events and Information	Remarks and references to Appendices
ALFTER.	2		Battalion is now comfortably settled down. The daily scheme of parades is as follows 8.45 – 9.45. Education A Grant (Compulsory). 10.00 – 12.00 P.T. Close Order + Saluting Drill. Musketry. 14.00 – 16.00 Recreational Training. Each Company spends one whole morning a week 8.45–12.45 on Education (Enlightenment) when Lectures are given and debates on subjects of general interest are held. In the evenings there are voluntary classes in special subjects. Four football grounds have been found and a Platoon League Competition (Soccer) is in full swing.	
	1		25 O.R.'s left for Demobilization.	
	4		4 O.R's left for Demobilization. 2Lt J.A. DRAPKIN. M.M. went with the party as Conducting Officer	

D. D. & L., London, E.C.
(A8004) Wt. W1771/M2031 750,000 5/17 Sch. 52 Forms/C2118/14

Army Form C. 2118.

Instructions regarding War Diaries and Intelligence Summaries are contained in F. S. Regs., Part II. and the Staff Manual respectively. Title pages will be prepared in manuscript.

WAR DIARY
or
INTELLIGENCE SUMMARY.
(Erase heading not required.)

Place	Date	Hour	Summary of Events and Information	Remarks and references to Appendices
ALFTER.	6		2Lt R.E. PALLETT, T.O.S. WHITE, W.E. BOOTH, and 139 O.R.'s joined from HAVRE.	
	7		15. O.R's left for Demobilization	
	8		Lt. C.T. MASON and 10. O.R's joined.	
	12		Lt J.A. RALPH, 2Lt D.C. FINCHAM and 43. O.R's left for Demobilization 9. O.R's joined.	
	14.		4. O.R's joined	
	16.		Capt D.H. BUCKLAND rejoined the Battalion from 2nd Bde H.Q. where he had been acting Brigade Major.	
	17.		An officers Pierrot Troupe, which had been practising assiduously for the last 3 weeks, ~~gave~~ ~~a~~ performance to the Battalion, which was thoroughly appreciated. The Brigadier General was present at the show and he invited the party to give performances to the other two Battalions in the Brigade. These took place early the next week and were apparently much enjoyed by the audiences and the performers.	

D. D. & L., London, E.C.
(A8004) Wt. W1771/M2-31 750,000 5/17 Sch. 52 Forms/C2118/14

Instructions regarding War Diaries and Intelligence Summaries are contained in F. S. Regs., Part II. and the Staff Manual respectively. Title pages will be prepared in manuscript.

WAR DIARY
or
INTELLIGENCE SUMMARY.
(*Erase heading not required.*)

Army Form C. 2118.

January 1919.

Place	Date	Hour	Summary of Events and Information	Remarks and references to Appendices
ALFTER.	18		Capt D.H. BUCKLAND and 33 O.R. left for Demobilization.	
			2Lt A.E.P. ROSE (Rifle Brigade attd 2nd K R R Corps) and 49. O.R.s joined Battalion from Divnl Reception Camp.	
	21.		53. O.R.'s left for Demobilization.	
	26		2Lt's J.H. JONES PARRY and H.H. ROBINSON rejoined from drafts conducting duties.	
	29.		2. O.R. left for Demobilization.	
	31.		2Lt G.H. SKINNER left to go on a one months course at Oxford under Army Education Scheme.	

H. F. Smith
Lieut Col.
Comdg 2nd Bn K.R.R. Corps

D. D. & L., London, E.C.
(A8004) Wt. W1771/M2 31 750,000 5/17 Sch. 52 Forms/C2118/14

Vol 53

Army Form C. 2118.

WAR DIARY
or
~~INTELLIGENCE~~ SUMMARY.
(Erase heading not required.)

Instructions regarding War Diaries and Intelligence Summaries are contained in F. S. Regs., Part II. and the Staff Manual respectively. Title pages will be prepared in manuscript.

2nd Bn K R R Corps — February 1919

Place	Date	Hour	Summary of Events and Information	Remarks and references to Appendices
ALFTER.			At the beginning of the month we had a good spell of cold frosty weather with occasional snowfalls. A small pond was found quite close at hand & all officers who could skate spent very pleasant afternoons there. Our ice-hockey team arranged three or four matches and came through undefeated. Football was hardly interrupted at all, & though the ground was frozen hard and there were 4 inches of snow lying on it, games were played quite cheerfully. The Battalion football team suffered very considerably from the effects of Demobilization and in the Brigade League we lost 2 matches and only succeeded in making the third a draw. In the Company-teams knockout competition we did better. C. and D Coys met each other in the semifinals. After an even game C Coy won by the odd goal & had to meet the 2nd Field Ambulance in the Final. Here they came against a considerably stronger side & lost 3-1.	

D. D. & L., London, E.C. (A8004) Wt. W1771/M2131 750,000 5/17 Sch. 52 Forms/C2118/14

Army Form C. 2118.

Instructions regarding War Diaries and Intelligence Summaries are contained in F. S. Regs., Part II. and the Staff Manual respectively. Title pages will be prepared in manuscript.

WAR DIARY
or
INTELLIGENCE SUMMARY.

(Erase heading not required.)

Place	Date	Hour	Summary of Events and Information	Remarks and references to Appendices
ALFTER			In the tug-of-war our lightweight team won two of its pulls and in the cross country run we supplied two men in the Brigade team, who came in 6th and 16th in the Divisional race. In the Brigade boxing we won the Bantam-weights & we supplied the runners up for the Welter & Middle-weights.	
			The remainder of the month's events is a catalogue of men leaving ~~the~~ Bn for Demobilization and of Officers going to hospital with influenza.	
	5th		2. O.R's to Demob. Camp.	
	9th		13. O.R's to Demob. Camp	
	11th		Lt C. H Freshwater & 2Lt J. H. Jones Parry to Hospital	
			Lt W. J. D. Sneddon. M.C and 4. O.R's to Demob Camp.	
	15th		15 O.R's to Demob. Camp with Lieut T. C. Stephen as draft conducting Officer.	
	17		Lieut C Savin D.C.M to hospital. Capt A. J. Fletcher M.C. rejoined.	

D. D. & L., London, E.C.
(A8004) Wt. W1771/M2731 750,000 5/17 Sch. 52 Forms/C2118/14

Army Form C. 2118.

2nd Batt R K R C

March 1919

Vol 54

Instructions regarding War Diaries and Intelligence Summaries are contained in F. S. Regs., Part II. and the Staff Manual respectively. Title pages will be prepared in manuscript.

WAR DIARY
or
~~INTELLIGENCE SUMMARY.~~
(Erase heading not required.)

Place	Date	Hour	Summary of Events and Information	Remarks and references to Appendices
ALFTER.	1		Major B.C. JUDD. O.B.E and 11 O.R. to Demobilization Camp.	
	3		Lt E.A. WARNER rejoined Battalion.	
	17		13. O.R. to Demobilization Camp	
	19		2 O.R to Demobilization Camp	
	20		Bandmaster W.J. Dunn M.C. and a band, 51 strong, joined the Battalion.	
			Accepting the challenge of 1st Divn H.Q. an Officers Hockey Team went over to RHEINBACH and after a good game won by 14 goals to 4.	
	22		3 O.R to Demobilization Camp	
			The officers' Pierrot Troupe went over to the 6th Bde and gave a performance to the 17th Royal Fusiliers.	
	25		The Battalion moved to DRANSDORF about 1½ miles near BONN.	

D. D. & L., London, E.C.
(A8004) Wt. W1771/M2 31 750,000 5/17 Sch. 52 Forms/C2118/14

Army Form C. 2118.

Instructions regarding War Diaries and Intelligence Summaries are contained in F. S. Regs., Part II. and the Staff Manual respectively. Title pages will be prepared in manuscript.

WAR DIARY
or
INTELLIGENCE SUMMARY.
(Erase heading not required.)

Place	Date	Hour	Summary of Events and Information	Remarks and references to Appendices
DRANSDORF	26		53rd Bn Welch Regt arrived and took over our billets at ALFTER.	[illegible] Lt.
			2 O.R. to Demobilization Camp.	
	28th		9. O.R. to Demobilization Camp.	
	29th		8 O.R. to Demobilization Camp.	
	31st		Battalion moved to WITTERSCHLICK. about 5 miles S.W. of BONN. taking over from 52nd S.W.B.	
			Lt J. GOURDIE to Demobilization Camp.	

H. J. E. Smith Lieut Col
The Kings Royal Rifle Corps
Comdg 2nd Batn.

D. D. & L., London, E.C.
(A8004) Wt. W1771/M2 31 750,000 5/17 Sch. 52 Forms/C2118/14

1

Instructions regarding War Diaries and Intelligence Summaries are contained in F. S. Regs., Part II. and the Staff Manual respectively. Title pages will be prepared in manuscript.

WAR DIARY or ~~INTELLIGENCE SUMMARY.~~

(Erase heading not required.)

Army Form C. 2118.

2ND BATTN THE. KINGS ROYAL RIFLE CORPS

APRIL 1919 VOLUME NO. NIL

9848

Place	Date	Hour	Summary of Events and Information	Remarks and references to Appendices
WITTERSCHLICK	2nd		13 Officers and 336 ORanks (retainable for service with Army of occupation) transferred to 9th Bn London Regt (Q.V.R.)	
			Lt. J. C Stephen and 10. ORanks to Demobilization Camp.	
	3rd.		20. ORanks to Demobilization Camp	
	4th.		3 ORanks to Demobilization Camp	
	5th.		8. ORanks to Demobilization Camp	
	6th.		Lt. J. A Warner. Capt P. D Ravenscroft MC. Lt. C. S. Mason 2/Lt J. G Young Capt. A Cook MC Lt. A Blackett MC and 31 ORanks to Demobilization Camp.	
	10th.		Cadre and Band (4 officers and 101. ORanks). left for JOLIMETZ FRANCE to take over transport etc of 4th Bn the KRRif C	
JOLIMETZ	11th		Arrive Jolimetz	
	21st.		Band visited Battlefields where Battalion fought in october and november 1918	
			H J E Smith Lieut Col Comdg 2nd KRR Corps	

D. D. & L., London, E.C. (A8004) Wt. W1771/M2 31 750,000 5/17 Sch. 52 Forms/C2118/14

Instructions regarding War Diaries and Intelligence Summaries are contained in F. S. Regs., Part II. and the Staff Manual respectively. Title pages will be prepared in manuscript.

WAR DIARY
or
INTELLIGENCE SUMMARY.
(Erase heading not required.)

Army Form C. 2118.

2ND BN. The KING'S ROYAL RIFLE CORPS

MAY 1919

Volume No. 56

Place	Date	Hour	Summary of Events and Information	Remarks and references to Appendices
JOLIMETZ			During the month, eight Other ranks were demobilized. On the 7th the Division held the eliminating contests for the Corps Sports, at which a large number competed. The Corps Sports were held on the 10th inst. and about 20 from the Battalion went over by Lorry. During the month, all men of the cadre were employed. The Band practised in the mornings and the afternoons they bathed or played football. H. S. E. Smith Lieut Colonel The Kings Royal Rifle Corps Comdg 2nd Battn 31.5.19.	

D. D. & L., London, E.C.
(A8004) Wt. W1771/M2731 750,000 5/17 Sch. 52 Forms/C2118/14

CENTRAL REGISTRY
HEADQUARTERS
WIMEREUX.
26 JUL 1919
No.

The Deputy Adjutant General.

British Troops in France & Flanders.

The attached original copy of the Battalion War Diary, covering period from 1st to 10th June 1919, is forwarded for favour of disposal, please.

H Wake

Lieut-Colonel

Winchester.
23rd July 1919.

The King's Royal Rifle Corps......
Commanding 2nd Battalion......

2 K.R.R.C.
95/27
Ceases
1.6.19

33

Instructions regarding War Diaries and Intelligence Summaries are contained in F. S. Regs., Part II. and the Staff Manual respectively. Title pages will be prepared in manuscript.

WAR DIARY
or
INTELLIGENCE SUMMARY.
(Erase heading not required.)

Army Form C. 2118.

Place	Date	Hour	Summary of Events and Information	Remarks and references to Appendices
			On ~~1st~~ June 1st 1919. The cadre and band entrained at LE QUESNOY and arrived at HAVRE on the afternoon of June 2nd and marched to the Base Camp at HARSFLEURS. June 3rd was spent in bathing and being reclothed. On June 4th we embarked for SOUTHAMPTON where we arrived ~~on~~ at 7.30 am June 5th. The night of June 5th was spent at the REST CAMP and on June the 6th the cadre and band arrived at the Rifle Depot WINCHESTER. On MONDAY June 9th LIEUT.GENERAL Sir E. Hutton K.C.B. K.C.M.G. Colonel Commandant addressed the 2nd Bn and welcomed them home. On June 10th all ranks dispersed for leave or demobilization.	
			July 16th 1919. H. G. E. Smith Lieut Col. 2nd K.R.R Corps	

D. D. & L., London, E.C. (A10266) Wt W5300/P713 750,000 2/18 Sch. 52 Forms/C2118/16.

BEF

1 DIVISION

2 BRIGADE

51 WELSH R.

1919 MAR to 1919 JULY

MARCH

Army Form C. 2118.

WAR DIARY
or
INTELLIGENCE SUMMARY.
(*Erase heading not required.*)

Instructions regarding War Diaries and Intelligence Summaries are contained in F. S. Regs., Part II, and the Staff Manual respectively. Title pages will be prepared in manuscript.

BATTN. WELCH REGIMENT No. 0R15 -5 APR 1919

Place	Date	Hour	Summary of Events and Information	Remarks and references to Appendices
MÜNSTEREIFEL	17th	0700	Bn arrived at MUNSTEREIFEL RHINELAND by train from DUNKIRK	
"	"	1000	Proceeded to billets.	
"	"	1100	Major Gen STRICKLAND Cmdg WESTERN DIV & Brig Gen ST AUBYN Cmdg 3rd Bgde visit the C.O. Weather – bad	MHL
"	18th	0900	Re-arrangement of billets	
"	"	1000	Bn Route March	
"	"	1500	Brig Gen ST AUBYN – Staff Captain – C.O. 2nd WELSH & Civil Staff Captain visit Bn	
"	"	–	Supplies of food – bad. Weather – fine.	MHL
"	19th	0900	Bn Route March and Capt. W.T. GREENWOOD. D.S.O. M.C.	
"	"	1500	Bgde Major & Staff Capt arrive for conference	
"	"	–	Mens food again bad. Weather – good	MHL
"	20th	0900	Bn Parade	
		1000	Coy Parades – men wash in stream near recreation fields	
		–	Mens food greatly improved	
		–	Capt. POYSER. R.A.M.C. returned to ENGLAND	
		–	Lt. M.R. RICHARDS R.A.M.C. reported for duty. Weather good.	MHL

(A9475) Wt W2358/P360 600,000 12/17 D. D. & L. Sch. 52a. Forms/C2118/15.

Army Form C. 2118.

Instructions regarding War Diaries and Intelligence Summaries are contained in F. S. Regs., Part II. and the Staff Manual respectively. Title pages will be prepared in manuscript.

WAR DIARY
or
INTELLIGENCE SUMMARY.
(Erase heading not required.)

BATTN. WELCH REGIMENT No. OR15 -5 APR 1919 51st

Place	Date	Hour	Summary of Events and Information	Remarks and references to Appendices
MÜNSTEREIFEL	21st	0900 1400	Coy Parades	
"	"	1430	C.O. Adjt & Lt CORY rode over to FLAMERSHEIM to see 2nd WELSH	
"	"	–	2 O.R. proceed to 3rd Bgde H.Q as runners. Weather. Fine	[initials]
"	22nd	0900	Coy Kit inspections & interior economy	
"	"	1100	Brig Gen CUBITT assumes command of 3rd Bgde & visits C.O.	
	"	1400	Football Matches inter company. Weather fine	[initials]
"	"	1600	Canteen Stores arrive	
"	23rd	1000	C of E Parade Service	
"	"	1400	Football Matches inter company Weather fair	[initials]
"	24th	0900	Route March abandoned on account of heavy snow – Coy Parades Weather bad.	[initials]
"	25	1000	Bn moved by Route March from MUNSTEREIFEL to FLAMERSHEIM, inspected	
		"	en route by Gen BRAITHWAITE Cmdg IXth CORPS	
		–	Brig Gen CUBITT saw C.O during afternoon	
FLAMERSHEIM		1600	16 Mules arrive & are taken on strength	
"		1600	Men proceed into billets in FLAMERSHEIM	
		–	2/Lt L P L LLOYD admitted to Hospital Weather – fair	[initials]

Instructions regarding War Diaries and Intelligence Summaries are contained in F. S. Regs., Part II, and the Staff Manual respectively. Title pages will be prepared in manuscript.

WAR DIARY
or
INTELLIGENCE SUMMARY.
(Erase heading not required.)

Army Form C. 2118.

BATTN. WELCH REGIMENT No. OR15. –5 APR 1919 61st

Place	Date	Hour	Summary of Events and Information	Remarks and references to Appendices
FLAMERSHEIM	26	0700	Capt E. ROBINSON, Lt TUDOR & 14 O R proceed on leave to COLOGNE.	
"	"	0900	A & B Coys bathe & change underclothes at RHEINBACH.	
"	"	–	7 Z.D animals proceed to ESSIB for destruction	
–	–	–	Lt T.L ~~[illegible]~~ JONES appointed L.G. Officer 2/Lt F M CAREFULL appointed	
–	–	"	Mining Officer	
–	–	"	2 O R per Platoon instructed in loading Pack Mules ammunition	
–	–	"	1st Mail received since leaving ENGLAND Weather bad.	MHt
–	27	0900	Parades under Coy arrangements	
–	–	1245	Dental Inspection	
–	–	1400	Football Match 2nd WELSH v 51st WELSH	
–	–	–	17 Mules arrived from EUSKIRCHEN	
–	–	–	Major M H MERRY 13th WELSH reported for Duty Weather bad.	MHt
"	28	0700	Lt WARDWALKER proceeds to MONTJOIE on scouting Course	
"	"	1000	20 Offs 400 O.R. proceed to KÖLN to see final of Football Cup Arrive back	
–	"	–	22.50. Hot food for men.	
–	"	–	1 Pack pony proceeds to 2 MVS. ESSIG & is struck off strength. Weather bad	MHt

Instructions regarding War Diaries and Intelligence Summaries are contained in F. S. Regs., Part II, and the Staff Manual respectively. Title pages will be prepared in manuscript.

WAR DIARY
or
INTELLIGENCE SUMMARY.
(*Erase heading not required.*)

BATTN. WELCH REGIMENT No. OR15 -5 APR 1919 51st

Army Form C. 2118.

Place	Date	Hour	Summary of Events and Information	Remarks and references to Appendices
FLAMERSHEIM	29th	0900	Parades under Cy arrangements.	
	-	1020	Bgde cancels baths for C & D Cy	Weather Bad RHL
	30th	09.30	C of E Parade	
	-	1030	Conference at Bg H.Q of C.O's	
		1200	Lecture to A & B Cy on Historical records of WELSH Rgt	
		1500	" 'C & D Cys " " "	
		1930	Prepare for move to MECKENHEIM.	Weather Bad RHL
	31st	0930	Move from FLAMERSHEIM	
		1200	Inspected in RHEINBACH by G.O.C WESTERN DIV	
		1330	Dinners en route	
MECKENHEIM		1500	Arrive in MECKENHEIM.	
		1600	Lt WARD WALKER returns as Course is cancelled	
		1730	All Coys settled in	Weather good. RHL

Instructions regarding War Diaries and Intelligence Summaries are contained in F. S. Regs., Part II, and the Staff Manual respectively. Title pages will be prepared in manuscript.

WAR DIARY of 51st Welsh Regt. or INTELLIGENCE SUMMARY.

(Erase heading not required.)

April 1919

Army Form C. 2118.

Place	Date	Hour	Summary of Events and Information	Remarks and references to Appendices
MECKENHEIM	1	0900	D Coy bathed at RHEINBACH.	
		1000	All web equipment scrubbed steel helmets painted.	
		1400	Coys rearrange billets. Weather good	KHL
	2	0900	C Coy & casuals of A B & C Coys bathed at RHEINBACH	
		1000	1 Off 34 OR 14 horses of 76 Field Coy RE attached for rations & accomodation	
		1400	2/Lt L.C. GARBETT proceeds on P T Course COLOGNE 2/4.19 - 17/4/19.	
		1500	8 OR proceed to Div H.Q for Div Employ	
		—	2 — — Bgde H.Q — Bgde —	
		1530	Adjt sees Staff Capt at Bgde. Weather good	KHL
	3	0700	2 Offs & 14 OR proceed to COLOGNE on leave	
		0900	C.O inspects Coys in fighting order	
		1400	Bn Parade in fighting order	
		—	4 Military Police attached. Weather good	KHL
	4	1000	G.O.C 2nd Bgde inspects Battn in fighting order	
		1200	G.O.C inspects Billets, Mess Rooms Cook Houses etc & lunches in mess.	
		1415	Battn Parade in full marching order. Weather good	KHL

(A9175) Wt W2358/P360 600,000 12/17 D. D. & L. Sch. 52a. Forms/C2118/15.

WAR DIARY
or
INTELLIGENCE SUMMARY.
(Erase heading not required.)

Army Form C. 2118.

Instructions regarding War Diaries and Intelligence Summaries are contained in F. S. Regs., Part II. and the Staff Manual respectively. Title pages will be prepared in manuscript.

Place	Date	Hour	Summary of Events and Information	Remarks and references to Appendices
MECKENHEIM	5	1030.	Inspection by G.O.C IX Corps	
		1430	Football Match 104 Brigade R.F.A v 51st Welch 1-4	
		–	G.S.O.1 Division visits C.O.	
		–	20 Other ranks detached Weather bad	C.H.
	6	1030	Church Parade	
		–	Rugger Match A v D Soccer B v C	
			2 L.D. horses to 2nd M.V.S Weather good	
			85794 Pte ANDERSON V.W. attached to 2nd Brigade for all purposes from 6-4-19	C.H.
	7	0900	Parade under Company arrangements	
		1100	G.S.O.1 inspected billets etc	
		1230	C.O's Orderley Room	
		1400-1600	Organised Games Weather good	C.H.
	8	0715	Short run for all Companies	
		0930	Route March, Fighting order	
		1400	Organised games	
		–	2 O.R's to No 2 Field Ambulance for 14 days instruction Weather fair	C.H.

Instructions regarding War Diaries and Intelligence Summaries are contained in F. S. Regs., Part II. and the Staff Manual respectively. Title pages will be prepared in manuscript.

WAR DIARY
or
INTELLIGENCE SUMMARY.
(Erase heading not required.)

Army Form C. 2118.

Place	Date	Hour	Summary of Events and Information	Remarks and references to Appendices
MECKENHEIM	9	0930	Battalion Route march, strong as possible	
		0900	85995 Sergt Gordon 86232 Pte Morgan, to 2nd Army Concentration Camp, Cologne	
		-	Officers servants to attend Educational Training with their Coys.	
		13.30	Capt E.A.K. Robinson, Lieuts Davis, Tudor, & Jones proceed to Level Crossing S.E	
			of IMPEKOVEN Railway Station to witness Lewis Gun Demonstrations	
		1400	Organised games. Weather good.	E.J.H.
	10	0900	Parade under Company arrangements	
		1000-1130	A. Coy bathed at RHEINBACH	
			2/Lt A. Quaintrill & 85971 L/Cpl Urmston to Agricultural College	
		1330	Capt R.U. Thomas Lts C.C. Cory, T.L. Jones & H.C. Laycock to level crossing S.E of	
			IMPEKOVEN Station to witness Lewis Gun, demonstration.	
			Lieut R.W. Thomas appointed Acting Capt.	
		1400	Organised games Weather good	E.J.H.
	11	0900	Battalion parade, Coy training	
			3 L.D. horses proceeded to Deutz collecting Camp. Cologne	
			6. O.R. by 094 train to Rosberg for pioneer course.	

(A9175) Wt W2358/P360 600,000 12/17 D. D. & L. Sch. 52a. Forms/C2118/15.

Instructions regarding War Diaries and Intelligence Summaries are contained in F. S. Regs., Part II. and the Staff Manual respectively. Title pages will be prepared in manuscript.

WAR DIARY
or
INTELLIGENCE SUMMARY.
(Erase heading not required.)

Army Form C. 2118.

Place	Date	Hour	Summary of Events and Information	Remarks and references to Appendices
MECKENHEIM.	11.	–	10. O.R. attached to 2nd Light Trench Mortar Battery.	
		1400	Football. Weather Good.	O.S.H.
	12.	09.30	B.C.D. Coys bathe at Reichbach various times	
		1400	Football. Batt v 1st M.G. Corps Weather Good.	O.S.H.
	13	1745	Voluntary Church Service.	
			2 O.R. attached to No. 3. Coy Div: Train for Lorry driving. Weather bad.	O.S.H.
	14	0900	Coy training.	
		1000	Inspection of training by Brigadier General	
		0940	1 Sergt to Commandant Gas School, Glendbach	
		1400	Football. Weather good.	O.S.H.
	15.	–	Audit Board for P.R.I. Officers & Sergts Mess.	
		0930	Companies go through gas	
		0940	3 Officers & 17 other ranks to Cologne 48 hours leave. Weather showery	O.S.H.
		–	2/Lieut Lewis to Regular Unit	
		1400	1 Mule to 2nd M.V.S & struck off strength Weather Wet	O.S.H.

(A9475) Wt W2358/P360 600,000 12/17 D. D. & L. Sch 52a. Forms/C2118/15.

Army Form C. 2118.

Instructions regarding War Diaries and Intelligence Summaries are contained in F. S. Regs., Part II. and the Staff Manual respectively. Title pages will be prepared in manuscript.

WAR DIARY
or
INTELLIGENCE SUMMARY.
(Erase heading not required.)

Place	Date	Hour	Summary of Events and Information	Remarks and references to Appendices
MERKENHEIM	16.	0930	Battalion parade cancelled. Route march by Coys	
			2 Riders from 1st Northants taken on strength	
		0940	2/Lts Williams & Gibbon to Concentration Camp, Cologne for Demobilisation	
			2/Lt. A. H. Levers to Regtl Depot, Welch Regt.	
			5 mules to 53rd Welch & 4 mules to 52nd Welch Regt. Weather showery.	O.E.H.
	17	0900	Bathing whole day A. B. C & D Coys	
			1 Mule to 53rd Welch.	
		1930	Lieut Col Owen C.M.G. D.S.O arrived and takes over command. Weather fine	O.E.H.
	18	1010	Church of England Service (Good Friday)	
			Lieut J. T. Richards to No 1. Concentration Camp, Cologne for demobilisation	
			2 O.R to Wiesling for duty at Div H.Q. Weather good	O.E.H.
	19	1045	Church of England Service	
		0940	1 OR proceeded Friday for duty at Signal School.	
			Lieut W. R. Richards R.A.M.C to No 2 Field Ambulance	
			2/ Lieut W. Glen Williams reported for duty as Education Officer	
			Weather good	O.E.H.

(A9475) Wt W2358/P360 600,000 12/17 D. D. & L. Sch. 52a. Forms/C2118/15.

Instructions regarding War Diaries and Intelligence Summaries are contained in F. S. Regs., Part II. and the Staff Manual respectively. Title pages will be prepared in manuscript.

WAR DIARY
or
INTELLIGENCE SUMMARY.
(Erase heading not required.)

Army Form C. 2118.

Place	Date	Hour	Summary of Events and Information	Remarks and references to Appendices
MECKENHEIM	20	1045	Church Parade.	
			Organised games Weather good	O.H.
			Football.	
	21	0900	Company Training	
		0915	3 O.R's to No 3 Company, Western Divisional Train, as Loader.	
		1430	Football. 51st Welch v 1st M.G.C. Weather good.	O.H.
	22	0915	Battalion Route march.	
		0940	5 O.R's to No 2 Concentration Camp for demobilization Weather bad	O.H.
	23	0900	Battalion Training, all companies.	
		–	85361 Sergt Ellis to Educational Course, Newmarket, England.	
		–	85910 Pte Johnson to Detention Barracks, Schangasse, Cologne. Weather good	O.H.
	24	0900	Company training.	
			85774 Pte Barlow to No 2 Concentration Camp Cologne for Demobilisation	
		1400	Organised Games. Weather fine	O.H.

(A9475) Wt W2358/P360 600,000 12/17 D. D. & L. Sch. 52a. Forms/C2118/15.

Instructions regarding War Diaries and Intelligence Summaries are contained in F. S. Regs., Part II, and the Staff Manual respectively. Title pages will be prepared in manuscript.

WAR DIARY
or
INTELLIGENCE SUMMARY.
(Erase heading not required.)

Army Form C. 2118.

Place	Date	Hour	Summary of Events and Information	Remarks and references to Appendices
MECKENHEIM	25	0900	Company training	
		1400	Organised Games. Weather bad	[illegible]
	26	0900	Company Training	
		1400	Arms Inspection by Armourer Sergt.	
			Organised games. Weather good	[illegible]
	27	1045	Church Parade	
			Football	
		0715	Short run for Coys	
	28	0900	Coy. Training	
		1400	Organised games Weather good	[illegible]
	~~28~~	0715	Short run for Coys	
		0915	Coy training	
		1400	Organised games Weather good	[illegible]

(A9175) Wt W2358/P360 600,000 12/17 D. D. & L. Sch. 52a. Forms/C2118/15.

Instructions regarding War Diaries and Intelligence Summaries are contained in F. S. Regs., Part II, and the Staff Manual respectively. Title pages will be prepared in manuscript.

WAR DIARY
or
INTELLIGENCE SUMMARY.
(Erase heading not required.)

Army Form C. 2118.

Place	Date	Hour	Summary of Events and Information	Remarks and references to Appendices
MECKENHEIM	29	0715	Short run for Coys.	
		0915	Coy Training	
		1400	Lecture to Battalion by Mr. Masterman Smith. Subject: Alsace Lorraine	
	30	0715	Short run for all Coys. Weather good	[illegible]
		0915	Route March	
		1400	Football. Weather good	[illegible]

(A9175) Wt W2358/P360 600,000 12/17 D. D. & L. Sch. 52a. Forms/C2118/15.

(6339) Wt. W160/M3016 1,500,000 10/17 McA & W Ltd (E 1898) Forms W3091. Army Form W.3091.

Cover for Documents.

SECRET

Nature of Enclosures.

WAR DIARY

of

the 51st BATTALION, THE WELSH REGIMENT,

----

from 1st May 1919......to 31st May 1919.

---------oOo---------

Notes, or Letters written.

51st Batt. Welsh Regt.

Instructions regarding War Diaries and Intelligence Summaries are contained in F. S. Regs., Part II. and the Staff Manual respectively. Title pages will be prepared in manuscript.

WAR DIARY
or
~~INTELLIGENCE SUMMARY.~~

(Erase heading not required.)

Army Form C. 2118.

THE 51st BATTALION THE WELCH REGT. [stamp]

Place	Date	Hour	Summary of Events and Information	Remarks and references to Appendices
Meckenheim	1/5/19	09.30	"B" + "C" Coy marched off to Musketry at Witterschlick	
		08.30	Coy Training + Education	
		14.00	Organised Games — Weather showery	C.J.H.
	2/5/19	07.15	Short run for boys	
		08.30	Coy training + Education	
		14.00	Organised games. — Weather fine	C.J.H.
	3/5/19	07.15	Short run for boys	
		09.00	A + D Coys bathing — Weather fine	C.J.H.
	4/5/19	09.45	Divine Service C of E. R.C.	
		11.00	do do Nonconformists — Weather wet	C.J.H.
	5/5/19	07.15	Short run for boys	
		08.30	Musketry. + Education	
			C.O. held Summary Court — Weather fine	C.J.H.
		14.00	Organised games	
	6/5/19	07.15	Short run for boys	
		08.30	Musketry + Education	

(A9475) Wt W2358/P360 600,000 12/17 D. D. & L. Sch. 52a. Forms/C2118/15.

Instructions regarding War Diaries and Intelligence Summaries are contained in F. S. Regs., Part II, and the Staff Manual respectively. Title pages will be prepared in manuscript.

WAR DIARY
or
INTELLIGENCE SUMMARY.
(Erase heading not required.)

Army Form C. 2118.

Place	Date	Hour	Summary of Events and Information	Remarks and references to Appendices
Meckenheim	6/5/19	14.00	Organised Games. Weather Fine.	
			1 "Z" L.D. Horse & 1 "Z" Mule to Animal Collecting Station.	[illegible]
	7/5/19	07.15	Short run for boys	
		09.15	Musketry & Education	
		11.00	G.O.C. visited	
		14.00	Organised games. Weather Fine	[illegible]
	8/5/19	07.15	Short run for boys	
		09.00	Musketry & Education	
		09.30	C.O. visited from [illegible]	
		10.00	G.O.C. Brigade visited. Weather Fine	[illegible]
	9/5/19	07.15	Short run for boys	
		09.00	Boys bathing	
		09.00	Major [illegible] to Cologne for cookery demonstration.	
		14.00	Organised games. Weather Fine	[illegible]
	10/5/19	09.15	Short run for boys	
		09.00	Bathing. Weather Fine	[illegible]

Army Form C. 2118.

WAR DIARY
or
INTELLIGENCE SUMMARY.
(Erase heading not required.)

Instructions regarding War Diaries and Intelligence Summaries are contained in F. S. Regs., Part II, and the Staff Manual respectively. Title pages will be prepared in manuscript.

Place	Date	Hour	Summary of Events and Information	Remarks and references to Appendices
Meckenheim	10/5/19	09.00	Bathing. Weather Fine	O.F.H.
	11/5/19	10.45	Divine Service C of E. R.C. & Non Conformist	—
		12.45	Capt Cary to H.Q. 2nd Brigade as A/Staff Captain. Weather Showery	O.F.H.
	12/5/19	07.15	Short run for boys	
		09.00	Musketry.	
		10.30	C.O. visited & held Summary Court.	
		14.00	Organised games. Weather Showery	O.F.H.
	13/5/19	07.15	Short run for boys	
		08.30	Musketry & Education	
		14.00	Organised Games. Weather Fine	O.F.H.
	14/5/19	07.15	Short run for boys	
		09.30	Musketry & Education	
		09.00	B & C Boys returned from Witterschlick Rifle Range. Weather Fine.	O.F.H.
	15/5/19	07.15	Short run for boys.	
		09.00	Coy training & fitting web equipment.	
		09.30	5 O.R's to Cyclists Corps.	

(A9475) Wt W2358/P360 600,000 12/17 D. D. & L. Sch. 52a. Forms/C2118/15.

Army Form C. 2118.

Instructions regarding War Diaries and Intelligence Summaries are contained in F. S. Regs., Part II, and the Staff Manual respectively. Title pages will be prepared in manuscript.

WAR DIARY
or
INTELLIGENCE SUMMARY.
(Erase heading not required.)

Place	Date	Hour	Summary of Events and Information	Remarks and references to Appendices
Beckenheim	16/5/19	07.30	13 Officers & 170 O.R's trip down Rhine to Coblenz. Weather fine.	[illegible]
	17/5/19	07.15	Short run for Boys	
		09.00	"B" & "C" Coys. Bathing. Weather fine	[illegible]
	18/5/19	10.00	Divine Service C of E. R.C. & Nonconformist	
		16.00	A/Staff Capt visited. Weather fine	[illegible]
	19/5/19	07.15	Short run for Boys	
		08.30	Boy training	
		10.00	G.O.C. visited & inspected training	
		11.00	C.O. held summary court.	
		16.00	Divisional Concert Party gave a Concert. Weather fine	[illegible]
	20/5/19	07.15	Short run for Boys	
		08.30	Organised Games	
	21/5/19	07.15	Short run for Boys	
		08.30	Route March for Boys	
		09.00	4 Officers & 28 O.R's to Cologne.	[illegible]

(A9175) Wt W2358/P360 600,000 12/17 D. D. & L. Sch. 52a. Forms/C2118/15.

Instructions regarding War Diaries and Intelligence Summaries are contained in F. S. Regs., Part II, and the Staff Manual respectively. Title pages will be prepared in manuscript.

WAR DIARY
or
INTELLIGENCE SUMMARY.
(*Erase heading not required.*)

Army Form C. 2118.

Place	Date	Hour	Summary of Events and Information	Remarks and references to Appendices
Meckenheim	22/5/19	07.15	Short run for boys.	
		08.30	Training & Education Weather fine	O.H.
	23/5/19	07.15	Short run for boys	
		08.30	Training ~~of~~ & Education. Weather fine.	O.H.
	24/5/19	07.15	Short run	
		08.30	Boys bathing	
	25/5/19	09.45	Divine Service Weather fine.	O.H.
	26/5/19	07.15	Short run	
		08.30	Training & Education	
		11.30	100 men from 1/4 Cheshire Regt arrived & taken on Strength.	
	27/5/19	07.15	Short run for boys Weather fine.	O.H.
		08.30	Training & Education	
		11.00	Corps Commander visited & inspected education. Weather fine	O.H.
	28/5/19	07.15	Short run for boys	
		08.30	Training & Education Weather fine	O.H.

(A9475) Wt W2358/P360 600,000 12/17 D. D. & L. Sch. 52a. Forms/C2118/15.

Instructions regarding War Diaries and Intelligence Summaries are contained in F. S. Regs., Part II. and the Staff Manual respectively. Title pages will be prepared in manuscript.

Army Form C. 2118.

WAR DIARY
or
INTELLIGENCE SUMMARY.
(*Erase heading not required.*)

Place	Date	Hour	Summary of Events and Information	Remarks and references to Appendices
Moeckenheim	29/5/19	07.15	Short men for Coys	
		08.30	Coy Training	
		11.30	G.O.C. visited + inspected draft from Cheshire Regt.	
		12.00	A + D Coys returned from Musketry at Wildenschlick. Weather fine	O.R.H.
	30/5/19	07.15	Short men	
		08.30	Coy training + education	
		11.30	Capt Cary returned from Brigade + resumed duty as Adjutant	O.R.H.
	31/5/19	07.15	Rifle Inspection	
		08.30	Bathing for Coys. Weather fine.	O.R.H.

[signature]
Commanding 51st Bn. Welsh Regt.

(A9175) Wt W2358/P360 600,000 12/17 D. D. & L. Sch 52a. Forms/C2118/15.

CONFIDENTIAL.

War Diary of

51st Battalion The Welch Regiment.

from 1st June 1919. to 30th June 1919.

Lieutenant-Colonel.
COMMANDING 51st BATTN. WELCH REGT.

Instructions regarding War Diaries and Intelligence Summaries are contained in F. S. Regs., Part II. and the Staff Manual respectively. Title pages will be prepared in manuscript.

WAR DIARY
or
INTELLIGENCE SUMMARY.
(Erase heading not required.)

Army Form C. 2118.

51st Batt. Welch Regt.

Place	Date	Hour	Summary of Events and Information	Remarks and references to Appendices
Meckenham	1/6/19	10.30	Divine Service, C of E. R.C's & Nonconformists. Weather fine.	O.E.H.
"	2/6/19	07.15	Short run for boys.	O.E.H.
		09.30	Coy training. 4 Officers & 30 OR's to Cologne on leave.	O.E.H.
			Examination for 2nd & 3rd Class Army Certificates of Education.	O.E.H.
		10.45	Divisional General visited. Weather fine.	O.E.H.
	3/6/19	07.15	Short run for Boys	O.E.H.
		08.45	Ceremonial parade (King's Birthday) Weather dull & showery.	O.E.H.
	4/6/19	10.00	Regtl: Sports. G.O.C. presented prizes. Weather dull showers in evening	O.E.H.
	5/6/19	07.15	Short run for boys	O.E.H.
		08.30	Coy training & Education. Weather dull, slight showers	O.E.H.
	6/6/19	07.15	Short run for boys.	O.E.H.
		08.30	Coy training & Education.	O.E.H.
		14.00	Bathing.	O.E.H.
	7/6/19	07.15	Short run for boys	O.E.H.
		08.30	Coy training & education	O.E.H.
		14.00	Bathing. Weather fine.	O.E.H.

(A9475) Wt W2358/P360 600,000 12/17 D. D. & L. Sch. 52a. Forms/C2118/15.

Army Form C. 2118.

Instructions regarding War Diaries and Intelligence Summaries are contained in F. S. Regs., Part II. and the Staff Manual respectively. Title pages will be prepared in manuscript.

WAR DIARY
or
INTELLIGENCE SUMMARY.
(*Erase heading not required.*)

51st Batt: Welch Regt.

Place	Date	Hour	Summary of Events and Information	Remarks and references to Appendices
Meckenheim	7/6/19	10.45	G. O. C visited & inspected training.	O.J.H.
		12.00	C. O to Brigade Head Quarters. Weather fine	O.J.H.
	8/6/19	10.30	Devine Service. Weather fine	O.J.H.
	9/6/19		Whit Monday. General holiday.	O.J.H.
		17.00	Cross Country run. Won by "C" Coy. Weather fine.	O.J.H.
	10/6/19	07.15	Short run	O.J.H.
		08.30	Coy training	O.J.H.
		10.45	C. O visited	O.J.H.
		14.00	Organised games. Weather fine	O.J.H.
	11/6/19	07.15	Short run for Coys.	O.J.H.
		12.00	Education. Weather fine.	O.J.H.
	12/6/19	07.15	Training & Education Weather fine (thunderstorm 16.00)	O.J.H.
	13/6/19	08.30	Platoon training & education. Fine	O.J.H.
	14/6/19	08.30	Training & Education Weather fine	O.J.H.
	15/6/19	09.30	Church Services Weather fine	O.J.H.

(A9475) Wt W2358/P360 600,000 12/17 D. D. & L. Sch 52a. Forms/C2118/15.

Instructions regarding War Diaries and Intelligence Summaries are contained in F. S. Regs., Part II. and the Staff Manual respectively. Title pages will be prepared in manuscript.

WAR DIARY
or
INTELLIGENCE SUMMARY.
(Erase heading not required.)

Army Form C. 2118.

51st Bn The Welsh Regt.

Place	Date	Hour	Summary of Events and Information	Remarks and references to Appendices
Mockenheim	16/6/19	08.30	Training & Education — Weather fine	RAAL
"	17/6/19	08.30	Training & Education — Weather fine	RAAL
		5K.	Preparation for move	
Bonn	18.6.19		Move by Route march to BONN. Billeted in PROIVANT MAGAZIN	
	"		Foot Inspection	
	"		1 off & 30 Rs to SEIGBURG for billeting 1 off to TROISDORF for billeting — Weather fine	RAAL
Troisdorf	19.6.19		Bn moved from BONN to TROISDORF by Route March. — Weather fine	RAAL
			1 Coy dropped at SEIGBURG	
			Relieving guards proceeded by lorry to SEIGBURG, WAHN & LINDF. & took over guards of E Div	
"	20.6.19	1400	Baths (open air) allotted to Coys — Weather fine	RAAL
			Training (Platoon)	
"	21.6.19	0900	Training & Baths	
			One off leave to England	
			2 OR to IX Corps for duty as Clerks — Weather fine	RAAL
			3 OR to Course at Army Technical College — Weather fine	RAAL
"	22.6.19		Church Services	
"	23.6.19	0900	Training (Platoon & Coy) — Weather showery	RAAL
		1000	Massed PT in large hall	
"	24.6.19	0900	Massed P.T.	
		1000	Training Platoon & Coy	
			3 offs & 10 OR to Artillery Demonstration at ELSENBORN — Weather showery	RAAL
			1 off & 12 OR to Cologne Hostel.	
"	25.6.19	0900	Training & Bathing	
			1 OR to 2nd Western Bde as Clerk — Weather showery	RAAL
			2 offs leave to England	

A7092. Wt W128 9/M1293 750,000. 1/17. D. D & L., Ltd. Forms/C2118/14.

Instructions regarding War Diaries and Intelligence Summaries are contained in F. S. Regs., Part II. and the Staff Manual respectively. Title pages will be prepared in manuscript.

WAR DIARY
or
INTELLIGENCE SUMMARY.

(*Erase heading not required.*)

Army Form C. 2118.

51st Bn The Welch Rgt.

Place	Date	Hour	Summary of Events and Information	Remarks and references to Appendices
TROISDORF	26/6/19	0900	Training (Platoon & Coy) — Weather Showery	RHH
		0945	3 offrs & 10 O R to COLOGNE Hostel.	
"	27/6/19	0900	Training 2 offs leave to England. 2 OR for A S Special Certificate to Bonn. — Weather Showery	RHH
"	28.6.19	0900	Training (Platoon & Coy). 1 Off leave to England. 2/Lt CAREFULL attached to 403 Coy Train W DW. — Weather Showery	RHH
"	29/6/19	1030	Peace signed. Church Parades. — Weather Showery	RHH
"	30/6/19	1300	Move to BONN en route for MECKENHEIM. B Coy M G C detached Billeting party to MECKENHEIM — Weather Showery	RHH

[signature]
Lieutenant-Colonel.
COMMANDING 51st BATTN. WELCH REGT.

LT [initials]

A7092. Wt W128 9/M1293 750,000. 1/17. D. D & L., Ltd. Forms/C2118/14.

C O N F I D E N T I A L.

War Diary of

51st Battn. The Welch Regt.

from 1st July 1919 to 31st July 1919.

Major.
Commanding 51st Battalion The Welch Regt.

Instructions regarding War Diaries and Intelligence Summaries are contained in F. S. Regs., Part II. and the Staff Manual respectively. Title pages will be prepared in manuscript.

~~WAR DIARY~~ or INTELLIGENCE SUMMARY.

(Erase heading not required.)

Army Form C. 2118.

51st Batt Welch Regt

Place	Date	Hour	Summary of Events and Information	Remarks and references to Appendices
Meckenheim	1/7/19	07.00	The Battalion arrived at Meckenheim from Troisdorf & took over billets. Weather fine	O.B.H.
"	2/7/19	07.00	Training & Education	O.B.H.
		09.30	27 O.Rs to dispersal stations for demobilisation.	O.B.H.
		12.00	3 O.Rs to Train for transfer to R.A.S.C. Weather fine	O.B.H.
"	3/7/19	07.00	Training & Education	O.B.H.
		10.30	Commanding Officers kit inspection Weather fine	O.B.H.
"	4/7/19	07.00	Training & education	O.B.H.
		08.00	100 All ranks for Rhine trip	O.B.H.
			Lt Tudor granted leave to U.K	O.B.H.
		09.30	4 O.Rs to IX Corps Cyclists Battalion	O.B.H.
			4 O.Rs to Signal School	O.B.H.
			Capt Robinson to Signal School for duty. Weather fine	O.B.H.
"	5/7/19	09.00	Battalion Bathing	O.B.H.
			Lt. O.K	O.B.H.
			Weather fine	O.B.H.

(A9475) Wt W2358/P360 600,000 12/17 D. D. & L. Sch. 52a. Forms/C2118/15.

Instructions regarding War Diaries and Intelligence Summaries are contained in F. S. Regs., Part II. and the Staff Manual respectively. Title pages will be prepared in manuscript.

~~WAR DIARY~~
or
INTELLIGENCE SUMMARY.
(Erase heading not required.)

Army Form C. 2118.

5/1st Battalion Welch Regt.

Place	Date	Hour	Summary of Events and Information	Remarks and references to Appendices
Meckenheim	6/7/19	10.30	Devine Service for all for all denominations.	
"	7/7/19	07.30	Training & Education. Weather fine.	[illegible]
			Capt. Greenwood. D.S.O. M.C. & 4 N.C.O's to Paris for Victory march.	[illegible] [illegible]
"	8/7/19	07.30	Training & Education Weather showery	[illegible]
			2 O.R's to Rhine Army Detention Barracks Weather fine	[illegible]
"	9/7/19	07.30	Training & Education	[illegible]
			16 O.R. granted leave to England. Weather fine	[illegible]
"	10/7/19	07.30	Training & Education.	[illegible]
			2 OR's. R.E attached to the Battalion	[illegible]
			6 O.R's granted leave to United Kingdom. Weather fine	[illegible]
"	11/7/19	07.30	Training & Education	[illegible]
"			2 OR's from 6th Welch attached	[illegible]
"			10 O.R's granted leave to United Kingdom.	[illegible]
			10 O.R's to Dispersal Station for Demobilisation Weather fine	[illegible]
"	12/7/19	07.30	Training & Education	[illegible]
			3 OR's to Poultry keeping course	[illegible]
			Sergt Hemsley to R.G.A. Siege Battery for 1 weeks Musketry course. Weather fine	[illegible]
			8 O.R's to United Kingdom on leave.	[illegible]
			Weather fine.	[illegible]

A7092. Wt W128 9/M1293 750,000. 1/17. D. D & L., Ltd. Forms/C2118/14.

Instructions regarding War Diaries and Intelligence Summaries are contained in F. S. Regs., Part II. and the Staff Manual respectively. Title pages will be prepared in manuscript.

~~WAR DIARY~~
or
INTELLIGENCE SUMMARY. 51st Batt: Welch Regt.
(Erase heading not required.)

Army Form C. 2118.

Place	Date	Hour	Summary of Events and Information	Remarks and references to Appendices
Meckenheim	13/7/19	10·30	Divine Service. Weather ~~fine~~ showery	O.E.J.S.
"	14/7/19	07.30	Training & Education.	O.E.J.S.
			2/Lts Hill & Lloyd to Regtl. Depot. Cardiff. Weather fine	O.E.J.S.
			2/Lt Badcoe & 7 O.Rs granted leave to U. K. Weather fine	O.E.J.S.
"	15/7/19	07.30	Training & Education. Weather fine	O.E.J.S.
			2/Lt Coatham & 7 O.Rs to U K on leave.	O.E.J.S.
"	16/7/19	07·30	Training & Education Weather fine	O.E.J.S.
"	17/7/19	07.30	Training & Education	O.E.J.S.
			Brigade Platoon drill competition at Flerzheim, won by	O.E.J.S.
			No 13 Platoon (Sergt Humphreys)	O.E.J.S.
			Capt Fowler, Inspector of Catering visited. Weather fine	O.E.J.S.
"	18/7/19	07.30	Training.	O.E.J.S.
			Examination for 2nd & 3rd Class Army Certificates	O.E.J.S.
			Capt Fowler, Inspector of Catering visited.	O.E.J.S.
"	19/7/19	07·30	Bathing.	O.E.J.S.
			Brigade Sports at Alfter Weather fine. Weather fine. Heavy thunderstorm in afternoon	O.E.J.S. O.E.J.S.
"	20/7/19	10·30	Divine Service. Weather	

A7092. Wt W128 9/M1293 750,000. 1/17. D. D & L., Ltd. Forms/C2118/14.

Instructions regarding War Diaries and Intelligence Summaries are contained in F. S. Regs., Part II. and the Staff Manual respectively. Title pages will be prepared in manuscript.

Army Form C. 2118.

~~WAR DIARY~~
or
INTELLIGENCE SUMMARY. 51st Batt: Welch Regt.
(Erase heading not required.)

Place	Date	Hour	Summary of Events and Information	Remarks and references to Appendices
MECKENHEIM	21/7/19	07.30	Training & Education	O.J.S.
		08.00	27 O.R's to Reinbach for Medical Inspection	O.J.S.
		09.15	1 Officer & 16 O.R's to Divisional Hostel Cologne.	O.J.S.
		09.30	Summary Court.	O.J.S.
			Capt Cary granted leave to England. Weather showery.	O.J.S.
"	22/7/19	07.30	Training & Education	O.J.S.
			9 O.R's granted leave to United Kingdom. Weather fine	O.J.S.
"	23/7/19	07.30	Training & Education	O.J.S.
		18.00	Divisional Cinema. Weather fine	O.J.S.
"	24/7/19	07.30	Training & Education	O.J.S.
			Capt W. F. Greenwood granted leave to U.K.	O.J.S.
			Pte Hughes tried by F.G.C.M. Weather fine	O.J.S.
"	25/7/19	07.30	Training & Education. Weather fine	O.J.S.
"	26/7/19	07.30	Training & Education	O.J.S.
"			Bathing Weather fine	O.J.S.
"	27/7/19		Divine Service Weather fine	O.J.S.
"	28/7/19		Training & Education	O.J.S.
			C.O. held Summary Court	O.J.S.
			Audit Board on Regtl Accounts. Weather fine.	O.J.S.

A7092. Wt W128 9/M1293 750,000. 1/17. D. D & L., Ltd. Forms/C2118/14.

Instructions regarding War Diaries and Intelligence Summaries are contained in F. S. Regs., Part II. and the Staff Manual respectively. Title pages will be prepared in manuscript.

~~WAR DIARY~~
or
INTELLIGENCE SUMMARY. 51st Battalion Welch Regt.

(Erase heading not required.)

Army Form C. 2118.

Place	Date	Hour	Summary of Events and Information	Remarks and references to Appendices
MECKENHEIM	29/7/19	07.30	Training & Education Weather fine	O.H.S.
"	30/7/19		Lt Col Owen C.M.G. D.S.O. granted leave to U.K.	O.H.S.
			Lieut Morris & Sergt Jenkins to Cologne for demobilisation	O.H.S.
"			2/Lt W.V. Evans to Chinese Labour Corps Weather fine	O.H.S.
"	31/7/19		Training & Education	O.H.S.
"		11.30	G.O.C. visited Weather fine	O.H.S.

H S [illegible] Major,
Commanding 51st Welch Regt.

A7092. Wt W128 9/M1293 750,000. 1/17. D. D & L., Ltd. Forms/C2118/14.

BEF

1 DIVISION

2 BRIGADE

52 WELSH R.

1919 MAR to 1919 JULY

(6339) Wt. W160/M3016 1,500,000 10/17 McA & W Ltd (E 1898) Forms W3091. Army Form W.3091.

Cover for Documents.

SECRET

Nature of Enclosures.

WAR DIARY

of

the 52nd BATTALION, THE WELSH REGIMENT.

from ~~1st May~~ MARCH 1919........to 31st May, 1919.

-----------oOo-----------

Notes, or Letters written.

W

Instructions regarding War Diaries and Intelligence Summaries are contained in F. S. Regs., Part II. and the Staff Manual respectively. Title Pages will be prepared in manuscript.

WAR DIARY of 52nd Bn. Welsh Regt.

~~or~~

~~INTELLIGENCE SUMMARY~~

(Erase heading not required.)

Army Form C. 2118

Volume I. from 1-3-19 to 31-3-19

Vol I

Place	Date	Hour	Summary of Events and Information	Remarks and references to Appendices
LOWESTOFT	1-3-19	12.55.	Orders received for Battalion to proceed to GERMANY to form part of Army of Occupation.	A.B.
LOWESTOFT.	2-3-19	0955.	Battalion entrained at LOWESTOFT CENTRAL Railway Station and proceeded to DOVER. Arrived DOVER 1730 and accommodated for night 2/3rd March in barracks	A.B.
DOVER	3-3-19	1230	Embarked in H.T. "SCOTIA" for conveyance to DUNKIRK.	
DUNKIRK	3-3-19	1600	Disembarked at DUNKIRK and accommodated at No 3 Rest Camp for night 3/4th March.	A.B.
DUNKIRK.	4-3-19	1030	Entrained at SAND SIDING. Proceeded up country VIA BAILLEUL, ARMENTIERES, LILLE to COLOGNE, GERMANY.	A.B.
COLOGNE	5-3-19	2330	Arrived COLOGNE. Battalion ordered to proceed to DUISDORF.	
DUISDORF	6-3-19	0230	Arrived DUISDORF. Battalion detrained at 0530. "A" "B" and "C" Companies took over billets from 1st Northampton Regt in DUISDORF. "D" Coy billeted in the village of LESSENICH. Strength of Battalion 42 officers 685 other ranks	A.B.
DUISDORF	7-3-19.		Companies employed on general clean up.	A.B.
DUISDORF	8-3-19.		2nd Lieut A. L. DYER placed under close arrest for being Drunk on duty.	A.B.
DUISDORF	10-3-19	13-45	Battalion inspected in "Drill Order" by ~~[illegible]~~ Genral Sir Herbert C.O. PLUMER, G.C.B., G.C.M.G., G.C.V.O., ADC. (AB)	A.B.
DUISDORF	12-3-19	1800	2nd Infantry Brigade Scheme No G10/10 (Copy No. 6) received dealing with the Defence of BONN.	A.B.
DUISDORF	14-3-19.		Lieut-Colonel B.E. CROCKER, D.S.O. reconnoitred the BONN bridge defences.	
	14-3-19		Captain LAWSON, R, (RAMC) left the Battalion for ENGLAND.	
	14-3-19		Captain HAYES, H (RAMC) joined for duty from the 1st Northampton Regt.	
	14-3-19		Rev. H.H.L. LONGUET HIGGINS, C.E. joined the Battalion.	A.B.
DUISDORF	15-3-19		All Company Commanders reconnoitred the BONN bridge defences.	
DUISDORF.	16-3-19	1300	52nd Welsh Regt Secret Orders No S 100/2 issued, re defence of the BONN Bridge.	A.B
DUISDORF	17-3-19	1000	Reconnaissance of the BONN bridge carried out by Commanding Officer, 2nd in Command and Adjutant.	
	17-3-19	1800	Lieut J. W. O. CANDY, Royal Welsh Fusiliers reported for duty with Unit from ENGLAND	A.B.

1875 Wt. W593/826 1,000,000 4/15 J.B.C. & A. A.D.S.S./Forms/C. 2118.

Instructions regarding War Diaries and Intelligence Summaries are contained in F. S. Regs., Part II. and the Staff Manual respectively. Title Pages will be prepared in manuscript.

WAR DIARY

~~or~~ of 52nd Bn. Welsh Regt.

~~INTELLIGENCE SUMMARY~~

(Erase heading not required.) from 1-3-19 to 31-3-19.

Army Form C. 2118

Place	Date	Hour	Summary of Events and Information	Remarks and references to Appendices
DUISDORF	21-3-19		The Battalion was inspected by G.O.C. 2nd Infantry Brigade on Battalion Parade Ground in Battle Order.	
			5 other ranks struck off the strength having been in hospital 7-days.	A.B.
DUISDORF	24-3-19		One other rank taken on the strength on discharge from hospital.	
			Three other ranks struck off the strength having been in hospital 7-days.	A.B.
DUISDORF	25-3-19		Two other ranks struck off the strength having been in hospital 7 days.	
			Orders received from G.H.Q. letter No A.G/2158/9947 (O) dated 16-3-19, ordering Lieut-Colonel B. E. CROCKER, D.S.O. Commanding 52nd Welsh Regt, to proceed to ENGLAND with a view to assuming command of the 1st Bn. Welsh Regt.	A.B.
			~~One other rank taken on strength on discharge from hospital~~ A.B.	
		A.B.	~~Three~~ Two other ranks struck off the strength having been in hospital 7 days.	A.B.
DUISDORF	26-3-19		One other rank taken on strength on discharge from hospital	
			Four other ranks struck off the strength having been in hospital 7 days.	A.B.
DUISDORF	27-3-19	1700	2nd Inf. Bde (Defence of BONN) Instructions No 3 (Copy No 6) received.	A.B.
DUISDORF	28-3-19		One other rank taken on strength on discharge from hospital.	A.B.
DUISDORF	29-3-19		Two other ranks taken on strength on discharge from hospital	A.B.
DUISDORF	30-3-19	1600	Lieut-Colonel B E. CROCKER, D.S.O. left Unit to proceed to England	
			Major W.A.V. FINDLATER, Royal Irish Fusiliers, assumes command of the 52nd Welsh Regt, vice Lt-Colonel CROCKER.	A.B.
DUISDORF	31-3-19		One other rank struck off the strength.	A.B.

W A V Findlater Major
Commdg 52nd Welsh Regt

1875 Wt. W593/826 1,000,000 4/15 J.B.C. & A. A.D.S.S./Forms/C. 2118.

S E C R E T .

Copy No.....11....

Date:- 16th March 1919.

DEFENCE OF BONN.

52nd Battalion Welsh Regiment. No. S.100/ 2

1. In the event of action taking place on the perimeter of the COLOGNE Bridgehead it may be necessary for the 2nd Infantry Brigade to take over the defence of BONN bridge and some of the duties in the neighbourhood of BONN.

NOTE:- The conditions assumed in the event of hosyile action against BONN bridge are:-
(a) That the enemy has rifles, machine guns, bombs and explosives, but not artillery.
(b)That the garrison must be prepared to hold out for about 48 hours.

2. The task of the battalion would then be:-
(a) To proceed forthwith and relieve the 12th L.N.Lancs.Regt.
(b) To ensure communication across the bridge at BONN and to close the bridge to any unauthorised persons.
(c)To maintain order in that part of the town allotted to the battalion.

3. Companies on receipt of message " PREPARE TO MOVE" will take action as follows:-
(i) Parade their companies on Battalion Parade Ground immediately and report to B.O.R. when ready to move.
(ii) E nsure that all surplus stores, baggage, etc, are dumped in the yard at the Quartermaster's Stores.
(iii) All sick men and men unable to march to be ordered to report at Battalion Headquarters.
(iv) O.C."A" Company will detail 1 Officer, 3 N.C.O's and nine men for Guard duties at DUISDORF.

4. For the purpose of defence the bridge is divided into two Sectors at the centre, and companies are distributed as under:-

EASTERN SECTOR

"A" Company.- 1 Platoon in houses South of the corner of COMBAHN and RHEIN STRASSE.

1 Platoon in houses at North end of RHEIN STRASSE.

1 Platoon at corner of RHEIN and BRUCKEN STRASSE.

1 P latoon at corner of RHEIN and WILHELM STRASSE.

Company Headquarters at corner of RHEIN and BRUCKEN STRASSE.

" B" Company.-

1 Platoon at corner of COMBAHN and KAISER STRASSE.

1 Platoon at junction of KAISER and WILHELM STRASSE

1 Platoon at corner of KAISER and BRUCKEN STRASSE.

1 Platoon in support in BRUCKEN STRASSE.

Company Headquarters with support Platoon.

WESTERN SECTOR.

"C" Company.- 1 Platoon at corner of RHEINWERFT and MUHLEN GASSE.

1 Platoon in Tower 70 yards South of Abutment.

1 Platoon at junction of RHEINWERFT and BRUCKEN STRASSE.

1 Platoon at corner of RHEINWERFT and JOSEPH STRASSE.

Company Headquarters at junction of RHEINWERFT and BRUCKEN STRASSE.

" D" Company.-

1 Platoon at corner of MUHLEN GASSE and DOETSCH STRASSE.

1 Platoon at junction of BRUCKEN and DOETSCH STRASSE.

1 Platoon at corner of JOSEP H and DOETSCH STRASSE.

1 Platoon in support in BRUCKEN STRASSE.

Company Headquarters with support platoon.

NOTE:- If on arrival in BONN it is ascertained that the 12th L.N.Lancs.Regt, have not taken over the BONN bridge Defences, the O.C."C" Company will immediately despatch a party of 1 Officer, 2 Sergeants, 2 Corporals and 18 Privates to relieve the Guard at the Western end of BONN Bridge, the remainder of the Battalion proceeding to the MUSEUM KONIG, COBLENZ STRASSE and take over billets from 19th Lancs.Fusiliers.

5. Officers Commanding Companies will reconnoitre their areas for additional Lewis Gun positions and report same to B.O.R.immediately.

6. Each company will detail one complete A.A.Lewis Gun team (with gun) to report to Battalion Headquarters.

7. O's.C.Companies at each end of the bridge will arrange for frequent patrolling for some distance outside the defended area of all roads leading into it.

8. A Dressing Station will be established at whichever end of the bridge the trouble is taking place.
In the event of trouble at both ends of the bridge at the same time a second Aid Post will be established.

9. Houses in defended areas will be cleared of inhabitants as quickly as possible.
They may be turned out of the Area or collected in suitable places, under cover, in the defended area at each end of the bridge.
No Civilian is to cross the bridge under any circumstances once the order to defend it has reached the Guard.

10. The following ammunition etc, has been stored in equal proportions at the Guard House at the BONN end of the bridge and at the Headquarters of the 5/6th Royal Scots at BEUEL end of the bridge.

- 120,000 Rounds S.A.A. - 300 rounds per man.
- 36,000 rounds S.A.A. for Lewis Guns.
- 160 Boxes Mills grenades.
- 2,000 sandbags.
- 150 knife rests
- 30 bundles of barbed wire.
- 12 crow bars.
- 12 buckets each with 100 feet rope.

Rations for 400 men for two days.

These will eventually be distributed as follows:-
One third S.A.A., 60 Boxes Mills, 6 Crowbars and half the rations, sandbags and wire will remain in the Guard House at the BONN end of the bridge, and similar quantities at the present Headquarters of the 5/6th Royal Scots; the remainder with the buckets and rope will be stored in the Towers nearest the banks.

Orders as to storage of knife rests will be issued later.

P ositions of knife rests are shewn in attached map in blue.

The garrisons of the sectors are responsible for putting out the knife rests on the first alarm.

11. All reports to Battalion Headquarters in the W estern Tower.

12. ACKNOWLEDGE.

A.Bridgens Captain & Adjutant,

52nd Battalion The W elsh Regiment.

Issued by runner at 1300 hours 16th March 1919.

Copy No. 1 to......2nd Infantry Brigade.
" 2 ........O.C."A" Company.
" 3 ........O.C."B" Company.
" 4 ........O.C." C" Company
" 5 ........O.C." D" Company.
" 6 ....Q uartermaster.
" 7 ....Transport Officer.
" 8 ,,,,,,,, Lewis Gun Officer.
" 9 ....Signalling Officer.
" 10 .... Battalion Headquarters.
" 11 .... W ar Diary.
" 12 .... File.

Instructions regarding War Diaries and Intelligence Summaries are contained in F. S. Regs., Part II. and the Staff Manual respectively. Title pages will be prepared in manuscript.

Army Form C. 2118.

ORDERLY ROOM
30 APR 1919
52nd BATT. WELSH REGT.

WAR DIARY of 52nd Welsh Regt.

~~or INTELLIGENCE SUMMARY.~~

(Erase heading not required.)

Volume II from 1-4-19 to 30-4-19.

Place	Date	Hour	Summary of Events and Information	Remarks and references to Appendices
DUISDORF	1-4-19.		One other rank taken on the strength on discharge from hospital.	A.B.
DUISDORF	2-4-19		Two other ranks taken on the strength on discharge from hospital.	
			Two other ranks struck off the strength having been in hospital 7 days.	A.B.
DUISDORF	3-4-19	1030	The Battalion was inspected on Battn Parade Ground by G.O.C., IX Corps. Dress F.S.M.O. After the inspection the Battalion marched passed in "Column of Route."	
			Capt J.A.L DRAFFIN, Capt R.H. LINDSAY, and Lieut W.T. SHANNON and 15 other ranks proceeded to COLOGNE on 48 hours leave.	A.B.
DUISDORF	4-4-19.		8 R.E Sappers attached to Battalion for rations & accommodation.	
			Companies were bathed at Brigade Baths.	
			Three other ranks taken on the strength on discharge from hospital	A.B.
DUISDORF	5-4-19		Colonel FAWKES lectured to the Bn. in the Recreational Room. Subject - "Temperance".	
			Lieut W. COWPER proceeded to EUSKIRCHEN for duty to teach "METHOD" (Educational Trg)	
			Battalion was issued with Webbing Equipment.	
			22 officers and 290 other ranks proceeded on a trip on the RHINE.	
			Brevet Lieut-Colonel J.R.M. MINSHULL FORD, D.S.O, M.C joined on the afternoon of the 4-4-19 and assumed Command of the Battalion vice Lt Col R.H. CROCKER	A.B.
DUISDORF.	6-4-19		Commanding Officer met Company Commanders and discussed training matters.	A.B.
DUISDORF	7-4-19		Chaplain H.H. LONGUET HIGGINS (C.E) left the Battalion for duty at HARVE.	
			2 other ranks taken on the strength on discharge from hospital	
			5 other ranks (one shoeing smith and four cooks) taken on the strength on transfer from 1st Bn. Northamptonshire Regt.	
			One other rank struck off the strength having been in ~~on discharge from~~ hospital 7 days.	
			Battn. rugger team defeated 13th King's Liverpool Regt at BONN - 12 points to NIL	A.B.

A7092. Wt W1319/M1293 750,000. 1/17. D. D & L., Ltd. Forms/C2118/14.

Sheet 2.

Instructions regarding War Diaries and Intelligence Summaries are contained in F. S. Regs., Part II. and the Staff Manual respectively. Title pages will be prepared in manuscript.

WAR DIARY 52nd Welsh Regt.

or

~~INTELLIGENCE SUMMARY.~~

Volume II. (Erase heading not required.) 1-4-19 to 30-4-19

Army Form C. 2118.

Place	Date	Hour	Summary of Events and Information	Remarks and references to Appendices
DUISDORF	8-4-19		Commanding Officer and 2nd in Command reconnoitred the BONN Bridge defences.	A.B.
			Battalion ordered to detail a working party of 100 other ranks daily to help to construct a rifle range at WITTERSCHLICK.	A.B.
DUISDORF	9-4-19		2nd Lieutenant T. MOLLOY proceeded to No 2 Concentration Camp, DUREN, for demobilization.	
			Plan of DUISDORF and house to house inspection for billeting purposes completed.	
			Ditto for LESSENICH. Commanding Officer lectured to all officers. Subject – "Training".	A.B.
DUISDORF	10-4-19		IX Corps Concert Party gave a performance to the Battalion at DUISDORF.	
			One other rank struck off the strength having been in hospital 7 days.	A.B.
			Commanding Officer and 2nd in Command completed a reconnaissance of the BONN Bridge defences.	
DUISDORF	11-4-19		Four other ranks proceeded to ROSBERG to be attached to R.E for a course of instruction in Carpentry.	
			Battalion Route March. – DUISDORF – ENDERNICH – DRANSDORF – ALFTER – Billets	A.B.
			Steel helmets to be worn by all ranks when "On Guard", on Wednesdays and Route Marches	A.B.
DUISDORF	12-4-19		Commanding Officer had a heart to heart talk with the men of "D" Company.	
			All subaltern officers detailed for one hours musketry instruction daily under Lieut E.J JAMES.	A.B.
DUISDORF	13-4-19	1200	Commanding Officer saw all N.C.O's and explained system of Examinations for promotion which are to be held monthly.	
DUISDORF	14-4-19		The Commanding Officer had a heart to heart talk with the men of "C" + "B" Coy Drummers and Signallers. Adjutants Class for N.C.O's commenced	A.B.

A7092. Wt. W128 9/M1293 750,000. 1/17. D. D & L., Ltd. Forms/C2118/14.

Sheet 3.

Instructions regarding War Diaries and Intelligence Summaries are contained in F. S. Regs., Part II. and the Staff Manual respectively. Title pages will be prepared in manuscript.

WAR DIARY
or
INTELLIGENCE SUMMARY.
(Erase heading not required.)

52nd Welsh Regt.

Army Form C. 2118.

Volume II 1-4-19 to 30-4-19

Place	Date	Hour	Summary of Events and Information	Remarks and references to Appendices
DUISDORF	15.4.19		Battalion Route March :- DRANSDORF - ROISDORF - ALFTER - Billets.	A.B.
DUISDORF	16.4.19		The Battalion was engaged in Baths and Training. The Commanding Officer spoke to the Transport Section at 1730 hours, on Interior Economy and horse management.	A.B.
DUISDORF	17.4.19		The Battalion was engaged in Baths, and working party. The G.O.C. 2nd Infantry Brigade visited the Battalion. He inspected the limbers and the Battalion Quarter-Guard; and also visited the site of the proposed new Battalion Training Ground and ground to be set apart for the Battalion Garden. The Divisional Cinema (Travelling) visited Duisdorf and shewed good pictures in the Battn. Recreation Room. Dr. W. J. Dyson lectured to the Officers, N.C.O.s & men of the Battalion on "Health & Citizenship", and the lecture was enjoyed and appreciated by all ranks attending it. Captain The Rev. C. M. Smith, C of E. Chaplain reported for duty.	A.B.
DUISDORF	18.4.19		This date being Good Friday no ordinary parades were carried out. There was a Church parade held in the morning - Church of England service at 1000 Roman Catholic at 1100.	A.B.

Sheet 4

Instructions regarding War Diaries and Intelligence Summaries are contained in F. S. Regs., Part II. and the Staff Manual respectively. Title pages will be prepared in manuscript.

WAR DIARY 52nd Welsh Regt
or
~~INTELLIGENCE SUMMARY.~~
(Erase heading not required.)

Army Form C. 2118.

Volume II — 1-4-19 to 30-4-19

Place	Date	Hour	Summary of Events and Information	Remarks and references to Appendices
DUISDORF	18·4·19		Lieut Southall, M.C. Rifle Brigade joined the Battalion for duty as Educational Instructor. Authy. Western Div. No. G.E. 88/3 dated 17-4-19.	
			Major W.A.V. Findlater, proceeded to England and is struck off the strength of the Battalion accordingly. (Authy A.G. 2158/109670 dated 31-3-19)	A.B.
DUISDORF	19·4·19		The Commanding Officer and Captain J.A.L. Draffin proceeded to BORNHEIM as members of a F.G.C.M. and returned at 1720 hours.	A.B.
DUISDORF	20·4·19		The G.O.C. attended divine Service in the Battalion Recreation Room at 1100. This was Easter Sunday.	
			After divine Service the Commanding Officer addressed all Officers on matters connected with training and interior economy in the Battalion.	A.B.
DUISDORF	21·4·19		The Commanding Officer addressed "A" Coy in their Company mess Rooms, — subject "The British Empire and Patriotism".	
			In the afternoon, this day being Easter Monday the Battalion Sports were run off on the Battalion Recreation Ground.	
			The Divisional photographer photographed one man per company in different orders of kit. The Commanding Officer and Adjutant were present.	A.B.

A7092 Wt. W128 9/M1293 750,000. 1/17. D. D & L., Ltd. Forms/C2118/14.

Instructions regarding War Diaries and Intelligence Summaries are contained in F. S. Regs., Part II. and the Staff Manual respectively. Title pages will be prepared in manuscript.

Sheet 5

WAR DIARY 52nd Welsh Regt.

or

~~INTELLIGENCE SUMMARY.~~

(*Erase heading not required.*)

Volume II. 1-4-19 to 30-4-19

Army Form C. 2118.

Place	Date	Hour	Summary of Events and Information	Remarks and references to Appendices
DUISDORF	21.4.19		The Battalion Sports were a great success, the day being bright and sunny. The G.O.C. 2nd Infantry Bde. attended and distributed the prizes. "C" Company led, followed by A, B & D. The Band of the 1st Battalion ~~1st~~ Northamptonshire Regiment played throughout the afternoon, and were entertained at tea by the Battalion.	A.B.
DUISDORF	22.4.19		Officers Lewis Gun Class under the Battalion Lewis Gun Officer started, to have all officers qualified in the Lewis Gun.	A.B.
DUISDORF	23.4.19		The Commanding Officer attended a conference at Bde. H.Q. Matters of training were discussed, and it was decided that the Battalion would fire its Annual Musketry Course between May 1st & May 31st. Lieut. H.M. Hake, Intelligence Officer, Western Division, lectured to the Battalion in the Battalion Recreation ~~Officers~~ Room at 1430 hours. The Commanding Officer drew up and arranged the training programme for the Battalion's firing of the Annual Musketry Course with the Musketry Officer.	A.B.
DUISDORF	25.4.19		The Battalion was engaged in Intensive Musketry Training for G.M.C. and baths.	

A7092. Wt. W128 9/M1293 750,000. 1/17. D. D & L., Ltd. Forms/C2118/14.

Sheet 6

Instructions regarding War Diaries and Intelligence Summaries are contained in F. S. Regs., Part II. and the Staff Manual respectively. Title pages will be prepared in manuscript.

Army Form C. 2118.

WAR DIARY 52nd Welsh Regt
or
~~INTELLIGENCE SUMMARY~~.

(Erase heading not required.)

Volume II

1-4-19 to 30-4-19

Place	Date	Hour	Summary of Events and Information	Remarks and references to Appendices
			It was arranged that the Lewis Gun Course would be fired by Companies directly they had fired the G.M.C. Parts I-II-and III, and that Part I would be fired on the 30 yards range, part II on the Rifle Range.	
DUISDORF	27-4-19		Sunday Divine services were held in the morning. After services the Battalion was inspected by the Medical Officer.	K.
DUISDORF	28-4-19		Dates of firing for this Unit & 51st Welsh Regiment were arranged. It was arranged that the Battalion Alarm Post would be on the Battalion Parade Ground. It was decided by G.O.C. Western Division that Category "B" personnel be examined for reclassification, & that they would fire the G.M.C. and be eligible for all training. Battalion Barber shop was started.	K.
DUISDORF	29-4-19		Notice was given that the 2nd Western Infantry Brigade would be inspected by the Commander-in-Chief, British Army of the Rhine.	K.
DUISDORF	30-4-19		The Brigade (minus 51st Welsh Regt) was inspected by the Commander-in-Chief on the Parade Ground of this Unit. Battalions were drawn up in mass, 466th Battery R.F. on right, 2nd T.M. Battery on left. The Commander-in-chief arrived at 0950 hours. After inspection the Brigade marched past in column of ~~fours~~ route, the saluting base being near DUISDORF station. For the remainder of the day Companies carried out training as per programme of work.	K.

[illegible signature]
LIEUT.-COLONEL
COMMG. 52ND BN. THE WELCH REGT.

A7092. Wt W128 9/M1293 750,000. 1/17. D. D & L., Ltd. Forms/C2118/14.

Army Form C. 2118

WAR DIARY
of 53rd Welch Regiment.
~~INTELLIGENCE SUMMARY~~
(Erase heading not required.)

Instructions regarding War Diaries and Intelligence Summaries are contained in F. S. Regs., Part II. and the Staff Manual respectively. Title Pages will be prepared in manuscript.

Sheet 1. Volume III From 1.5.19 to 31.5.19.

Place	Date	Hour	Summary of Events and Information	Remarks and references to Appendices
DUISDORF	1.5.19		The Divisional Cinema visited DUISDORF. There was a good attendance. No 84724 Sergt. O.H Williams, Orderly Room Sergt returned from 3rd Echelon.	KFCm
DUISDORF	3.5.19		"B" and "D" Coys. started firing the G.M.C. on WITTERSCHLICK Long Range. The weather was dull but cleared up during the afternoon. Practices 1; 2; 3; and 4 fired.	KFCm
DUISDORF	5.5.19		"D" and "B" Coys. continue firing the G.M.C. Practices 5; 6; 7; and 12; fired light - good. The B.G.C. 2nd Western Infantry Brigade addressed the Officers of this Unit at 1000 hrs. in the Corpls. Room. "Platoon Training", "Hints on Training" "The Sgt-Spot" were issued to Coys preparatory to intensive platoon training.	KFCm
DUISDORF	6.5.19.		"D" and "B" Coys. on G.M.C. Light - good.	KFCm
DUISDORF	7.5.19.		D and B Coys on G.M.C. Light - good. Instructions received from 2nd Western Infantry Bde. that Officers when firing part III G.M.C. would wear same order as the men.	KFCm
DUISDORF	8.5.19.		"D" and "B" Coys. finish firing G.M.C. The light was bad, but improved later in the day. STRENGTH - DECREASE - OFFICERS. - Lieut W.T Shannon was cross-posted to the 1/4th Cheshire Regt.	KFCm

1875 Wt. W593/826 1,000,000 4/15 J.B.C. & A. A.D.S.S./Forms/C. 2118.

Instructions regarding War Diaries and Intelligence Summaries are contained in F. S. Regs., Part II. and the Staff Manual respectively. Title Pages will be prepared in manuscript.

WAR DIARY
or
~~INTELLIGENCE SUMMARY~~
(Erase heading not required.)

52nd Welch Regiment

Sheet II. Volume III — From 1.5.19 to 31.5.19

Army Form C. 2118

Place	Date	Hour	Summary of Events and Information	Remarks and references to Appendices
DUISDORF	8.5.19		Lieut. W A Crupwell proceeded to join the 2nd Western T.M. Battery for duty on a month's probation. Kit Inspection, one company each day each week was introduced on this date. A Battalion Paper Chase took place at 1500 hrs.	KFCm
DUISDORF	9.5.19		"D" & "B" Coy Lewis Gunners started firing on 30x Range. Information was received that the G.O.C. Western Division would address the Officers of this and other units in the Brigade on Saturday, 10th inst at 0945 in "D" Coy. Mess Room at LESSENICH.	KFCm
DUISDORF	10.5.19		Major General E.P. Strickland, C.B.; C.M.G.; DSO: Commanding the Western Division addressed the Officers of this and other Units in the Brigade as above.	
DUISDORF	11.5.19		Divine Services and Medical Inspection of the Battalion. STRENGTH-DECREASE. 4 O.R's proceeded for demobilization in April, were struck off strength of the Battalion.	KFCm
DUISDORF	12.5.19		"B" Coy. Lewis Gunners fired Part II of the L.G.C. on WITTERSCHLICK Long Range on the 12th and 13th insts.	KFCm
DUISDORF	13.5.19		Amendments to Infantry Training were issued to all Coys & Specialist Officers. The Commanding Officer decided on Battalion Bathing place near LESSENICH. The Battalion Notice Board was erected near the Guard Mounting Square, & instructions issued re posting up of B.O. thereon. Barricades were erected at suitable points in the village to prevent speeding of motor cars and motor cycles.	KFCm

1875 Wt. W593/826 1,000,000 4/15 J.B.C. & A. A.D.S.S./Forms/C. 2118.

Army Form C. 2118

WAR DIARY
of 52nd Welch Regiment
~~INTELLIGENCE SUMMARY~~

Instructions regarding War Diaries and Intelligence Summaries are contained in F. S. Regs., Part II. and the Staff Manual respectively. Title Pages will be prepared in manuscript.

Sheet III Volume III (Erase heading not required.) From 1.5.19 to 31.5.19

Place	Date	Hour	Summary of Events and Information	Remarks and references to Appendices
DUISDORF	14.5.19		"D" Coy Lewis Gunners fired Part II of the L. G. C. on WITTERSCHLICK Long Range on the 14th and 15th insts.	KFCm
DUISDORF	15-5-19		The preliminary rounds for the Battalion Cup for Boxing were fought in the Battalion Recreation Room. The Divisional Cinema visited DUISDORF.	KFCm
DUISDORF	16.5.19.		"A" and "C" Coys commenced firing the G.M.C. on WITTERSCHLICK Long Range. Light – bright.	KFCm
DUISDORF	17.5.19.		"A" and "C" Coys continue firing the G.M.C. Light – bright. STRENGTH DECREASE – OFFICERS. Capt. E.D.T. Hayes R.A.M.C. left this unit on this date.	KFCm.
DUISDORF	18.5.19.		STRENGTH. INCREASE – OFFICERS Capt. F. Godson. R.A.M.C. reported for duty. Divine Services & Medical Inspection of the Battalion.	KFCm
DUISDORF	19.5.19		"A" and "C" Coys. continue firing the G.M.C. Light – bright.	
DUISDORF	20.5.19		All available Officers & N.C.O's of "B" and "D" Coys attended a lecture by Lt. Col. TYSHAM at Bornheim.	KFCm
DUISDORF	21.5.19.		"A" and "C" Coys continue firing the G.M.C. Light – bright. The N.C.O's examination commenced this day. Practical in the morning written exam. in the afternoon in the Battalion Recreation Room	KFCm

1875 Wt. W593/826 1,000,000 4/15 J.B.C. & A. A.D.S.S./Forms/C. 2118.

Instructions regarding War Diaries and Intelligence Summaries are contained in F. S. Regs., Part II. and the Staff Manual respectively. Title Pages will be prepared in manuscript.

WAR DIARY or ~~INTELLIGENCE SUMMARY~~ of 52nd Welch Regt

Army Form C. 2118.

Sheet IV Volume III (Erase heading not required.) From 1.5.19 to 31.5.19

Place	Date	Hour	Summary of Events and Information	Remarks and references to Appendices
DUISDORF	22.5.19		"A" and "C" Coys continue firing the G.M.C. Light – bright. N.C.O's examination finished.	KFCw
DUISDORF	23.5.19		"A" and "C" Coys continue firing the G.M.C. – Light – bright. The Commanding Officer, the adjutant, the acting 2nd in Command and the Quartermaster reconnoitred the BONN defences.	KFCw.
DUISDORF	24.5.19		Information was received that reinforcements – 200 – O.R's would reach the Unit on Monday 26th inst. "C" Coy Lewis Gunners fired on the 30x Range during the morning.	KF Cw
DUISDORF	25.5.19		Divine Services & Medical Inspection.	
DUISDORF	26.5.19		STRENGTH – INCREASE – 200 O.R's arrived in the Station and are taken on strength from this date.	KF Cw.
KFCw ~~DUISDORF~~			Mr Arthur Dorsy lectured to the Battalion in the Battalion Recreation Room. Subject – "The Mystery of the Maya". The lecture proved interesting and was enjoyed by all ranks.	
DUISDORF	27.5.19		The Corps Commander was present while "B" and "D" Coys were firing the L.G. Course on WITTERSCHLICK Long Range	KFCw

1875 Wt. W593/826 1,000,000 4/15 J.B.C. & A. A.D.S.S./Forms/C. 2118.

Instructions regarding War Diaries and Intelligence Summaries are contained in F. S. Regs., Part II. and the Staff Manual respectively. Title Pages will be prepared in manuscript.

Army Form C. 2118.

WAR DIARY
of 52nd Welch Regiment
~~INTELLIGENCE SUMMARY~~
(Erase heading not required.)

Sheet V Volume III From. 1.5.19 to 31.5.19.

Place	Date	Hour	Summary of Events and Information	Remarks and references to Appendices
DUISDORF	28.5.19		The Battalion was engaged in Baths and Training.	KFCm
DUISDORF	29.5.19		The Battalion was engaged in Route marching ROUTE: PARADE GROUND; ROCHUSTRASSE; ROAD JUNCTION 800x N. of ROTTGEN; IPPENDORF; LENGSDORF; BILLETS.	KFCm
			The B.G.C. 2nd Western Infantry Brigade inspected the drafts received from the Cheshire Regiment. After inspection the B.G.C. addressed the drafts. Before ~~they~~ dismissing the Parade the Commanding Officer said a few words.	
DUISDORF	30.5.19		Books and Training Manuals were issued to all Companies	KFCm
DUISDORF	31.5.19		The Battalion Sports were held on this date. The day was warm & sunny, and the Sports were a great success. They were attended by the B.G.C. 2nd Western Inf. Bde. In the evening the "Rhinedrops" - the Battalion Concert Party - gave a show in "C" Coy. Dining [illegible] which was attended by Major-General E.P. Strickland, CB, CMG, DSO. G.O.C. Western Division, and Brigadier-General T.O. Marden, C.B.; C.M.G. The Battalion Boxing Cup & Special Prizes given by the Commanding Officer to special boxers were presented by General Strickland, who [illegible] short address before the presentation. The Boxing Cup was ~~won~~ for the month of May by "B" Coy. Capt. G.L. Warlock, M.C. received the cup for his Company.	KFCm.

[Signature], Lieut. Colonel, Commdg. 52nd Bn. Welch Regt.

1875 Wt. W593/826 1,000,000 4/15 J.B.C. & A. A.D.S.S./Forms/C. 2118.

ORDERLY ROOM
2 JUN 1919
52nd
BATT. WELSH REGT.

(6414) Wt. W3906/P1607 2,500,000 7/18 McA & W Ltd (E 3591) Forms W3091/4. Army Form W.3091.

Cover for Documents.

Nature of Enclosures.

CONFIDENTIAL.

War Diary

of

52nd Battn Welsh Regiment

from 1st June 1919 to 30th June 1919

(Volume IV)

Notes, or Letters written.

R H Montgomery Major

Commanding 52nd Bn Welsh Regt.

Instructions regarding War Diaries and Intelligence Summaries are contained in F. S. Regs., Part II. and the Staff Manual respectively. Title Pages will be prepared in manuscript.

ORDERLY ROOM
1 JUL 1919
B121
52nd BATT. WELSH REGT.

WAR DIARY
of 52nd Welch Regiment
~~INTELLIGENCE SUMMARY~~
(Erase heading not required.)

Army Form C. 2118

Sheet 1. - Volume IV From 1.6.19 to 30.6.19

Place	Date	Hour	Summary of Events and Information	Remarks and references to Appendices
DUISDORF	1.6.19		Divine Services & Medical Inspection of the Battalion.	KFCm.
DUISDORF	2.6.19		"B" and "D" Coys. start platoon training. The Commanding Officer was present with both companies during the morning.	KFCm.
DUISDORF	3.6.19		In recognition of the birthday of His Majesty the King, Brigadier General T.O. Marden, C.B.; C.M.G. held a ceremonial parade for Units of the Brigade on the Parade Ground of this Unit. After the Royal Salute Units marched past the B.G.C. in column of companies. The remainder of the day was a general holiday.	KFCm.
DUISDORF	4.6.19		The G.O.C. Western Division inspected B. Coy on Platoon Training Area in Platoon Training.	
			STRENGTH. - DECREASE. 1 O.R. proceeded to rejoin 1/4 Battalion Cheshire Regt and is struck off strength from this date.	KFCm.
DUISDORF	5.6.19		It was decided that all ranks would carry Box Respirators on the early morning parade and that five minutes training (Rapid adjustment) in the Box Respirator would be done.	
			It was ordered that all Guards would mount in Marching order wearing caps.	
			"B" & "D" Coys. struck off all duties while doing Platoon Training.	
			It was decided that Platoon Training would be carried out in Fighting order, wearing steel helmets.	KFCm.

Instructions regarding War Diaries and Intelligence Summaries are contained in F. S. Regs., Part II. and the Staff Manual respectively. Title Pages will be prepared in manuscript.

Army Form C. 2118

WAR DIARY
of 53rd Welch Regiment
~~INTELLIGENCE SUMMARY~~
(Erase heading not required.)

Sheet II Volume IV From. 1.6.19 to 30.6.19

Place	Date	Hour	Summary of Events and Information	Remarks and references to Appendices
DUISDORF	6.6.19.		O's. C. "A" & "C" Coys with their platoon Commanders reconnoitred Training Areas "A" and "B", and it was decided that Platoon Training for these Companies would commence on June 16th. - DRESS. - Fighting Order.	
DUISDORF	8.6.19.		Divine Services and Medical Inspection of the Battalion. It was decided that Coys. doing platoon training would use area "A" only.	RFCW
DUISDORF	9.6.19.		Whit Monday. This day was a holiday. In the afternoon this unit played a cricket match against 53rd Welch Regt at ALFTER in the BONN League, we being the victors.	RFCW. RFCW
DUISDORF	10.6.19		Twenty Men were tested for entry in Swimming Competition at BONN. STRENGTH-INCREASE-OFFICERS- 2nd Lieut P. MacTavish, M.C. reported back from sick leave. Scout Training under this Officer was continued.	
DUISDORF	14.6.19.		The Commanding Officer and Adjutant were present and judged all Companies in the Platoon Competition. "A" Coy. had the best platoon.	
DUISDORF	16.6.19		"A" and "C" Companies commence platoon training and are struck off all duties.	
DUISDORF	17.6.19.		Word was received that "J" Day would be "A" i.e. 20th June 1919. The Commanding Officer held a conference of 2nd in Command, Company Commanders, Adjutant, Transport Officer, Lewis Gun Officer, Signalling Officer, and Lieut E. J. James, Officer i/c Details, when all arrangements for the move were completed. Captain J.A.L. DRAFFIN and 2nd Lieut F. RATCHIFFE proceeded to ENGLAND on 14 days leave.	AB

1875 Wt. W593/826 1,000,000 4/15 J.B.C. & A. A.D.S.S./Forms/C. 2118.

Instructions regarding War Diaries and Intelligence Summaries are contained in F. S. Regs., Part II. and the Staff Manual respectively. Title Pages will be prepared in manuscript. Sheet 3, Volume IV

WAR DIARY
or
~~INTELLIGENCE~~ SUMMARY

52nd Welsh Regt.

(Erase heading not required.) From :- 1-6-1919 to 30-6-1919

Army Form C. 2118

Place	Date	Hour	Summary of Events and Information	Remarks and references to Appendices
DUISDORF	18/6/1919		Lieut W.R.D. COOPER and Lieut R. PARRY proceeded to ENGLAND on 14 days leave. Six other ranks admitted to hospital. Three other ranks discharged from hospital. One other rank returned from leave to U.K. One other rank sent to COLOGNE for demobilization. One other rank sent to ENGLAND to join Coldstream Guards. The Battalion took over the BONN Bridge Guard from 16th Lancashire Fusiliers Strength of Guard one Officer two sergeants, 2 Corporals and sixteen men. The Battalion furnished the Guard for the X Corps Commander at PALACE SCHOMBURG, BONN.	
			The Battalion was employed preparing for the move by march route to BONN.	A.B. Capt
DUISDORF	19/6/1919		Lieuts F.W. MOORSOM, J.C. FERNELEY and H. PARRY proceeded to ENGLAND on 14 days leave.	
DUISDORF	19-6-19	0815	The Battalion left DUISDORF by march route to BONN. Dress.- F.S.M.O carrying one blanket	
BONN	19-6-19	0930	Arrived BONN. "B" and "D" Coys, transport and half Battn Head Qrs Company were billeted in INFANTERIE CASERNA under command of Major R.H. MONTGOMERY. "A" and "C" Coys, signallers and ½ Bn H.Q. Company billeted at the Schools, DOETSCH STRASSE under the command of Bt Lt-Colonel J.R. MINSHULL FORD, DSO, M.C. Companies were employed in cleaning equipment & settling down in new billets. The Commanding Officer, Adjutant and Company Commanders reconnoitred the BONN Bridge defences	A.B. Capt

1875 Wt. W593/826 1,000,000 4/15 J.B.C. & A. A.D.S.S./Forms/C. 2118.

Army Form C. 2118

WAR DIARY
or
~~INTELLIGENCE SUMMARY~~

52nd Welsh Regt

(Erase heading not required.)

Instructions regarding War Diaries and Intelligence Summaries are contained in F. S. Regs., Part II. and the Staff Manual respectively. Title Pages will be prepared in manuscript.

Sheet 4, Volume IV, From 1-6-19 to 30-6-1919.

Place	Date	Hour	Summary of Events and Information	Remarks and references to Appendices
BONN	20/6/1919.		6 other ranks discharged from hospital. "A" + "C" Coys furnished a working party (24 O. Ranks) to construct machine gun emplacements on the BONN Bridge. Remainder of Battn. did Guard Drill on the RHINEWERFT under the Adjutant. X Corps Commanders Guard relieved by 16th Lancs Fus. Company Commanders took their section leaders around the BONN Bridge defences.	A.B. Capt
BONN	20/6/1919.		6 other ranks tried by F.G.C.M for breaking arrest. 5 other ranks discharged hospital All companies bathed in the floating baths on the RHINE.	A.B. Capt.
BONN	22/6/1919.		Divine Services were held after which companies bathed.	A.B. Capt
BONN	23/6/1919		Two other ranks discharged hospital. One other rank evacuated to ENGLAND sick. R.S.M. LEWIS transferred from the 1/7th Cheshire Regt to 52nd Welsh. Companies received clean underclothing + bathed in the RHINE. Guard Drill was carried out by all companies. Bt. Lt-Colonel J.R. MINSHULL FORD, DSO, MC. assumed temporary command of the 2nd Western Infantry Brigade. Major R.H. MONTGOMERY assumed temporary command of the Battalion. Captain G.L. WORLOCK, M.C. assumed command of the detachment at INFANTERIE CASERNA.	A.B. Capt.
BONN	24/6/1919		Lieut H HUNT returned from U.K. leave and proceeded to join the 154th Labour Coy. Captain R.H. LINDSAY proceeded to U.K. on 14 days leave. One other rank transferred to 1/8th London Regt. The Battalion carried out training at EXERZIER PLATZ, BONN.	A.B. Capt

1875 Wt. W593/826 1,000,000 4/15 J.B.C. & A. A.D.S.S./Forms/C. 2118.

Instructions regarding War Diaries and Intelligence Summaries are contained in F. S. Regs., Part II. and the Staff Manual respectively. Title Pages will be prepared in manuscript.

Army Form C. 2118

WAR DIARY
or
~~INTELLIGENCE SUMMARY~~ 52nd Welsh Regt.
(Erase heading not required.)

Sheet 5. Volume IV From 1-6-19 to 30-6-1919

Place	Date	Hour	Summary of Events and Information	Remarks and references to Appendices
BONN	24/6/1919.		A great improvement in the turn out and general smartness on parade has taken place. The men are very keen to perform guard duty on the BONN Bridge. The change of surrounding has worked wonders and they appear to be very contented although guard duty is very frequent. 52nd Welsh Operation Order No 3 issued	A.B. Capt.
BONN	25/6/1919.		Captain R.H. LINDSAY posted to Depôt Royal Irish Fusiliers and struck off the strength. Companies carried out training on the RHINEWERFT. One other rank proceeded on leave to ENGLAND. A regimental concert was held in the School Lecture Room and was enjoyed by a large audience.	A.B. Capt.
BONN	26/6/1919.		10 other ranks proceeded on 14 days leave to ENGLAND. Two other ranks discharged hospital. The Battalion marched to EXERZIER PLATZ and carried out Battalion Drill under the Adjutant. Lieut L. BELL admitted to hospital	A.B. Capt.
BONN	27/6/19.		Three other ranks taken on the strength from 3rd Welsh Regt. Four officers and 200 other ranks went for a trip on the RHINE to COBLENZ. The Battalion took over the Divisional Commanders Guard at WESSELING. Strength of guard – one platoon. The O.C. 'C' Coy reports that his men were very anxious to be selected for this duty.	A.B. Capt.
BONN.	28/6/19		8 other ranks rejoined from leave. 2 other ranks admitted to hospital. Battalion Drill under the Adjutant was carried out at EXERZIER PLATZ. The Brigade Commander was present.	A.B. Capt.

1875 Wt. W593/826 1,000,000 4/15 J.B.C. & A. A.D.S.S./Forms/C. 2118.

Army Form C. 2118

Instructions regarding War Diaries and Intelligence Summaries are contained in F. S. Regs., Part II. and the Staff Manual respectively. Title Pages will be prepared in manuscript. Sheet 6, Volume IV

WAR DIARY
or
~~INTELLIGENCE SUMMARY~~
(Erase heading not required.)

52nd Welsh Regt
~~From~~ 1-6-19 to 30-6-1919

Place	Date	Hour	Summary of Events and Information	Remarks and references to Appendices
BONN	28/6/1919		Two other ranks proceeded on leave to ENGLAND.	
			The Battalion Cricket Team played H^d Qrs, Lancashire Division at SIEGBURG in the BONN League Tournament.	AB Capt
			52nd Welsh Administrative Instructions No 1 in connection with Operation Order No 3 issued.	
BONN	29/6/1919		Divine Services were held for all denominations	AB Capt
BONN	30/6/1919		The Battalion was employed preparing for move to DUISDORF.	
			Addendum to Operation Order No 3 issued	AB Capt

R H Montgomery
Major
Comdg 52nd Bn Welsh Regt.

W.

(6414) Wt. W3906/P1607 2,500,000 7/18 McA & W Ltd (E 3591) Forms W3091/4.

Army Form W.3091.

Cover for Documents.

CONFIDENTIAL.

Nature of Enclosures.

War Diary

of

52nd Battalion The Welch Regiment.

from 1-7-1919 to 31-7-1919

Volume V.

A Bridgens
Captain
1-8-19 Commdg. 52nd Battalion The Welch Regt.

Notes, or Letters written.

Army Form C. 2118.

Instructions regarding War Diaries and Intelligence Summaries are contained in F. S. Regs., Part II. and the Staff Manual respectively. Title pages will be prepared in manuscript. Sheet I. Vol. V

WAR DIARY of 52nd Welch Regiment ~~INTELLIGENCE SUMMARY.~~

(Erase heading not required.)

From 1-7-19 to 31-7-1919.

Place	Date	Hour	Summary of Events and Information	Remarks and references to Appendices
DUISDORF	1-7-19		The Battalion moved from BONN to DUISDORF. The move was completed by 0930 hours.	
			Capt. G. L. Worlock proceeded to England on 14 days leave.	KFCm H.
DUISDORF	2-7-19		"A" & "C" Coys recommence Platoon Training on Area "A".	
			Lieut E. J. James proceeded to England to attend the meeting at Bisley.	KFCm H.
			18 other ranks proceeded on leave to United Kingdom. Two other ranks admitted hospital.	
			Two other ranks discharged hospital.	
			"B" and "C" Coys employed finishing duties & platoon drill.	A.B. Capt
			Seven other ranks sent to No 3 Coy. Train, R.A.S. Corps, IMPECOVEN for duty.	
DUISDORF	3-7-19		8 other ranks proceeded on leave to United Kingdom. Two other ranks returned from U.K. leave.	
			~~Lieut E. J. JAMES~~ AB. One other rank discharged hospital.	A.B. Capt
DUISDORF	4-7-19		Observed as a holiday in commemoration of the signing of Peace. One officer and 100	
			other ranks went for a RHINE trip. Sports were held in the afternoon. The	
			Regtl. Jazz Band proved a great success. Twenty other ranks proceeded to	
			England on leave. Nine other ranks proceeded to WIDDIG on a signalling Course.	A.B. Capt
DUISDORF	5-7-19		One other rank admitted to hospital. One other rank discharged hospital.	
			"A" & "C" Coys exercised at Platoon Training. "B" & "D" Kit inspection & drill.	A.B. Capt
DUISDORF	6-7-19		Divine Services for all denominations. Medical Inspection for all companies carried out.	
			Two other ranks admitted hospital. One other rank discharged hospital.	A.B. Capt
DUISDORF	7-7-19		"B", "D" and "C" Coys were bathed & received clean underclothing.	
			Lieut J. W. O. CANDY rejoined the Battalion from duty as R.T.O. COLOGNE.	
			9 other ranks proceeded to U.K. on leave, also Captain J. A. GILBERT and Lieut T. M. JARRETT.	A.B. Capt

D. D. & L., London, E.C. (A5003) Wt. W1 71/M2031 750,000 5/17 Sch. 52 Forms/C2118/14

Army Form C. 2118.

WAR DIARY
or
~~INTELLIGENCE SUMMARY.~~

Instructions regarding War Diaries and Intelligence Summaries are contained in F. S. Regs., Part II. and the Staff Manual respectively. Title pages will be prepared in manuscript. Sheet II. Volume V.

(Erase heading not required.) 52nd Welsh Regiment From 1-7-1919 to 31-7-1919.

Place	Date	Hour	Summary of Events and Information	Remarks and references to Appendices
DUISDORF.		7-7-19	Board of Officers assembled to examine and report on state of webbed equipment.	A.B. Capt
DUISDORF		8-7-19	One other rank discharged hospital. 44 (Forty four other ranks proceeded on leave to United Kingdom. Brigade Commander and Adjutant visited WESSELING to inspect quarters etc of the Divisional Commanders Guard. 'A' Coy. bathed at Brigade Baths.	A.B. Capt
DUISDORF		9-7-19	Twenty other ranks proceeded on leave to United Kingdom. One other rank discharged hospital. Lieut. S. J. NEEDHAM, M.C., and 15 other ranks proceeded on 48 hours leave to COLOGNE. 'A' and 'C' Coys ordered to continue platoon training till 12-7-1919. B and D Coys. drill, duties etc.	A.B. Capt
DUISDORF		10-7-19.	Ten other ranks proceeded on leave to U.K. One other rank discharged hospital, two other ranks admitted hospital. Divisional Cinema visited DUISDORF and gave a very good show.	A.B. Capt.
DUISDORF		11-7-19	Coy. Sergt-Majors Chignell, Davies and Sergts Blything and Bownes proceeded to take part in Allies Victory March, in PARIS on the 14-7-1919. One other rank proceeded on demobilization. One other rank evacuated sick to U.K. Eleven other ranks returned from U.K. leave.	A.B. Capt.
DUISDORF.		12-7-19	The Brigade Commander inspected cookhouses etc. Everything was in order and clean. Eight other ranks proceeded on leave to U.K. An examination for promotion of N.C.O's was ~~[illegible]~~ held.	A.B. Capt
DUISDORF		13-7-19	Divine Services for all denominations were held. All Companies were medically inspected. 8 other ranks proceeded on leave to United Kingdom. 2/Lieut. E. EVANS proceeded on an Educational Course to COLOGNE	A.B. Capt

D. D. & L., London, E.C. (A8001) Wt. W1-71/M2031 750,000 5/17 Sch. 52 Forms/C2118/14

Army Form C. 2118.

WAR DIARY ~~or INTELLIGENCE SUMMARY.~~

(Erase heading not required.)

52nd Bn Welsh Regt.

Instructions regarding War Diaries and Intelligence Summaries are contained in F. S. Regs., Part II. and the Staff Manual respectively. Title pages will be prepared in manuscript. Sheet III, Volume V

From 1-7-1919 to 31-7-1919

Place	Date	Hour	Summary of Events and Information	Remarks and references to Appendices
DUISDORF		14-7-19	8 other ranks proceeded on leave to United Kingdom. 3 other ranks admitted to hospital. 2 other ranks discharged hospital. Examination of N.C.O's for promotion continued by the Adjutant.	A.B. Capt.
DUISDORF		15-7-19	"A" and "C" Coys bathed and had clean underclothing issued. The Brigade Commander examined all officers + sergeants mess accounts. Captain A.W. FISH, MC and 8 other ranks proceeded on leave to U.K. 3 other ranks proceeded on courses of instruction. One other rank discharged hospital.	A.B. Capt.
DUISDORF		16-7-19	One other rank admitted to hospital. Ten other ranks proceeded on leave to U.K. Two other ranks sent for demobilization. Six other ranks proceeded to England on re-enlistment leave.	A.B. Capt.
DUISDORF		17-7-19	Lieut W.H CORNER, M.C. rejoined from leave to U.K. Captain A.G.J. OWEN M.C. and 9 other ranks proceeded on leave to United Kingdom. Steps taken through Battalion Orders to ensure a better attendance at Educational Training. Brigade Drill Competition held at FLERZHEIM	A.B. Capt.
DUISDORF		18-7-19	A distinguishing badge (green cloth 2 inches square) authorised and issued to Companies. This badge to be sewn on right sleeve of jacket two inches below the shoulder strap. One other rank discharged from hospital. 2nd Lieut E J PETERS admitted to hospital. Captain G.L WORLOCK, M.C. and 2nd Lieut S.E. HARPER returned from leave to United Kingdom	A.B. Capt.
DUISDORF		19-7-19	A holiday to commemorate the signing of peace. Brigade Sports were held at ALFTER. It was a great success and was very well attended. Nine other ranks proceeded on leave to the United Kingdom. The Germans are now allowed to hold Private and Public Dances and Meetings without special sanction providing the British authorities are notified 4 days beforehand	A.B. Capt.

D. D. & L., London, E.C. (A7004) Wt. W1771/M2031 750,000 5/17 Sch. 52 Forms/C2118/14

Instructions regarding War Diaries and Intelligence Summaries are contained in F. S. Regs., Part II. and the Staff Manual respectively. Title pages will be prepared in manuscript. Sheet IV. Volume V

WAR DIARY

~~or~~

~~INTELLIGENCE SUMMARY.~~

(Erase heading not required.) 52nd Bn Welsh Regt From 1-7-1919 to 31-7-1919.

Army Form C. 2118.

Place	Date	Hour	Summary of Events and Information	Remarks and references to Appendices
DUISDORF		20-7-19	Divine Services for all denominations were held. All companies were medically examined. 7 other ranks proceeded on leave to U.K. Five other ranks returned from leave to U.K. 4 other ranks discharged hospital. LIEUT R. CROW, Welsh Regt, reported for duty from 3rd Bn Welsh Regt, England.	A.B. Capt
DUISDORF		21-7-19	3 other ranks returned from leave to U.K. 6 other ranks joined for duty from 2nd Welsh Regt, ENGLAND. 7 other ranks proceeded on leave to U.K. One other rank admitted to hospital. One other rank transferred to Depot, Welsh Regt, England. Three other ranks transferred to R.E's (Signals.)	A.B. Capt
DUISDORF		22-7-19	3 other ranks admitted to hospital. Seven other ranks proceeded to U.K. on leave. One other rank returned from leave to U.K. All defective box respirators examined by Brigade Gas N.C.O. Battalion Baths and Delouser completed by R.E's.	A.B. Capt
DUISDORF		23-7-19	Divisional Commander inspected Cook houses + some of the billets. Ten other ranks proceeded on leave to U.K, and ten returned off leave. One other rank admitted and one discharged hospital. Lieut + Qr Mr T.M. JARRETT returned from leave to U.K.	A.B. Capt
DUISDORF		24-7-19	All companies bathed and received clean under clothing. Two officers and 15 other ranks returned from leave to U.K. Five Other ranks proceeded on leave to U.K. Two other ranks discharged hospital. Three other ranks transferred to Details, Welsh Regt, FRANCE. Divisional Travelling Cinema visited DUISDORF and gave a show	A.B. Capt
DUISDORF		25-7-19	Lieut E. EVANS rejoined from Educational Course. Four other ranks proceeded and five returned from leave to U.K.	A.B. Capt

D. D. & L., London, E.C.
(A8001) Wt. W1771/M2031 750,000 5/17 Sch. 52 Forms/C2118/14

Instructions regarding War Diaries and Intelligence Summaries are contained in F. S. Regs., Part II. and the Staff Manual respectively. Title pages will be prepared in manuscript. Sheet V. Volume V.

WAR DIARY
or
INTELLIGENCE SUMMARY.
(*Erase heading not required.*) 52nd Bn Welsh Regt From 1-7-1919 to 31-7-1919

Army Form C. 2118.

Place	Date	Hour	Summary of Events and Information	Remarks and references to Appendices
DUISDORF		26-7-19	Lieut L. BELL discharged hospital and placed under close arrest for Alcoholism. One other rank to hospital. 16 other ranks returned from leave to U.K. Orders received from War Office ordering Major R H MONTGOMERY to ENGLAND to join the 2nd Welsh Regt.	A.B. Capt.
DUISDORF.		27-7-19	Divine Services were held for all denominations. Medical Inspection for all companies. 27 other ranks returned and 6 proceeded on leave to U.K. One other rank admitted to hospital. One other rank struck off as a deserter.	A.B. Capt.
DUISDORF		28-7-19	2nd Lieut. H. TAYLOR, DCM, M.M, Shropshire Light Infantry joined for duty. Lieut S.J. NEEDHAM, MC, and 2nd Lieut T. POSTLETHWAITE and 6 other ranks proceeded on leave to U.K. Thirty six other ranks rejoined from U.K. leave. B and D Coys continued company training, "A" and "C" Coys duties guards etc.	A.B. Capt.
DUISDORF		29.7.19	The G.O.C. Western Division inspected 'B' & 'D' Coys at training on Area A. Captain A. Bridgens assumed Command of the Battalion vice Major R.H. Montgomery who proceeded to England to join the 2nd Welch Regt. Lieut R.F.C. MacIver assumed the duties of adjutant. 2 O.Rs returned and 2 O.Rs proceeded to EUSKIRCHEN for police duty with IX Corps. 1 O.R. discharged from hospital, 1 O.R. transferred to 47th C.C.S. 6 O.Rs returned and 6 proceeded on leave to the U.K.	R.F. Cmdt.
DUISDORF		30.7.19	Two German motor lorries reported for use in motor engineering classes under Lt. R. Crow	

D. D. & L., London, E.C. (A8005) Wt. W1 71/M2031 750,000 5/17 Sch. 52 Forms/C2118/14

Army Form C. 2118.

WAR DIARY

~~or~~ 52nd Welch Regiment

~~INTELLIGENCE SUMMARY.~~

(*Erase heading not required.*) From 1-7-1919 to 31-7-1919

Instructions regarding War Diaries and Intelligence Summaries are contained in F. S. Regs., Part II. and the Staff Manual respectively. Title pages will be prepared in manuscript. Sheet VI. Vol. V.

Place	Date	Hour	Summary of Events and Information	Remarks and references to Appendices
DUISDORF		30.7.19	6 O.R's proceeded on leave to 8 O.R's returned from leave to the U.K. 1 Officer (Lieut. Capt. Nicholson) discharged from hospital. 1 Officer (2/Lt. S.G. Harper) admitted to hospital. 1 O.R. proceeded to No1 Concentration Camp, COLOGNE for demobilization and is struck off strength.	R.F. Cm Lieut
DUISDORF		31.7.19	The Divisional Cinema showed at DUISDORF. There was a good attendance. 1 Officer (2/Lt. Dow Candy) transferred to Chinese Labour Corps. struck off strength. 7 O.R's proceeded on leave to and 2 O.R's returned from leave to the U.K. 1 O.R. returned from a course at ROSBERG. 1 O.R. discharged from hospital. 1 O.R evacuated sick to the U.K. and struck off strength.	R.F. Cm Lieut

1-8-1919.

A. Bridgens Captain ~~LIEUT.-COLONEL~~
COMMG. 52ND BN. THE WELCH REGT.

D. D. & L., London, E.C.
(A8001) Wt. W171/M2031 750,000 5/17 Sch. 52 Forms/C2118/14

BEF

1 DIVISION

2 BRIGADE

53 WELSH R.

1919 MAR to 1919 JULY

1/11

CONFIDENTIAL

WAR DIARY

— of the —

53rd Batt THE WELSH REGT

from 23rd March 1919. To 31st March 1919.

W

Instructions regarding War Diaries and Intelligence Summaries are contained in F. S. Regs., Part II. and the Staff Manual respectively. Title pages will be prepared in manuscript.

WAR DIARY
or
~~INTELLIGENCE~~ SUMMARY.

(*Erase heading not required.*)

Army Form C. 2118.

Place	Date	Hour	Summary of Events and Information	Remarks and references to Appendices
Shoreham by Sea.	22/3/19	1130 1200	Battalion entrained in two parties at 1130 and 1200 for Dover.	
Dover	22/3/19	1605	1st Party arrived at 1605 2nd party at 1655. Battalion was accommodated for the night at Victoria Barracks Dover.	
Dover	23/3/19	1300	Battalion embarked at 1300 with the 52nd Leicesters.	
Dunkerque	23/3/19	1700	Batt. disembarked at 1700 and Marched to No 3 Rest Camp, a distance of about 5 miles, where accommodation was provided for the night.	
Dunkerque	24/3/19	1040	Batt. paraded at 1040 ready to entrain at SAND SIDING. ~~at~~ This order was cancelled & arrangements were made for the men to have dinner. This in turn was cancelled and the Batt. paraded & entrained at SAND SIDING at 13.00.	
	25/3/19	0145	0145 where a meal was provided. Left BAISSIEUX at 0245. Arrived at BAISSIEUX at 1715 where another meal was provided. Arrived CHARLEROI at Left latter place at 1815 & arrived HUY 2245. Departed from HUY 2345	
DUISDORF	26/3/19		Arrived DUISDORF 1415 and marched to ALFTER where the Battalion took over billets from the 2nd K.R.R.C.	
ALFTER	27/3/19		Billeted here	
ALFTER	28/3/19		do.	
do	29/3/19	1000	Battalion was to be inspected at 1000 by Brig. General F.O. Marden, C.B, C.M.G. but this was cancelled.	
do	31/3/19	1000	Bat. was inspected by Brig. Gen. F.O. Marden C.B. C.M.G.	

D. D. & L., London, E.C.
(A10266) Wt W5300/P713 750,000 2/18 Sch. 52 Forms/C2118/16.

Instructions regarding War Diaries and Intelligence Summaries are contained in F. S. Regs., Part II. and the Staff Manual respectively. Title pages will be prepared in manuscript.

WAR DIARY
or
INTELLIGENCE SUMMARY.
(Erase heading not required.)

Army Form C. 2118.

Place	Date	Hour	Summary of Events and Information	Remarks and references to Appendices
Shoreham by Sea	22/3/19	1130 1200	Battalion entrained in two parties at 1130 and 1200 for Dover.	
Dover	22/3/19	1605	1st Party arrived at 1605 2nd party at 1655. Battalion was accommodated for the night at Victoria Barracks, Dover.	
Dover	23/3/19	1300	Battalion embarked at 1300 with the 52nd Leicesters	
Dunkerque	23/3/19	1700	Batt. disembarked at 1700 and marched to No 3 Rest Camp, a distance of about 5 miles, where accommodation was provided for the night.	
Dunkerque	24/3/19	1040	Batt. paraded at 1040 ready to entrain at SAND SIDING. This order was cancelled & arrangements were made for the men to have dinner. This in turn was cancelled and the Batt. paraded & entrained at SAND SIDING at 1300. Arrived at BAISSIEUX at	
	25/3/19	0145	0145 where a meal was provided. Left BAISSIEUX at 0245. Arrived CHARLEROI at 1715 where another meal was provided. Left latter place at 1815 & arrived HUY 2245. Departed from HUY 2345	
DUISDORF	26/3/19		Arrived DUISDORF 1415 and marched to ALFTER where the Battalion took over billets from the 2nd KRRC.	
ALFTER	27/3/19		Billeted here	
ALFTER	28/3/19		do	
do	29/3/19	1000	Battalion was to be inspected at 1000 by Brig General J.O. Marden CB CMG but this was cancelled	
do	31/3/19	1000	Batt was inspected by Brig Gen J.O. Marden, CB CMG	[signature]

D. D. & L., London, E.C.
(A10266) Wt W5300/P713 750,000 2/18 Sch. 52 Forms/C2118/16.

(6414) Wt. W3906/P1607 2,500,000 7/18 McA & W Ltd (**E 3591**) Forms W3091/4. Army Form W.3091.

Cover for Documents.

Nature of Enclosures.

CONFIDENTIAL.

WAR DIARY

of

53rd Batt WELSH REGIMENT.

1st – 30th April 1919.

Notes, or Letters written.

Instructions regarding War Diaries and Intelligence Summaries are contained in F. S. Regs., Part II. and the Staff Manual respectively. Title pages will be prepared in manuscript.

WAR DIARY
or
~~INTELLIGENCE SUMMARY.~~
(Erase heading not required.)

Army Form C. 2118.

Place	Date	Hour	Summary of Events and Information	Remarks and references to Appendices
ALFTER	1/4/19		Strength of Batt 34 Officers + 601 other ranks.	
"	3/4/19		The Battalion was inspected by Lt Gen Sir Walter Braithwaite KCB., Comdg IX Corps who expressed himself as well satisfied with the parade. "The General turn out, the packing of the packs, the steadiness shown on parade and the March past" to quote the words of the Corps Commander "reflected the greatest credit on the officers NCO's + men of the Batt."	
"	7/4/19		Provisional orders were issued for the defence of BONN	Appendix I
"	10/4/19		Lt Col C.C. Norman, DSO. RWF. reported for duty.	
"	12/4/19		Lt Col C.C. Norman assumed command of the Batt. vice Lt Col E.H.C.P. Bellingham CMG DSO Royal Scots	
"	13/4/19		2/Lt G.H.S. BURROWS reported from Course of Education at OXFORD.	
"	15/4/19		LT R.P. HUGHES, RWF. + 2/Lt E.W. ALEXANDER, EAST LANCS left Batt for demobilisation 2 Lt M.B. DOWSE, RWF. proceeded to ENGLAND to rejoin Depot.	
"	16/4/19		2LT. B.H. HOPKINS " " " " " "	
"	17/4/19	1100	Dr W.J. Tyson delivered a lecture on "Health + Citizenship" to the Batt.	
"	18/4/19		2/Lt E. BEYNON left for demobilisation	
"	25/4/19		Lt H.M. HAKE, Intelligence Officer, WESTERN DIVISION delivered an interesting lecture on the "general situation in EUROPE"	
"	27/4/19		LT T.T. DAVIES rejoined from School of Instruction (Education) Newmarket.	
"	29/4/19	9.30	The Batt was inspected by the General Officer Comdg in Chief RHINE ARMY at DUISDORF with other units of the Brigade.	

[initials]

D. D. & L., London, E.C.
(A8004) Wt. W1771/M2 31 750,000 5/17 Sch. 52 Forms/C2118/14

SECRET.

REFERENCE PROVISIONAL SCHEME FOR D E F E N C E OF B O N N

A M E N D M E N T S.

Sheet I. Para.1.(b) In first line for "three" substitute "Two".

-do- Delete "Scheme Z Riots in BONN"-Code word Riots".

Para.11 (b) For "3 N.C.Os & 10 Ptes."D" Coy.substitute "1 Lewis Gun & 1 Rifle Sections."

(c) For "1 N.C.O.& 6 Ptes. "D" Coy. substitute "1 Rifle Section

(d) For "3 N.C.Os & 18 other ranks "D" Coy. substitute "2 Lewis Guns & 1 Rifle Sections.

Para.111 For "3 N.C.Os & 10 other ranks "D" Coy. substitute "1 Lewis Gun & 1 Rifle Section.

For "1 N.C.O.& 6 Ptes."D" Coy." substitute 1 Rifle Section.

Para.IV. Delete "Scheme Z upon receipt of code word "Riots" the same action will take place as set forth in para.3.

SHEET 11.Para.VI, Delete words "Riots" "Prepare to move".

" VII. Delete words "Reports-Scheme Z"

[signature]
Captain
Adjt. 53rd (Y.S.) Bn. Training Res. (Welsh Regt.)

ISSUED TO.

No.1. C. O.	No.2. 2nd In Command.
No.3. Adjutant.	No.4. O.C. "A" Coy.
No.5. O.C. "B" Coy.	No.6. O.C. "C" Coy.
No.7. O.C. "D" Coy.	No.8. Quartermaster.
No.9. Transport Officer.	No10. M. O.
No11. Master Tailor.	No12. 2nd Infantry Brigade.
No13. War Diary.	No14. File.

****

SECRET. 13.

PROVISIONAL SCHEME FOR

D E F E N C E   O F   B O N N.

1. (a) In the event of hostile action taking place on the perimeter of COLOGNE Bridgehead, The 2nd Infantry Brigade will be required to take over the defence of BONN Bridge.

(b) There are ~~three~~ two contingencies which may occur:-

Scheme X. Hostile Action on the Perimeter-Code Word "PERIMETER".

Scheme Y. Hostile Action on the Perimeter together with Riots in BONN. . Code Word "PERIMETER RIOT

~~Scheme Z. Riots in BONN. - Code Word "RIOTS".~~

11. Scheme X.(a) Upon receipt of the code word "Perimeter" the Battali. will proceed to the Artillerie Kaserne(Rheindorfed Strasse)BONN and take over from the Battalion quartered there, except,

(b) COYS.	LOCATION & DUTIES.	WHERE BILLETED.
B.&.C.	Picquet under A.P.M.BONN	Konelgasse, Fort Buildi. G. 5&6.
1 Lewis Gun + 1 Rifle Sectn ~~3 N.C.O's 10 Privates~~ "D" Coy.	Adolf Platz BONN Lorry Park Guard.	Konigwilhelm Kaserne Rheindorfed Strasse, BONN H.8.
1 Rifle Section (c) ~~1 N.C.O 6 Privates~~ "D" Coy.	HUSSALLEE, BONN H.5. Lorry Park Guard.	Hut near Lorry Park . off HUSSALLEE.
2 Lewis Gun (d) ~~3 N.C.O's & 18 other ranks~~ + 1 Rifle Section. "D" Coy.	Goods Station, BONN H.5. Guard over Goods.	In Station.

The above duties will be taken over from whatever Battalion is fi.. The Town Guard for the week.

BATTN.H.Q.	BATTN.H.Q.
"A" & Remainder of "D" Coy.	Artillerie KASERNE In Reserve.

111. SCHEME.Y. Upon receipt of code word "Perimeter Riots" The Battalio. will march to BONN and take over the following duties and quarters.

COMPANY.	LOCATION AND DUTIES.	BILLETS
A.	Electricity & Gas Works BONN. Put in state of Defence	Gas Works Buildings
B.&.C.	Picquet under A.P.M.	Same as before.
1 Lewis Gun 1 Rifle Sectn ~~3 N.C.O's 10 other ranks~~ "D" Coy.	Adolf Platz, BONN H.6.	ditto.
1 Rifle Section ~~1 N.C.O 6 Ptes.~~ "D" Coy.	HUSSALLEE.	ditto.
Batt.H.Q.& remainder of "D" Coy.	MARKT.F,6. (Report to Brigade H.Q. ar Rathaus.	

NOTE. O.C. "A" Coy, as soon as relief of Company in Gas Works is complete will authorize in writing The Guard over Goods Station to report to its unit.

IV. ~~SCHEME.Z. Upon receipt of code word "Riots" The same action will tak place as set forth in Para.3.~~

V. DRESS Batt-le Order (Steel Helmets, Box Respirators, Haversack containing emergency ration(2) Towel, (3) Soap, (4) Holdall, (5) Housewife, (6) Paid of Socks, (7) Unexpired portion of days rations, canteens slung outside Haversack Filled Water Bottles, 120 rounds of S.A.A. per man.

VI Upon receipt of warning orders:,

"Perimeter"	Prepare to move	The alarm having previously sounded.
or		
"Perimeter" Riots"	Prepare to move.	
~~or~~		
~~"Riots".~~	~~Rapare to move.~~	

The following action will take place.

(1) All men return to their Billets.

(2) Draw Box Respirators.

(3) Draw 60 rounds of S.A.A. per man.

(4) 1st Line Transport will be made ready to move at short notice.

(5) All Stores will be dumped in billets occupied by each Company. Battn.H.Q. Stores will be dumped at THE SCHEOSS.

(6) Guard of 1 N.C.O. and 3 men per Company and Headquarters to be left over dumps.

(7) 1 Officer and 2 N.C.O's to be left to take charge of all Battalion & Government property, and superintend the guards.

(8) Officers and other ranks mentioned in the foregoing sub-paras, will be supplied with two days rations.

(9) As soon as Companies are ready to move, the following word will be sent to Battn.H.Q" Coy.READY" and the Company without further orders will proceed to the Battn.Parade Ground.

VII (a) The Officer mentioned in para 10 (7) will be the Ordorly Officer.

(b) The N.C.O's " " " " " " " Master Tailor, ~~and~~ Sergt.Sinnott.

VIII Any Officers or men away from the vicinity, on duty or on leave will be recalled and will report on arrival to the Officer i/c Details left behind.

IX Administration, Medical, and other Details will be issued seperately.

X Reg. Aid Post in all 3 schemes at Battn.H.Q.

XI Reserve S.A.A." " " " " " "

XII Reports (Scheme X) to Artillerie KASERNE.

" (Scheme Y) } to MARKT.
" (Scheme ~~Z~~)

(SIGNED) W.Y.P..ICE.
CAPTAIN & ADJUTANT.
53rd BATT, THE WELSH REGIMENT.

ISSUED TO,

Copy	- No.1. C.O.	Copy	- No.2. 2nd.In Command.
"	- No.3. Adjutant.	"	- No.4. O.C. "A" Coy.
"	- No.5. O.C. "B" Coy.	"	- No.6. O.C. "C" Coy.
"	- No.7. O.C. "D" Coy.	"	- No.8. Quartermaster.
"	- No.9. Transport Officer	"	- No.10.M.O.
"	- No.11.Master Tailor.	"13	- War Diary.
"	- No.12.Brigade for information.	"	- No.14. File.

(6339) Wt. W160/M3016 1,500,000 10/17 McA & W Ltd (E 1898) Forms W3091.

Army Form W.3091.

Cover for Documents.

SECRET.

Nature of Enclosures.

WAR DIARY.

of.

53rd BATT. THE WELSH REGIMENT.

From 1st May 1919 to 31st May 1919.

VOL. I.

Notes, or Letters written.

C. C. Norman

LIEUT. COL.
CMDG 53 BATT THE WELSH REGT.

Instructions regarding War Diaries and Intelligence Summaries are contained in F. S. Regs., Part II. and the Staff Manual respectively. Title pages will be prepared in manuscript.

WAR DIARY
~~or~~
~~INTELLIGENCE SUMMARY.~~
(*Erase heading not required.*)

Army Form C. 2118.

53rd Batt THE WELSH REGT.

Place	Date	Hour	Summary of Events and Information	Remarks and references to Appendices
ALFTER GERMANY	1 May		Strength of Batt on this date 28 officers 671 other ranks	
	1st May		2/Lts E. Ashby, R SMITH + P.E. DOSWELL proceeded to No 2 Concentration Camp, DUREN for demobilisation.	
	11th May		Lt Col A.C. CORFE, DSO Royal WEST KENT Regt took over duty as Second in Command	
	26th May		'B' Coy vacated billets in ALFTER + moved to GIELSDORF	
	28th May		Battalion Sports were held on this day. All events were well contested. Major GEN. E.P. STRICKLAND C.B. C.M.G. D.S.O. Cmdg WESTERN DIVISION + BRIG. GEN. TOM ARDEN C.B. C.M.G. were present.	
		2pm	A draft of 200 other ranks arrived from the 51st + 52nd S. W. BORDS	
	30th May	11.45	Sir HARRY JOHNSON lectured to the Batt on "The Races of Africa"	
	31 May		Strength 26 officers. 873 Other ranks	

C. [illegible] Norman
LIEUT. COL.
CMDG. 53rd Batt. THE WELSH REGT.

D. D. & L., London, E.C.
(A8004) Wt. W1771/M2-31 750,000 5/17 Sch. 52 Forms/C2118/14

(6339) Wt. W160/M3016 1,500,000 10/17 McA & W Ltd (E 1898) Forms W3091. Army Form W.3091.

Cover for Documents.

Nature of Enclosures.

WAR DIARY

of

53rd Batt THE WELSH REGT.

From 1st June 1919 to 30 June 1919.

Notes, or Letters written.

[signature] Lt Col.

Comdg 53 Batt the Welsh Regt

[initials]

Instructions regarding War Diaries and Intelligence Summaries are contained in F. S. Regs., Part II. and the Staff Manual respectively. Title pages will be prepared in manuscript.

WAR DIARY

~~or~~

~~INTELLIGENCE SUMMARY.~~

(Erase heading not required.)

Army Form C. 2118.

53rd Batt THE WELSH REGT.

Hour, Date, Place	Summary of Events and Information	Remarks and references to Appendices
1.6.19 ALFTER.	Strength 29 officers 873 Other Ranks. E.L.K.W.	
18.6.19 ALFTER	On instructions received from 2nd Western Infantry Brigade the move into BONN was commenced in accordance with 53 WELSH REGT operation Order No I (Appendix I) B Coy marched from GIELSDORF to BONN and were quartered at UNIVERSITY BUILDINGS for duty under the A.P.M. The guards detailed in appendix I to operation order No I also proceeded on this day. E.L.K.W.	Appendix I.
19.6.19. ALFTER	The remainder of the Battalion marched to BONN and relieved the 1/5 BORDER REGT at the ARTILLERIE KASERNE E.L.K.W.	
30.6.19	Strength 30 officers 856 Other ranks. E.L.K.W.	

A. Norman Lt. Col.
53 Batt the Welsh Regt.

(73989) W4141—463. 400,000. 9/14. H.&J.Ltd. Forms/C. 2118/10.

SECRET

Copy No. 15

HEADQUARTERS,
2nd WESTERN INFANTRY BRIGADE

APPENDIX I

OPERATION ORDERS NO.1.
53rd Batt. THE WELSH REGIMENT.

Reference Sheet 2.L.1./100.000.

1. In the event of the Germans not signing the Peace Terms the Battalion will be ordered to move to BONN. Battalion Headquarters and "A" "C" &."D" Companies will move to the ARTILLERIE KASERNE.

"B" Company will move indopondantly to UNIVERSITY BUILDINGS.
"D" Company will find the Guards detailed in appendix 1.

2. The Battalion will parade in full marching order.

The Transport will accompany the Battalion. Company Lewis Gun Limbers and Travelling Kitchens will march in rear of their Companies and remainder of Transport in rear of Battalion.

1 Blanket per man loaded on 2 G.S. Waggons will accompany the Battalion.
These Blankets rolled in bundles of 10 will be dumped at the Transport Lines under Company arrangements. They will be loaded by a fatigue Party to be detailed by the Adjutant.

3. All surplus baggage will be collected into a central dump at and near the Battalion Orderly Room, under arrangements to be made by Lieut.Brown.

A Guard consisting of 1 N.C.O. and 5 men per Company under Lieut. Brown will remain behind to look after and load the baggage.

The Baggage will on arrival in the New Area be stacked in the ARTILLERIE KASERNE and will not be issued to Companies until further orders.

4. In the event of the breaking off of the Armistice and the advance of the Allied Troops causing a change in the attitude of the population of the Occupied Territory, the following disposisitions will be taken by "C" &."A" Companies.

"C" Company is RESPONSIBLE FOR:-

1. The prtection of the Railway from BONN STATION (inclusive) to the GOODS STATION.(exclusive)

2. The Defence of the Post and Telegraph Office in MUNZER PLATZ.

3. GUARDING the POPPLESDORFER ALLEE.

Company Headquarters at BONN STATION.

1 Platoon protecting Railway from BONN STATION (exclusive)

1 Platoon MUNSTER PLATZ.

1 Platoon (less 2 Rifle Sections) Railway Crossing in POPPLESDORFER ALLEE to deal with any hostile body moving up the ALLEE.

2 Rifle Sections to Guard the Railway Station.

1 Platoon in reserve in BONN STATION.

Continued.

SHEET 2.

"A" COMPANY IS RESPONSIBLE FOR:-

1. The Defence of BONN GOODS STATION.

2. The protection of the Railway From BONN GOODS STATION (inclusive) to the crossing ¼ mile North of the N in DRANSDORF.

3. The Defence of the Gas and Electricity Works.

Company Headquarters at BONN GOODS STATION.

1 Platoon Guarding Railway from GOODS STATION (exclusive) to level crossing.

1 Platoon guarding Gas and Electricity Works.

1 Platoon guarding The GOODS STATION.

1 Platoon in reserve at the GOODS STATION.

"B" Company will proceed to the UNIVERSITY BUILDINGS. O.C. "B" Company will report to the A.P.M. for Orders.

"D" Company will find the Guards as already detailed. Remainder of the Company will proceed(with Battalion Headquarters) to ARTILLERIE KASERNE.

"D" Company and Battalion Headquarters will remain at the ARTILLERIE KASERNE unless ordered to move to the RATHAUS HOUSE in which case "D" Company will leave a Guard of 1 Platoon at the ARTILLERIE KASERNE.

Platoon Commanders and Company Commanders of "A" & "C" Companies will carry out reconnaissance and submit detailed plans to the Commanding Officer for their dispositions described in para 4 forthwith.

(signed) W.Y.PRICE Captain,
Adjutant 53rd Batt.THE WELSH REGIMENT.

53rd BATT THE WELSH REGIMENT.
APPENDIX 1.

Battalion Headquarters. Transport. Battalion less the Duties below. — ARTILLERIE KASERNE.

~~Outpost Guard~~.

D U T I E S.

Coy. or Guard.	Nature of duty.	Place.	Route by which Party proceeds from ALFTER.
"B" Company.	Piequets under A.P.M. BONN.	University Buildings.	
2 N.C.Os. 6 men "D" Company.	Lorry Park Guard	ADOLF PLATZ.	Light Railway to Ellerbahnhof, then via VORGEBUG STRASSE.
1.N.C.O. 6 men "D" Company.	~~Lorry Park Guard.~~ Cancelled	~~HAYDN STRASSE.~~	~~Light Railway to ELLERBAHNHOF, then via ELLERSTRASSE. WESTSTRASSE. NEDEGGER STRASSE, and JAEGER STRASSE.~~
3.N.C.Os.18 men "D" Company.	GOODS STATION.	BONN GOODS STATION.	Light Railway to ELLERBAHNHOF then via ELLERSTRASSE.WESTSTRASSE
1.N.C.O.3 men "D" Company.	AMMUNITION GUARD.	CAVALRY BARRACKS.	(To be notified later)
1.N.C.O. 3 men "D" Company.	Ordnance Stores.	26.BRUHLER STRASSE.	Light Railway to ELLERBAHNHOF then back along the line to BRUHLER STRASSE.
1.N.C.O. 6 men "D" Company.	POPPLESDORFER ALLEE.	POPPLESDORFER. ALLEE.	Light Railway to FREDRICHSPLATZ then via BONN STATION, BAHNHOF STRASSE into POPPLESDORFER ALLEE.

****

COPIES ISSUED TO.

Copy No.1.	C.O.	Copy No.2.	2nd in Command.
" " 3.	Adjutant.	" " 4.	O.C. "A" Company.
" " 5.	O.C."B" Coy.	" " 6.	O.C. "C" Company.
" " 7.	O.C."D" Coy.	" " 8.	O.C."HQ" Company.
" " 9.	Quartermaster.	" "10.	Transport Officer.
" "11.	Medical Officer.	" "12.	Lewis Gun Officer.
" "13.	Signalling "	" "14.	Brigade for information.
" "15.	War Diary.	" "16.	FILE.

--*-*-*-*

(6414) Wt. W3906/P1607 2,500,000 7/18 McA & W Ltd (E 3591) Forms W3091/4. Army Form W.3091.

Cover for Documents.

53rd BATTALION
THE WELSH REGT.
- 3 AUG 1919
ORDERLY ROOM No.

Nature of Enclosures.

WAR DIARY

of the

53rd Batt THE WELSH REGT.

From 1st July 1919 to 31st July 1919.

Notes, or Letters written.

E [illegible]
Major
Cmdg 53rd Batt The Welsh Regt.

Instructions regarding War Diaries and Intelligence Summaries are contained in F. S. Regs., Part II. and the Staff Manual respectively. Title pages will be prepared in manuscript.

WAR DIARY
or
INTELLIGENCE SUMMARY.
(Erase heading not required.)

53 Welsh Regt

Army Form C. 2118.

Hour, Date, Place	Summary of Events and Information	Remarks and references to Appendices
1st July 1919 ALFTER	The Btn moved in from BONN to ALFER at about 0900 B Coy proceeded to GIELSDORF & took over their old billets	WJP Capt & Adj
4th July 1919 "	A general holiday proclaimed in commemoration of the signing of the peace	WJP Capt & Adj
5th July 1919 "	General Marden inspected the Platoon which was going to represent the Btn in the Platoon Drill competition	WJP Capt & Adj
13th July " "	Lt Col Norman proceeded on leave & Capt Daniels assumed Command	WJP Capt & Adj
15th July	Major E J de Pentheny O'Kelly DSO assumed command	
18th July 1919 "	2nd & 3rd Class Army Examinations were held at ALFTER about 300 candidates entered from the Btn	WJP Capt & Adj
19th " " "	The 2nd Western Bde Sports took place at ALFTER. The Btn easily came out top. We won seven of the nine events which counted towards the divisional championship. We also won the best turned out section. Lt T.T. Davies MC won the Victor Ludorum Cup	WJP Capt & Adj
21st " " "	A regimental boxing contest was held at the Recreation room. Major Delaney refereed. Excellent boxing resulted & a good team has been selected for the Bde Contest	WJP Capt & Adj
26th " " "	A & B Coys commenced firing at the Range.	WJP Capt & Adj

Army Form C. 2118.

Instructions regarding War Diaries and Intelligence Summaries are contained in F. S. Regs., Part II. and the Staff Manual respectively. Title pages will be prepared in manuscript.

WAR DIARY
or
INTELLIGENCE SUMMARY.

(*Erase heading not required.*)

53 Welsh Regt.

Hour, Date, Place	Summary of Events and Information	Remarks and references to Appendices
30th July 1919 ALFTER	Bde Boxing Contest at DUISDORF Btn won three out of the seven weights contested	[illegible] Adj.
	3/8/19 E [illegible] Major Comdg 53 Welsh Regt.	

(73989) W4141—463. 400,000. 9/14. H.&J.Ltd. Forms/C. 2118/10.

1ST DIVISION
2ND INFY BDE

2ND TRENCH MORTAR BATTERY

1917 JUL - ~~DEC 1917~~ 1918 DEC

~~Dec~~ 1918

W A R   D I A R Y.

2nd.T.M.Battery.

2nd. INFANTRY BRIGADE.

1st.DIVISION.

JULY.1917.

CONFIDENTIAL.   2nd Brigade No. G. 20/6.

Headquarters,

1st Division.

Reference 1st Division No. T.F.302 of 9th inst:

Herewith War Diary of 2nd Trench Mortar Battery for month of July.

R. C. Chichester-Constable Capt.

for Brigadier General,
Commanding 2nd Infantry Brigade.

10th August, 1917.

Instructions regarding War Diaries and Intelligence Summaries are contained in F. S. Regs., Part II. and the Staff Manual respectively. Title pages will be prepared in manuscript.

WAR DIARY

or

~~INTELLIGENCE SUMMARY.~~

(Erase heading not required.)

Army Form C. 2118.

Place	Date	Hour	Summary of Events and Information	Remarks and references to Appendices
Bader Camp	1/7/17			
Coxyde Bains Area	to 2/7/17		Training in Camp.	
Nieuport Bains Area	3/7/17		Relieved 1st T.M.B. in Nieuport Bains Sector.	
	8/7/17		One gun destroyed by direct hit on Emplacement. No casualties.	
	9/7/17	5.30pm	2 Officers and 9 OR killed, and 4 OR wounded (2 of whom died of wounds) and 4 guns put out of action by Enemy shell fire.	
		11.30pm	2 Guns assisted 2nd King's Royal Rifle Corps raid.	
	10/7/17	1 am	C Section relieved by B Section.	
		8 am	Heavy Enemy shelling.	
		11.30am	Bridges across Yser destroyed. Communication cut.	
		7.30am	Enemy attacked and captured our trench system on Eastern side of Yser. 1 Officer 7 OR Missing. 7 guns lost including the four put out of action 9th inst.	
Coxyde Bains Area	14/7/17	14/7/17	C Section withdrawn from Line. Rear Headquarters established at Lefevre Camp Coxyde Bains.	
			2 Officers 28 OR joined as reinforcements.	
	16/7/17		Relieved by 197th T.M. By.	
Effrinckhoucke Area	17/7/17		Left Coxyde Bains and marched to Effrinckhoucke Area.	
St Pol sur Mer area	18/7/17		Left Effrinckhoucke Area and marched to St Pol sur Mer Area.	

Army Form C. 2118.

Instructions regarding War Diaries and Intelligence Summaries are contained in F. S. Regs., Part II. and the Staff Manual respectively. Title pages will be prepared in manuscript.

WAR DIARY
or
~~INTELLIGENCE SUMMARY.~~
(Erase heading not required.)

Place	Date	Hour	Summary of Events and Information	Remarks and references to Appendices
St Pol sur Mer area	19/7/17 to 30/7/17		Training	
Le Clipon Camp area	30/7/17		Left St Pol sur Mer area and marched to Le Clipon Camp	

M. A. Reade Capt. Cmdg.
2nd TRENCH MORTAR BATTERY.

A5834 Wt. W4973 M687 750,000 8/16 D. D. & L. Ltd. Forms C.2118/13.

W A R   D I A R Y.

2nd. T. M. Battery.

2nd. INFANTRY BRIGADE.

1st. DIVISION.

SEPTEMBER. 1917.

Army Form C. 2118.

Instructions regarding War Diaries and Intelligence Summaries are contained in F. S. Regs., Part II. and the Staff Manual respectively. Title pages will be prepared in manuscript.

WAR DIARY
or
~~INTELLIGENCE SUMMARY.~~

(Erase heading not required.)

2 Bde T M B.

Sept 1917

Place	Date	Hour	Summary of Events and Information	Remarks and references to Appendices
Le Clipon Camp	Sept 1st to 30th		Training.	

A5834 Wt. W4973 M687 750,000 8/16 D. D. & L. Ltd. Forms C.2118/13.

W A R D I A R Y.

2nd.T. M. Battery.

2nd. INFANTRY BRIGADE.

1st. DIVISION.

OCTOBER. 1917.

Instructions regarding War Diaries and Intelligence Summaries are contained in F. S. Regs., Part II, and the Staff Manual respectively. Title pages will be prepared in manuscript.

WAR DIARY

~~or~~

~~INTELLIGENCE SUMMARY.~~

(Erase heading not required.)

Army Form C. 2118.

Place	Date	Hour	Summary of Events and Information	Remarks and references to Appendices
Le Clipon Camp	Oct 1st to 21/10/17		Training	
Le Clipon Camp	22/10/17	9am	Move to Zeggars Cappel.	
Zeggars Cappel	23/10/17		Training.	
Zeggars Cappel	24/10/17	8.45am	Move to Herzelle Area	
Herzelle	25/10/17	7.45am	Move to School Camp 1½ miles West of Poperhinge.	
School Camp	26/10/17 to 31/10/17		Training at School Camp.	

[illegible] Capt. Cmdg.
2nd TRENCH MORTAR BATTERY.

D. D. & L., London, E.C.
(A7283) Wt W809/M1672 50,000 4/17 Sch. 52a Forms/C/2118/14

W A R   D I A R Y.

2nd. T.M.Battery.

2nd. INFANTRY BRIGADE.

1st. DIVISION.

NOVEMBER. 1917.

Army Form C. 2118.

Instructions regarding War Diaries and Intelligence Summaries are contained in F. S. Regs., Part II. and the Staff Manual respectively. Title pages will be prepared in manuscript.

WAR DIARY
or
~~INTELLIGENCE~~ SUMMARY.

(*Erase heading not required.*)

Place	Date	Hour	Summary of Events and Information	Remarks and references to Appendices
School Camp	1.11.17 to 5.11.17		Training	
	6.11.17		Move from School Camp at 9.45 am to Poperinghe. Billeted in the town.	
Poperinghe	7.11.17		Move from Poperinghe by rail to Reigersburg Camp. Camp bombed by hostile Aeroplanes. No casualties.	
Reigersburg	9.11.17		1 NCO and 18 men sent to Divisional Signals to act as Orderlies. Lt Norman took charge of Stretcher Bearers at Irish Farm. Battery on Ration Fatigue.	
	10/11/17		Ration fatigue	
	11/11/17		— do —	
	12/11/17		— do — 1 NCO and 18 men rejoined from Div. Signal Coy. Lt Norman rejoined from Stretcher Bearing.	
	13/11/17		Ration fatigue	
	14/11/17		— do — Lt Watkin and 6 OR took over camp at St Julien.	
	16/11/17		Coal fatigue	
	17/11/17		— do —	
	18/11/17		— do —	

A5834 Wt. W4973/M687 750,000 8/16 D. D. & L. Ltd. Forms/C.2118/13

Instructions regarding War Diaries and Intelligence Summaries are contained in F. S. Regs., Part II. and the Staff Manual respectively. Title pages will be prepared in manuscript.

WAR DIARY

or

~~INTELLIGENCE SUMMARY.~~

(*Erase heading not required.*)

Army Form C. 2118.

Place	Date	Hour	Summary of Events and Information	Remarks and references to Appendices
Reigersburg	20/11/17		Ration fatigue. 1 OR. wounded. 1 Gun attached to 1st L. N. Lancs for Anti Aircraft work.	
	21/11/17		Ration fatigue. Gun attached to L. N. Lancs destroyed by hostile shell fire. No Casualties.	
	22/11/17		Ration fatigue. 1 OR wounded.	
	23/11/17		— do —	
	25/11/17		Marched to Brielen and entrained for Poperinghe. From Poperinghe marched to Tunnelling Camp.	
Tunnelling Camp	26.11.17		Tunnelling Camp.	
	27/11/17		Marched from Tunnelling Camp to Herzeele.	
Herzeele	28/11/17 to 30th/11/17		Training	

Capt. Cmdg.
2nd TRENCH MORTAR BATTERY.

A5834 Wt. W4973/M687 750,000 8/16 D. D. & L. Ltd. Forms/C.2118/13.

W A R D I A R Y.

2nd. T. M. Battery.

2nd. INFANTRY BRIGADE.

1st. DIVISION.

DECEMBER. 1917.

Army Form C. 2118.

Instructions regarding War Diaries and Intelligence Summaries are contained in F. S. Regs., Part II. and the Staff Manual respectively. Title pages will be prepared in manuscript.

WAR DIARY

~~or~~

INTELLIGENCE SUMMARY.

(Erase heading not required.)

2nd Trench Mortar Battery

Place	Date 1917	Hour	Summary of Events and Information	Remarks and references to Appendices
Herzeele	Dec 1st to Dec 5th		Training.	
Herzeele	Dec 6		Marched from Herzeele to Crombeke.	
Crombeke	Dec 7		Marched from Crombeke to Woesten.	
Woesten	Dec 8th 9th		Training.	
Woesten	Dec 10		Marched from Woesten to Canal Bank.	
Canal Bank	Dec 12 13		Laying Duckboards & Wire on Valley of Steenbeek	
Canal Bank	Dec 14		Moved from Canal Bank to Charpentier Cross Roads	
Charpentier Cross Roads	Dec 14th to 31st		Laying duckboards and Wire from Valley of Steenbeek to Charpentier Cross Roads and Canal Bank	

31/12/17

J W Watkin Lieut Adjt.
2nd TRENCH MORTAR BATTERY.

A5834 Wt. W4973 M687 750,000 8/16 D. D. & L. Ltd. Forms C.2118/13.

1st Division

War Diaries

2nd Trench Mortar Battery

From 1st January, To 31st December 1918

Army Form C. 2118.

Instructions regarding War Diaries and Intelligence Summaries are contained in F. S. Regs., Part II, and the Staff Manual respectively. Title pages will be prepared in manuscript.

WAR DIARY ~~or~~ ~~INTELLIGENCE SUMMARY.~~

(*Erase heading not required.*)

2nd Trench Mortar Battery

Place	Date 1918	Hour	Summary of Events and Information	Remarks and references to Appendices
CHARPENTIER CROSS ROADS	Jan 1st – 29th		Laying Duckboard Tracks.	
"	30th		Work around Camp.	
"	31st		Moved from CHARPENTIER CROSS ROADS to STABLE FARM EIKHOEK.	

D. D. & L., London, E.C. (A7883) Wt W8c9/M1672 350,000 4/17 Sch 52a Forms/C/2118/14

[signature] Capt. Cmdg.
2nd TRENCH MORTAR BATTERY.

Instructions regarding War Diaries and Intelligence Summaries are contained in F. S. Regs., Part II. and the Staff Manual respectively. Title pages will be prepared in manuscript.

WAR DIARY
or
INTELLIGENCE SUMMARY.
(Erase heading not required.)

Army Form C. 2118.

2nd T.M. BATTERY.

FEBRUARY, 1918.

Place	Date	Hour	Summary of Events and Information	Remarks and references to Appendices
			2nd Trench Mortar Battery	
			1918 Month ending 28th February	
			Feby 1st STABLE FARM Training	
			2nd moved to S.22.d	
			3rd to 6th " Training	
			7th Moved by bus to HILLtop FARM	
			8 Cleaning up around Camp 6 Guns in the line.	
			9th to 14th Improving and draining Camp	
			14th to 19 Revetting huts.	
			20th Moved to SIEGE CAMP	
			21 Clothing & kit inspection afternoon, bathing parade.	
			22nd & 23rd — Training	
			24. Cleaning up preparatory to going on Course to II Corps School MILAIN	
			25 to 28. Receiving Course of instruction at II Corps School.	

[illegible] Capt. [illegible]
2nd TRENCH MORTAR BATTERY.

A5834 Wt. W4973/M687 750,000 8/16 D. D. & L. Ltd. Forms/C.2118/13.

Army Form C. 2118.

Instructions regarding War Diaries and Intelligence Summaries are contained in F. S. Regs., Part II. and the Staff Manual respectively. Title pages will be prepared in manuscript.

WAR DIARY
or
~~INTELLIGENCE SUMMARY.~~

(Erase heading not required.)

2nd T.M. Battery.
March 1st – 31st, 1918.

Place	1918 Date	Hour	Summary of Events and Information	Remarks and references to Appendices
	March 1st		Battery on course (Trench mortar) at 2nd Corps school MILLAIN	
	2nd		Completed Course.	
	3rd		Moved by bus to SIEGE CAMP.	
	4th		Moved from SIEGE CAMP to CANAL BANK	
	6th		1 NCO + 6 OR reported to 409th Lowland RE's at CORNER COT	
	"		1 " 10 OR " Officer in Charge of DUMP " "	
	"		1 " 24 OR " Divisional Salvage officer at TURCO FARM.	
	8th to 15th		Battery on fatigue as on the 6th. On 13th Capt. H.C. Barnes, M.C. took over command of the Battery from Capt. A.W.D. Watten.	
	16th		Battery moved to HILL TOP FARM. 8 Guns + 23 men in the line.	
	16th to 21st		Left half Battery working in Camp, Draining and revetting huts. 18th - 20th Rations to line.	
	22nd		Right half battery relieved by Left half.	
	22 to 27th		Work continued in Camp. Rations to the line 24th + 26th.	
	28th		Battery relieved by 3rd T.M. Battery	
	29th		Battery moved to CANAL BANK	
	30th		Rifle Inspection, Arms drill. (Afternoon) Equipment, Kit, and clothing inspection.	
	31		Improvements to Camp (morning) (Sunday) afternoon Church Services. Easter Services in evening	

Hugh C Barnes Capt. Cmdg.

D. D. & L., London, E.C.
(A7883) Wt W809/M1672 550,000 4/17 Sch. 52a Forms/C/2118/14

Instructions regarding War Diaries and Intelligence Summaries are contained in F. S. Regs., Part II. and the Staff Manual respectively. Title pages will be prepared in manuscript.

WAR DIARY for month of APRIL 1918.
or
~~INTELLIGENCE SUMMARY.~~
(Erase heading not required.)

Army Form C. 2118.

Place	Date	Hour	Summary of Events and Information	Remarks and references to Appendices
Canal Bank YPRES.	1st & 2nd		Training (gun drill, squad & arms drill, musketry, etc) Baths, Salvage Fatigues, and Reconnaissance of "Army Battle Zone" by Officers.	
do	3rd & 4th		ditto. 75% of Battery inoculated. Warning order to move received on 4th	
MARLES LES MINES	5th		Moved by rail from BOESINGHE to CHOQUES and then by road to billets in MARLES LES MINES	
do	6th		Inspection of Guns, Gas Helmets, Iron Rations etc. Reconnaissance of line by Officers	
LINE and ANNEQUIN	7th		Moved by lorry to BEUVRY thence by road to ANNEQUIN and line. Seven guns in line. One gun, two teams and HQ at ANNEQUIN in billets.	
Line	8th		Hostile attack from LA BASSEE CANAL northwards. Heavy gas shelling of back areas including ANNEQUIN and bombardment of line	
do.	9th to 17th		Seven guns in line until 11th after which all guns and teams in the line. Work on emplacements & carrying and fusing ammunition. Firing to Hostile Trenches, T.Ms. T.M.Gs.	
do	18th		Hostile attack on GIVENCHY accompanied by heavy bombardment and gas shelling S of Canal	
do	19th to 21st		Hostile aeroplane brought down by Stokes AA Fire. Work & Firing in line continued	
do	22nd		4 guns & teams withdrawn from line on 21st went into line N of Canal at GIVENCHY	
do.	to 24th		returning to Battery on 24th. H.Q. moved to WIMPOLE ST. on 23rd from ANNEQUIN	
do	24th to 30th		Battery continued in line without relief, firing, working etc.	

Hugh [illegible] Capt. Cmdg.
2nd TRENCH MORTAR BATTERY.

D. D. & L., London, E.C. (A7883) Wt W809/M1672 50,000 4/17 Sch 52a Forms/C/2118/14

Instructions regarding War Diaries and Intelligence Summaries are contained in F. S. Regs., Part II, and the Staff Manual respectively. Title pages will be prepared in manuscript.

WAR DIARY or INTELLIGENCE SUMMARY.

2nd T.M. Battery for Month of May 1918

(Erase heading not required.)

Army Form C. 2118.

Place	Date	Hour	Summary of Events and Information	Remarks and references to Appendices
In the Line CAMBRIN SECTOR	1st		8 guns in the Line. Good weather – some gas shelling by night	
NOEUX LES MINES	2nd		Battery relieved in the Line by 1st T.M. Battery and moved to NOEUX LES MINES (billets) on completion of relief (5pm)	
do.	3rd		Day spent in cleaning up, kit inspections etc.	
do	4th to 8th		Training commenced and carried out on following general lines:- Setting up Drill, Rifle Exercises, Musketry, Bayonet Fighting, Gun Drill, Mechanism, Range Practices, Gas Drill, Extended Order. Officers reconnoitred Reserve Area.	
do.	9th to 11th		Battery "Stood By". Men wore boots & clothing by night, all surplus stores deposited at Transport Lines. Officers reconnoitred special areas. Training continued by day	
In the Line HOHENZOLLERN.	12th		Battery moved into the Line in the HOHENZOLLERN SECTOR, relieving 3rd T.M. Battery. 8 guns in the line, 6 in Offensive positions and 2 in Defensive Positions. Work was organised re-building & improving emplacements and in cleaning ammunition.	
do.	13th to 23rd		Battery remained in line carrying out harassing & retaliatory schemes of fire, and continuing work on improving positions – 1000 rounds had been fired by evening of the 23rd.	
do	24th		A successful raid was carried out by 2nd K.R.R.C. in which 6 guns carried out co-operating fire. 4 unwounded prisoners were captured. The Battery fired 850 rounds.	
do	25th to 27th		Battery remained in line continuing usual routine & harassing fire	
NOEUX LES MINES	28th		The Battery was relieved in the line by 1st T.M. Battery moving back at about 4pm to previous Billets in NOEUX LES MINES. During the 16 days in the line 2175 rounds were fired.	
do	29th		Day spent cleaning up and with kit Inspections etc. Men requiring new clothing refitted. Gas Helmets were inspected.	
do	30th & 31st		Training commenced on following general lines. 6.15 am Daily – Rouse Parade – ½ hour alternate Run & Brisk Walk. In addition 4 to 5 hours daily on same programme as is given above for 4th to 8th	

Hugh C Barnes
Capt. Cmdg.
2nd TRENCH MORTAR BATTERY.

D. D. & L., London, E.C.
(A7883) Wt W809/M1672 350,000 4/17 Sch. 52a Forms/C/2118/14

Instructions regarding War Diaries and Intelligence Summaries are contained in F. S. Regs., Part II. and the Staff Manual respectively. Title pages will be prepared in manuscript.

WAR DIARY or ~~INTELLIGENCE SUMMARY.~~ 2nd T. M. Battery for Month of June 1918.

(Erase heading not required.)

Army Form C. 2118.

Place	Date	Hour	Summary of Events and Information	Remarks and references to Appendices
NOEUX LES MINES	1st to		Training (on the following general lines) 6-15 am daily Rouse Parade ½ hour Run + Brisk Walk,	
do	3rd		Setting up Drill, Rifle Exercises, Musketry, Bayonet Fighting, L.T.M.s in attack, Dummy Firing, Misfire + Gun Drill, Compass Work, Mechanism,	
do	3rd		Practice A.A. firing.	
do	4th		Training continued, Reconnaissance of the line by Officers.	
CAMBRIN SECTOR	5th		Battery moved into the Line in the CAMBRIN SECTOR, relieved 3rd T. M. Btty & guns in the line,	
do	6th		All guns registered, and Work organised of rebuilding + improving emplacements, cleaning + fusing ammun.	
do	7th to		Battery remained in the line carrying out harrassing + retaliatory schemes of fire, Improving	
do	13th		positions, gun pits, + emplacements, Firing A.A. at low flying hostile aircraft, carrying and fusing ammunition.	
do	13th		No 7 Gun pit was blown in by hostile shell fire, 1 OR killed + one wounded.	
do	14th to 19th		Battery in the line continuing the usual routine + harrassing fire	
do	19th		Premature occurred at No 3 gun position, while firing at low flying hostile aircraft one killed, one wounded,	
	20th		Battery in the line continuing the usual routine + harrassing fire.	
NOEUX LES MINES	21st		The Battery was relieved in the line by 1st T. M. Battery, + moved back to previous billets at NOEUX LES MINES arriving about 4 pm, During the 16 days in the line about 1500 rounds were fired	
do	22nd		Day spent cleaning up, Kit inspections etc. Men requiring clothing were refitted. Gas helmets inspected	
do	23rd to 30th		Training on the following general lines was commenced + continued, 6-30 daily Rouse Parade Brisk Run and Walk, Rifle Exercises, Squad Drill, Misfire Drill, Gun Drill, Dummy Firing Range Practice, Physical Training, Bayonet Fighting, Musketry, Gas Drill, Mechanism, Map Reading Rapidity in action etc. —	

Hugh C Barnes Capt. Cmdg.
2nd TRENCH MORTAR BATTERY.

A5834 Wt. W4973/M687 750,000 8/16 D. D. & L. Ltd. Forms/C.2118/13.

Instructions regarding War Diaries and Intelligence Summaries are contained in F. S. Regs., Part II, and the Staff Manual respectively. Title pages will be prepared in manuscript.

WAR DIARY ~~or INTELLIGENCE SUMMARY.~~

(*Erase heading not required.*)

2nd T M Battery

for Month of July

Army Form C. 2118.

Place	Date	Hour	Summary of Events and Information	Remarks and references to Appendices
NOEUX LES MINES	1st		25 O.Rs reported to Brigade Staff Captain for fatigue	
HOHENZOLLERN SECTOR	2nd		The Battery moved into the line in the HOHENZOLLERN SECTOR relieved the 3rd TM Battery. 8 guns in the line.	
do	3rd		All guns registered and work organised for improving gun positions and emplacements.	
do	4th to 6th		Battery remained in the line carrying out harassing and retaliatory schemes of fire. Cleaning fusing + carrying ammunition	
do	7th		The Battery co-operated in the 1st Brigade Raid. 4 guns fired 440 rounds on selected targets and continued harassing fire during night and day, firing a total of 640 rounds.	
do	9th to 16th		Continued the usual routine in the line, Harassing fire on Trench targets M.Gs: TMs. carrying cleaning ammunition, exchanging Bickford fuzes at gun position and dumps.	
do	17th to 20th		The Battery continued harassing fire by night and day. Total rounds fired during the month to date being 3219 on selected targets, also preparing forward emplacements forward.	
do	20/21st		The Battery co-operated with the 2nd Royal Sussex Regt in raid on the enemy's front line and support trenches, 8 guns in action fired 2206 rounds on selected targets as per T.M. 174. The forward gun position A28 c 12.57 was destroyed by enemy shell fire, Capt H.C. Barnes M.C. also 2 O.R.s were killed.	
do	21st		The Battery was relieved in the line by the 1st TM Battery + moved back to previous Billets at NOEUX LES MINES arriving about 4 pm.	
NOEUX LES MINES	22nd		The day spent cleaning up Kit and Clothing inspections etc.	
do	23rd to 30th		Training on the following general lines was commenced and continued 6-30 am daily Running Parade Rifle Exercises, Squad Drill, Misfire Drill Gun Drill, Range Practise Musketry Mechanism, Rapidity in action etc. On the 24th the men attached to the battery returned to their respected units	
do	29th		4 Section of the Battery co-operated with the 2nd Royal Sussex Regt in training operations	
			Lieut W.F. Barfoot took over the command of the Battery.	
CAMBRIN SECTOR	31st		The Battery moved into the line CAMBRIN SECTOR and relieved the 3rd T.M. Battery H.Q. Wimpole St. 2 Offensive and 4 Defensive Guns –.	

W.F. Barfoot Lt ~~Capt~~ Cmdg.
2nd TRENCH MORTAR BATTERY.

D. D. & L., London, E.C. (A7883) Wt W809/M1672 350,000 4/17 Sch 52a Forms/C/2118/14

Instructions regarding War Diaries and Intelligence Summaries are contained in F. S. Regs., Part II, and the Staff Manual respectively. Title pages will be prepared in manuscript.

WAR DIARY 2nd Trench Mortar Battery

or

~~INTELLIGENCE SUMMARY.~~

(*Erase heading not required.*)

Army Form C. 2118.

for Month of August 1918.

Place	Date	Hour	Summary of Events and Information	Remarks and references to Appendices
CAMBRIN SECTOR	1st		Battery in the line in the CAMBRIN SECTOR. 6 guns and 2 guns at H.Q. WIMPOLE ST in reserve. All guns were re-registered + work of organising the improvement of gun positions etc. commenced	
do	2nd to 14th		The Battery remained in the line carrying out harrassing or retaliatory schemes of fire improving emplacements etc	
do	15th to 21st		C.O went on course. The Battery remained in the line, firing + carrying out the usual routine. During the 22 days in the line the battery fired about 2,000 rounds on selected targets.	
	22nd		The Battery was relieved by the 49th T.M. Battery + proceeded to DIEVAL by route march and bus for a course of training	
DIEVAL				
do	23rd		Day spent cleaning up. Clothing inspection etc	
do	24th to 30th		Training commenced + was carried out on the following lines; Musketry, Gun Drill, etc special attention being given to the Employment of Light Mortars in open warfare	
do	31st		The Battery entrained for ARRAS, part of the Battery having previously proceeded by road with the handcarts.	

M. A. Barford. Capt. Cmdg.
2nd TRENCH MORTAR BATTERY.

D. D. & L., London, E.C.
(A7283) Wt W809/M1672 350,000 4/17 Sch 52a Forms/C/2118/14

Instructions regarding War Diaries and Intelligence Summaries are contained in F. S. Regs., Part II. and the Staff Manual respectively. Title pages will be prepared in manuscript.

Army Form C. 2118.

WAR DIARY
or
~~INTELLIGENCE SUMMARY.~~
(*Erase heading not required.*)

for month of September 1918

Place	Date	Hour	Summary of Events and Information	Remarks and references to Appendices
ARRAS	1st to 3rd		Arrived at ARRAS and billeted for day marching to rendezvous at night for operation in conjunction with Canadian and 4th British Division – The Battery advanced during the day and night of the 2nd and 3rd and billeted on the 3rd at ENTERPIGNO	
ENTERPIGNO	4th to 7th		2 guns under Lieut G N D Walters in the front line position	
	8th		The Battery was relieved by 168th T.M. Battery & proceeded by route march and bus to HARBCQ	
HARBCQ	9th 10th		Billets at HARBCQ cleaning up and refitting etc	
	10th 11th		On the night of the 11th entrained at ACQ for GUILLAUCOURT & marched to billets at PROYART	
ATHIES	13th		Embussed for ATHIES 14th Marched to TERTERY	
TERTERY	15th & 16th		In billets at TERTERY & on the 17th proceeded to VERMAND by route march prior to operations	
GRICOURT SECTOR	18th		Brigade attacked North and South of the Omignon River 2 guns attached to each of the two front Battalions. Subsections moved in the advance with front line companies. Two right guns got into action twice during the advance	
	19th		When the days objectives were reached effective fire was brought to bear on active enemy M.G.s.	
VERMAND	20th		Relieved by the 139th T.M. Battery & returned to former billets at VERMAND	
GRICOURT SECTOR	20th/21st		~~Relieved~~ On the night of the 23rd relieved the 1st T.M. Batty in the line. Brigade attacked South of the Omignon River, 2 guns attached to each of the two Battalions in front. During the advance no opportunity for the use of guns.	
	1st		When objective was reached fire was brought to bear on active M.G.s in PONTRUET	
			During the advance the sections did mopping up work, Dugouts were cleared of prisoners	
	28th		Remained ~~in~~ the line carrying out harrassing fire and keeping down fire of active M.G.s until the 29th	
VERMAND	29th/29th		Relieved by the 3rd T.M. Battery & Returned to Billets at VERMAND	
	30th		Cleaning up & refitting. S.B.R. inspections etc.	

[signature] Capt. Comdg.
2nd TRENCH MORTAR BATTERY.

D. D. & L., London, E.C.
(A7883) Wt W809/M1672 50,000 4/17 Sch. 52a Forms/C/2118/14

Instructions regarding War Diaries and Intelligence Summaries are contained in F. S. Regs., Part II. and the Staff Manual respectively. Title pages will be prepared in manuscript.

WAR DIARY
or
~~INTELLIGENCE SUMMARY.~~
(Erase heading not required.)

for month of October 1918

2nd Trench Mortar Battery

Army Form C. 2118.

Place	Date	Hour	Summary of Events and Information	Remarks and references to Appendices
MARTEVILLE	1st/3rd		The Battery in billets following the usual routine of training etc.	
CAULLINCOURT	4th/7th		Moved to new billets at CAULLINCOURT. The Battery training for open warfare	
do	8th		The Battery stood to for a forward move.	
BELLINGLASE	9th/15th		Moved to BELLINGLASE and carried out special training for open warfare, the battery co-operated with battalions in schemes of training.	
BOHAIN	16th		The Battery moved to BOHAIN + on the evening of the 16th, two sections of the battery were attached to the two front battalions for operations on the 17th	
VAUX ANDIGNY	17th		The four guns attached to the battalions moved forward with the support line, leap frogged the 6th Division, doing some mopping up on the advance, and when the infantry were held up by enemy M.G's + strong points went forward and subdued the enemy resistance. The section attached to the right front battalion when the advance reached LA VALLÉE MULÂTRE though suffering heavy casualties including the section commander put an enemy M.G. out of action with a direct hit. In the evening the guns were dug in on S.O.S. lines. H.Q. moved to VAUX ANDIGNY.	
do	18th		Four guns remained in the line on S.O.S. lines in support of infantry	
do	19th		During the evening of the 19th the battery moved to ARBRE DE GUISE	
ARBRE DE GUISE	20th/21st		Spent in reorganising and refitting for operation in conjunction with the infantry.	
do	22nd/23rd		Battery co-operated with Battalions in Front line and at the end of the operation dug in on S.O.S. lines	
do	23rd		The guns in the line relieved by 1st T.M. Battery.	
	24th		Moved to Billets at LA VALLÉE MULATRE	
LA VALLÉE MULATRE	/27th		Reorganising + refitting etc.	
MAZINGHEN	28th		Relieved the 1st T.M.B in the line	
	29th		One gun attached to each battalion in support of front line. The gun attached to the centre battalion went forward when the enemy attacked + assisted in holding the line, in one enemy attack the gun put up a barrage which greatly helped to repel the enemy, + in one counter attack on enemy M.G's + strong points reinforced by the gun from the left put up a barrage on the enemy lines where the artillery was not effective.	
VAUX ANDIGNY	30th		The Battery was relieved by the 3rd T.M. Battery + moved to billets at VAUX ANDIGNY.	
	31st		Battery cleaning up refitting	

[illegible signature] Capt. Cmdg. 2nd TRENCH MORTAR BATTERY.

A5834 Wt. W4973/M687 750,000 8/16 D. D. & L. Ltd. Forms/C.2118/13.

Instructions regarding War Diaries and Intelligence Summaries are contained in F. S. Regs., Part II. and the Staff Manual respectively. Title pages will be prepared in manuscript.

WAR DIARY for the month of November 1918
or
~~INTELLIGENCE SUMMARY.~~
(Erase heading not required.)

Army Form C. 2118.

2nd Trench Mortar Battery

Place	Date	Hour	Summary of Events and Information	Remarks and references to Appendices
VAUX AUDIGNY	1st		The Battery preparing gun positions in the line for operation	
"	2nd		The Battery digging gun positions, fusing ammunition etc for operation	
MAZINGHEN	3rd/4th		The Battery moved up for operations on the 4th 8 guns in the line which put up a barrage on the Canal Lock, Houses etc which were held as enemy M.G. positions + strong points, targets which the artillery could not reach, firing in all about 600 rounds. When the infantry advanced over the canal, one section was attached to the right front battalion and one section to the left front battalion went forward + fired on enemy strong positions thus enabling the infantry to advance at several points where they were held up. AT FERMY several enemy Machine Guns + teams were put out of action by direct hits	
FERMY				
LAVALÉE MULATRE	5th		The guns in the line were withdrawn + the battery moved to billets at LAVALLÉE MULATRE	
FERNOY LE GRAND	6th		The battery proceeded by route march to billet at FERSNOY LE GRAND	
do	7th/11th		The battery cleaning up, refitting etc. a scheme of training was carried out special attention being given to "Stokes in open warfare"	
	11th	11.00	Armistice began. Usual routine of training etc was carried out until the 13th	
FAYRIL	13th		The Battery moved by bus to FAYRIL.	
DOMIPERRE	15th		The March to the Rhine ~~out~~ commenced + the battery moved to billet at DOMIPERRE by route march	
SARS POTTERES	16th		The Battery moved with the Brigade to SARS POTTERES by route march	
MARZELLE	18th		" " " " MARZELLE	
WALLCOURT	19th		" " " " WALLCOURT	
"	20th/22nd		The Battery carried out the usual routine of Training etc	
MORALINE	23rd		" moved to MORALIVE by route march	
ANTHÉE	24th		" " ANTHÉE by " "	
"	25th/30th		A scheme of training was carried out, special attention being given to guard duties, arms drill etc and short route marches	

M.H. Bartlett Capt. Cmdg.
2nd TRENCH MORTAR BATTERY.

D. D. & L., London, E.C.
(A10266) Wt W53 10/P713 750,000 2/18 Sch. 52 Forms/C2118/16

Instructions regarding War Diaries and Intelligence Summaries are contained in F. S. Regs., Part II. and the Staff Manual respectively. Title pages will be prepared in manuscript.

WAR DIARY *or* INTELLIGENCE SUMMARY.

(*Erase heading not required.*)

for Month of December 1918 — Army Form C. 2118.

2nd Trench Mortar Batty

Place	Date	Hour	Summary of Events and Information	Remarks and references to Appendices
WHIELLEN	1		March to the RHINE continued The Battery moved by route march to WHIELLEN	
SOINNE	2		" " " " " SOINNE	
JAMBLINNE	3		" " " " " JAMBLINNE	
do	4/8th		The Battery carried out the usual routine of cleaning, refitting, training etc	
SIN SIN	9th		March to the RHINE resumed The Battery moved by route march to SINSIN	
HUTTON	10th		do do do continued " " " HUTTON	
ERAZEE	11th		do do do do " " " ERAZEE	
do	12th/13th		Spent in Billets cleaning, refitting etc	
GRANDMENIL	14th		March to the RHINE resumed The Batty moved by route march to GRANDMENIL	
HEBRONVALE	15th		" continued " " " HEBRONVALE	
BEHO	16th		" " " " BEHO	
GRUFFLINGE	17th		" " " " GRUFFLINGE	
LOSHEIM	18th		" " " " LOSHEIM	
HAMMERHUTTE	19th		" " " " HAMMERHUTTE	
"	20th		Spent in Billets cleaning refitting etc	
SCHMIETHEIM	21st		March to the RHINE resumed The Batty moved by route march to SCHMIDTHEIM	
MUNSTEREIFEL	22nd		continued " " " to MUNSTEREIFEL	
ESSIG	23rd		" " " ESSIG	
DUISDORF	24th		" " " DUISDORF	
do	25th/31st		The Battery carried out the usual routine of cleaning refitting training etc	

2/1/19

[signature] Capt. Cmdg.
2nd TRENCH MORTAR BATTERY.

D. D. & L., London, E.C.
(A10266) Wt W5300/P713 750,000 2/18 Sch. 52 Forms/C2118/16

1ST DIVISION
2ND BRIGADE

2ND MCHINE GUN COMPANY

JAN - DEC 1916

2nd Brigade.

1st Division.

Formed in France 26.1.16.

2nd MACHINE GUN COMPANY

26th JANUARY to 30th APRIL 1916.

Instructions regarding War Diaries and Intelligence Summaries are contained in F. S. Regs., Part II. and the Staff Manual respectively. Title Pages will be prepared in manuscript.

WAR DIARY ~~or INTELLIGENCE SUMMARY~~

(Erase heading not required.)

Army Form C. 2

Place	Date	Hour	Ref. 1/100 000. HAZEBROUCK 5A — Summary of Events and Information	Remarks and references to Appendices
LILLERS PAS-DE-CALAIS FRANCE	26/1/16		The 2nd Infantry Brigade Machine Gun Company was formed on 26th January 1916 under the command of CAPT. E. A PEARSON, 2nd KING'S ROYAL RIFLES.	
			The Company was inspected in the Square, LILLERS by BRIG GEN. THUILLIER, commanding 2nd INFANTRY BRIGADE) after which the Company marched to billets in ECQUEDECQUES.	
			The composition of the Company was as follows:-	
			Machine Gun Sections of	
			2nd BATT ROYAL SUSSEX REGT renamed A SECTION (Sub-sections	1 & 2)
			1st - LOYAL NORTH LANCASHIRE REGT - B - -	3 & 4
			1st - NORTHAMPTONSHIRE REGT - C - -	5 & 6
			2nd - KING'S ROYAL RIFLES. - D - -	7 & 8
ECQUEDECQUES:	27/1/16 to 4/2/16.		Training. Nothing of interest.	
-do-	5/2/16.		Tactical march by the 2nd INF BRIGADE.	
			The company paraded at 7.10 am. and joined the 2nd BRIGADE in LILLERS at 8 am. They marched to BUSNES via LE CORNET BOURDOIS and LA. MIQUELLERIE returning via LILLERS.	

2449 Wt. W14957/M90 750,000 1/16 J.B.C. & A. Forms/C.2118/12.

Instructions regarding War Diaries and Intelligence Summaries are contained in F. S. Regs., Part II. and the Staff Manual respectively. Title Pages will be prepared in manuscript.

WAR DIARY
or
~~INTELLIGENCE SUMMARY~~
(Erase heading not required.)

Army Form C. 2118.

Feby

Place	Date	Hour	Summary of Events and Information Ref. 1/100000. HAZEBROUCK 5A	Remarks and references to Appendices
ECQUEDECQUES.	5/2/16.		After leaving LILLERS the Brigade received the order to attack a position on the ridge S.W. of ECQUEDECQUES. The Machine Gun Company supported the infantry in that attack and on the position being taken limbered up and moved forward to consolidate.	
—"—	6/2/16 to 12/2/16		Training. Nothing of interest.	
—"—	13/2/16		The Company marched into billets at BURBURE. No. 8 Sub-section marched to RAIMBERT to report to the officer commanding 2ND BATT WELCH REGT for duty with the LOOS DEFENCES. The sub section with two (2) Vickers guns to be permanently attached while the 1st DIVISION is in the Line.	
BURBURE	14/2/16		Training.	
—"—	15/2/16		The Company marched into billets in LES BREBIS	
LES BREBIS	15/2/16	9.15pm	Ref. 1/40000. 36 B.C. The Company relieved 141st BDE M.G. Coy. in the MAROC SECTOR of the 47TH DIVISION Line.	

2449 Wt. W14957/M90 750,000 1/16 J.B.C. & A. Forms/C.2118/12.

Army Form C. 2118.

Instructions regarding War Diaries and Intelligence Summaries are contained in F. S. Regs., Part II. and the Staff Manual respectively. Title Pages will be prepared in manuscript.

WAR DIARY
or
INTELLIGENCE SUMMARY
(Erase heading not required.)

Feb. & Mar.

Place	Date	Hour	Summary of Events and Information	Remarks and references to Appendices
			Ref. 1/40000 36 B.C.	
LES BREBIS	16/2/16 & 21/2/16		Company in the Line. Nothing of interest. Much work done on new emplacements. No casualties – due to new pattern emplacement (protected by steel rails)	
	21/2/16	6 pm	Relieved by 1st BDE M.G. Coy.	
–"–	22/2/16 & 27/2/16		Rest, cleaning & training.	
–"–	27/2/16	6 pm	Company relieved 3rd BDE M.G. Coy in LOOS SECTOR.	
–"–	27/2/16 & 10/3/16		Company in the Line. Nothing of interest. Continuous work on emplacements. No casualties.	
–"–	10/3/16	6 pm	Relieved by 1st BDE M G Coy.	
–"–	11/3/16 & 14/3/16		Rest cleaning & training.	

2449 Wt. W14957/M90 750,000 1/16 J.B.C. & A. Forms/C.2118/12.

Army Form C. 2118. 4

Instructions regarding War Diaries and Intelligence Summaries are contained in F. S. Regs., Part II. and the Staff Manual respectively. Title Pages will be prepared in manuscript.

WAR DIARY
~~or~~
~~INTELLIGENCE~~ SUMMARY

(Erase heading not required.)

Place	Date	Hour	Summary of Events and Information — Ref. 1/40,000, 36, B.C.	Remarks and references to Appendices
LES BREBIS	14/3/16		Orders were received that the machine gun company in Reserve should move up to GRENAY so as to be able to line up positions assigned in the Reserve Line in the shortest possible space of time. The idea being to have a heavy reserve of fire while the infantry in Reserve were being brought up.	
LES BREBIS GRENAY	15/3/16		Company moved up to GRENAY	eh
GRENAY	16/3/16	6.30 pm	Company relieved 3rd BDE M.G. Coy in MAROC SECTOR.	
LES BREBIS	16/3/16 to 28/3/16		Company in the Line. nothing of interest. Continuous work on emplacements. No casualties	eh
GRENAY	28/3/16	6.20 pm.	Relieved by 1st BDE M.G. Coy.	
GRENAY	29/3/16 to 3/4/16		Rest, cleaning and training.	
GRENAY.	3/4/16	7.30 pm.	Relieved 3rd BDE M.G. Coy in LOOS SECTOR.	eh

2449 Wt. W14957/M90 750,000 1/16 J.B.C. & A. Forms/C.2118/12.

Army Form C. 2118.

Instructions regarding War Diaries and Intelligence Summaries are contained in F. S. Regs., Part II. and the Staff Manual respectively. Title Pages will be prepared in manuscript.

WAR DIARY
~~or~~
INTELLIGENCE SUMMARY

(Erase heading not required.)

Place	Date	Hour	Summary of Events and Information	Remarks and references to Appendices
			Ref. 1/40,000 36 B.C.	
LES BREBIS	4/4/16 to 5/4/16		Company in the Line. Nothing of interest. Work on emplacements.	
–"–	6/4/16	12.30 AM to 1.30 AM	The enemy exploded a mine between positions occupied by the two guns of No 7 Sub-section. The guns opened immediate fire.	
–"–	6/4/16 to 15/4/16		Company in the Line. Much work on emplacements. Casualties: 1 man killed. 1 officer & 3 men wounded.	
GRENAY	15/4/16	7.30 pm	Relieved by 1st BDE M.G. Coy	
GRENAY	16/4/16 to 21/4/16		Rest, cleaning and training.	
–"–	21/4/16	7 pm	Relieved 3rd BDE M.G. Coy. in MAROC SECTOR.	

2449 Wt. W14957/M90 750,000 1/16 J.B.C. & A. Forms/C.2118/12.

Instructions regarding War Diaries and Intelligence Summaries are contained in F. S. Regs., Part II. and the Staff Manual respectively. Title Pages will be prepared in manuscript.

WAR DIARY or INTELLIGENCE SUMMARY

(Erase heading not required.)

Army Form C. 2118.

2 Bde M G Coy

6

Vol

Place	Date	Hour	Summary of Events and Information	Remarks and references to Appendices
			Ref 1/40.000 36 B.S.	
LES BREBIS	22/4/16 to 3/5/16		In the Line. Nothing of Interest.	
	3/5/16		Relieved by 1st Brigade M. G. Coy.	
GRENAY	3/5/16 to 9/5/16		In Reserve. Training	
	9/5/16	8.30pm.	Relieved 3rd Brigade M.G. Coy in LOOS sector	
LES BREBIS	10/5/16 to 18/5/16		Company in the Line. Nothing of interest	
	18/5/16	8.45pm.	Relieved by 49th Bde. M.G. Coy.	
GRENAY	19/5/16 to 26/5/16		Company in reserve.	

REGISTRY
MACHINE GUN CORPS
6 - JUL 1916
RECORD OFFICE
No.

Instructions regarding War Diaries and Intelligence Summaries are contained in F. S. Regs., Part II. and the Staff Manual respectively. Title pages will be prepared in manuscript.

WAR DIARY
or
INTELLIGENCE SUMMARY.
(Erase heading not required.)

Army Form C. 2118.

HOUR PLACE DATE	INFORMATION	REFERENCES REMARKS
10.4.16 1035	One aeroplane was observed to be up in a southerly direction from Coy H.Q. the same was very heavily shelled it was impossible to note the marks on plane about this time a stray shell (possibly one that had been fired at the plane) fell in the direction of La Brique & exploded.	SHEET 5A 1/100000 I 4
1100	Six observation Balloons were up one to the N. NNE NE. E. SE. & SW of Coy H.Q.	
1200	At 1200 the ?? Howitzer Bde consisting of 3 complete Batteries passed No 2 Billet going East	
	Weather. Fine clear & warm Wind from East.	

(A9175) Wt W2358/P360 600,000 12/17 D. D. & L. Sch. 52a. Forms/C2118/15.

Instructions regarding War Diaries and Intelligence Summaries are contained in F. S. Regs., Part II, and the Staff Manual respectively. Title pages will be prepared in manuscript.

WAR DIARY
or
INTELLIGENCE SUMMARY.
(Erase heading not required.)

Army Form C. 2118.

Date Place	INFORMATION.	REFERENCE REMARKS
11. 4. 16	Our aeroplanes have made very few and only short flights during the day	
	No Observation balloons have been seen up	
	No Enemy's aircraft has been observed.	
	Occasional bursts of artillery fire during the afternoon were heard.	
0900	Some Mounted Infantry about 30 strong passed No 2 Billet from W to E about 0900	
	Weather – Rainy. Cold + dull with wind from the west. Reserve Section of 2 officers and 31 other ranks arrived for training	Arrivals
1945. 12. 4. 16	men of Coy were innoculated for the second time.	TAB 2
1800	One Officer + 26 other ranks arrived with 52 horses 12 Limber waggons 1 Water Cart + 1 Baggage Cart at 1800	Arrivals
	Weather. Cold, rain Windy + dull wind from a N.W. direction	

(A9475) Wt W2358/P360 600,000 12/17 D. D. & L. Sch. 52a. Forms/C2118/15.

Instructions regarding War Diaries and Intelligence Summaries are contained in F. S. Regs., Part II. and the Staff Manual respectively. Title pages will be prepared in manuscript.

WAR DIARY
or
INTELLIGENCE SUMMARY.

(Erase heading not required.)

Army Form C. 2118.

Place	Date	Hour	Summary of Events and Information	Remarks and references to Appendices

DATE, PLACE	INFORMATION	REMARKS REFERENCES
13.4.16.	Very quiet all day & night. Weather conditions very [illegible] dull strong winds at intervals during the afternoon. Wind from N.W. No aircraft of any description observed. [initials]	
14.4.16. 0730	1 Officer + 4 other ranks despatched as advance Guard to new billeting area at ERQUINHEM. One Officer to [illegible] + One [illegible] Weather conditions dull + showery Wind from N.W.	Departures. SHEET 5a 1/40,000 1C4.
15.4.16 0930	Company comprising 9 Officers + 169 other ranks including [illegible] and 3 attached A.S.C. also 16 Waggons + 57 horses proceeded to starting point A.9.D.0.4 + then to fresh billets in Erquinghem area Via STEENWERCK, LE SEQUEMEAU and BAC. ST MAUR. [initials]	SHEET 36 1/40,000 A.9.D.0.4.

(A9475) Wt W2358/P360 600,000 12/17 D. D. & L. Sch. 52a. Forms/C2118/15.

Instructions regarding War Diaries and Intelligence Summaries are contained in F. S. Regs., Part II. and the Staff Manual respectively. Title pages will be prepared in manuscript.

WAR DIARY
or
INTELLIGENCE SUMMARY.
(Erase heading not required.)

Army Form C. 2118.

DATE PLACE	INFORMATION	REMARKS REFERENCE
15.4.16	arrived about 1730 at new billets and were joined by advance party of 1 NCO and 3 other ranks [illegible] also school of Instruction of 7 officers + 50 other ranks Weather cold + windy but fine	SHEET 36 1/40,000 H-9-B-7-8.
16.4.16	One Armourer departed for Calais for instruction Two Signallers from Div Sig Coy attached to Bn for duty Considerable activity of aeroplanes	
1600	noticed during the afternoon as many as 10 friendly planes were up at one time + were heavily shelled. 3 Observation Balloons were up in the Westerly direction of Bn HQ possibly Hoskle a farm about 3/4 of a mile	

(A9475) Wt W2358/P360 600,000 12/17 D. D. & L. Sch. 52a. Forms/C2118/15.

Instructions regarding War Diaries and Intelligence Summaries are contained in F. S. Regs., Part II. and the Staff Manual respectively. Title pages will be prepared in manuscript.

WAR DIARY
or
INTELLIGENCE SUMMARY.
(Erase heading not required.)

Army Form C. 2118.

DATE PLACE	INFORMATION	REFERENCE REMARKS.
	awayane West of Coy Billets was set on fire about 1530.	
	Weather Dull but fine. [initials]	
17/4/16	Everything appears very quiet	
	Weather Dull showery & cold nothing otherwise of any importance [initials]	
18/4/16	17/4/16 2 Cooks from 6th Bn attached to School [initials]	
	One Officer returned from visit to trenches.	
	School of Instruction attached to Billets finished up at 1200 & moved to their respective Units at 1430. leaving behind the 2 attached Cooks for the next school to be formed.	
	Weather dull showery & cold wind from N W	
	[initials]	

Instructions regarding War Diaries and Intelligence Summaries are contained in F. S. Regs., Part II. and the Staff Manual respectively. Title Pages will be prepared in manuscript.

WAR DIARY
or
INTELLIGENCE SUMMARY
(Erase heading not required.)

Army Form C. 2118.

Place	Date	Hour	Summary of Events and Information	Remarks and references to Appendices
ERQUINGHEM	19.4.16.		10 Officers and 48 other ranks reported to Billets for Instruction School (Bayonet fighting etc), classes. no of Instructors 3.	
			Everything appears very quiet. No aeroplanes or observation Balloons observed at all.	
			One man returned from hospital.	
			Weather Showery + dull with Strong S.W. winds	
ERQUINGHEM	20.4.16		One man to Hospital. 1 Officer + 4 men arrived + joined School of Instruction	
		1535	A German plane appeared from S.W. but our artillery quickly drove him away	
		1810.	The Enemy shelled a point in the L'ERINNETT district. Belgium + pt France Edition 6 Sheet 36 1/40,000 B.27.D. North East corner. About 21 Shells all told were sent over at intervals of about 4 minutes. Shells appeared to be between 4 + 5 inch size. ceasing about 19.15. Weather Conditions Dull + Slight Showers with N West Wind afternoon fine	Pt Belg + Pt France 36. 1/40,000 B 27 D NE Corner

2449 Wt. W14957/M90 750,000 1/16 J.B.C. & A. Forms/C.2118/12.

Army Form C. 2118.

WAR DIARY
or
INTELLIGENCE SUMMARY
(Erase heading not required.)

Instructions regarding War Diaries and Intelligence Summaries are contained in F. S. Regs., Part II. and the Staff Manual respectively. Title Pages will be prepared in manuscript.

Place	Date	Hour	Summary of Events and Information	Remarks and references to Appendices
ERQUINGHEM	21.4.16		One man sent to Hospital, sick	
			Aeroplanes fairly active in the forenoon (Both friendly & Hostile)	
		0920	An Enemy plane was chased by two friendly planes, in the direction of Armentiers result unknown	
			Occasional Artillery fire noticed to the West of ARMENTIERS during the day	
			Machine Gun + Rifle fire have also been very noticeable during parts of the morning + afternoon.	
		1200	Two observation ballons West of Armentiers, seen up.	
			Weather morning dry + fine afternoon dull & showery	
ERQUINGHEM	22.4.16	0700	Artillery fire noticed to the West of Armentiers	AA
			No Aircraft observed during the day, Artillery active in direction of	
		1500 to 1900	Armentiers, from 1500 to 1900.	
			2 Reserve Officers & 2 Batmen returned to units.	
			Weather Wet & Cold Wind N.E.	AA

2449 Wt. W14957/M90 750,000 1/16 J.B.C. & A. Forms/C.2118/12.

Instructions regarding War Diaries and Intelligence Summaries are contained in F. S. Regs., Part II. and the Staff Manual respectively. Title Pages will be prepared in manuscript.

WAR DIARY
or
INTELLIGENCE SUMMARY
(Erase heading not required.)

Army Form C. 2118.

Place	Date	Hour	Summary of Events and Information	Remarks and references to Appendices
ERQUINHEM	23 4 16		Occasional Hostile aeroplanes up during the forenoon but were shelled + did not stay long.	
			Company's Strength —	
	Permanent		Officers 9 · O Ranks 133 · attached 2 ASC, 1 Div Sig · on Instruction Calais 1 Armourer · in Hospital local 2	
	Reserves		O Ranks 29	
	Total		9 · 162 · 3 · 1 · 2	
			Grand Total: Off 9 · other ranks 168 · Horses 52	
			Nothing else of any importance occurred during the day	
			[signature]	

2449 Wt. W14957/M90 750,000 1/16 J.B.C. & A. Forms/C.2118/12.

Instructions regarding War Diaries and Intelligence Summaries are contained in F. S. Regs., Part II. and the Staff Manual respectively. Title Pages will be prepared in manuscript.

WAR DIARY
or
INTELLIGENCE SUMMARY

(Erase heading not required.)

Army Form C. 2118.

Place	Date	Hour	Summary of Events and Information	Remarks and references to Appendices
ERQUENHEM.	24.4.16	0745	A Hostile aeroplane that was being shelled was brought down in the direction of Nieppe.	
			Our aeroplanes were up the best portion of the day and were occasionally heavily shelled	
			Weather fine & warm.	
	25.4.16		Enemy's planes were over our lines about 0900. 0930 & 130. friendly Guns opened fire but no results	
			Our planes were very active between ARMENTIERS & FLEUR BAIX. and drew a considerable volume of enemy's fire but without doing any apparent damage	
		1700	Enemy heavy guns were searching a small area south of Erquinghem by Pont about half way between Armentiers & Erquinghem. about 160 shells were sent over about 25 failed to explode	
			Weather fine warm & dry	

2449 Wt. W14957/M90 750,000 1/16 J.B.C. & A. Forms/C.2118/12.

Army Form C. 2118.

Instructions regarding War Diaries and Intelligence Summaries are contained in F. S. Regs., Part II. and the Staff Manual respectively. Title Pages will be prepared in manuscript.

WAR DIARY
or
INTELLIGENCE SUMMARY
(Erase heading not required.)

Place	Date	Hour	Summary of Events and Information	Remarks and references to Appendices
ERQUINHEM	26.4.16		Aircraft quiet all day Nothing of Importance to report Weather fine Dry & Warm. [initials]	
ERQUINHEM	27.4.16		3 of our planes were observed during the morning and were twice shelled by the enemy.	
		1100	An Enemy's plane was observed overhead our guns opened fire on it & it cleared behind enemy's lines.	
		1400	Some shells about 5 or 6 were dropped on the WEST end of ERQUINGHEM. damage unknown. Inspected by General D Haig during afternoon. Our Guns N.E. of Billets were firing at intervals during the afternoon about 6.15 Enemy replied with about 4 shells at position. Our aircraft were up during the evening & were heavily shelled without any apparent result	
		2240	Wire received from B.H.Q. that gas attack imminent, Left Bdg Second Division report attack. all Officers & other ranks were at once warned	

2449 Wt. W14957/M90 750,000 1/16 J.B.C. & A. Forms/C.2118/12.

Instructions regarding War Diaries and Intelligence Summaries are contained in F. S. Regs., Part II. and the Staff Manual respectively. Title Pages will be prepared in manuscript.

WAR DIARY
or
INTELLIGENCE SUMMARY
(Erase heading not required.)

Army Form C. 2118.

Place	Date	Hour	Summary of Events and Information	Remarks and references to Appendices
ERQUINHEM	27.4.16	2318	Wire received Division that gas attack passed. [initials]	
ERQUINHEM	28.4.16	0800	4 Officers & half fighting personnel departed for firing line minus Guns ammunition & transport, to relieve part of 6th Bde M.G. Coy & take over positions.	
ERQUINHEM	28.4.16	2000	Balance of 2nd M.G. Coy with transport moved at 2000 from ERQUINHEM via FORT ROMPU to PORT A CLOUS FARM the Hdqrs of 6th Bde M.G. Coy. Column moved in small bodies when South of ARMENTIERES, BAC ST. MAUR railway. Last party arrived at 2050. Transport unloaded & returned to old Billets H9B.2.8.	[initials]
FLEURBAIX	29-4-16	1800	Balance of 1st, 2nd, 3rd Sections moved at 1800 to front line to relieve the remaining half of the 6th Bde M.G. Coy. Relief was complete & positions finally taken over by 2030. Last of 6th Bde M.G. Coy reported at PORT A CLOUS FARM at 2215 & then proceeded to ERQUINHEM. 4th Section remains at Hdqrs in Reserve.	
		1100	Enemy shelled M.O. HOUSE and BRICK KILN with H.E and Shrapnel shells. M.G. Emplacement knocked out in M.O. HOUSE. Gun was dismounted. Shelling repeated at 1730. No other damage done.	[initials]
		1730		
FLEURBAIX	[crossed out]	[crossed out]	[crossed out, illegible]	
	30-4-16	0337	Following message received from L. "Gas attack against right Bde 34th Division is developing AAA Locality square C 36. A.11 AAA Attack may be of some magnitude AAA Be prepared and take all precautions AAA Acknowledge". 0315. On receipt of this message all ranks were duly warned & necessary precautions taken.	B.M.207. [initials]

2449 Wt. W14957/M90 750,000 1/16 J.B.C. & A. Forms/C.2118/12.

Army Form C. 2118.

Instructions regarding War Diaries and Intelligence Summaries are contained in F. S. Regs., Part II. and the Staff Manual respectively. Title Pages will be prepared in manuscript.

WAR DIARY
or
INTELLIGENCE SUMMARY
(Erase heading not required.)

Place	Date	Hour	Summary of Events and Information	Remarks and references to Appendices
FLUERBAIX	30-4-16		Everything Quiet.	
		2324	Following message received from 1.A.20. Second Army: Div advises gas attack due north of ARMENTIERES AAA Please warn all ranks and take necessary precautions. 2310.	
			All ranks were warned + precautions taken.	
	1-5-16	0005	Following message Rcd. from 1.A.20. Div advises that gas attack passed. 2010	[illegible initials]
	30-4-16		The following is the distribution of this unit after relieving the 6th Bde M. Gun Company:—	
			No. 1 Section. M.O. HOUSE. BRICK KILN. ELBOW FARM. and SMITH VILLA.	Reference Maps
			No. 2 Section. JAYS POST. and the two guns in left Battn Section.	1/10000 S.W. Sheets 1 + [illegible]
			No. 3 Section. Two right guns in left Battn Section + the two Guns in right Battn Section.	1/10000 N.W. Sheet 3
			No. 4 Section. at Hdqrs in Reserve.	
			Locality Square of Hdqrs of Company H.15.c.1.0.	[illegible initials]
	30-4-16	1430	Lieut. Hogg + 1 N.C.O. returned to unit from School of Instruction NEAUVEAU MONDE.	

2449 Wt. W14957/M90 750,000 1/16 J.B.C. & A. Forms/C.2118/12.

2nd Brigade.

1st Division.

----- -----

2nd MACHINE GUN COMPANY

MAY 1916.

V/145

Instructions regarding War Diaries and Intelligence Summaries are contained in F. S. Regs., Part II. and the Staff Manual respectively. Title Pages will be prepared in manuscript.

WAR DIARY
or
INTELLIGENCE SUMMARY
(Erase heading not required.)

2 Bde M G Coy
Vol 5

Army Form C. 2118. 1

Place	Date	Hour	Summary of Events and Information	Remarks and references to Appendices
FLEURBAIX	1-5-16		During Day very quiet, little shelling & sniping. During night enemy traversed Trench 38 with Machine gun fire. Road East of M.O. HOUSE was also swept by Machine gun fire, irregularly during the night.	
		1905	Following message recd "Div. advises enemy artillery registering on the right trenches of Division on our left AAA This may be preparatory to an attack of some kind AAA For your information AAA All observers to be particularly alert. 1905." —	
			One N.C.O sent on leave to ENGLAND.	42R 659
FLEURBAIX	2-5-16	0630	Enemy bombarded the vicinity of BRICK POST until 0930 firing about 70 H.E. Shells, no appreciable damage. Between 0800 and 0900 they also bombarded Artillery observation Post about 300 yds East of M.O. HOUSE with about 50 H.E. Shells. The strengthening of No 2 Gun emplacement was carried out.	[initials]
		1400	Five friendly aeroplanes observed over our lines, & remained in view during our artillery bombardment which lasted for about 3 hours. During night enemy carried on usual sniping.	[initials]
		2006	Vickers gun placed in position in Trench 47 (This trench has just been taken over by 2nd Bde).	
FLEURBAIX	3.5.16	1500	Our Artillery bombarded enemy's positions for about 2 hours, otherwise day was quiet, during night rifle & Machine gun fire was rather less than usual.	
		1500	2 Aeroplanes observed direction South of ARMENTIERES, one about 5000 feet up, other much higher, lower one was apparently hit, it was seen to catch fire & volplane to earth.	[initials]
			1 Man sent on leave to ENGLAND.	
		1100	One Third of Company sent to Baths.	
FLEURBAIX	4.5.16		Quiet during day and night.	
		1100	One Third of Company sent to Baths at SAILLY.	
			1 man went to ENGLAND on leave.	[initials]

2449 Wt. W14957/M90 750,000 1/16 J.B.C. & A. Forms/C.2118/12.

Instructions regarding War Diaries and Intelligence Summaries are contained in F. S. Regs., Part II. and the Staff Manual respectively. Title Pages will be prepared in manuscript.

WAR DIARY
or
INTELLIGENCE SUMMARY

(Erase heading not required.)

Army Form C. 2118.

Place	Date	Hour	Summary of Events and Information	Remarks and references to Appendices
FLEURBAIX	5-5-16		Quiet during day usual sniping.	
		1945	Enemy commenced bombardment on front line & communication trenches, bombardment ceased at 2115. Reserve Section standing to from 2010 until 2215 at Coy Hdqrs.	
		2010	Verbal message from Bde Hdqrs per Lt Barker "stand to, await further orders".	
		2215	Message Recd "Carry On" 1.A.20. 2200"	
			1 N.C.O. sent on leave to England.	
		1100	Bathing party (1/2 of Company) proceeded to SAILLY.	
FLEURBAIX	6-5-16		Quiet during day. Wind S.W. showery during morning.	
		0630	Two friendly aeroplanes observed flying towards German lines.	
			One man sent to Hospital. One N.C.O. returned off leave at 1600.	
			Battery near PORT A CLOUS FARM fired a few rounds during day at 1000 and 1800.	
		1830	One N.C.O. went on leave to England.	
		2130	Machine Gun did indirect fire from position H.35.D.1.3. on Targets N.17.A.8.5 and N.17.B.4.0. from 2130 until about 2320 firing in all about 750 Rds. Result unobtainable, but as considerable movement is observed at Targets during day, it is to be assumed that movement would be there at night.	Reference Maps 1/10,000 Sheets N.W.4 and S.W.2

STATE.

	Officers	O.R.'s	Guns	G.S. Limbered Wagons	Horses Rdg	L.D.
Establishment	10	147	16	17	10	43
Duties	9	136	-	-	-	-
Leave	-	1	-	-	-	-
Hospital	-	1	-	-	-	-
Reqd. to Complete	1	4	-	-	1	-
Attached Reserves	-	27	-	-	-	-

2449 Wt. W14957/M90 750,000 1/16 J.B.C. & A. Forms/C.2118/12.

Instructions regarding War Diaries and Intelligence Summaries are contained in F. S. Regs., Part II. and the Staff Manual respectively. Title Pages will be prepared in manuscript.

WAR DIARY
or
INTELLIGENCE SUMMARY
(Erase heading not required.)

Army Form C. 2118.

Place	Date	Hour	Summary of Events and Information	Remarks and references to Appendices
FIEURBAIX				
7.5.16			Generally quiet all day, Light Showers S Wind.	
			Our planes were observed over enemy's line early in the morning	
		0730	Mr S.B. Hill returned from leave.	
		0815	Cpl McFadden returned from leave had one day extra granted.	
		1200	Bombardment to our right ended.	
		1500	Our plane up over lines.	
		1800	Signaller Butler went on leave	
			Bombardment going on in the direction of La Bassee.	
		1700	Enemy's Machine Guns active during the night one of their guns enfiladed portion of Sector 40 of 6th Battn	
		2030 to 2230	Machine Gun did indirect fire from H.35 . D.13 range 1875 + 2000 result unknown Targets. O 13 A 45.4 O 13 A 14. [initials]	reference map 1/10,000 SHEET 36 NW + S.W. 2.
FLEURBAIX. 8.5.16		0700	Cpl Smith returned from leave.	
			Our artillery were registering on enemy's line at Corner Fort in front of 6th Bn extreme right flank.	
		1600	About 6 shots were fired by our artillery to the right of our HQ.	

2449 Wt. W14957/M90 750,000 1/16 J.B.C. & A. Forms/C.2118/12.

Instructions regarding War Diaries and Intelligence Summaries are contained in F. S. Regs., Part II. and the Staff Manual respectively. Title Pages will be prepared in manuscript.

WAR DIARY
or
INTELLIGENCE SUMMARY
(Erase heading not required.)

Army Form C. 2118.

Place	Date	Hour	Summary of Events and Information	Remarks and references to Appendices
8.5.16 FLEURBAIX.		1700.	Sgt O Donnell went on leave	
		2230	Bombardment fairly heavy slightly to the right of Coy H.Q. by enemy	
		2030 – 2300	Machine Gun did Indirect fire on N.12 D Tramline 750 rounds	
			Wind S.W. Weather cool	
			No Enemys or friendly planes observed during the day.	
FLEURBAIX.	9.5.16.		Showery & Windy	
		0800	Pte A/ Dunn returned from leave	
			Enemy shelled communication trench leading into Sector H1	
			plenty of sniping by both sides.	
		1345	Artificer Page returned from course of Instruction Calais	
		1500	Dr McCasker left for A.P.M. Sailly under Guard	
			Pte Hoare (reserve Section) to hospital	
		2030 – 2300	Indirect fire by MG 750 rounds	Targets. 0.13.A 4.5 + 0.13.A.8.4.

2449 Wt. W14957/M90 750,000 1/16 J.B.C. & A. Forms/C.2118/12.

Instructions regarding War Diaries and Intelligence Summaries are contained in F. S. Regs., Part II. and the Staff Manual respectively. Title Pages will be prepared in manuscript.

WAR DIARY
or
INTELLIGENCE SUMMARY

(Erase heading not required.)

Army Form C. 2118.

Place	Date	Hour	Summary of Events and Information	Remarks and references to Appendices
FLEUBAIX	10.5.16.		Weather fine + Warm.	
		0930	10 men of No 4 Section left for trenches to relieve No 2 Section	
		1145	our planes up but flying very low	
		1350	Enemy Shelled in the vicinity of BOUTILLERIE AVENUE for about 30 minutes, Our Artillery replied enemy's guns ceased fire as soon as our plane came in sight which was flying very low + was fired at by M.G. + Shrapnell	
		1555	three of our planes were up our Artillery continued to shell the enemy's rear positions	
		1600	remainder of no 4 Section proceeded to trenches.	
		1800	No 4 Section duly relieved No 2 Section who proceeded to [illegible] + arrived about 1930	
			Snipers were very active during the night on both sides, M.G. fire quiet	
		2045 2300	Indirect fire by our M.G. at Targets H 35 D.1.3. N.12 A.7.5 Tramline 750 rounds	

2449 Wt. W14957/M90 750,000 1/16 J.B.C. & A. Forms/C.2118/12.

Army Form C. 2118.

WAR DIARY
or
INTELLIGENCE SUMMARY
(Erase heading not required.)

Instructions regarding War Diaries and Intelligence Summaries are contained in F. S. Regs., Part II. and the Staff Manual respectively. Title Pages will be prepared in manuscript.

Place	Date	Hour	Summary of Events and Information	Remarks and references to Appendices
FLEURBAIX.	11.5.16	0930	Enemy put a few shrapnel at the entrance to TIN BARN AVENUE and also a few H.E. about RUE JONATHON. Our aeroplanes then appeared + enemy at once stopped shelling	
		1200	Two of our planes up were being shelled by enemy.	
		1545	One of our planes was seen to come down in the rear of Junction line but later was seen to rise again about 1700 + flew back in the direction of BAILLEUL.	
			M.G. positions were inspected by Brigade staff between 1500 + 1730	
			Our artillery active with aeroplane assistance	
			Quiet generally all night with the exception of sniping on both sides	
		2100 2300	Indirect fire by our M.G. at Target N.12.A.7.5 Tramline range 1900 to 1900 x results unknown	REFERENCE 1/10,000 SHEET N.W. 4 + S.W. 2.
			Weather fair + calm.	

Instructions regarding War Diaries and Intelligence Summaries are contained in F. S. Regs., Part II. and the Staff Manual respectively. Title Pages will be prepared in manuscript.

WAR DIARY
or
INTELLIGENCE SUMMARY

(Erase heading not required.)

Army Form C. 2118.

Place	Date	Hour	Summary of Events and Information	Remarks and references to Appendices
FLEUBAIX.	12.5.16.	0930.	in retaliation to a few rifle grenades fired by our people this morning enemy sent over some large bombs wounding 3 of 6th Bn only one seriously. Our trench mortar opened fire with something larger than the enemy the enemy then quieted down	
			Dr Hill departed from leave having one day extra granted.	
		1500.	Two of our planes were up	
			Our artillery active during the afternoon no retaliation	
		1800	S/c [illegible] went on leave to U.K.	
		2115	Word received (from B.H.Q.) at Coy H.Q. to stand to	
		2145	Word received (from B.H.Q.) at Coy H.Q. to carry on.	
		2050 + 2300.	Indirect fire was carried out from position 4.36.A.4.4. at Targets 0.7.4.9.6. and 0.7.A.3.5. 500 rounds each results unknown.	
			Weather dull cool very little wind	
			[initials]	

2449 Wt. W14957/M90 750,000 1/16 J.B.C. & A. Forms/C.2118/12.

Instructions regarding War Diaries and Intelligence Summaries are contained in F. S. Regs., Part II. and the Staff Manual respectively. Title Pages will be prepared in manuscript.

WAR DIARY
or
INTELLIGENCE SUMMARY
(Erase heading not required.)

Army Form C. 2118.

Place	Date	Hour	Summary of Events and Information	Remarks and references to Appendices
FLEUBAIX.	13.5.16		Weather dull & wet all day	
			No aeroplanes were observed during the day	
		1400	Our Artillery opened fire position & targets [illegible]	
		1430	Enemy Light & heavy artillery retaliated dropping a few shells about Tardy House and further towards Croix MARECHAL, result unknown. Our artillery was active all the afternoon the enemy's fire was rather spasmodic	
		1800	The Enemy put in about 9 HE & some shrapnel along City Road.	REFERENCE 1/10,000 SHEET N.W.4 & S.W.2.
			Continued movement of enemy noticed road junction O.I.C 6.5 & 3.5.	
		2000 2030	Indirect fire by our M.G. at targets CROSS ROADS. N.12.A.1.2.	

	Officers.	ORRS	Guns	GS Limb Wagons	Horses RD	Horses LD
Establishment	10	147 ~~136~~	16	12	10	43
Details	9	136				
LEAVE		8				
MG School.		1				
Req'd to Complete	1	3			1	
Attached Reserves		22				
Non Combatants.		3				

2449 Wt. W14957/M90 750,000 1/16 J.B.C. & A. Forms/C.2118/12.

Army Form C. 2118.

Instructions regarding War Diaries and Intelligence Summaries are contained in F.S. Regs., Part II, and the Staff Manual respectively. Title pages will be prepared in manuscript.

WAR DIARY

or

INTELLIGENCE SUMMARY.

(Erase heading not required).

Hour, Date, Place.			Summary of Events and Information.	Remarks and references to Appendices.
0800	14/3/16	FLEURBAIX.	Enemy shelled position no N.5.C.10.5 with about 20 shells of various size no damage done Generally quiet along the line all day our Artillery fired occasionally without any retaliation at all The Infantry of B Battn were very quiet owing to the fact of changing over	REFERENCE 1/10000 SHEET N W 4 + S W.
0900			Enemy shelled M O House with HE and Shrapnel	
2000 and 2400			Indirect fire was carried out by our Machine Guns at Targets N12 B 4.1. CORNER ROAD (E.4.16.5.) result unknown	ditto
			Weather dull & showery	

[illegible signature]

Army Form C. 2118.

WAR DIARY
or
INTELLIGENCE SUMMARY.
(Erase heading not required).

Instructions regarding War Diaries and Intelligence Summaries are contained in F.S. Regs., Part II, and the Staff Manual respectively. Title pages will be prepared in manuscript.

Hour, Date, Place.	Summary of Events and Information.	Remarks and references to Appendices.
FLEUBAIX. 15/5/16 –	Sgt THOMPSON returned from leave also Pte Warne Pte William to hospital slightly wounded. 2/Lt Honeyburn went on leave to U.K.	
1100	Enemy shelled Convent Avenue with HE.	
1200	Enemy shelled communication trench about 400x SE of M.D. HOUSE.	
1230	Enemy sent over a few bombs killing 3 + wounding 3 about 7 bombs in all were fired	
2000–2100 (Stand To)	Enemy again started bombing but without any damage	
	There was plenty of M G fire during the night also Enemy very active with snipers (probably fresh troops)	
1900–2400	Indirect fire was carried out by our M Gs. from [illegible] FARM (H.35.D.1.3) at Target ROAD + TRAMLINE. N.12.B.D. range 2000 rounds expended 1000	REFERENCE 1/10000 SHEET N.W.4 + S.W. 2
	Weather ~~[illegible]~~ Very showery + dull.	
	[illegible initials]	

Army Form C. 2118.

Instructions regarding War Diaries and Intelligence Summaries are contained in F. S. Regs., Part II. and the Staff Manual respectively. Title Pages will be prepared in manuscript.

WAR DIARY
or
INTELLIGENCE SUMMARY
(Erase heading not required.)

Place	Date	Hour	Summary of Events and Information	Remarks and references to Appendices
FLEURBAIX.	16.5.16	0700	Our Machine Guns did Indirect Fire at intervals from 0700 to 1200 from Brick POST at targets H.36. A4.4 MARTINS CORNER fired about 220 rounds	
		1200	Enemy shelled support trenches 350x SW of M.O. HOUSE with HE + Shrapnel	
			Aeroplanes both enemy + friendly were very active all day at times as many as 6 of ours were observed at one time	
		1230	about a dozen shells were fired into + about roadby Port a Colons Farm	
		1745	A friendly plane came down in a field NW of PORT A COLOUS FARM.	
		2200	Enemy? aeroplane dropped some coloured lights	
		2300	Droning of either Zepp or aeroplane heard lights on parachutes dropped over ARMENTIERES + FLEURBAIX. also over German lines one Red Light is reported to have dropped in no mans land question machine seemed to be taking N.W to SE	
			Bomb dropped in C Coy B. Battn killed one + 2 wounded	
			MG (Enemy active all night)	
			Sgt Watson returned from leave being granted one day extra.	
		2000 + 2400	Indirect fire was carried out at targets N11.D.2.6 Communication Trench + Road range 2000x from position N4 B.1.8.	REFERENCE 1/10000 SHEET NW4 SHEET SW.2
			Weather Fine + Warm.	

2449 Wt. W14957/M90 750,000 1/16 J.B.C. & A. Forms/C.2118/12.

Instructions regarding War Diaries and Intelligence Summaries are contained in F. S. Regs., Part II. and the Staff Manual respectively. Title Pages will be prepared in manuscript.

WAR DIARY
or
INTELLIGENCE SUMMARY
(Erase heading not required.)

Army Form C. 2118.

Place	Date	Hour	Summary of Events and Information	Remarks and references to Appendices
FLEURBAIX.	17.5.16		Weather fine & warm very little wind at all.	
		1130.	Enemy shelled communication trenches to the right of M.O. HOUSE with HE. also some shrapnel. no damage done.	
		1200	Enemy shelled to the right of Post a Clons on heavy guns replied.	
		1300	Enemy shelled (Sector 37. A Batt.) N.C. 5.0.2. with HE no damage done	REFERENCE 1/10000 NW. 4 SW. 2
		1500	Enemy shelled in the vicinity of Brick Post & Foray House with HE NO DAMAGE	
		2000	Gas alarm was sounded no gas was noticed carry on passed along at 2115.	
			Sgt Watson & Sig Butler returned from leave	
			Mc Pompa went on leave.	
		2000 & 2400	Indirect fire was carried out by our M.G. Target N.11.D.2.6. communication Trench & Road. 1000 rounds fired. results unknown.	Reference 1/10000 NW. 4. SW. 2
FLEURBAIX.	18.5.16		0015 Gas alarm given (Cay H 2) FLEURBAIX.	
			0030 Carry on given.	
			Weather fine but a distinct Haze hung over Enemy's lines making it very difficult to observe far	
	1100		Two Enemy aeroplanes were observed going in a westerly direction	
	1415		One Enemy plane seen going west then turned & flew due North	

2449 Wt. W14957/M90 750,000 1/16 J.B.C. & A. Forms/C.2118/12.

Instructions regarding War Diaries and Intelligence Summaries are contained in F. S. Regs., Part II. and the Staff Manual respectively. Title Pages will be prepared in manuscript.

WAR DIARY
or
INTELLIGENCE SUMMARY
(Erase heading not required.)

Army Form C. 2118.

Place	Date	Hour	Summary of Events and Information	Remarks and references to Appendices
FLEUBAIX.	18.5.16	1700	Our heavy artillery very active in this area.	REFERENCE 0.7.A.9.6 1/10,000 SHEET NW 4, SW 2.
		2000 + 2400	Indirect fire carried out by our M G on MARTINS CORNER between hours of 2000 & 2400 1000 rounds expended. [initials]	
FLEUBAIX	19.5.16	1130	Enemy plane driven off by our shell fire.	
		1600	3 men reported from 5th Bn for duty with reserve section	
			Pte Smith left for leave.	
			Sgt O'Donnell returned from leave	
			Haze lifted making it good for observation	
		615	2 enemy observation balloons up.	
		1830	Enemy shelled CROIX MARACHAL with about 20 HE SHELLS two of these did not explode.	
			Our planes were up most of the day light artillery active	
			Weather fine & warm WIND N.E. – Hazy up to 1600 [initials]	
	20.5.16	1000	Pte McCasker returned from [illegible] under escort.	
			Small parties seen about Martins Corner at intervals	
			No 1 & No 3 Sections changing over completed at 1700.	

Instructions regarding War Diaries and Intelligence Summaries are contained in F. S. Regs., Part II. and the Staff Manual respectively. Title Pages will be prepared in manuscript.

WAR DIARY
or
INTELLIGENCE SUMMARY
(Erase heading not required.)

Army Form C. 2118.

Place	Date	Hour	Summary of Events and Information	Remarks and references to Appendices
FLEUR BAIX.	30.5.16	1700	Indirect fire was done on Martins Corner by our M.G. results not seen about 600 rounds fired	1/10,000 SHEET N.W.4 SW.2.
			Our aeroplanes up (4) flying very low and occasionally shelled	
		1800	Enemy shelled Fleurbaix with heavy shells 26 in all & only 5 burst & they seemed very weak in explosion	
		1900	Enemy shelled house to the N of SMITHS VILLA. Could not see which one.	
		2000 to 2300	Indirect fire was carried out against MARTINS CORNER about 700 rounds being fired results unknown H 36 a.	1/10,000 SHEET N.W.4 SW.2.
			Weather fine warm & very little wind	
		2000	Enemy threw over two fairly large bombs in B Battn line killing one & wounding four. This mortar can be heard going off & noise sounds as if it were fired from a deep pit & it is thought to be the same gun that fires most of the bombs.	
			Aerial searchlight seen on enemy side towards RADINGHAM.	
FLEURBAIX.	31.5.16	0700	[illegible] returned from leave.	
		1030	Our 18pr. Artillery & Medium T.M.B. & trench howitzers on an arranged signal opened out on the enemy front line & evidently did considerable damage to enemy trenches. Enemy retaliated with about 12 bombs but did no damage.	

Instructions regarding War Diaries and Intelligence Summaries are contained in F. S. Regs., Part II. and the Staff Manual respectively. Title Pages will be prepared in manuscript.

WAR DIARY
or
INTELLIGENCE SUMMARY
(Erase heading not required.)

Army Form C. 2118.

Place	Date	Hour	Summary of Events and Information	Remarks and references to Appendices
FLEURBAIX	21/5/16	—	Our people fired 33 Light & 4 heavy bombs over this sector (B.Bn)	
		1500	Enemy shelled battery to the left of ELBOW FARM. Results not known	
		1130	German 77 opened fire on portion of Pays Post where heavy mortar emplacement has been constructed they also fired 16 HE at from 10x to 40x from M.G. position at Pays Post. NO DAMAGE DONE.	
		2100	Our Light mortars again opened fire on working parties repairing parapets and M.Gs also fired at same, Enemy retaliated by firing [illegible] to our fifteen (15) bombs.	
		2100 2200 2400 0200	Two of our M.G. opened fire from over parapet sweeping enemy's parapet and wire about 1000 rounds being fired. Enemy's [illegible] blown in after bursts of our fire [illegible] of casualties	
			Enemy working all night either inside or outside his trench.	
			Disappearing mounting proved a great success.	
			Weather Warm fine & very little wind	
			Aeroplanes were fairly active during the day no Enemy machines were seen	

Army Form C. 2118.

Instructions regarding War Diaries and Intelligence Summaries are contained in F. S. Regs., Part II. and the Staff Manual respectively. Title Pages will be prepared in manuscript.

WAR DIARY
or
INTELLIGENCE SUMMARY
(Erase heading not required.)

Place	Date	Hour	Summary of Events and Information	Remarks and references to Appendices
FIEURBAIX.	21.5.16.		Sgt Watson sent to Hospital. V.	P
	22.5.16		Pte Henderson to Hospital	
			Reserves started training again.	
			2/Lt Oliver + 2 Guns + crews to Pigy House for duty.	
		0530	1 Enemy machine (aeroplane) driven off by artillery fire	
		0700	Enemy plane above + firing down on one of ours.	
		1200	2 Enemy observation balloons up.	
		1530	Enemy shelled H.29. C 03. / 8 Shrapnel all exploded	REFERENCE
		1630	Enemy shelled H.29 C.33. with 2 HE and 8 Shrapnel all exploded.	1/10000
		2030	Our M.G. fired over the parapet SECTOR 41. BAY 3. at enemys parapet + wire between CLAPHAM JUNCTION and THE NEEDLE	NW + SW. 2
		2115	One of our M.G. fired at THE ANGLE + LOZENGE from over the parapet covering patrol	
			Weather fine + warm very little wind at all.	
	23.5.16		0930. Enemy shelled our plane without doing any damage	
		1100	THE BREWERY was shelled by enemy at 1100 with HE	
			Working Parties were observed at ~~martins~~ MARTINS CORNER 0327.	
		1200	Enemy shelled to the rear of M.O. HOUSE + did not explode. 12 shells fired	
		~~1400~~ 1500	Enemy shelled JAYS POST with 77° getting 2 direct hits on 1 MG gun emplacements	

2449 Wt. W14957/M90 750,000 1/16 J.B.C. & A. Forms/C.2118/12.

Instructions regarding War Diaries and Intelligence Summaries are contained in F. S. Regs., Part II. and the Staff Manual respectively. Title Pages will be prepared in manuscript.

WAR DIARY
or
INTELLIGENCE SUMMARY

(Erase heading not required.)

Army Form C. 2118.

Place	Date	Hour	Summary of Events and Information	Remarks and references to Appendices
FLEURBAIX	23.5.16		about 10 light HE dropped very close NO DAMAGE DONE H.36 C.6.1	REFERENCE 1/10000 NW4 SW2.
	1945	—	Enemy sent over 3 fair sized bombs which exploded about 20x behind sector 43 "B" Bath without doing any damage	
	2030 to 2230		Night firing by our MG over parapets was carried out from SECTOR NO Box 29. TARGETS ENEMY'S PARAPET. between CLAPHAM JUNCTION and TURKS POST had one stoppage one Broken LOCK SPRING	
		2/15 2300	INDIRECT FIRE was carried out at TARGETS N H.D.9.6. N 12 A 2.2½. N.12 A 6.6 1000 being expended	do
		2/15 2345	Played on Enemys parapets were between and about the ANGLE + LOZENGE patrol reports our fire on wire was perfect Fired 3000 rounds	
			Weather Fine & warm very little wind	
	24.5.16		2/Lt. Honeyborn returned from leave	
			Cpl. Dennan departed for leave	
		0600	Enemys planes passed over our line (A Bath) going WEST but was turned off by our planes	
		0815	Enemy fired 8 HE shells at H.28.A.8.1 all exploded very little damage done	do
		0830	Enemy fired 3HE shells on H28 C.7.8 all exploded no damage at all	
		1030	ENEMY Shelled JAYS POST getting 2 direct hits on dug out vacated by MG gun crew short night the position was wrecked H 36.5.0.	do
		1100	Enemy fired 3 H E shells on H 28. A8.3 and set fire to shed on NORTH side of building	

2449 Wt. W14957/M90 750,000 1/16 J.B.C. & A. Forms/C.2118/12.

Instructions regarding War Diaries and Intelligence Summaries are contained in F. S. Regs., Part II. and the Staff Manual respectively. Title Pages will be prepared in manuscript.

WAR DIARY
or
INTELLIGENCE SUMMARY
(Erase heading not required.)

Army Form C. 2118.

Place	Date	Hour	Summary of Events and Information	Remarks and references to Appendices
FLEURBAIX.	24.5.16	1130	Enemy fired 8 HE shells on H 29.B.2.2. + set fire to the HOUSE	REFERENCE 1/10000
		1300	Enemy fired one HE shell at H 29.C.0.1. did not explode	SHEET N.W.H. S.W. 2.
		1330	Enemy fired one HE shell at H 28. B.2.1 no damage done.	
		1400	Started raining making observation difficult	do
		1500	Enemy shelled about 200x in front of FORAY HOUSE NO DAMAGE.	do.
		1715	INDIRECT FIRE was carried out during the afternoon on MARTINS CORNER + TRAMLINE 0.7A.44 0.7A.10.7 on the second burst the enemy's artillery searched for us with Shrapnel but was 300x over. we fired 450 rounds SAA.	do
		1725	Enemy fired 8 Shrapnel shells on H 29.C.8.8 + 3 on H 29.C.7.3. all exploded	
		1750	Enemy fired 4 Shrapnel Shells on H.28.A.8.3 also 1. HE. which did not explode	
		2015 to 2230	Our MGs fired over the parapet from Sector 38 BAY 5. at targets enemy's wire + parapets. expended 500 rounds SAA. also from Sector 44 BAY 19. on same targets. The two ENEMY MG which usually traverse the portion of trench from which we fired were very quiet	
		2030	Indirect fire was carried out on targets MARTINS CORNER + TRAMLINE 0.7A.44 + 0.7A.10.7 fired 1750 rounds in all	
	25.5.16		Pte McFarlane to Hospital – 1 Pte Henderson returned from Hospital	
			Weather showery towards evening	
		0830	Started raining a little making observation difficult	

2449 Wt. W14957/M90 750,000 1/16 J.B.C. & A. Forms/C.2118/12.

Army Form C. 2118.

WAR DIARY
or
INTELLIGENCE SUMMARY

(Erase heading not required.)

Instructions regarding War Diaries and Intelligence Summaries are contained in F. S. Regs., Part II. and the Staff Manual respectively. Title Pages will be prepared in manuscript.

Place	Date	Hour	Summary of Events and Information	Remarks and references to Appendices
FLEURBAIX.	25/5/16	1045	Our Artillery shelled the POTTERIES.	REFERENCE 1/10,000 SHEET NW4 SW2.
		1120	Enemy fired 2 Shrapnel shells on H.28 C.8.1.	
		1200	Enemy fired 15 Shrapnel shells on and between H.35 A.10.5 and H.35.A.5.0.	
		1215	2 Enemy shrapnel fell on H.28.D.8.7	
		1345	16 Enemy HE fell between H.35.A.10.5 and H.35 A.5.0. two failed to explode	do
		1130	Individual movements were noticed at MARTINS CORNER	
		1400	A number of parties were noticed by the tramway and WHITE HOUSE	
		1845	Enemy shelled H.29.C.2.8 with 4 HE shells fairly large + 4 shrapnel.	do
		2000 / 2205	Indirect fire was carried out from positions H.35 B.3.4 at target O.7.A.2½.8½. (TRAM TRACK) expenditure 800 rounds SAA.	
		2015 / 2230	Our M.G. fired over parapet in sector 41. at Enemy's parapet + wire from CLAPHAM JUNCTION to the NEEDLE Enemy MG very quiet in this sector.	
			Our MG also fired at intervals during darkness in B Batt. Sector at Enemy's parapet [illegible] about 1800 rounds expended.	
	26.5.16	0830	Brigade emergency rounds were inspected by 1 Officer + 4 NCO's	
			2/Lt Bowman went on Leave	
			Sgt Watson struck off strength	
		1500	Enemy troops were seen passing MARTINS CORNER.	
		1800	Enemy fired about 24 Shrapnel shells on H.28.B.2.0.	
		1630	Enemy shelled MG HOUSE and buildings in rear without effect	do
		1500 / 1600	Indirect fire was done from MG gun position H34.B.3.4 at Target O.7.A.2½.8½ (500 rounds)	

2449 Wt. W14957/M90 750,000 1/16 J.B.C. & A. Forms/C.2118/12.

Instructions regarding War Diaries and Intelligence Summaries are contained in F. S. Regs., Part II. and the Staff Manual respectively. Title Pages will be prepared in manuscript.

WAR DIARY
or
INTELLIGENCE SUMMARY

(Erase heading not required.)

Army Form C. 2118.

Place	Date	Hour	Summary of Events and Information	Remarks and references to Appendices
FLEURBAIX.	26.5.16	1930	Enemy opened out on our trenches with HOWITZERS. sending about 40 at the entrance to BAY AVENUE no real damage done H.36.D.7.0.	REFERENCE 1/10000 SHEET NW.4 SW.2
		2015 2230	Our M.G. fired from over the parapet Sector 37 Bay 2 target enemy's wire + parapet 750 rounds being expended another Gun fired from Sector 43 Bay 8 during the night Target enemy's wire + parapets 1000 rounds were expended. Enemy's M.G. sweeping our parapet during night.	
		2000 2200	Indirect fire was carried out from position H.34.B.3.4. at targets N.6.C.3½.7 (Intersection Tramline) + N.12.A.6.6. (Communication Trench) 450 rounds expended.	
	27.5.16	0330	Enemy Artillery opened fire on our parapet from SECTOR 45 to BRIDS Salient. Weather fair and a little wind.	
	27.5.16	1200	Enemy fired 9 shrapnel shells at our plane over H.29 it is noticed that whenever a plane passes square H.29 it is always shelled by the enemy	
		1600 1700	Indirect fire was carried out from positions H.35.B.3.4. at targets O.7.A.2½.8½ (Turn Trench) also O.7.A.4.4. (Batt H2) O.7.A.1.7 (MARTINS CORNER) 500 rounds being expended. The Enemy again searched for positions with HE + shrapnel but could not [illegible] at all	
		2000	Enemy fired 69 H.E shells at H.29.A.8.2 (4 of which failed to explode	
		2010	about 200 shrapnel shells were sent at our plane over H.29	
		2015 2330	Firing was carried out over the parapet from Sect. 36 Bay 5 Target enemy's parapet and wire. 1000 rounds expended. also fired from B Batt. Dukes at enemy's parapets + wire. 2000 rounds.	

2449 Wt. W14957/M90 750,000 1/16 J.B.C. & A. Forms/C.2118/12.

Army Form C. 2118.

WAR DIARY
or
INTELLIGENCE SUMMARY

(Erase heading not required.)

Instructions regarding War Diaries and Intelligence Summaries are contained in F. S. Regs., Part II. and the Staff Manual respectively. Title Pages will be prepared in manuscript.

Place	Date	Hour	Summary of Events and Information	Remarks and references to Appendices
FLEURBAIX	27.5.16		Strength for week ending 27/5/16	

	Officers	O. Ranks	Guns	Limbers	Horses R	Horses L.D.
On Establishment	10	144	16	12	11	45
Duty Depot		1				
On Leave	1	4				
Fighting Strength	9	134			10	44
Required to complete	1	7			1	1
Attached reserves		28				
Noncombatants		3				
Hospital (sick)		3				
Total Rationed	9	160			10	44 X

X 1 Horse Hospital sick

Place	Date	Hour	Summary of Events and Information	Remarks and references to Appendices
	28.5.16		Weather fine + warm little wind from N.W.	REFERENCE 1/10000 NW4 SW 2
			Casual movements were noticed at the TRAMWAY N12.A and the SAP at MARTINS CORNER this seems to be the most used round this part O.7.A.10.7.	
		1700	Enemy fired 20 HE SHELLS on H.29.C3.6	
		1715	10 Shrapnel shells burst over H.28.D.8.4 and 10? HE SHELLS on H.28.C9.2 (3 of which failed to explode	
		0735	Enemy aeroplane passed over H.29 travelling South then changed + went EAST.	

2449 Wt. W14957/M90 750,000 1/16 J.B.C. & A. Forms/C.2118/12.

Instructions regarding War Diaries and Intelligence Summaries are contained in F. S. Regs., Part II. and the Staff Manual respectively. Title Pages will be prepared in manuscript.

WAR DIARY
or
INTELLIGENCE SUMMARY
(Erase heading not required.)

Army Form C. 2118.

Place	Date	Hour	Summary of Events and Information	Remarks and references to Appendices
FLEURBAIX	28.5.16	1910	Enemy very busy shelling our aeroplane about 150 shells were fired at it also M.G. Batteries opened up on same all without any outward sign of damage.	
		2015	Fire over the parapet was carried out against targets Enemy's wire & parapet	REFERENCE
		10 0200	this was carried out from SECTORS 42 Bay 2 & SECTOR 43 BAY 19. ammunition expended 1500 rounds SAA.	10,000 SHEET NW4 SW2
			Fire over the parapet was also carried out in 'B' Battns Sector 250 rounds	
			Pte Pumpa returned from leave	
	29.5.16	0745	3 enemy's planes passed over H.29.C & D they were fired on without result	do
		0830	30 Shrapnel shells burst over M.O. HOUSE and about 40x in rear.	
		0900	Enemy aeroplane flew over our lines going East	
		0930	About 50 Shrapnel shells were fired at H.34.A.10.8.	do
			Enemy shelled WYE FARM with HE. H35.B9.2.	"
		1000	Enemy fired 8 shrapnel shells on H.29.C.3.8.	
		1015	Enemy aeroplane passed over H28 & 29 they were fired at and driven off by our artillery	"
		1100	Five HE shells fell on H.29.C.3.6. & 13 were fired at H28.D8.5	"
			Enemy put about 60 Shrapnel shells into H.34.A.10.8.	

2449 Wt. W14957/M90 750,000 1/16 J.B.C. & A. Forms/C.2118/12.

Instructions regarding War Diaries and Intelligence Summaries are contained in F. S. Regs., Part II. and the Staff Manual respectively. Title Pages will be prepared in manuscript.

WAR DIARY
or
INTELLIGENCE SUMMARY
(Erase heading not required.)

Army Form C. 2118.

Place	Date	Hour	Summary of Events and Information	Remarks and references to Appendices
FLEURBAIX	29.5.16	1100	5 HE were fired into Chapel Farm H.29.C.3.6. and 13 were fired at H.29.D.8.5.	REFERENCE 1/10000 SHEET NW 4 SW 2
		1125	12 HE were fired on ROAD about H.28.D.8.5.	
		1145	One of our planes passed over Enemy's line low down & was fired on by Enemy with about 30 shrapnel without any outward sign of damage	
			A number of the enemy were seen at Marlin's Corner during the forenoon	
		1300	Enemy shelled our heavy battery WEST of PORT A CLOUS.	
		1315	Enemy shelled FLEURBAIX with 12 Shrapnel shells S of TOWN.	do
		1330	20 Shrapnel shells fell on H.28 D9.4	
		1515	A Working party of 15 to 20 were seen at BATT HOUSE and were at once shelled by our artillery	
			Pte Willet went on leave & Cpl Smith returned from leave	
	30.5.16.		Raining during morning but fine afternoon Wind N.W.	
			Sjt Phelan sent to Hospital.	
		0815	1 Large HE Burst behind M.O HOUSE	
		1515	Enemy fired on our plane when over H.28 & 29. without doing any damage	do
		1530 to 1630	Indirect fire was carried out against Targets & fired 500 rounds	
		1930 to 2035	Indirect Fire was carried out against targets N.11.C.9.6 N.11.D.5.7. N12 A1.2. N.12.A.7.6½. & fired 1750 rounds	

2449 Wt. W14957/M90 750,000 1/16 J.B.C. & A. Forms/C.2118/12.

Army Form C. 2118.

Instructions regarding War Diaries and Intelligence Summaries are contained in F. S. Regs., Part II. and the Staff Manual respectively. Title Pages will be prepared in manuscript.

WAR DIARY
or
INTELLIGENCE SUMMARY

(Erase heading not required.)

Place	Date	Hour	Summary of Events and Information	Remarks and references to Appendices
FLEURBAIX.	30.5.16.	2020	Enemy bombarded Battn to the right of A Battn a few Shrapnel shells fell on A Battn lines & about 25 Trench Mortar Bombs without doing much damage	
		2210	Heavy mist enveloped the trenches [initials]	
	31.5.16	0300	Our M.G. fired over the parapet at Enemy's wire & parapet 1000 rounds being expended also in "B" Battns sector firing 750 rounds.	
			Owing to Mist observation was difficult until about midday	
		0930	Enemy aircraft flew over our positions going EAST returning about 1015.	
		1030	10 Shrapnel burst on batteries at rear of M.O. HOUSE	
		1100	47 HE shells fell on H.29.A.7.2.	
		1640	20 Shrapnel shells were fired at one of our planes over H.28 & 29	
		1815	18 HE shells were fired at H.28 D.9.7. one failed to explode	
		1915 to 2015	about 173 large sized HE shells were fired at H.28.D.9.7. 12 failed to explode	
		2100 to 0130	Our M.G. fired over parapet Sector 43 BAY 8. Target Enemy's wire & parapet	
			Lt Poynder returned from leave. [initials]	

2449 Wt. W14957/M90 750,000 1/16 J.B.C. & A. Forms/C.2118/12.

2nd Bde.

1st Div.

WAR
DIARY

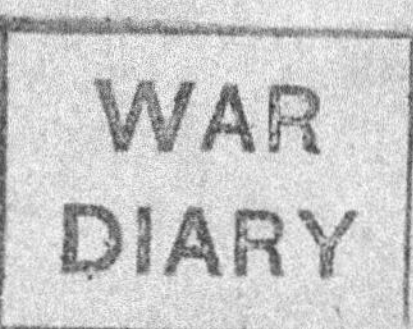

2nd MACHINE GUNE COMPANY.

JUNE & JULY 1916.

2nd
MACHINE GUN
COMPANY
No. 485
Date -/16

2nd Infantry Brigade.

Attached I beg to hand you AF C 2118 - War Diary - in duplicate from 24/5/16 to 30/7/16.

[illegible]
Captain
Cmdg. No 2 M.G. Coy

2nd Aug 1916

Instructions regarding War Diaries and Intelligence Summaries are contained in F. S. Regs., Part II. and the Staff Manual respectively. Title Pages will be prepared in manuscript.

WAR DIARY
or
INTELLIGENCE SUMMARY
(Erase heading not required.)

Army Form C. 2118.

2 M G Coy

Vol 6

Ref 1/40,000 36 B C

Place	Date	Hour	Summary of Events and Information	Remarks and references to Appendices
GRENAY	26/5/16	4 30 pm	Relieved 3rd Bde M.G. Coy in MAROC SECTOR	
LES BREBIS	27/5/16 to 11/6/16		Company in the Line.	
			G.O.C. 2nd Inf. Bde. expressed his appreciation of the work done by the 2nd Bde M.G. Coy. in preparing special emplacements in the Line	el
BULLY-GRENAY	11/6/16	4 pm	Relieved by 1st Bde M. G. Coy	
-"-	12/6/16 to 19/6/16		Company in Reserve. Training.	el
LES BREBIS	19/6/16	4 pm	Relieved 1st Bde M.G. Coy. in MAROC SECTOR	
LES BREBIS	19/6/16 to 3/7/16		Company in the Line. Company guns took part in attack on a section of the enemy's line by the 2nd Infantry Brigade.	el
-"-	3/7/16		Relieved by 121st Brigade M. G. Coy. 40th Division.	

2449 Wt. W14957/M90 750,000 1/16 J.B.C. & A. Forms/C.2118/12.

Army Form C. 2118.

Instructions regarding War Diaries and Intelligence Summaries are contained in F. S. Regs., Part II. and the Staff Manual respectively. Title Pages will be prepared in manuscript.

WAR DIARY or INTELLIGENCE SUMMARY

(Erase heading not required.)

Place	Date	Hour	Summary of Events and Information	Remarks and references to Appendices
			Ref 1/40.000 36 B C	
GRENAY	26/5/16	4 30 pm	Relieved 3rd Bde M.G. Coy in MAROC SECTOR	
LES BREBIS	27/5/16 to 11/6/16		Company in the Line. G.O.C. 2nd Inf Bde. expressed his appreciation of the work done by the 2nd Bde M.G. Coy in preparing special emplacements in the Line.	el
BULLY-GRENAY	11/6/16	4pm	Relieved by 1st Bde M.G. Coy	
-"-	12/6/16 to 19/6/16		Company in Reserve. Training.	el.
LES BREBIS	19/6/16	4pm	Relieved 1st Bde M.G. Coy. in MAROC SECTOR.	
LES BREBIS	19/6/16 to 3/7/16		Company in the Line. Company guns took part in attack on a section of the enemy's line by the 2nd Infantry Brigade.	el.
-"-	3/7/16		Relieved by 121st Brigade M.G. Coy 40th Division.	

2449 Wt. W14957/M90 750,000 1/16 J.B.C. & A. Forms/C.2118/12.

Army Form C. 2118.

Instructions regarding War Diaries and Intelligence Summaries are contained in F. S. Regs., Part II. and the Staff Manual respectively. Title Pages will be prepared in manuscript.

WAR DIARY
or
~~INTELLIGENCE SUMMARY~~
(Erase heading not required.)

Place	Date	Hour	Summary of Events and Information	Remarks and references to Appendices
			Ref 1/100,000 LENS 11	
LES BREBIS	3/7/16	11.30 pm.	Company marched to billets at HAILLICOURT. Arrived 3.30 AM.	
HAILLICOURT	4/7/16	5.15 pm.	Company marched to billets at FERME DE LABIETTE (BRUAY) Arrived 7.15 pm.	eS
BRUAY	6/7/16	2.15 AM.	Company marched to LILLERS. Arrived 7.15 AM. Entrained 10 AM. Detrained CANDAS 5 pm. Marched to billets at FLESSELLES. Arrived 9.30 pm.	eS
FLESSELLES	8/7/16	8.25 pm.	Company marched to billets at FRÉCHENCOURT (Ref. 1/100,000. AMIENS 17) arrived 1.30 am.	
FRÉCHENCOURT. (Ref. 1/100,000 AMIENS 17.)	9/7/16	5.40 pm.	Company marched to billets at BRESLE. arrived 8.30 pm.	eS
BRESLE (Ref. 1/100000 AMIENS 17.)	10/7/16.	10.15 pm.	Company marched to MAXSE REDOUBT, due East of ALBERT (Ref. 1/100,000 LENS 11) arrived 2 am. 11/7/16	eS
MAXSE REDOUBT	11/7/16 to 17/7/16		Bivouacked in MAXSE REDOUBT. Company in Reserve	
	17/7/16	6.45 pm.	Company moved to ~~sec~~ British Line, in Reserve.	eS

2449 Wt. W14957/M90 750,000 1/16 J.B.C. & A. Forms/C.2118/12.

Instructions regarding War Diaries and Intelligence Summaries are contained in F. S. Regs., Part II. and the Staff Manual respectively. Title Pages will be prepared in manuscript.

WAR DIARY
or
INTELLIGENCE SUMMARY
(Erase heading not required.)

Army Form C. 2118.

Place	Date	Hour	Summary of Events and Information	Remarks and references to Appendices
			Ref 1/100000 LENS 11	
LES BREBIS	3/7/16	11.30pm	Company marched to billets at HAILLICOURT. Arrived 3.30 AM.	
HAILLICOURT	4/7/16	5.15pm	Company marched to billets at FERME DE LABIETTE (BRUAY) Arrived 7.15 pm.	
BRUAY	6/7/16	2.15AM	Company marched to LILLERS. Arrived 7.15 AM. Entrained 10 AM. Detrained CANDAS 5 pm. Marched to billets at FLESSELLES. Arrived 9.30 pm.	
FLESSELLES	8/7/16	8.25pm	Company marched to billets at FRÉCHENCOURT (Ref 1/100000 AMIENS 17) arrived 1.30 am.	
FRÉCHENCOURT. (Ref 1/100000 AMIENS 17)	9/7/16	5.40pm	Company marched to billets at BRESLE. arrived 8.30 pm.	
BRESLE (Ref 1/100000 AMIENS 17)	10/7/16	10.15pm	Company marched to MAXSE REDOUBT, due East of ALBERT (Ref 1/100000 LENS 11) arrived 2 am. 11/7/16	
MAXSE REDOUBT	11/7/16 to 17/7/16		Bivouacked in MAXSE REDOUBT. Company in Reserve	
	17/7/16	6.45pm	Company moved to old British Line, in Reserve.	

2449 Wt. W14957/M90 750,000 1/16 J.B.C. & A. Forms/C.2118/12.

Instructions regarding War Diaries and Intelligence Summaries are contained in F. S. Regs., Part II. and the Staff Manual respectively. Title Pages will be prepared in manuscript.

WAR DIARY
or
INTELLIGENCE SUMMARY
(Erase heading not required.)

Army Form C. 2118.

A 9

Place	Date	Hour	Summary of Events and Information — Ref. 1/100000 LENS 11	Remarks and references to Appendices
	18/7/16	3.30 pm.	Company moved into Line. HQ. at CONTALMAISON.	
	18/7/16 to 23/7/16.		Company in Line.	
			On the night 21st/22nd July the 2nd Infantry Brigade made an attack, and eight guns were told off to form defensive flanks, should the attack succeed. The attack failed and the guns did not come into action.	
	23/7/16.		Company relieved by 3rd Bde M. G. Coy & moved to billets in ALBERT.	
ALBERT	23/7/16 to 26/7/16		Company in Reserve.	
	26/7/16	11 am.	Relieved by 69th Bde M. G. Coy. 23rd Division. Marched to billets in FRANVILLERS (Ref 1/100,000 AMIENS 17)	
FRANVILLERS	26/7/16 to 30/7/16		Division resting. Training	
			Name changed to No. 2 Machine Gun Company (G.R.O. 27/7/16.)	
	30/7/16	6.55 pm.	Company moved to bivouac in HENENCOURT WOOD. (Ref 1/100000. LENS 11)	

2449 Wt. W14957/M90 750,000 1/16 J.B.C. & A. Forms/C.2118/12.

Instructions regarding War Diaries and Intelligence Summaries are contained in F. S. Regs., Part II. and the Staff Manual respectively. Title Pages will be prepared in manuscript.

WAR DIARY
or
INTELLIGENCE SUMMARY
(Erase heading not required.)

Army Form C. 2118.

Place	Date	Hour	Summary of Events and Information (Ref. 1/100000 LENS 11.)	Remarks and references to Appendices
	18/7/16	3.30 pm	Company moved into Line. H.Q. at CONTALMAISON.	
	18/7/16 to 23/7/16		Company in Line.	
			On the night 21st/22nd July the 2nd Infantry Brigade made an attack, and eight guns were told off to form defensive flanks, should the attack succeed. The attack failed and the guns did not come into action.	
	23/7/16		Company relieved by 3rd Bde M.G. Coy. & moved to billets in ALBERT.	
ALBERT	23/7/16 to 26/7/16		Company in Reserve.	
	26/7/16	11 am	Relieved by 69th Bde M.G. Coy. 23rd Division. Marched to billets in FRANVILLERS (Ref 1/100,000 AMIENS 17)	
FRANVILLERS	26/7/16 to 30/7/16		Division resting. Training.	
			Name changed to No 2 Machine Gun Company (G.R.O. 27/7/16.)	
	30/7/16	6.55 pm	Company moved to bivouac in HENENCOURT WOOD. (Ref 1/100000 LENS 11)	

2449 Wt. W14957/M90 750,000 1/16 J.B.C. & A. Forms/C.2118/12.

2nd Brigade.
1st Division.

2nd BRIGADE MACHINE GUN COMPANY

AUGUST 1 9 1 6

Army Form C. 2118.

Instructions regarding War Diaries and Intelligence Summaries are contained in F. S. Regs., Part II. and the Staff Manual respectively. Title Pages will be prepared in manuscript.

WAR DIARY
or
INTELLIGENCE SUMMARY

(Erase heading not required.)

No 2 Machine Gun Coy. 10

Vol 8

Place	Date	Hour	Summary of Events and Information (Ref 1/100000 LENS 11.)	Remarks and references to Appendices
HENENCOURT WOOD	30/7/16 to 13/8/16		On Rest. Training.	
	1/8/16	4.15pm	2nd Infantry Brigade inspected by III Corps Commander	
	2/8/16	10am	Company inspected by G.O.C. 2nd Infantry Brigade.	
	13/8/16	5.40pm	Company moved to MAXSE REDOUBT.	
MAXSE REDOUBT	14/8/16	8am	No 2 M.G. Coy relieved No 111 M.G. Coy in ~~MAMETZ WOOD~~ the front line.	
MAMETZ WOOD.	14/8/16 to 20/8/16		Company in the Line. (Ref 1/20000 FRANCE. 57D SE)	
	18/8/16 / 19/8/16		Company's guns supported an attack by 2nd Inf Bde on the Enemy Intermediate Line. The attack was partially successful, and the machine guns inflicted heavy losses on the enemy.	
			Casualties: 3 Officers wounded. 8 O.R. Killed 11 O.R. wounded.	

2449 Wt. W14957/M90 750,000 1/16 J.B.C. & A. Forms/C.2118/12.

Army Form C. 2118.

10

WAR DIARY
or
~~INTELLIGENCE SUMMARY~~

(Erase heading not required.)

Instructions regarding War Diaries and Intelligence Summaries are contained in F. S. Regs., Part II. and the Staff Manual respectively. Title Pages will be prepared in manuscript.

Place	Date	Hour	Summary of Events and Information (Ref 1/100000 LENS 11.)	Remarks and references to Appendices
HENENCOURT WOOD	30/7/16 to 13/8/16		On Rest Training	[initials]
	1/8/16	4.15pm	2nd Infantry Brigade inspected by III Corps Commander	
	2/8/16	10am	Company inspected by GOC 2nd Infantry Brigade	
	13/8/16	5.00pm	Company moved to MAXSE REDOUBT	
MAXSE REDOUBT	14/8/16	8am	No 2 MG. Coy relieved No 111 MG. Coy in ~~[illegible]~~ the front line	[initials]
MAMETZ WOOD	14/8/16 to 20/8/16		Company in the Line (Ref 1/20000 FRANCE 57° SE)	
	18/8/16 / 19/8/16		Company guns supported an attack by 2nd Inf Bde on the Enemy Intermediate Line. The attack was partially successful, and the machine guns inflicted heavy losses on the enemy.	[initials]
			Casualties:- 3 Officers wounded. 8 OR killed 11 OR wounded.	

2449 Wt. W14957/M90 750,000 1/16 J.B.C. & A. Forms/C.2118/12.

Army Form C. 2118.

·11

Instructions regarding War Diaries and Intelligence Summaries are contained in F. S. Regs., Part II. and the Staff Manual respectively. Title Pages will be prepared in manuscript.

WAR DIARY
or
INTELLIGENCE SUMMARY
(Erase heading not required.)

Place	Date	Hour	Summary of Events and Information	Remarks and references to Appendices
			Ref 1/100000 LENS 11.	
	20/8/16	10 am.	No. 2 M.G. Coy relieved by No. 3 M.G. Coy	
			Company moved to quarters in MAXSE REDOUBT	
MAXSE REDOUBT	20/8/16 to 27/8/16		Company in Reserve.	eb
	27/8/16	2.30 pm.	Company relieved No. 1 M.G. Coy. in Support in MAMETZ WOOD.	
MAMETZ WOOD	27/8/16 to 31/8/16		Company in Support. (Ref. 1/20000 FRANCE. 57D S.E.)	eb
	31/8/16	10 am	Company relieved No. 1 M.G. Coy in the Front Line.	
BAZENTIN LE GRAND	31/8/16 to 2/9/16		Company in Line. Nothing of interest. (Ref 1/20000 FRANCE. 57C S.W.)	
			Casualties 2 OR. Killed	
			2 OR. wounded.	
	2/9/16	10 am	Company relieved by No. 1 M.G. Coy	eb

2449 Wt. W14957/M90 750,000 1/16 J.B.C. & A. Forms/C.2118/12.

Army Form C. 2118.

11

Instructions regarding War Diaries and Intelligence Summaries are contained in F. S. Regs., Part II. and the Staff Manual respectively. Title Pages will be prepared in manuscript.

WAR DIARY
or
INTELLIGENCE SUMMARY

(Erase heading not required.)

Place	Date	Hour	Summary of Events and Information	Remarks and references to Appendices
			Ref 1/100000 LENS 11.	
	20/8/16	10am	No 2 MG Coy relieved by No 3 MG Coy	
			Company moved to quarters in MAXSE REDOUBT.	
MAXSE REDOUBT	20/8/16 to 27/8/16		Company in Reserve.	eb
	27/8/16	2.30pm	Company relieved No 1 MG Coy in Support in MAMETZ WOOD.	
MAMETZ WOOD	27/8/16 to 31/8/16		Company in Support (Ref 1/20000 FRANCE 57D SE)	
	31/8/16	10am	Company relieved No 1 MG Coy in the front line.	eb
BAZENTIN LE GRAND	31/8/16 to 2/9/16		Company in Line. Nothing of interest (Ref 1/20000 FRANCE 57C SW)	
			Casualties 2 OR killed, 2 OR wounded	
	2/9/16	10am	Company relieved by No 1 MG Coy	eb

2449 Wt. W14957/M90 750,000 1/16 J.B.C. & A. Forms/C.2118/12.

2nd Brigade

1st Division.

2nd MACHINE GUN COMPANY ::: SEPTEMBER 1916.

No 2 M.G. Coy

Instructions regarding War Diaries and Intelligence Summaries are contained in F. S. Regs., Part II. and the Staff Manual respectively. Title Pages will be prepared in manuscript.

WAR DIARY or ~~INTELLIGENCE SUMMARY~~

(Erase heading not required.)

Army Form C. 2118.

2 M G Coy Vol 9

Place	Date	Hour	Summary of Events and Information	Remarks and references to Appendices
			Ref. 1/100000 LENS 11	
MAXSE REDOUBT	2/9/16 to 5/9/16		Company in Reserve.	
	5/9/16	2pm.	Company relieved No 3 M.G. Coy. in Support. (MAMETZ WOOD) (Ref. 1/20000 FRANCE 57D SE)	
	5/9/16 to 8/9/16		In support.	
	8/9/16		Company relieved No 3 M.G. Coy in Front Line. H.Q. BAZENTIN LE GRAND.	
BAZENTIN LE GRAND.	8/9/16 to 11/9/16.		Company in the Line.	
	9/9/16.		2nd Bde attacked Intermediate Line.	
			Company's guns in action:	
			4 guns attached to 2nd ROYAL SUSSEX REGT	
			2 " " " 1st NORTHAMPTONSHIRE REGT.	
			2 " " " 2nd K.R.R.C.	
			CASUALTIES. 1 Officer wounded. 3 O.R. Killed 1 O.R. missing 18 O.R. wounded.	
			Attack partially successful.	
	11/9/16	8pm.	Relieved by 142nd Bde M G Coy and 3rd N.Z. Bde MG Coy.	
	12/9/16.		On relief Company moved to Billets in BAIZIEUX	
BAIZIEUX	12/9/16 to 17/9/16		Company in Corps Reserve.	
			Training.	

2449 Wt. W14957/M90 750,000 1/16 J.B.C. & A. Forms/C.2118/12.

No. 2 M.G. Coy

Army Form C. 2118.

Instructions regarding War Diaries and Intelligence Summaries are contained in F. S. Regs., Part II. and the Staff Manual respectively. Title Pages will be prepared in manuscript.

WAR DIARY
or
INTELLIGENCE SUMMARY
(Erase heading not required.)

Place	Date	Hour	Summary of Events and Information	Remarks and references to Appendices
			Ref 1/100000 LENS. 11	
MAXSE REDOUBT	2/9/16 to 5/9/16		Company in Reserve.	
	5/9/16	3 pm.	Company relieved No. 3 M.G. Coy in Support. (MAMETZ WOOD) (Ref 1/20000 FRANCE 57D SE)	
	5/9/16 to 7/9/16		In support.	
	8/9/16		Company relieved No. 3 M.G. Coy in Front Line. H.Q. BAZENTIN LE GRAND	
BAZENTIN LE GRAND	8/9/16 to 11/9/16		Company in the Line.	
	9/9/16		2nd Bde attacked Intermediate Line.	
			Company's guns in action.	
			4 guns attached to 2nd Royal Sussex Regt	
			2 " " 1st Northamptonshire Regt	
			2 " " 2nd K.R.R.C.	
			CASUALTIES. 1 Officer wounded, 3 O.R. killed, 1 O.R. missing, 15 O.R. wounded	
			Attack partially successful.	
	11/9/16	8 am.	Relieved by 142nd Bde M.G. Coy and 3rd N.Z. Bde M.G. Coy.	
	12/9/16		On relief Company went to billets in BAIZIEUX	
BAIZIEUX	14/9/16 to 19/9/16		Company in Corps Reserve.	
			Training.	

2449 Wt. W14957/M90 750,000 1/16 J.B.C. & A. Forms/C.2118/12.

No 2. M.G. Coy

Instructions regarding War Diaries and Intelligence Summaries are contained in F. S. Regs., Part II. and the Staff Manual respectively. Title Pages will be prepared in manuscript.

WAR DIARY or INTELLIGENCE SUMMARY

(Erase heading not required.)

Army Form C. 2118.

13

Place	Date	Hour	Summary of Events and Information	Remarks and references to Appendices
			Ref. 1/100,000 LENS 11	
BAIZIEUX	19/9/16	1-50pm	Company relieved 140th Bde M.G. Coy in MAMETZ WOOD (in Reserve).	
MAMETZ WOOD	19/9/16 to 26/9/16		Company in Reserve and Support.	ed
BAZENTIN LE GRAND	26/9/16	5-30am	Relieved No 3 M.G. Coy in Front Line.	
	27/9/16		Two guns supported an attack by the 2nd Royal Sussex Regt. Attack successful. Casualties 1 Officer Killed, 1 O.R. Killed, 2 O.R. missing, 10 O.R. wounded	ed
	29/9/16.	4am.	Company relieved by No. 141 M.G. Coy. On relief Company marched to billets in MILLENCOURT.	
MILLENCOURT	29/9/16 to 2/10/16.		Company in Corps Reserve	ed

No. 2. M.G. Coy.

Instructions regarding War Diaries and Intelligence Summaries are contained in F. S. Regs., Part II. and the Staff Manual respectively. Title Pages will be prepared in manuscript.

WAR DIARY
or
INTELLIGENCE SUMMARY
(Erase heading not required.)

Army Form C. 2118.

13

Place	Date	Hour	Ref. 1/100,000 LENS 11. Summary of Events and Information	Remarks and references to Appendices
BAIZIEUX	19/7/16	1-50pm	Company relieved 140th Bde MG Coy in MAMETZ WOOD (in Reserve).	
MAMETZ WOOD	19/7/16 to 26/7/16		Company in Reserve and Support.	[illegible]
BAZENTIN LE GRAND	26/7/16	5.30am	Relieved No 3 MG Coy in Front Line	
	27/7/16		Two guns supported an attack by the 2nd Royal Sussex Regt. Attack successful. Casualties: 1 Officer Killed, 1 OR Killed, 2 OR missing, 10 OR wounded	[illegible]
	29/7/16	4am	Company relieved by No 141 MG Coy. On relief company marched to billets in MILLENCOURT.	
MILLENCOURT	29/7/16 to 2/8/16		Company in Corps Reserve	[illegible]

2449 Wt. W14957/M90 750,000 1/16 J.B.C. & A. Forms/C.2118/12.

2nd Brigade

1st Division.

2nd MACHINE GUN COMPANY ::: OCTOBER 1916.

Army Form C. 2118.

WAR DIARY ~~or~~ INTELLIGENCE ~~SUMMARY~~

(Erase heading not required.)

Instructions regarding War Diaries and Intelligence Summaries are contained in F. S. Regs., Part II. and the Staff Manual respectively. Title Pages will be prepared in manuscript.

No 2 Machine Gun Coy. Original 14

Vol 10

Place	Date	Hour	Summary of Events and Information	Remarks and references to Appendices
			Ref. 1/100000 ABBEVILLE 14.	
MILLENCOURT	3/10/16	6.15 am.	Company proceeded to TOURS-EN-VIMEU in busses.	
TOURS	3/10/16 to 31/10/16		Company in Army Reserve. attached X Corps.	el.
			Training.	
	19/10/16		Brigade Route march.	
	27/10/16		Divisional Route march.	el.
	28/10/16		Company inspected by G.O.C. 1st Division.	
	31/10/16	6 am.	Company proceeded to BRESLE in busses.	
			(Ref. 1/100000. AMIENS. 17)	
BRESLE	1/11/16		Company in Corps Reserve, attached III Corps.	el.
	2/11/16		Training.	

A. W. Robinson Lt. Adj. 2nd M.G. Coy.

2449 Wt. W14957/M90 750,000 1/16 J.B.C. & A. Forms/C.2118/12.

2nd Brigade.

1st Division.

2nd MACHINE GUN COMPANY :: NOVEMBER 1916.

Army Form C. 2118.

2 M G Coy
Vol XI

Instructions regarding War Diaries and Intelligence Summaries are contained in F. S. Regs., Part II. and the Staff Manual respectively. Title Pages will be prepared in manuscript.

WAR DIARY
or
INTELLIGENCE SUMMARY

(Erase heading not required.)

Place	Date	Hour	Ref 1/10,000 ABBEVILLE 14. Summary of Events and Information	Remarks and references to Appendices
BRESLE	5/11/16		No 9 M.G. Cy proceed to ALBERT	
ALBERT	5/11/16 to 18/11/16		Company training.	
	18/11/16		Company proceed to BAZENTIN-LE-GRAND in Support (Ref 1/20,000 FRANCE 57c. S.W.)	
BAZENTIN LE GRAND.	22/11/16		Company relieved 5th & 6th Australian Bdes in Line.	
	23/11/16 to 28/11/16		Company in line. - Nothing of interest - Casualties 1 man wounded 1 gun put out of action by direct hit.	
	29/11/16		Company less 2 Sections relieved by Composite M.G. Cy proceed to MAMETZ WOOD in Reserve. (Ref 1/20,000 FRANCE 57D SE)	
	1/12/16		Two Sections of Company in line relieved by 3rd Bde M G Cy	
MAMETZ WOOD	3/12/16		Company in Reserve	

F.W. Robinson Lt. Adjt.
No 2. M. G. Coy

2449 Wt. W14957/M90 750,000 1/16 J.B.C. & A. Forms/C.2118/12.

2nd Brigade.

1st Division.

<u>2nd MACHINE GUN COMPANY ::: DECEMBER 1916.</u>

Army Form C. 2118.

Instructions regarding War Diaries and Intelligence Summaries are contained in F. S. Regs., Part II. and the Staff Manual respectively. Title Pages will be prepared in manuscript.

WAR DIARY

~~or~~

~~INTELLIGENCE SUMMARY~~

(Erase heading not required.)

No 2. M.G. Company

Vol 12

Place	Date	Hour	Summary of Events and Information	Remarks and references to Appendices
MAMETZ WOOD	5-12-16		Company, less one Section moved to High Wood East Camp into support	
HIGH WOOD	5-12-16 to 13-12-16		One Section in the Line	
	10-12-16		Work on Flers Line commenced.	
	14-12-16		One Section moved up to Flers Line in reserve	
	14-12-16 to 29-12-16		Two Sections in the Line.	
	29-12-16		Two Sections in the Line relieved by two Sections of No 151 MG Coy. Casualties 1 O.R. [Wounded	
	31-12-16		Company, less two Sections, relieved by No 151 M.G. Coy, less two Sections, moved into reserve billets at Millencourt (Ref. $\frac{1}{100,000}$ Lens)	
	1/1/17		Remaining Sections relieved by two Sections of No 151 M G Coy proceeded to Millencourt.	

[illegible]
for Major Cmdg
No 2 M.G. Coy

2449 Wt. W14957/M90 750,000 1/16 J.B.C. & A. Forms/C.2118/12.

1ST DIVISION
2ND INFY BDE

2ND MACHINE GUN COMPANY.

1917 JAN - ~~DEC 1917~~ 1918 FEB

W A R   D I A R Y.

2nd. M. G. Company.

2nd. INFANTRY BRIGADE.

1st. DIVISION.

JANUARY. 1917.

Army Form C. 2118

Instructions regarding War Diaries and Intelligence Summaries are contained in F. S. Regs., Part II. and the Staff Manual respectively. Title Pages will be prepared in manuscript.

WAR DIARY
or
INTELLIGENCE SUMMARY
(Erase heading not required.)

2 M. G. Coy

Vol 13

Place	Date	Hour	Summary of Events and Information	Remarks and references to Appendices
MILLENCOURT	2·1·17		Elementary Training 3 O R proceeded on leave to U.K	RAAT
	3·1·17		Coy Training. 2 reinforcements arrived from the base.	–
	4·1·17		Elementary Training. Sgt RAINFORD proceeded U.K, on being transferred to home establishment	
	5·1·17		Elementary Training : 5 O R sick to hospital.	–
	6·1·17		~~Elementary Training~~ Church Parade.	–
	7·1·17		Elementary Training ~~Church Parade~~ ~~Etc~~ 5 O R proceeded on leave.	–
	8·1·17		Inspection by G O C, & coy training.	–
	9·1·17		Elementary Training.	
	10·1·17		Firing on Range: Training	–
	11·1·17		Elementary Training	–
	12·1·17		Elementary Training LT PRITCHARD arrived from the base.	–
	13·1·17		Elementary Training.	–

2449 Wt. W14957/M90 750,000 1/16 J.B.C. & A. Forms/C.2118/12.

Army Form C. 2118.

WAR DIARY
or
INTELLIGENCE SUMMARY
(Erase heading not required.)

Instructions regarding War Diaries and Intelligence Summaries are contained in F. S. Regs., Part II. and the Staff Manual respectively. Title Pages will be prepared in manuscript.

No 2 Machine Gun Coy

Place	Date	Hour	Summary of Events and Information	Remarks and references to Appendices
MILLENCOURT	14.1.17		Church Parade: Major Pearson returned, & resumed command of the Coy	RA&T
	15.1.17		Coy Training	—
	16.1.17		Coy Training 4 O.R proceeded on leave to U.K	—
	17.1.17		Coy Training. 1 reinforcement arrived from ABBEVILLE	—
	18.1.17		Inspection by G.O.C, 2nd Inf Bde Coy Training	—
	19.1.17		Coy Training 2 reinforcements arrived from the base	—
	20.1.17		Coy Training	—
	21.1.17		Church Parade	—
	22.1.17		Coy Training 4 O.R proceeding on leave to U.K	—
	23.1.17		Inspection by G.O.C; 2nd Inf Bde. Coy Training	—
BRESLE	24.1.17	9.10am	The Coy proceeded to BRESLE & took over billets, from the 3rd Australian M.G. Coy	—
	25.1.17		A & C sections attended a Brigade Scheme. remainder Coy Training	—

2449 Wt. W14957/M90 750,000 1/16 J.B.C. & A. Forms/C.2118/12.

Army Form C. 2118.

Instructions regarding War Diaries and Intelligence Summaries are contained in F. S. Regs., Part II. and the Staff Manual respectively. Title Pages will be prepared in manuscript.

WAR DIARY
or
INTELLIGENCE SUMMARY
(Erase heading not required.)

2nd Machine Gun Coy

Place	Date	Hour	Summary of Events and Information	Remarks and references to Appendices
BRESLE	26.1.17		Firing on range & Coy Training	RAAT
	27.1.17		Brigade Route March: 6 reinforcements arrived from the base	—
	28.1.17		Voluntary Church Service	—
	29.1.17		B & D sections attended a Brigade Scheme: Remainder Coy Training	—
	30.1.17		Firing on Range & Coy Training	—
	31.1.17		Brigade Route March	—

R. Turnig Lt & Adjt

No 2 M. G. Coy

2449 Wt. W14957/M90 750,000 1/16 J.B.C. & A. Forms/C.2118/12.

W A R D I A R Y.

No.2. M. G. Company.

2nd. INFANTRY BRIGADE.

1st. DIVISION.

FEBRUARY. 1917.

ORIGINAL

Instructions regarding War Diaries and Intelligence Summaries are contained in F. S. Regs., Part II. and the Staff Manual respectively. Title Pages will be prepared in manuscript.

WAR DIARY
or
INTELLIGENCE SUMMARY
(Erase heading not required.)

No2 M.G. Coy.

Army Form C. 2118.

Vol 14

Place	Date	Hour	Summary of Events and Information	Remarks and references to Appendices
MERICOURT	3/2/17		Coy took up billets in MERICOURT	
CHIGNOLLES	4/2/17		Coy proceeded to CHIGNOLLES & took up billets there	
	6/2/17		Coy relieved French in sector PERONNE	
	5-13/2/17		Coy in line no firing done	
	13/2/17		Coy relieved by 1st Coy & took up billets in CHIGNES	
	14/2/17		Coy inspected by Major E.A. Pearson	
	15/2/17		Draft of 17 O.R. arrived from Base	
	15-22/2/17		Coy took up Antiaircraft work by section reliefs	
	22/2/17		Coy relieved No3 Coy in sector from N12 central to N.17.C.4.2	
	23/2/17		No1 gun C section put out of action by shell fire in position N17C65 Sat 21 bis Lieut Reynolds wounded Pte Hawkins killed. Pte Young B section wounded	
	26/2/17		Inter section reliefs. Two guns D section kept open gap in German wire.	

H Grange Lt
For Major Commanding
No2 M.G. Coy

2449 Wt. W14957/M90 750,000 1/16 J.B.C. & A. Forms/C.2118/12.

WAR DIARY.

No.2. M.G.Company.

2nd. INFANTRY BRIGADE.

1st.DIVISION.

MARCH.1917.

Instructions regarding War Diaries and Intelligence Summaries are contained in F. S. Regs., Part II. and the Staff Manual respectively. Title Pages will be prepared in manuscript.

WAR DIARY or INTELLIGENCE SUMMARY

(Erase heading not required.)

Army Form C. 2118.

No 2. M. G. Coy.

Vol 15

Place	Date	Hour	Summary of Events and Information	Remarks and references to Appendices
CHUIGNES	3.3.17	–	B section fired on gap in German wire.	RAHT
	4 —	–	B section fired on gap in German wire: one hostile aircraft fired on by our antiaircraft guns.	
	5 –	–	B section fired on gap in German wire.	–
	6 –	–	B section fired on gap in German wire.	–
	7 –	—	D & A assisted a raid by direct & indirect barrage on German Trenches & BARLEUX	–
	8 –	–	A section did indirect fire on approaches to BARLEUX.	–
	9 –	–	B, D, & A sections assisted a raid by firing on the approaches to BARLEUX	–
	10 –	–	The Coy was relieved by No 1. M G Coy at 12 midnight, & returned to billets in CHUIGNES. Casualties nil.	–
	11 –	–	Cleaning of clothes and equipment.	–
	12 –	—	" " "	–
	13 –	–	Training: fitting of small box respirators.	–
	14 –	–	Coy inspection by O. C. Coy: Training	–
	15 –	–	Coy Training.	–
	16 –	–	Coy Training.	–
	17 –	–	The Coy relieved the No 3. M. G Coy at GRAND-BOIS: A section took up positions in VILLERS-CARBONNEL, which had been vacated by the Germans the same morning.	–
	18 –	–	C section was withdrawn to Coy HQ, as mobile reserve	–
	19 –	–	A & D sections were withdrawn to Coy HQ	
	20 –	–	The Coy improved the ESTREES-VILLERS CARBONNEL road.	

2449 Wt. W14957/M90 750,000 1/16 J.B.C. & A. Forms/C.2118/12.

Instructions regarding War Diaries and Intelligence Summaries are contained in F. S. Regs., Part II. and the Staff Manual respectively. Title Pages will be prepared in manuscript.

WAR DIARY

INTELLIGENCE SUMMARY

(Erase heading not required.)

Army Form C. 2118.

No 2 M. G. Coy

Place	Date	Hour	Summary of Events and Information	Remarks and references to Appendices
CHUIGNES	21	—	The Coy worked on the ESTREES-VILLERS CARBONNEL road: C section took up anti-aircraft positions at BRIE to guard the SOMME bridge.	RAHT
	22	—	Coy continued work on the road	—
	23	—	" " " " " "	—
	24	—	" " " " " "	—
	25	—	" " " " " "	—
	26	—	" " " " " "	—
	27	—	" " " " " "	—
	28	—	" " " " " "	—
	29	—	" " " " " "	—
	30	—	" " " " " "	—
	31	—	" " " " " "	—
	1.4.17	—	" " " " " "	—
	2.4.17	—	A section relieved C section at BRIE	—

R Turing Lt & Adjt

No 2 M. G. Coy

2449 Wt. W14957/M90 750,000 1/16 J.B.C. & A. Forms/C.2118/12.

W A R   D I A R Y.

No.2. M. G. Company.

2nd. INFANTRY BRIGADE.

1st. DIVISION.

APRIL. 1917.

Army Form C. 2118

WAR DIARY
or
INTELLIGENCE SUMMARY
(Erase heading not required.)

Instructions regarding War Diaries and Intelligence Summaries are contained in F. S. Regs., Part II. and the Staff Manual respectively. Title Pages will be prepared in manuscript.

2 M G Coy
Vol 16

Place	Date	Hour	Summary of Events and Information	Remarks and references to Appendices
GRAND BOIS Nr ASSEVILLERS	3·4·17 – 6·4·17		The Coy continued working on the ESTREES-VILLERS CARBONNEL road. Shell holes were filled in and road metal laid.	
CHUIGNES	7·4·17		The Coy was relieved by No 3 Machine Gun Coy and returned to billets in CHUIGNES.	
	8·4·17		Cleaning of Clothes and Equipment.	
	9·4·17		Inspection of Gun kit and Issue of Clothing.	
	10·4·17		Inspection by Lt Col Abadie D.S.O. Cmdg 2nd Bn K.R.R. (actg G.O.C. 2nd Infy Bde). Report satisfactory. Chief complaints. A few deficiencies in small kit. Clothing could have been cleaner. Arms Drill weak. Limbers and guns were inspected and reported satisfactory.	
	11·4·17 – 14·4·17		Elementary Training in Gun Drill. Stoppages. Mechanism. LT DIBDIN M.C. assumed command of the COY. vice MAJOR E.A PEARSON M.C. Evacuated sick 11·4·17.	
MORCOURT	15·4·17		The COY moved into huts S.W of MORCOURT.	
	16·4·17 – 19·4·17		Elementary Training in the field. Use of Cover. Selection of Gun Positions. Concealment from aircraft. Range firing up to 400x. Elementary tests completed.	
	20·4·17 – 22·4·17		Tactical Training with Battalions. Practiced Direct and indirect overhead fire. and communication. Discovered the value of mounting on the reverse slope of a hill when communication has to be kept up in the open over a considerable distance.	
	23·4·17		Brigade Scheme. Difficulty of communication between Sections and Coy HQ and between Gun detachments and limbers emphasised. Pack-saddle. Mules were not employed.	
	24·4·17 – 27·4·17		New System of M.G. visual signals inaugurated in the COY. Also new method of carrying gun (ie strapped in case on back) invented and adopted. This method is much less visible and can be carried greater distances. One sections' guns were camouflaged and were tested successfully against aeroplane observation. Communication by pack-saddle mules was tested and considered essential for long distance communication. Long Range Practices (680x-1020x). Training in Bomb Throwing.	
	28·4·17		Brigade Sports. Coy secured third place in Bde Cup. Won the Cross country race and was second in the COY tug of war.	
	29·4·17		Capt W.H.C. Hardy took over temporary command of the Coy. Authy G.O.C. 2nd Infy Bde. Administrative department of the Coy reorganised. Men's canteen opened. SGTS mess re-instituted.	
	30·4·17		T/MAJOR J. ANGELL M.C. took command of the Coy. Authy III Corps.	

D H Webb Lieut & Adj
No 2 Machine Gun Coy.
2/5/17

2449 Wt. W14957/M90 750,000 1/16 J.B.C. & A. Forms/C.2118/12.

W A R   D I A R Y.

No.2. M. G. COMPANY.

2nd. INFANTRY BRIGADE.

1st. DIVISION.

MAY. 1917.

Army Form C. 2118.

No 2 M.G. Coy

Vol 17

WAR DIARY
or
INTELLIGENCE SUMMARY

(Erase heading not required.)

Instructions regarding War Diaries and Intelligence Summaries are contained in F. S. Regs., Part II. and the Staff Manual respectively. Title Pages will be prepared in manuscript.

Place	Date	Hour	Summary of Events and Information	Remarks and references to Appendices
MORCOURT	1-5-17		Training - Tactical Exercises in the Field - Communication by pack mules practical - Company Tailor appointed - New Company standing order introduced forbidding Taking in of trousers. G.O.C 2nd INF. BDE. inspected transport. Report v satisfactory.	
	2-5-17	Coy.	Training. Sections co-operating with Battalions - Rapid calculations for overhead Fire. General Tactical Employment: two guns sent forward with 4th wave of assaulting line: two guns remaining behind to cover with overhead Fire - The latter do not advance to consolidate until definite information is received that O.C.1 is captured.	
	to	at	Regular System of Pay adopted - Men paid weekly - rate of: Privates 5 Fcs. L/Cpls 10 Fcs. Cpls 15 Fcs. - Sgts. 20 Fcs - Appointment of Provost Corporal and Coy. Pioneer - River Bathing in the SOMME started. Alterations in ROUTINE - Reveille 6.0 am. Lights out 9-30 pm. Fresh Orders with regard to Sanitation carried out - Flyproof Food boxes constructed	
	13-5-17	Rest.	Water tins painted & marked etc - Fresh Coy. order re. laying out of Kit adopted.	
	14-5-17		Coy. Boxing.	
	15-5-17	Coy.	Coy. returned to Camp 59 MORCOURT.	
	16-5-17		The proposed Inspection of Transport by G.O.C 2nd INF. BDE. notified in Orders was postponed "sine die"	
	17-5-17	at Rest.	Brigade Boxing Tournament. SERGT E. CROWDER beaten in semi final. by CPL CASEY 2nd K.R.R.C. SERGT E. CROWDER put up a very plucky fight, & was awarded a prize for best loser.	
	18-5-17		Two Sections practice River crossing with Limber (S.A.A) on improvised rafts. Experiment proved successful. Afternoon - Company Sports.	

Instructions regarding War Diaries and Intelligence Summaries are contained in F. S. Regs., Part II. and the Staff Manual respectively. Title Pages will be prepared in manuscript.

WAR DIARY
or
INTELLIGENCE SUMMARY
(Erase heading not required.)

Army Form C. 2118.

Place	Date	Hour	Summary of Events and Information	Remarks and references to Appendices
MORCOURT.	18.5.17	afternoon	Sports. 100x Lt LOCKHART. 440x Lt LOCKHART. 1 MILE. Pte DUCHARS. Cross Cty 3 MILES. A Section Pte Hopkins A. 1st man. Bowling Bomb Lt COLEMAN.	
	19.5.17		Inspection of Kit &c. (weekly institution).	
			Company moved to VILLERS BRETONNEUX arrived about 6 p.m. Very hot day. Two men only fell out. The Battalion had many stragglers.	
	20.5.17	Sunday.	Bells Inspection by C.O. No parades.	
	21.5.17		Route March. Land principally under cultivation. Open work hindered.	
	22.5.17		G.O.C. 2nd Infy Bde unable to inspect Company as arranged owing to temporary illness. Route march cancelled because of rain. Lectures & Mechanism.	
	23.5.17		Coy Training. Advance Scheme. Action. Marching Order to include 2 sandbags on braces in Fighting Order.	
	24.5.17		Coy Training. Divisional Sports. Coy Water Cart took 3rd Prize. & Coy team 3rd in 'Boat Race'. Officers' Cavalry [illegible]	
VILLERS-BRETONNEUX.	25.5.17		Coy Training. Attack. Afternoon Brigade Football Final. Company v 2 K.R.R. Corps. Company beaten 3–nil.	
	26 / 27		Company entrained and arrived 8.30 am 27/5/17 at FONTAINE HOUCK nr METEREN. Sheet 27 $\frac{1}{40.000}$ X 4. c 4.4. The move was expeditiously carried out.	
	28.5.17.		Coy Training. Mounting Gun on rough ground.	
METEREN.	29.5.17.		Route March. Bathing.	
	30.5.17.		Coy Training. Action. Direct & Indirect Laying. Inspection by Brigade Gas Sergt Instructor.	
	31.5.17.		Coy Training. Afternoon Recreation. Paid out Company.	

[illegible] 2nd Lt & Adjt
for O.C.
No 2 M.G. Coy.

2449 Wt. W14957/M90 750,000 1/16 J.B.C. & A. Forms/C.2118/12.

W A R   D I A R Y.

No.2. M. G. Company.

2nd. INFANTRY BRIGADE.

1st, DIVISION.

JUNE. 1917.

Instructions regarding War Diaries and Intelligence Summaries are contained in F. S. Regs., Part II. and the Staff Manual respectively. Title Pages will be prepared in manuscript.

WAR DIARY
or
INTELLIGENCE SUMMARY
(Erase heading not required.)

Army Form C. 2118.

No 2 M.G. Coy

Vol 18

Place	Date	Hour	Summary of Events and Information	Remarks and references to Appendices
FONTAINE HOUCK	1.6.17	5.15 pm	Inspection by G.O.C. 2nd Infantry Bgde, who congratulated Coy on its very fine turnout.	
"	2.6.17 to 10.6.17		TRAINING. Tactical Exercises in the field, advancing over open ground, use of ground & cover, & rapid construction of defilated emplacements. Instruction in overhead & indirect fire. N.C.O.s instructed in map reading & fire calculations.	
"	11.6.17		Company moved into billets in SAINT MARIE CAPELLE area	
SAINT MARIE CAPELLE	12.6.17 to 14.6.17		Training as for period 2.6.17 to 10.6.17	
"	15.6.17		Company moved into billets at WORMHOUDT. } During these 3 days Coy marched about 45 miles. Total casualties, one, caused by great heat	
WORMHOUDT	16.6.17		" " " " " MALO	
MALO	17.6.17		" " " " " CAMP ZEEPANNE	
CAMP ZEEPANNE	18.6.17		Limbers packed for trenches & Coy paid out.	
"	19.6.17 to 24.6.17		Coy moved into trenches, relieving 112th Regt of French Infantry. 16 guns in the line, 2 in each of 8 emplacements, & manned by half teams. French gun emplacements were reconstructed. Rations were carried up to gun positions by pack mule each night. Remainder of Coy training in back areas	
"	24.6.17		Coy relieved by No 1 M.G. Coy & moved into back area at LA FEIRE CAMP.	
LA FEIRE CAMP	25.6.17 to 30.6.17		2 sections, with 8 guns, relieved No 3 M.G. Coy in coast defence. 1 section in reserve. 2 guns employed in indirect fire for 3 nights & 2 employed on anti-aircraft duty. Nature of emplacements, concrete. Remaining section employed on general improvement of camp, erection of permanent latrines, incinerators, etc.	

2449 Wt. W14957/M90 750,000 1/16 J.B.C. & A. Forms/C.2118/12.

1st July 1917.

[signature]
Mt. for O.C.
No 2 M.G. Coy

W A R   D I A R Y.

No.2.M. G. COMPANY.

2nd. INFANTRY BRIGADE.

1st. DIVISION.

JULY. 1917.

Instructions regarding War Diaries and Intelligence Summaries are contained in F. S. Regs., Part II. and the Staff Manual respectively. Title Pages will be prepared in manuscript.

WAR DIARY
or
INTELLIGENCE SUMMARY

(Erase heading not required.)

Army Form C. 2118.

2 M.G. Co.
Vol 19

Place	Date	Hour	Summary of Events and Information	Remarks and references to Appendices
LA LEVRE CAMP	1-7-17 to 2-7-17		2 Sections in line on Coast defence. 1 Section in reserve. Remainder employed on improvement of camp.	
" "	3-7-17		Company relieved No 1 M.G. Coy in left sub sector NIEUPORT BAINS.	
NIEUPORT BAINS	7-7-17		Two Officers become casualties, 1 Killed & 1 wounded. The latter dying in hospital 10-7-17.	
" "	10/7/17	8.0am to 7.0pm	Enemy shells us heavily, & destroyed the three Bridges over the Yser, thus cutting our communication	
		7. pm	Enemy attacked & captured our first & second line on a 1400 yd front. Our 16 guns were lost. & 2 Officers & 55 OR missing. No 17054 PTE. F. HOLLOWAY volunteers to swim the river & carry information to Coy. H. Qrs. which he did under heavy shell & Machine Gun fire For this he was awarded the "Military Medal"	
RINCK CAMP	11/7/17 to 14/7/17		Reorganised & refitted.	
	15/7/17		Coy. marched into camp at GHYVELDE	
GHYVELDE	16/7/17		" " " billets " PONT DE PTE SYNTHE.	
PONT DE PTE SYNTHE	19/7/17		" " " Camp in ST. POL SUR MER AREA	
" "	to 30/7/17		Company Training	
ST. POL SUR MER	30/7/17		Coy. moved into Camp at LE CLIPON.	
LE CLIPON	to 31/7/17		Company Training.	

[signature] Lt & Adjt
No 2 M. G. Coy.

2449 Wt. W14957/M90 750,000 1/16 J.B.C. & A. Forms/C.2118/12.

W A R   D I A R Y.

No.2. M. G. Company.

2nd. INFANTRY BRIGADE.

1st. DIVISION.

AUGUST. 1917.

Headqrs
2nd Infantry Bde

War Diary for preceding month herewith

[illegible]
O/C Comdg
No 2 M.G. Coy

1/9/17

Instructions regarding War Diaries and Intelligence Summaries are contained in F. S. Regs., Part II. and the Staff Manual respectively. Title Pages will be prepared in manuscript.

WAR DIARY
or
~~INTELLIGENCE SUMMARY~~
(Erase heading not required.)

Army Form C. 2118.

V 8 20

Place	Date	Hour	Summary of Events and Information	Remarks and references to Appendices
LE CLIPON CAMP	1.5.17 to 6.5.17		Special training. Negotiating Obstacle Course, Scaling Sea Wall, etc. At second attempt whole Company scaled the Wall carrying extra full loads, two spare numbers per team carrying four belt boxes of S.A.A. each.	
"	7.5.17		Company inspected by G.O.C, 2nd Infantry Bde. Report very satisfactory	
"	8.5.17 to 10.5.17		~~Res~~ Special training as above	
"	11.5.17		Presentation of Medal Ribbons by G.O.C 1st Division	
"	12.5.17 to 13.5.17		Special training as above.	
"	14.5.17		Commander-in-Chief inspected one section scaling Sea Wall. Whole section went up carrying extra full loads.	
"	15.5.17 to 16.5.17		Brigade Boxing Tournament. Company secured first prize in Light Heavy weights & second prize in Light weights.	
"	18.5.17		Brigade competition over Obstacle course. Company obtained highest number of points for turn out, style, & for completing course in shortest time, but were disqualified for carrying Machine Gunners instead of Infantry loads.	
"	19.5.17 to 24.5.17		Special training as above.	
"	25.5.17		Division inspected by G.O.C 4th Army. Report highly satisfactory	
"	26.5.17 to 31.5.17		Special training as above	

J. Angell.
Major
Army No 2. M.G. Coy

2449 Wt. W14957/M90 750,000 1/16 J.B.C. & A. Forms/C.2118/12.

W A R   D I A R Y.

No.2. M. G. Company.

2nd. INFANTRY BRIGADE.

1st. DIVISION.

SEPTEMBER. 1917.

Instructions regarding War Diaries and Intelligence Summaries are contained in F. S. Regs., Part II. and the Staff Manual respectively. Title Pages will be prepared in manuscript.

WAR DIARY
or
~~INTELLIGENCE SUMMARY~~
(Erase heading not required.)

Army Form C. 2118.

9821

Place	Date	Hour	Summary of Events and Information	Remarks and references to Appendices
LE CLIPON CAMP	1.9.17 to 21.9.17		Company engaged on Special training Scaling sea-wall with full loads Crossing obstacle course etc etc.	
"	22.9.17		Inter M.G. Coy Sports. This Company took 1st prize (silver cup)	
"	23.9.17 to 30.9.17		Special training as for period 1st to 21st	

[signature] 2/Lt & Adjt
[illegible] 2 M G Coy

2449 Wt. W14957/M90 750,000 1/16 J.B.C. & A. Forms/C.2118/12.

W A R   D I A R Y.

No.2.M. G. Company.

2nd. INFANTRY BRIGADE.

LST. DIVISION.

OCTOBER. 1917.

Instructions regarding War Diaries and Intelligence Summaries are contained in F. S. Regs., Part II. and the Staff Manual respectively. Title pages will be prepared in manuscript.

WAR DIARY
or
INTELLIGENCE SUMMARY.
(Erase heading not required.)

Army Form C. 2118.

2 M.G. Coy

Vol 22

Place	Date	Hour	Summary of Events and Information	Remarks and references to Appendices
LE CLIPON CAMP	1-10-17 to 21-10-17		Special training. Scaling Sea Wall, Barrage drill etc etc	
-"-	22-10-17		Company moved into billets in ERINGHAM area. ~~HERZEELE area~~	
ERINGHAM	24-10-17		" " " " HERZEELE area	
HERZEELE	25-10-17		" " " camp " ST. JANSTER-BIEZEN area	
ST. JAN	26-10-17 to 31-10-17		Company training. Barrage drill, advancing over open country etc.	

F. [illegible]
Major
Comdg No 2 M.G. Coy

A5834 Wt. W4973 M687 750,000 8/16 D. D. & L. Ltd. Forms C.2118/13.

W A R D I A R Y.

No.2.M. G. COMPANY.

2nd. INFANTRY BRIGADE.

1st. DIVISION.

NOVEMBER.1917.

2 M.G. Coy

Vol 23

Army Form C. 2118.

WAR DIARY
or
~~INTELLIGENCE SUMMARY~~.
(Erase heading not required.)

Instructions regarding War Diaries and Intelligence Summaries are contained in F. S. Regs., Part II. and the Staff Manual respectively. Title pages will be prepared in manuscript.

Place	Date	Hour	Summary of Events and Information	Remarks and references to Appendices
	1/7 2 3		Company Training.	
	4		Church Parades.	
	5		Company Training	
	6		Company moved to POPERINGE.	
	7		" " " REIGERSBURG — Entrained at RAILHOEK detrained at REIGERSBURG	
	8		Cleaning billets. B & C SECTIONS (LIEUTS MEADOWS & SIMS) moved to Battery positions at D4.a.2.2.13 via IRISH FARM. Battery commander LIEUT. D.H. WEBB (REF map SPRIET Ed 2 1:10000)	
	9		Remainder of Company less transport moved to billets in CANAL BANK. Guns in the line prepared lines of fire.	
	10		Barrage Guns cooperate in attack by 3rd BDE. on enemy position in V.29 A & B (Ref Map SPRIET Ed 2 1:10000) Guns fired about 5.000 rounds each during attack and continued firing during afternoon on S.O.S line. Guns withdrawn at night. Our casualties amounting to 1 Officer LT. D.H. WEBB & 4 OR's killed. "D" section (Lt. REAY) relieved 2 Guns at D5 c 6 0 and 2 Guns at V5 c 11. Section H.Q at D5 a 9 0. Advance Coy. H.Q. at KANSAS HOUSE.	
	11		"A" Section (LIEUT. COLEMAN) relieved 2 Guns at BERKS HOUSES and 2 Guns at V28 c 4.4. Section H.Q at HUBNER FARM. LIEUT. PRITCHARD took over command of "D" section with section H.Q at D5 a 9 0. Lt. REAY remained in the line (Ref Map SPRIET Ed. 2. 1:10000	

A5834 Wt. W4973/M687 750,000 8/16 D. D. & L. Ltd. Forms/C.2118/13.

Army Form C. 2118.

Instructions regarding War Diaries and Intelligence Summaries are contained in F. S. Regs., Part II. and the Staff Manual respectively. Title pages will be prepared in manuscript.

WAR DIARY
or
INTELLIGENCE SUMMARY.
(*Erase heading not required.*)

Place	Date	Hour	Summary of Events and Information	Remarks and references to Appendices
	12		Remainder of teams of "D" Section relieved teams already in the line LT. REAY proceeded to CANAL BANK. Harassing fire carried out on road about WESTWOOD HOUSE. V17 a11 road MALLET COPSE – MALLET FARM and VOID FARM – VALUATION HOUSES (Ref Map SPRIET Ed 2 1:10000) Situation normal with periods of heavy enemy shelling especially toward evening	[illegible]
	13		"B" section (LT. MEADOWS) relieved "A" Section. LIEUT SIMS relieved LT. PRITCHARD. Gun positions now as follows:– "D" section guns D5 c6090 } D5 c6590 } MEETCHEELE. Section H.Qs at D5 a 9.00. "B" section 1 gun at D3 b9050, 1 " " D3 b8060, 2 " " BANFF HOUSE. Section H.Qs at HUBNER FARM. Ref Map SPRIET Ed 2 1:10000. Enemy attacked in strength on CORPS on our RIGHT but was repulsed by our barrage S.O.S sent up at 5.5 PM. Artillery fire intense until 6.30 pm when situation became practically normal. During day hostile E.A. flew over our line apparently meeting with no resistance. About 4 pm 30 hostile EA were flying low over our line. Harassing fire carried out as on previous night.	[illegible]
	14		"C" Section with LT. REAY relieved "D" Section. LT. SIMS remained in Command. LT. BOOTH reported for duty with LT. MEADOWS.	[illegible]

A5834 Wt. W4973/M687 750,000 8/16 D. D. & L. Ltd. Forms/C.2118/13.

Army Form C. 2118.

Instructions regarding War Diaries and Intelligence Summaries are contained in F. S. Regs., Part II. and the Staff Manual respectively. Title pages will be prepared in manuscript.

WAR DIARY
or
INTELLIGENCE SUMMARY.
(Erase heading not required.)

Place	Date	Hour	Summary of Events and Information	Remarks and references to Appendices
	14		Situation during day normal but hostile artillery fire considerably above normal especially at BELLEVUE MEETCHEELE spur and in battery positions. Harassing fire carried out on same points as on previous nights	
	15.		Shortly after 8 am. S.O.S. fired on front of Corps on our RIGHT. Situation became normal at 10. am. No attack took place on our front. Harassing fire carried out as usual.	
	16		A & D sections moved to DAMBRE CAMP B & C sections relieved by Teams from No 1 M.G. COY.	
	17		B & C section & H.Qs moved to DAMBRE CAMP.	
	18		Kit inspections	
	19		A, B & D. sections moved to CANAL BANK.	
	20		A. section (LT. COLEMAN) relieved 2 Guns of No 1 M.G. Coy at WALLEMOLEN and took up new position for 2 Guns at D4 a 83. B. section (LT. SIMS) relieved 4 Guns of No 1 M.G. COY. at YETTA HOUSES. D. section (LT. EDGELL) relieved 4 Guns of No 1 M.G. COY. at MEETCHEELE Situation normal with some Artillery activity	
	21		Situation generally normal	
	22		Remainder of A section (LT. WADLEY) relieved A section " B " " B " (LT. SIMS remained in the line) " D " (LT. PRITCHARD) " D "	

Instructions regarding War Diaries and Intelligence Summaries are contained in F. S. Regs., Part II. and the Staff Manual respectively. Title pages will be prepared in manuscript.

WAR DIARY
or
INTELLIGENCE SUMMARY.
(*Erase heading not required.*)

Army Form C. 2118.

Place	Date	Hour	Summary of Events and Information	Remarks and references to Appendices
	23		B section relieved by gun teams from No 97 M.G. COY.	
	24		A & D section relieved by gun teams from No 97 M.G. COY. Company moved to TUNNELLING CAMP. Entrained at BRIELEN and detrained at RAILHOEK. Transport by road via VLAMERTINGE & POPERINGE	
	25		Cleaning billets.	
	26		Inspection of gun kit, equipment etc	
	27		Company moved via WATOU – HOUTKERQUE to billets in HERZEELE.	
	28		Cleaning kit, equipment, limbers and billets.	
	29		Company training	
	30		" "	

[illegible] Comdg
No 2 Machine Gun Company

A5834 Wt. W4973/M687 750,000 8/16 D. D. & L. Ltd. Forms/C.2118/13.

W A R   D I A R Y.

No.2. M. G. Company.

2nd. INFANTRY BRIGADE.

1st. DIVISION.

DECEMBER. 1917.

No. 2 M.G. Coy.

WAR DIARY
or
INTELLIGENCE SUMMARY.
(Erase heading not required.)

Army Form C. 2118.

Instructions regarding War Diaries and Intelligence Summaries are contained in F. S. Regs., Part II. and the Staff Manual respectively. Title pages will be prepared in manuscript.

Vol 24

Place	Date	Hour	Summary of Events and Information	Remarks and references to Appendices
	1/12/17		Company Training.	WH
	2 "		Church Parades.	WH
	3 "		Company Training.	WH
	4 "		— " — — " —	WH
	5 "		Company moved via, BAMBECQUE – OUST-CAPPEL – TROUSBRUGGE – HARINGHE to billets near ZUYDHOEK. (Ref. map. HAZEBROUGH 5.a ED. II.)	WH
	6 "		Cleaning Camp and billets.	WH
	7 "		Company Training.	WH
	8.		Kit Inspections.	WH
	9.		Church Parades.	WH
	10.		Company Parades.	WH
	11.		Company moved, via:- CROMBEKE to billets at ZUIDHUIS FARM S22.c.4.2. (Ref. map BELGUIM SHEET 20.) Two Gun Teams of 'C' Section, under LIEUT. PRITCHARD relieved 2 gun teams of No. 3 M.G. COY. in A.A. defence at T29 c 9 7 (Ref. map BELGUIM SHEET 20)	WH
	12.		Cleaning billets.	WH

A5834 Wt. W4973 M687 750,000 8/16 D. D. & L. Ltd. Forms C.2118/13.

Army Form C. 2118.

Instructions regarding War Diaries and Intelligence Summaries are contained in F. S. Regs., Part II. and the Staff Manual respectively. Title pages will be prepared in manuscript.

WAR DIARY
or
INTELLIGENCE SUMMARY.
(Erase heading not required.)

Place	Date	Hour	Summary of Events and Information	Remarks and references to Appendices
	13/12/17		Company moved via NOESTAN to billets in Support Area at B 3 a 6.4 (Ref. Map. Sheet 28 BELGIUM) Transport moved to new lines in EIKHOEK area S21 a central. – Ref Map. BELGIUM Sheet 20	
	14		Cleaning billets.	
	15		Kit inspection and cleaning billets 2 guns of "A" Section relieved "C" Section on A.A. defence.	
	16.		Church Parades.	
	17		Fatigue Party.	
	18		Fatigue Party.	
	19		Company moved into the line in relief of No 3. M.G. Coy. "B" Section (2/Lt MEADOWS) relieved six gun team in left sector. 2 guns at CATINAT FARM. 2 guns at PAPEGOED. 2 guns at ISLANDE Section H.Q. at CATINAT FARM. Half "D" Section (Lt. EDGELL) relieved 4 guns in centre. 2 guns at LONELY MILL. 2 guns at MANGELARE Section H.Q. at MORTIER FARM.	

A5834 Wt. W4973 M687 750,000 8/16 D. D. & L. Ltd. Forms C.2118/13.

Instructions regarding War Diaries and Intelligence Summaries are contained in F. S. Regs., Part II. and the Staff Manual respectively. Title pages will be prepared in manuscript.

WAR DIARY
or
INTELLIGENCE SUMMARY.
(*Erase heading not required.*)

Army Form C. 2118.

Place	Date	Hour	Summary of Events and Information	Remarks and references to Appendices
	19 –		Half "C" section (2Lt PRITCHARD) relieved 3 guns on Right. 2 guns at HILL 20 POST 1 gun at FAIDHERBE POST. Coy. HQs at MONDOVI WOOD. Remainder of Company (less transport) moved to CANAL HOUSE (Ref. Map BIXSCHOOTE 1:10000) Situation very quiet, with occasional short bursts of L.H.V. shelling. Work on emplacements & latrines carried out.	
	20		One of our Machine Guns carried out, one minute bursts of indirect fire at 7.15pm. 8.30pm. 11.30pm road between O.34 a 51 and O34 b 15 20. Single guns fired on O33 b 64 70 and O34 b 19 in bursts at half hour intervals from 5.30pm to 11.30pm. Situation very quiet. Our position at HILL 20 shelled occasionally during afternoon. General improvements to gun positions carried out. Ref Map BELGIUM Sheet 20 S.W. Ed 5.	
	21		Our machine guns fired during early part of night on Road between O34 a 41 and O35 c 33 and on O33 b 47 and O34 b 22. Enemy Machine Guns replied during all three shoots. One E.A. flew at low altitude over our lines at 7.15am. Situation very quiet generally. Work on gun positions carried out (Ref. Map BELGIUM Sheet 20 S.W. Our A.A guns at T29 c 97 were relieved by No 3 M.G. Coy.	

A5834 Wt. W4973 M687 750,000 8/16 D. D. & L. Ltd. Forms C.2118/13.

Instructions regarding War Diaries and Intelligence Summaries are contained in F. S. Regs., Part II. and the Staff Manual respectively. Title pages will be prepared in manuscript.

WAR DIARY
or
INTELLIGENCE SUMMARY.
(Erase heading not required.)

Army Form C. 2118.

Place	Date	Hour	Summary of Events and Information	Remarks and references to Appendices
	22		Quiet day with somewhat disturbed evening and night. S.O.S. call was fired on our RIGHT at 4.15 pm. Enemy shelled vicinity of LONELY MILL between 4.15 pm and 5.30 pm. Our Machine Guns carried out shoots on Road between O34a41 and O28c33 and on PELICAN CORNER and FERRET JUNCTION. In all 25 000 rounds were fired. Enemy Machine Guns replied. E.A. extremely active during the day. Work carried on as usual. (Ref Map BELGIUM Sheet 20 S.W.)	[initials]
	23		'A' Section relieved 'B' section in the line. Lt MARDOWS remained in command. Remainder of 'D' section (Lt WADLEY) relieved teams of 'D' section in the line. Remainder of 'C' section (Lt BOOTH) relieved teams of 'C' section in the line. Out going teams proceeded to CANAL HOUSE. (Ref. Map. BIXSCHOOTE 1/10000) Situation very quiet. Few gas shells fell on Right of HILL 20 at 8 pm. Slight Artillery activity during day. Our Machine Guns fired on FERRET JUNCTION, pillboxes at O33b94. and on Area O28c. between 5.30 pm and 11.30 pm. 10,000 rounds were fired. Enemy Machine guns fired on HILL 20 area during the night. Aerial activity on both sides somewhat limited. 2 E.A. flew over our lines at 11 am. E.A. flew at low altitude over support area 5.30 pm to 7 pm. Work on Emplacements carried out as usual. (Ref. Map. BELGIUM SHEET 20. SW)	[initials]

A5834 Wt. W4973 M687 750,000 8/16 D. D. & L. Ltd. Forms C.2118/13.

Instructions regarding War Diaries and Intelligence Summaries are contained in F. S. Regs., Part II. and the Staff Manual respectively. Title pages will be prepared in manuscript.

WAR DIARY
or
INTELLIGENCE SUMMARY.
(Erase heading not required.)

Army Form C. 2118.

Place	Date	Hour	Summary of Events and Information	Remarks and references to Appendices
	24-		Situation very quiet. Our Machine Guns carried out indirect fire as on previous night. Artillery activity slight. One E.A flew over LANCIER X ROADS at 5.0pm. Work on emplacements carried out as usual. (Ref. Map BELGIUM. Sheet 20 S.W. 1:20000)	
	25-		Situation very quiet. Our Machine Guns fired on enemy tracks, ~~at~~ FERRET JUNCTION, and huts at O33 b 94 between 5.15pm and 11.30pm. 7.000 rounds were fired. Usual work carried out. (Ref. Map. BELGIUM Sheet 20. S.W 1:20000)	
	26-		Enemy showed unusual activity during the day which developed at 7.35pm into an attack on our RIGHT Division front. Enemy artillery extremely active. Our battery positions, tracks and organised areas shelled during the day and night. Enemy put down heavy barrage during attack. E.A extremely active chiefly spotting for artillery, but a few bombs were dropped. Our Machine Guns fired on FERRET JUNCTION and enemy tracks until 7.30pm when on account of situation they fired on S.O.S line. Firing was continued until 10.30pm. Work as usual. (Ref. Map BELGIUM, Sheet 20)	

Instructions regarding War Diaries and Intelligence Summaries are contained in F. S. Regs., Part II. and the Staff Manual respectively. Title pages will be prepared in manuscript.

WAR DIARY
or
INTELLIGENCE SUMMARY.
(Erase heading not required.)

Army Form C. 2118.

Place	Date	Hour	Summary of Events and Information	Remarks and references to Appendices
	27-		Situation quiet. Company was relieved in the line by No 1. M. G. Coy. Company moved into billets at B3a64 (Ref Map BELGIUM SHEET 28)	[initials]
	28-		Cleaning equipment. Camp. Etc	[initials]
	29.		Company moved via WOESTAN to billets at S22d50. Transport rejoined Coy. (Ref. Map. BELGIUM. Sheet 20. Ed 2)	[initials]
	30.		Church parades. – Cleaning billets	[initials]
	31		Kit inspection.	[initials]

[signature] Lieut
for Major
Comdg No 2 Machine Gun Company

A5834 Wt. W4973/M687 750,000 8/16 D. D. & L. Ltd. Forms/C.2118/13.

1st Division

War Diaries

No 2 Machine Gun Company

~~Feb~~ JAN - 1918

Instructions regarding War Diaries and Intelligence Summaries are contained in F. S. Regs., Part II. and the Staff Manual respectively. Title pages will be prepared in manuscript.

WAR DIARY
or
INTELLIGENCE SUMMARY.
(Erase heading not required.)

No 2 Machine Gun Company

Army Form C. 2118.

VA 25

Place	Date	Hour	Summary of Events and Information	Remarks and references to Appendices
	JANY.			
	1st		Kit Inspections.	
	2nd		Company Training.	
	3rd		Company Training	
	4th		Company Training	
	5th		Company Training. ½ B Section under 2nd Lt MEADOWS relieved No 3 M. GUN COY. on A.A duty at T29c97 (REF MAP SHEET 20).	
	6th		Company moved via WOESTEN to support Area at B3a64 Transport moved into lines vacated by No 1 M GUN COY at A6b48 (REF MAP SHEET. 28)	
	7th		Company Training & Cleaning billets.	
	8th		Company Training, ½ B Section under 2nd Lt BOOTH relieved 2nd Lt MEADOWS on A.A duty	
	9th		Company Training.	
	10th		Company Training.	
	11th		Fatigue Party	
	12th		Company relieved No 3 MACHINE GUN COY, in the line A. Section (Lt Coleman) relieved 6 guns in Left Sector, Portion of D Section (Lt Edgell) relieved 4 guns in Centre Sector, Portion of C Section (Lt Pritchard) relieved 3 guns in Right Sector. Left Sector Guns. 2 Guns at PAPEGOED. 2 Guns at ISLANDE. 2 Guns at CATINAT. Section H.Q at CATINAT. Centre Sector Guns. 2 Guns at MANGELARE. 2 Guns at LONELY MILL Section HQ at MORTIER FM.	

A5834 Wt. W4973 M687 750,000 8/16 D. D. & L. Ltd. Forms C.2118/13.

Army Form C. 2118.

Instructions regarding War Diaries and Intelligence Summaries are contained in F. S. Regs., Part II. and the Staff Manual respectively. Title pages will be prepared in manuscript.

WAR DIARY
or
INTELLIGENCE SUMMARY.
(*Erase heading not required.*)

Place	Date	Hour	Summary of Events and Information	Remarks and references to Appendices
	JANY 12th		Right Sector Guns. 2 Guns at HILL 20. 1 Gun at FAIDHERBE. Section HQ at HILL 20	
			Company HQ at MONDOVI FARM. SITUATION: Normal. (REF MAP BELGIUM SHEET 20 1:10,000).	
			A.A. Guns at T29 c 97 relieved by No 3 MACHINE GUN COY.	
	13th		Situation. Normal. Enemy Artillery lively at intervals during the day. At 8.0 am 3 E.A. flew in a S.E. direction over our lines. 10 of our aeroplanes were flying over HOULHULST FOREST during the morning.	
	14th		Situation Normal. Enemy Artillery slightly more active than on previous day. Snow started to fall between 4 + 5 pm.	
	15th		Situation. Quiet. Country flooded in low places + impassable in places.	
	16th		Situation Quiet. B SECTION (2Lt MEADOWS) relieved A section in Left Sector.	
			Portion of D SECTION (2Lt JAMES) relieved portion of D section in Centre Sector	
			Portion of C SECTION (2Lt BOOTH) relieved portion of C section in Right Sector	
	17th		Situation. Normal. Additional gun was put in at U2 c 71.69 (REF. MAP A.1. 1:10,000)	
	18th		Situation. Normal. Slight increase in activity.	
	19th		Situation. Fairly lively during day. Our aeroplanes active during day.	
	20th		Situation Lively. No 1. MACHINE GUN COY relieved this COMPANY in the line.	
			On relief Company moved into billets at CYRILLE VANDAMME CAMP.	
			C. Section (2nd Lt DINES) relieved No 1 MACHINE GUN COY on A.A duty at T29 c 97 (REF MAP BELGIUM SHEET 20)	
	21st		Cleaning equipment + billets.	
	22nd		Company moved via WOESTEN to Billets at ZUIDHUIS FM. S22 c 45 (REF MAP BELGIUM SHEET 20)	
			Transport moved to same Camp. No 3 MACHINE GUN COY relieved our A.A. teams at T29 c 97 (REF MAP BELGIUM SHEET 20). We relieved No 3 MACHINE GUN COY on A.A. duty at S22 a 8.4. (REF MAP SHEET 20).	

A5834 Wt. W4973 M687 750,000 8/16 D. D. & L. Ltd. Forms C.2118/13.

Instructions regarding War Diaries and Intelligence Summaries are contained in F. S. Regs., Part II. and the Staff Manual respectively. Title pages will be prepared in manuscript.

WAR DIARY
or
INTELLIGENCE SUMMARY.
(Erase heading not required.)

Army Form C. 2118.

Place	Date	Hour	Summary of Events and Information	Remarks and references to Appendices
	JANY			
	23rd		Company Training	
	24th		Company Training	
	25th		Company inspected by Brigadier General G. C. KEMP C.B. R.E. Commanding 2nd Infantry Brigade.	
	26th		Company Training.	
	27th		Church Parades.	
	28th		Company Training.	
	29th		Company Training.	
	30th		Company moved via WOESTEN to Billets at CYRILLE VANDAMME FM. No1. MACHINE GUN COY relieved our A. A. positions at S22 a 8 4. (REF MAP SHEET 20).	
	31st		Company Training.	

[signature] LIEUT.
COMMANDING No2 MACHINE GUN COMPANY.

A5834 Wt. W4973 M687 750,000 8/16 D. D. & L. Ltd. Forms C.2118/13.

Instructions regarding War Diaries and Intelligence Summaries are contained in F. S. Regs., Part II. and the Staff Manual respectively. Title pages will be prepared in manuscript.

WAR DIARY
or
INTELLIGENCE SUMMARY.
(Erase heading not required.)

2 M G Coy

Army Form C. 2118.

Vol 26

Place	Date	Hour	Summary of Events and Information	Remarks and references to Appendices
	1918. Feby. 1st		Company Training	
	2nd		Company Training	
	3rd		Church Parades	
	4th		Company Training	
	5th		Company Training	
	6th		Company Training	
	7th		Company relieved Nos 105 + 106 MACHINE GUN COYS, in the line. Part of 'A' Section (LIEUT COLEMAN) relieved 6 guns of No 106 M.G COY in right sector.	
			Part of 'C' Section (LIEUT JAMES) relieved 5 guns of No 105 M.G COY in centre sector	
			Part of 'D' Section (LIEUT DINES) relieved 4 guns of No 105 M.G COY in left sector	
			Right Sector Guns 2 Guns at BANFF, 4 Guns at VACHER. Section HQ at VACHER.	
			Centre Sector Guns. 1 Gun at TRACAS. 2 Guns at NORFOLK. 2 Guns at GLOSTER. SECTION HQ AT GLOSTER	
			Left Sector Guns. 1 Gun at STRING, 1 Gun at REQUETTE, 1 Gun at BREWERY	
			1 Gun at COURAGE POST. Section HQ at BREWERY.	
			Company HQrs established at CALIFORNIA DUGOUTS. SITUATION Normal.	
	8th		Situation Normal. V14d shelled at intervals (REF. MAP BI. 1/10,000)	
	9th		Situation Normal. Enemy Artillery fairly active.	
	10th		Situation Normal. Hostile Artillery below normal during day, but increased during night	
	"		Transport moved from EIKHOEK area to SIEGE CAMP	
	11th		Situation Quiet. V14d, V20A, + neighbourhood of VACHER, lightly shelled at 8.P.M.	

A5834 Wt. W4973 M687 750,000 8/16 D. D. & L. Ltd. Forms C.2118/13.

Army Form C. 2118.

Instructions regarding War Diaries and Intelligence Summaries are contained in F. S. Regs., Part II. and the Staff Manual respectively. Title pages will be prepared in manuscript.

WAR DIARY
or
INTELLIGENCE SUMMARY.
(Erase heading not required.)

Place	Date 1918	Hour	Summary of Events and Information	Remarks and references to Appendices
	Feby 12th	JH	Situation Normal. Hostile Artillery rather more active than previous day. BURNS HOUSES & YORK FARM, shelled several times with 5.9s. Enemy Machine Guns were active during the night, firing from direction of SPIDER X ROADS & CAMERON HOUSE.	
	13th	JH	Situation Normal, Guns at STRING, REQUETTE were withdrawn to NORFOLK HOUSE. 'B' SECTION (Lt MEADOWS) relieved A SECTION in Right sector. Lt Booth relieved Lt James in Centre sector. Gun teams 'C' Section relieved the team at TRACAS. Remainder of A & D Sections (LIEUT WADLEY) relieved 'D' Section in left sector.	
	14th	JH	Situation Normal. Area about D1b & D2a shelled intermittantly during the day	
	15th	JH	Situation Normal. The TRIANGLE, BREWERY & MEUNIER, shelled with 4.20. Hostile Aeroplane activity was about normal, E.As being over our lines at 12 noon, 2.30pm, 3.10pm & again at 3.50pm	
	16th	JH	Situation Normal. D1b, D2a & MEUNIER shelled with HE & Shrapnel during the day, one EA over our lines at 8.35 A.M	
	17th	JH	Situation fairly lively. The enemy raided our post at TRACAS MEBUS at 5.45 AM. Raiding party (about 40 strong) threw a bomb into gun emplacement putting the gun out of action, killing 1 man & wounding two. One of our men is missing. As enemy were retiring our Infantry opened fire on them killing 19 & taking one prisoner (wounded).	
	18th	JH	Situation Normal. Considerable Aeroplane activity on both sides, one EA brought down towards HOULTHURST FOREST about 3 0pm. TRACAS Gun withdrawn into reserve.	
	19th	JH	Situation Normal, GLOSTER MEUNIER, BANFF & BREWERY lightly shelled during the day. Three E.A passed over GLOSTER about 2.0 AM.	

A5834 Wt. W4973 M687 750,000 8/16 D. D. & L. Ltd. Forms C.2118/13.

Army Form C. 2118.

Instructions regarding War Diaries and Intelligence Summaries are contained in F. S. Regs., Part II. and the Staff Manual respectively. Title pages will be prepared in manuscript.

WAR DIARY
or
INTELLIGENCE SUMMARY.
(Erase heading not required.)

Place	Date 1918	Hour	Summary of Events and Information	Remarks and references to Appendices
	Feby 20th	JH	Situation Quiet. Enemy M.G Fairly active in vicinity of BANFF HOUSE	
	"	JH	Transport moved from SIEGE CAMP to HOSPITAL FARM. B19 d 1.2 (Ref/map 28NW (1/20,000))	
	21st	JH	Situation Normal. No1. Machine Gun Company relieved this Coy in the line. On relief Company moved into billets at SIEGE CAMP. A Section relieved No3 M.G Coy on A.A duty at A24 b 8.4 & B21 d 4.5 (REF. MAP 28.NW 1:20.000).	
	22nd	JH	Cleaning Billets & Equipment	
	23rd	JH	Company Training	
	24th	JH	Church Parades	
	25th	JH	Company Training. All Officers attended a lecture by G.O.C. Brigade on "Points noticed during recent tour in the line"	
	26th	JH	Company Training	
	27th	JH	Company Training. All Officers & senior N.C.O's attended a lecture on "Counter Battery Work"	
	28th	JH	Company Training. Inspection in F.S.M.O by Commanding Officer. Transport inspection by G.O.C. 2nd Inf Brigade	

J. H. [illegible] Capt.
COMMANDING No 2. MACHINE GUN COMPANY.

A5834 Wt. W4973 M687 750,000 8/16 D. D. & L. Ltd. Forms C.2118/13.

www.ingramcontent.com/pod-product-compliance
Lightning Source LLC
Chambersburg PA
CBHW082356010526
44111CB00041B/2562

* 9 7 8 1 4 7 4 5 0 2 7 3 3 *